T0280441

Pro PowerShell for Amazon Web Services

Second Edition

Brian Beach
Steven Armentrout
Rodney Bozo
Emmanuel Tsouris

Apress®

Pro PowerShell for Amazon Web Services

Brian Beach
Raleigh, NC, USA

Steven Armentrout
Mountlake Terrace, WA, USA

Rodney Bozo
Sterling, VA, USA

Emmanuel Tsouris
North Bend, WA, USA

ISBN-13 (pbk): 978-1-4842-4849-2
https://doi.org/10.1007/978-1-4842-4850-8

ISBN-13 (electronic): 978-1-4842-4850-8

Managing Director, Apress Media LLC: Welmoed Spahr
Acquisitions Editor: Susan McDermott
Development Editor: Laura Berendson
Coordinating Editor: Rita Fernando

Cover designed by eStudioCalamar

Distributed to the book trade worldwide by Springer Science+Business Media New York, 233 Spring Street, 6th Floor, New York, NY 10013. Phone 1-800-SPRINGER, fax (201) 348-4505, e-mail orders-ny@springer-sbm.com, or visit www.springeronline.com. Apress Media, LLC is a California LLC and the sole member (owner) is Springer Science + Business Media Finance Inc (SSBM Finance Inc). SSBM Finance Inc is a **Delaware** corporation.

For information on translations, please e-mail rights@apress.com, or visit http://www.apress.com/rights-permissions.

Apress titles may be purchased in bulk for academic, corporate, or promotional use. eBook versions and licenses are also available for most titles. For more information, reference our Print and eBook Bulk Sales web page at http://www.apress.com/bulk-sales.

Any source code or other supplementary material referenced by the author in this book is available to readers on GitHub via the book's product page, located at www.apress.com/9781484248492. For more detailed information, please visit http://www.apress.com/source-code.

Printed on acid-free paper

Table of Contents

About the Authors

Brian Beach has over 20 years of experience as a Developer and Architect and has spent the past 4 years focusing on Amazon Web Services. He holds a Computer Engineering degree from NYU-Poly and an MBA from Rutgers Business School. He published *Pro PowerShell for Amazon Web Services* in 2014. He is a regular author and has spoken at a number of events around the world. Brian lives in North Carolina with his wife and three kids.

Steven Armentrout is a Systems Engineer at a major cloud provider. He has over 15 years of experience in the public and private sectors with roles as System Administrator, Network Engineer, and Systems Engineer. Steven has earned over a dozen information technology certifications to include Microsoft Certified Solutions Expert (MCSE), Cisco Certified Network Associate (CCNA), and Certified Ethical Hacker (CEH). Steven has a BS in Business from Northern Arizona University.

Rodney Bozo is a Solutions Architect for a major public cloud provider. Previously, Rodney worked in the field supporting Microsoft services and technologies for almost 20 years. Rodney is an AWS Certified Solutions Architect and Developer and holds other AWS and Microsoft certifications. Rodney has a BS in Information Technology from George Mason University and an MS in Information Systems Technology and an MBA from George Washington University.

Emmanuel Tsouris is a Systems Development Engineer at a major cloud provider. Emmanuel builds scalable cloud computing services which enable running Windows Workloads on AWS, along with expanding compute services to customers in new regions around the globe. Previously, Emmanuel spent nearly two decades building enterprise solutions and applications at a Fortune 500 company.

About the Technical Reviewers

Eric Battalio has been working in software development for more than 25 years, most recently at Amazon. He has a degree in English Literature from Texas A&M and still enjoys working with technology through the perspective a liberal arts education provides.

Ryan Pothecary started using Amazon Web Services 6 years ago while working for a large UK-based NPO. There, he saw firsthand the benefit that a move to AWS could bring to a business, not only in cost reduction and becoming more agile but in the case of the business being able to use technology, such as machine learning, which was way outside their capability before.

Ryan has been with AWS Professional Services for nearly 3 years after being in the IT industry for over 25 years working predominantly on the Microsoft technology stack with a focus on Active Directory and Automation. Since joining AWS, he specializes in helping customers running Microsoft Workloads move to AWS working with some amazing customers delivering business-changing projects around EMEA.

Ryan has a beautiful wife and four children to keep him busy outside of work. He is also sometimes a roadie for his sons' band, The Pitchforks.

Acknowledgments

I would like to thank my wife, Karin. I know I said I would never write another book. I appreciate your support. I love you.

—Brian Beach

If not for my family, I wouldn't have been able to contribute to this project or have done many things in life and in my career. Thank you Chandana, Aparna, Karina, Federico, and Niam for being patient and encouraging.

I would also like to thank Brian Beach, who gave me an opportunity to help him in this endeavor. Also, thank you Steve and Emmanuel for joining me on this journey.

—Rodney Bozo

Introduction

Pro PowerShell for Amazon Web Services is for the Windows professional who is ready to make the leap to the cloud. While cloud computing has been around for a while now, enterprise adoption is just beginning. *Pro PowerShell for Amazon Web Services* is written specifically for Windows professionals who already know PowerShell and want to learn to host Windows workloads in the Amazon cloud.

Windows professionals find themselves under pressure to move workloads to AWS, but few books have been written for Windows users. *Pro PowerShell for Amazon Web Services* will introduce you to Amazon Web Services using a language you already know, Microsoft PowerShell.

This book assumes you have experience with Microsoft PowerShell. It will not teach you how to write PowerShell scripts. There are numerous excellent books on the market already. Apress offers a book titled *Pro Windows PowerShell* by Hristo Deshev.

On the other hand, we do not expect you to have any experience with AWS. We will start with the basics and build on that foundation. By the time you get to the end of the book, you will know everything you need to run Windows workloads.

What Does This Book Cover?

Amazon offers a wide selection of cloud services, enough to fill many books. This book focuses on running Windows workloads on AWS. The first version covered Elastic Compute Cloud (EC2), Virtual Private Cloud (VPC), Simple Storage Service (S3), Identity and Access Management (IAM), Simple Notification Service (SNS), Cloud Watch, Auto Scaling, and Elastic Load Balancing (ELB). As you likely know, AWS has been continuously innovating and these chapters have been updated to reflect the new features and capabilities. In addition, AWS has released numerous new services since the first edition was published. We have added additional chapters to cover this new material. These chapters include Systems Manager, Workspaces, AppStream, Lambda, and others.

In general, each chapter will introduce a specific topic (e.g., compute, storage, networking, etc.) and provide an overview of the capabilities. Then, we discuss the PowerShell commands available and how to use each. Each chapter ends with one or two exercises that bring together all of the commands introduced in the chapter.

In the early chapters, we begin by showing you how to use the Web Console and then introduce the various commands available in the PowerShell API. As the chapters progress and you get more comfortable with AWS, we will focus less on the Web Console and more on PowerShell. By the end of the book, we will be using PowerShell exclusively.

How Much Will This Cost?

In short, not much. AWS offers the "free tier" which allows you to use some resources for free each month. The free tier covers 30GB of storage and 750 hours of micro instance usage each month for the first year of your account. Micro instances are small servers ideal for getting started. These are too small to run most production workloads, but more than enough to launch a few servers and get comfortable with the platform.

The free tier does not cover everything, but if you use micro instances and are diligent about cleaning up after each exercise, your bill should be very small. Over the roughly 6 months I was writing the first edition, I spent a grand total of about $25. You should be able to complete the examples for much less.

A Note on the Code Examples

PowerShell is a complicated language with many tricks and shortcuts. Many developers, the authors included, pride themselves on being able to accomplish as much as possible with a single line of code. We have done our best to focus on readability and avoid complicated syntax. For example, the following code

```
$VPCFilter = New-Object Amazon.EC2.Model.Filter
$VPCFilter.Name = 'vpc-id'
$VPCFilter.Value = 'vpc-12345678'
Get-EC2SecurityGroup -Filter $VPCFilter
```

could have been written in one line like this:

```
Get-EC2SecurityGroup -Filter @{ Name='vpc'; Value='vpc-12345678' }
```

While we think the first version is easier to understand, don't assume that the AWS Toolkit does not support advanced syntax features. You are free to use pipelining, splatting, and so on.

In addition, we want to point out that the examples in this book are riddled with resource IDs. For instance, in the preceding example, 'vpc-12345678' is the ID of a Virtual Private Cloud (VPC). Your VPC would have a different ID. Every time you create a resource, it is assigned a new ID. As you are reading the book, be sure to replace the IDs with IDs specific to your resources.

CHAPTER 1

AWS Architecture Overview

If you are anything like us, you cannot wait to get started and launch an application in the cloud. But, before we dive in and start launching servers, let's take a step back and look at the big picture. Amazon Web Services (AWS) is a global platform with data centers around the globe. A little time spent on the architecture will help you understand why, and not just what, we are doing with AWS.

In this chapter, we will discuss the AWS global infrastructure, including regions and availability zones, and how to use them to design a robust application in the cloud. We will also introduce all of the services we are going to discuss throughout the book. Before we do, let's begin by defining cloud computing.

What Is Cloud Computing?

It seems that every company has a different definition of cloud computing. Amazon describes cloud computing as "the on-demand delivery of IT resources via the Internet with pay-as-you-go pricing" (http://aws.amazon.com/what-is-cloud-computing/).

Cloud computing is about leasing servers and storage from a provider like Amazon. But, it's also about so much more. The cloud offers information technology workers significant cost savings and unimaginable agility. Tasks that traditionally took weeks of work, costing thousands of dollars, can be completed in minutes for fractions of a penny.

In addition, cloud computing offers inconceivable scalability. With a single line of code, you can provision thousands of servers. Most important, you pay only for what you need and give the equipment back when you're done. Furthermore, because you are paying by the hour, running one server for a thousand hours costs the same amount as running a thousand servers for 1 hour. This is unthinkable in a traditional data center.

1

© Brian Beach, Steven Armentrout, Rodney Bozo, Emmanuel Tsouris 2019
B. Beach et al., *Pro PowerShell for Amazon Web Services*, https://doi.org/10.1007/978-1-4842-4850-8_1

Finally, cloud computing is often used in concert with automation. When we combine scalability with automation, we have the ability to build an application that responds to load. In Chapter 8, we will build a self-healing web application that automatically reconfigures itself in response to changes in load. That's what cloud computing is all about.

Regions

AWS is organized into multiple regions around the globe. Each region is designed to be independent of the others. This isolation allows us to design highly available applications that span the globe and ensure low-latency response times to our users.

All of the examples in this book were completed in Northern Virginia (us-east-1), but you can use the region closest to you. In fact this is the whole idea. By selecting a region closest to your users, you can deliver the best experience by minimizing latency.

Imagine you run an e-commerce site for a US-based clothing company. Most of your users are also in the United States, but recently you have had a small following in Australia. These users are complaining about the web site. They say it is slow and transactions often time out. Before the cloud, you would have to build another data center in Australia.

But using AWS, you can launch a few servers in Amazon's data center. Remember that you are only paying for what you use, so if you only need three or four servers in Australia, that's all you pay for. And it might cost just $1–2 an hour. This is one of the advantages of cloud computing.

Even more important, it may turn out that we are wrong. Maybe the users in Australia were just an anomaly. Within a month, all of the Australian users have moved on. We simply shut down the site in Australia and immediately stop paying. Cloud computing allows us to "fail fast," which lets the company try new things that would have been too expensive in the past.

Another reason you may want to use multiple regions is data privacy. Many companies are required to store data in a specific region. The European Union requires that data about its citizens be stored in Europe. In this case, the Ireland region (eu-west-1) would be a great choice.

As of this writing, there are 20 regions in production with 12 more planned. Two of these regions, GovCloud East and GovCloud West, are specifically designed to store data for the US government. If you are doing work for the US government, GovCloud may be an option for you.

Regions allow you to deliver your application from the location closest to your users and build redundant applications served from multiple regions. While this is great, Amazon also offers another layer of redundancy called availability zones.

Availability Zones

Each region is further organized into two or more availability zones (AZs). You can think of each AZ as a separate data center. The AZs within a region are isolated from failures but connected with high-speed, low-latency links.

Each AZ has separate power, cooling, and Internet access. In addition, their locations are chosen so they are never in the same flood plain and so on. This allows you to architect highly available applications that span multiple data centers.

Imagine we are deploying an application in a region with two availability zones (see Figure 1-1). We could deploy two servers, one in each AZ, and use an Elastic Load Balancer (ELB) to balance traffic between them. If one of the AZs suffered an outage, the ELB would automatically send all of the traffic to the other AZ. If we are using a Relational Database Service (RDS), we could also enable the multi-AZ option, and AWS will automatically replicate data between availability zones. (We will discuss ELB in Chapter 8 and RDS in Chapter 10.)

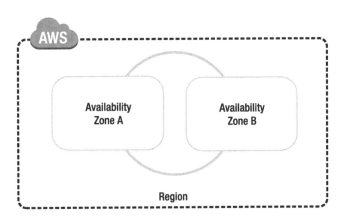

Figure 1-1. *Availability zones*

Regions and availability zones allow you to build a highly available, low-latency application that you could never dream of building in your own data center. Only a handful of companies around the globe have the resources to match this functionality in their own data centers. Before we wrap up, let's look quickly at the services available.

3

Services

AWS offers a lot of services and they are adding new services every day. This book is focused on Microsoft Windows, and I discuss only those services that are relevant to building Microsoft applications. Figure 1-2 provides an overview of the services we are going to use in this book. Note that there are many, many more services that we are not going to discuss.

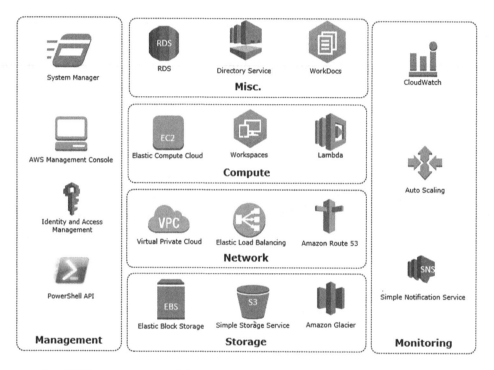

Figure 1-2. *AWS reference architecture*

Let's spend a minute discussing these options.

Management

The services in the management category are used to access and configure AWS:

- **AWS Management Console** – The console is the web GUI for configuring AWS. You can configure almost anything using the console, but this is a book on PowerShell. In the early chapters, I will show you how to get started using the console, but once we get comfortable, we will be using PowerShell almost exclusively.

- **Identity and Access Management (IAM)** – IAM allows you to control access to your account. You can create users and groups and write policies to control access to resources. (We will discuss IAM briefly in Chapter 2 and in detail in Chapter 9.)

- **PowerShell API** – PowerShell gives you full control over all services. You can do things in PowerShell that you cannot do in the AWS Management Console. AWS supports many scripting languages, but this book will focus on PowerShell.

- **Systems Manager** – Systems Manager allows you to manage your fleet of Windows and Linux servers. This includes patching, inventory management, maintenance windows, and much more. Chapters 15, 16, and 17 cover Systems Manager.

Storage

Starting at the bottom of Figure 1-2 and working up, we have multiple storage options:

- **Elastic Block Storage (EBS)** – EBS is a storage area network we use to create disks for our instances. EBS is a network-based solution similar to iSCSI. You can create volumes from 1GB to 1TB. You can also manage IO operations per second (IOPS). We will use EBS throughout the book, and focus on it in Chapter 4.

- **Simple Storage Service (S3)** – S3 is highly durable object storage in the cloud. You can use S3 to store an unlimited number of files up to 5GB each. S3 uses HTTP/HTTPS to read and write objects. Most important, you get 99.999999999% durability. (We will focus on S3 in Chapter 11.)

- **Amazon Glacier** – Glacier is a low-cost, cold-storage solution. Glacier offers the same high durability as S3 for about 1/10 the cost, but stores data offline and requires advanced notice to access your data. This is a great alternative to tape backup. (We will discuss Glacier in Chapter 11.)

Network

Moving up the stack in Figure 1-2, we have multiple network services that work together:

- **Virtual Private Cloud (VPC)** – VPC allows us to create a private network to isolate your instances from those of other AWS tenants. You can create a custom network topology and control network security. (We will use VPC throughout the book, but focus on it in Chapter 5.)

- **Elastic Load Balancer (ELB)** – ELB is a managed load balancing solution. You can balance traffic between multiple servers across availability zones. You can create public ELBs on the Internet or use a private ELB to balance traffic between layers of a multitier application. (We will discuss ELB in Chapter 8.)

- **Route 53** – Route 53 is Amazon's managed DNS solution. If you use Route 53, you can balance traffic between multiple regions, and AWS will determine which region is closest to the user and route them automatically. (We will discuss Route 53 briefly in Chapter 8.)

Compute

At the top of the stack, there are four compute services we will discuss:

- **Elastic Compute Cloud (EC2)** – EC2 is Amazon's virtual server service. This is how we launch servers, called instances, in the cloud. EC2 offers thousands of images and hardware configurations for every imaginable use case. This is the focus of the book, and we will use EC2 throughout.

- **WorkSpaces and AppStream** – WorkSpaces is a fully managed virtual desktop infrastructure (VDI) service. It allows you to manage Windows 7 and Windows 10 desktops at scale. AppStream allows you to stream Windows application into a browser. Both are covered in Chapter 13.

- **Lambda** – Lambda is serverless computing or functions as a service (FaaS). It allows you to run code in response to events using many languages including PowerShell and .Net. Lambda is covered in Chapter 18.

Monitoring

Finally, we have a collection of monitoring services:

- **CloudWatch** – CloudWatch is used to monitor the environment. CloudWatch allows you to create custom alarms and defines what actions to take when an issue arises. For example, you might raise an alarm when CPU utilization is above 80% for an extended period of time. (We will use CloudWatch to monitor instances in Chapter 8.)

- **Auto Scaling** – Auto Scaling, combined with CloudWatch, allows you to automatically respond to changing conditions. In Chapter 8 we will create an application that automatically launches new instances when the application is under high load.

- **Simple Notification Service (SNS)** – SNS is Amazon's notification system. CloudWatch can publish messages to SNS whenever an alarm occurs. You can use SNS to subscribe to events using e-mail, SMS text messages, and many other options.

Misc.

Finally, we have a few miscellaneous services:

- **Relational Database Service (RDS)** – RDS is Amazon's managed database service. RDS supports MySQL, Oracle, PostgreSQL, and Microsoft SQL Server. You can install any of these on an EC2 instance, but with RDS, Amazon manages the administration for you. (We will do a deep dive on RDS in Chapter 10.)

- **Directory Service** – Directory Service makes it easy to manage Active Directory in the cloud. Directory Service is used by many services including EC2, RDS, WorkSpaces, and WorkDocs. We cover Directory Service in Chapter 12.

- **WorkDocs** – WorkDocs is a service for secure collaboration in the cloud. You can use WorkDocs to store and manage documents. WorkDocs is covered in Chapter 14.

Summary

As you can see, Amazon offers everything you need to create a world-class application in the cloud. Regions and availability zones give you access to resources across the globe and allow you to build a highly available, low-latency application. In addition, Amazon offers numerous services that can be used in concert to create a robust application.

In the next chapter, we will create an account and configure our PowerShell environment. With this in place, we can begin using all the services we just discussed. What are we waiting for? Let's get going.

CHAPTER 2

Getting Started

In the previous chapter, we described cloud computing and then discussed the benefits of scripting your AWS configuration. Before we get started writing these scripts, we need to create an AWS account and prepare our PowerShell environment.

We will begin by creating a new AWS account and credentials for PowerShell. Then we will install the AWS Toolkit and configure a few default values. Although this might not be the most exciting chapter, it is an important one because the examples in the rest of the book assume that you have followed the steps in this chapter.

Creating an AWS Account

If you don't already have an Amazon Web Services (AWS) account, go to `http://aws.amazon.com` and click **Create a Free Account** to get started. If you already have one, skip ahead to the next section.

To create an AWS account, you will have to sign in using an `Amazon.com` account (see Figure 2-1). This can be the same account you use to shop on `Amazon.com`. If you are creating an AWS account for work, you might want to create a separate Amazon account using your work e-mail rather than using your personal account. If you want to create a new account, or have been living under a rock and don't have an Amazon account already, you can create one now.

After you create an AWS account, it's time to create an IAM account, which is discussed next.

© Brian Beach, Steven Armentrout, Rodney Bozo, Emmanuel Tsouris 2019
B. Beach et al., *Pro PowerShell for Amazon Web Services*, https://doi.org/10.1007/978-1-4842-4850-8_2

Creating an IAM User Account

Now that you have an AWS account, you will need to create a new IAM user. (IAM stands for Identity and Access Management.) AWS has two types of users: account credentials and IAM users. The e-mail address you used to create the AWS account is called an "AWS account credential." You should not use your account credentials for day-to-day activities on AWS. Save your AWS account credentials to change account options and access your bills. Create an IAM user for day-to-day activities instead.

IAM allows you to create multiple user accounts and configure the permissions of each user. If you already have an IAM user with administrator privileges, you can skip to the next section.

Open `http://console.aws.amazon.com`. If you are not already signed in, use your AWS account credential (i.e., the e-mail address used to create the account) to sign in. You will be taken to the AWS Management Console. Click **Services** from the menu bar at the top of the screen and search for IAM (see Figure 2-1).

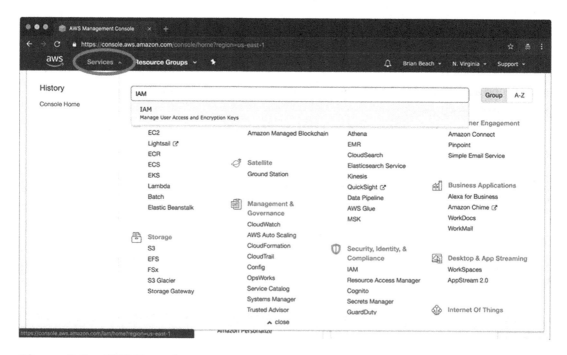

Figure 2-1. *AWS Console*

From the IAM dashboard, click the **Users** on the left navigation and then click the **Add User** button. This will start the add user wizard.

Enter **admin** as the User name and choose both **Programmatic access** and **AWS Management Console access**. You can enter a password here or let the wizard generate a random password for you. Click the **Next** button. (See Figure 2-2.)

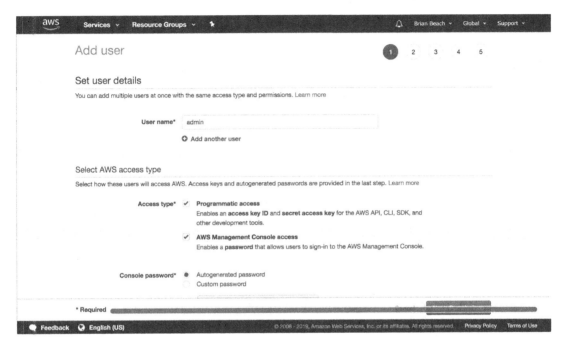

Figure 2-2. *Add user Step 1*

On the next page, click the **Create group** button. Enter the name **admins** and select the **AdministratorAccess** policy. Click **Create group** and then click **Next: Tags**. (See Figure 2-3.)

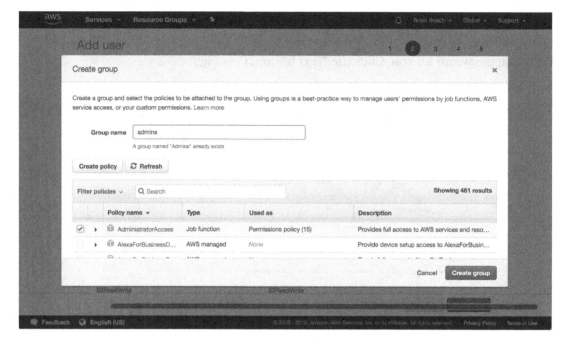

Figure 2-3. *Add user Step 2*

Skip the Tags screen by clicking the **Next: Review** button. Then, click the **Create User** button. Finally, click the **Download .csv** file. Keep this file somewhere safe. You will need it later.

TYPES OF CREDENTIALS

IAM users have three types of credentials, and each one is used for a different purpose:

Username and Password – The Username and Password are used to access the Web Console. In addition to the password, you can also opt for Multi-Factor Authentication (MFA). MFA uses an authentication code for extra security. MFA requires an authentication device or smartphone application like Google Authenticator.

Access Key ID and Secret Key – The Access Key ID and Secret Key are used to access the REST API. Both PowerShell and the AWS Command-Line Interface (CLI) use the REST API. Therefore, you need to download keys to use PowerShell.

Signing Certificates – Signing Certificates are used for the SOAP web services. The SOAP service is being deprecated, so I will not discuss it in this book.

Note that not all users will have all types of credentials. An administrator that does not use the API may only have a username and password, for example, while a developer that does not have access to the Web Console may only have an Access Key ID and Secret Key.

Logging in As an IAM User

The last thing we need to do is get the custom sign-in URL for your new account. In order to sign in using your IAM username and password, you must visit the account sign-in URL. Each account has a unique sign-in URL, but the default URL is very difficult to remember; let's change it to something we can remember.

To change the sign-in URL, return to the IAM dashboard and find the **IAM user sign-in link** (see Figure 2-4). Click the **Customize** link to specify a friendly account alias.

Welcome to Identity and Access Management

IAM users sign-in link:

https://beabrian.signin.aws.amazon.com/console | Customize

Figure 2-4. *Setting an account alias*

At this point you should sign out using the menu at the top right of the screen (see Figure 2-5).

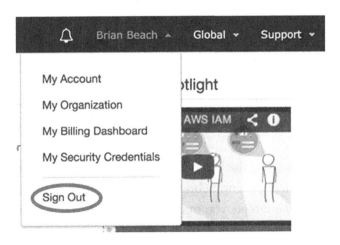

Figure 2-5. *Signing out*

Finally, navigate to the custom sign-in link and sign on as admin. If you let the wizard generate a password, you can find it in the csv file you downloaded earlier.

Note that you are now logged in as an IAM user. Compare the IAM user listed in the top right corner (see Figure 2-6) to the account credential in Figure 2-3. Note the IAM user includes the "@ alias."

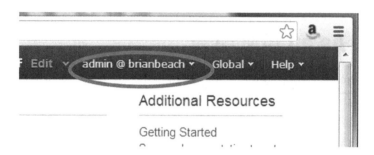

Figure 2-6. *Signed in as an IAM user*

At this point you have an AWS account and an IAM user with administrative privileges. Next, we are going to install the AWS Tools for PowerShell and configure a few default values.

Configuring PowerShell

You can download the AWS tools from `http://aws.amazon.com/powershell/`. If you are running your script on an AWS Windows instance (e.g., a server running in the AWS Cloud), the tools are already installed. If you want to run the tools on your own machine, download the installer from the preceding site.

The AWS tools are also available from the PowerShell gallery. There are two versions: **AWSPowerShell** and **AWSPowerShell.NetCore**. If you are running PowerShell on Linux, you will want to install AWSPowerShell.NetCore. For the rest of this book, I will assume you are running on Windows. However, nearly everything will work on PowerShell Core.

I usually write scripts using the PowerShell Integrated Script Environment (ISE) because it supports IntelliSense and debugging. The PowerShell ISE is a Windows feature. If it is not already enabled, you may need to enable the feature from Windows Server Explorer. This feature is enabled by default on AWS instances.

Let's check if the AWS tools are working. Type Get-AWSRegion at the PowerShell command prompt and press Enter, as shown here.

```
PS> Get-AWSRegion
```

Get-AWSRegion will list all of the AWS regions (described in Chapter 1) around the globe, as shown in the following code output:

```
Region                          Name
------                          ----
us-east-1                       US East (Virginia)
...
us-east-2                       US East (Ohio)
...
us-west-1                       US West (N. California)
...
us-west-2                       US West (Oregon)
...
eu-west-1                       EU West (Ireland)
...
...
```

If the command succeeds, your PowerShell environment is set up correctly. Notice that we did not use the credentials we downloaded earlier. The Get-AWSRegion method does not require authentication. Before you can do anything exciting, you are going to have to supply your credentials. Let's see how to do this in the next section.

Specifying Credentials and Region

Now that we have the AWS tools installed and PowerShell configured, let's try something more complicated. Type the Get-EC2Instance command to list all of the instances deployed in the cloud. Remember that an instance is Amazon's term for a server.

```
PS> Get-EC2Instance
```

Note that you have not deployed any instances yet, so this command is not expected to return anything. But when we run the command, we get the following error:

```
Get-EC2Instance : No credentials specified or obtained ...
```

15

Before you can use AWS, you need to log in. Remember that PowerShell uses the REST API. Therefore, you will need an access key and secret key in order to use PowerShell.

All of the AWS commands support the AccessKey and SecretKey parameters. You must include the keys you downloaded in the last section. For example, type

```
PS> Get-EC2Instance -AccessKey AKIA...ZHDA -SecretKey 9wVJ...iXdG
```

Note, however, that we still get an error:

```
Get-EC2Instance : No region specified or obtained ...
```

The credential error is gone, but now we have a new error – we also need to specify a region. Each AWS region is independent. You need to tell AWS which region you want to list the instances in. Note that you cannot list the instances in all regions in a single command. Let's list your instances in the Northern Virginia region. Type the following:

```
PS> Get-EC2Instance -AccessKey AKIA...ZHDA -SecretKey 9wVJ...iXdG -Region
us-east-1
```

This code produces the following results:

```
ReservationId   : r-12345678
OwnerId         : 123456789012
RequesterId     :
GroupId         : {}
GroupName       : {}
RunningInstance : {ip-10-1-1-5.brianbeach.com}
```

At this point, you should receive a list of your instances deployed in the specified region. If you just created a new account, you probably don't have any instances yet. As long as you don't get an error, it's working correctly. This is everything you need to execute the scripts in this book, but there are still a few things we can do make life easier. For example, it would be nice to save the default credentials and region so we don't have to add them to every command.

Setting Defaults

It can get cumbersome including the keys on every line of every script. Life would be easier if you had to specify the keys only once. Luckily, Amazon thought of this and included the Set-AWSCredentials and Set-DefaultAWSRegion commands.

Note   I am no longer including the command prompt (PS>) in my examples. From here on, most examples will be multiline scripts. I am using the PowerShell ISE to edit and run my scripts as a batch.

Just type the script into the top window and click the play button (or press the F5 key). If you prefer, you can enter these commands, one at time, at the command prompt. Personally, I prefer the IDE.

```
Set-DefaultAWSRegion us-east-1
Set-AWSCredentials -AccessKey ACCESS_KEY -SecretKey SECRET_KEY
Get-EC2Instance
```

This script results in the following:

```
ReservationId   : r-12345678
...
```

Notice that once I set a default region and credentials, I can run the Get-EC2Instance command without any parameters. This is so much easier. I can simply include these two lines at the top of the script, and I don't have to worry about it again.

If you want to clear the defaults, you can use the Clear-AWSCredentials and Clear-DefaultAWSRegion commands. For example:

```
Clear-AWSCredentials
Clear-DefaultAWSRegion
```

Setting defaults is great, but we have to remember to set them each time we start PowerShell. We can take it one step further and persist the defaults between PowerShell sessions.

Persisting Defaults

The Initialize-AWSDefaults command will persist the credentials and region between sessions. PowerShell will remember your defaults when you restart PowerShell or reboot your computer. Once you persist the credentials, you no longer need to specify them in your script. This makes the script portable between developers and AWS accounts. Note that unlike the PowerShell profiles, persisted defaults set in the ISE also affect the command line. Type the following:

```
Set-DefaultAWSRegion us-east-1
Set-AWSCredentials -AccessKey ACCESS_KEY -SecretKey SECRET_KEY
Initialize-AWSDefaults
```

Notice the results:

```
Credentials retrieved from Session
Region retrieved from Session
Credentials and region will be saved in this session
```

When you start a new PowerShell session, the default values will be loaded automatically. For example:

```
Get-EC2Instance
```

Now, if the defaults were not already loaded, they will be loaded as needed. This command now produces the following results:

```
Default credentials for this shell initialized from stored default profile
Default region for this shell initialized from stored default profile
ReservationId   : r-12345678...
```

If you want to clear the defaults, you can use the Clear-AWSDefaults command:

```
Clear-AWSDefaults
```

We are almost done discussing defaults, but there is one more option I want to mention: stored credentials. Stored credentials allow you to store multiple credentials and switch between them quickly.

Using Stored Credentials

You may find that you have more than one set of credentials to manage. Maybe you have separate AWS accounts for development and production servers; in my opinion, this is a really good idea. (And I hope you're not running these examples in the same account that you use to host production workloads.)

You can use the Set-AWSCredentials command we discussed earlier to create named profiles and quickly switch between them. To create a named profile, use the StoreAs attribute. For example:

```
Set-AWSCredentials -AccessKey ACCESS_KEY -SecretKey SECRET_KEY -StoreAs
"Production"
Set-AWSCredentials -AccessKey ACCESS_KEY -SecretKey SECRET_KEY -StoreAs
"Development"
```

Now we can use the stored credentials as an attribute to any command. For example, if you want to list the servers in the production environment, type

```
Get-EC2Instance -StoredCredentials Production
```

Here is the result:

```
ReservationId   : r-12345678...
```

And, if you want to list the servers in the development environment, type

```
Get-EC2Instance -StoredCredentials Development
```

The preceding script produces this result:

```
ReservationId   : r-87654321...
```

If you want to swap the default credentials between the development and production profiles, you can use the Set-AWSCredentials command with the StoredCredentials attribute. All subsequent commands will use the production credentials.

```
Set-AWSCredentials -StoredCredentials Production
```

You can list the various credentials you have stored using Get-AWSCredentials. For example, type

```
Get-AWSCredentials -ListStoredCredentials
```

to get this result:

```
Development
Production
```

Finally, you can remove credentials using the `Clear-AWSCredentials` command:

```
Clear-AWSCredentials -StoredCredentials Development
```

At this point your PowerShell environment is ready. In the next chapter, we are going to launch a few instances. Before you do that, however, you are going to need an EC2 key pair.

Using Key Pairs

Before we move on to creating instances, you will need a key pair. This key pair is used to encrypt the Windows Password for a new instance. AWS keeps the public key, and you keep the private key. When you create a Windows instance, AWS creates a local administrator account and generates a random password. It then encrypts the random password with the public key and stores the encrypted copy.

You can retrieve the password any time and decrypt it with your private key. Note that AWS does not keep the plain-text password. Therefore, only you can decrypt the password.

Caution   If you lose your private key, you will not be able to decrypt the password. Be careful with your keys!

To create a key pair, log in using your IAM admin user and choose a region. I will be using Northern Virginia, but you can select the location nearest you. Then, navigate to the EC2 service and choose **Key Pairs** from the left navigation. Click Create **Key Pair**.

Name the key pair and click Create. Your browser will download the private key. Make sure you save it. Note that the examples in this book assume your key is stored in c:\aws\mykey.pem.

You can also create a new key pair using the New-EC2KeyPair command. This command generates a new key pair and returns the private key. You can save the private key to a file using the Out-File command. Note that you must specify the encoding as ASCII. For example:

```
$KeyPair = New-EC2KeyPair -KeyName MyKey
$KeyPair.KeyMaterial | Out-File -FilePath 'c:\aws\MyKey.pem' -Encoding ASCII
```

That's everything you need to complete the exercises in this book. If you cannot wait any longer to launch an instance, feel free to move on to Chapter 3. But, if you have the patience, I would like to tell you about one more feature: IAM roles.

Using IAM Roles

We have covered a lot of material already in this chapter, but there is one more feature I want to discuss. It is a bad idea to have your production scripts running as an individual user. What happens if that user leaves the company? If you delete her account, all of your scripts will stop working.

You could create an additional IAM user just for running production scripts. But, how do you keep those keys secret? How do you keep a disgruntled administrator you fired from using the keys to terminate all your servers? Luckily, AWS provides a solution for this, too: IAM roles.

An IAM role allows you to grant permission to an EC2 instance. This way, you don't need keys to run PowerShell scripts. In other words, if you assign an IAM role to an instance, the instance has permission to run scripts rather than a user. Any scripts that are run on that instance are implicitly granted the permissions defined to the IAM role. Therefore, you don't have to bother with keys at all. Although you don't have to set credentials, you still need to set the region.

Of course this only works for instances running in AWS. You cannot use IAM roles for machines running in your data center. In addition, you have to assign the role when you create the instance; you cannot assign it later.

To create an IAM role, open the AWS Management Console and navigate to the IAM Console. (I assume you know how to do this by now. If not, go back to the "Creating a User Account" section at the beginning of this chapter.) Choose Roles from the left navigation. Then, click the **Create Role** button and name your new role (see Figure 2-6). I will use the name AdminRole for the scripts in this book.

There are many types of roles available. On the first screen of the create role wizard, choose **AWS Service** and **EC2**, then click **Next: Permissions**. (See Figure 2-7.)

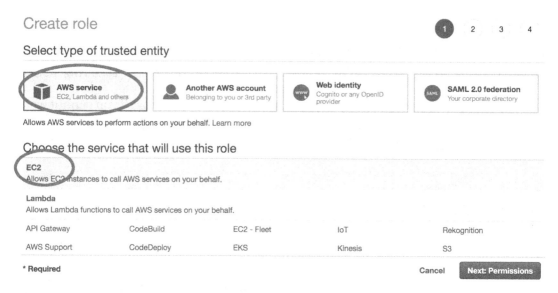

Figure 2-7. *Creating an IAM role*

On the next screen, choose **AdministratorAccess** and click **Next:Tags** (see Figure 2-8). Note that in a real-life scenario you would want to restrict the role. With administrator permissions assigned to an EC2 instance, anyone who runs a script on that instance will have full control over your account. For the purposes of this book, this is fine, but please be more restrictive in real life.

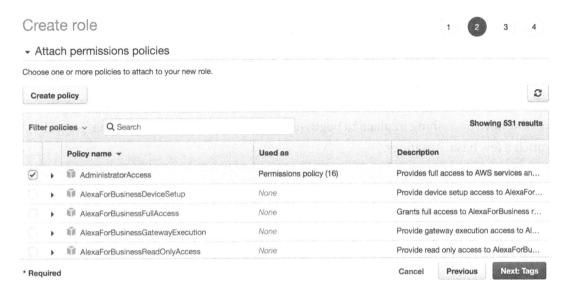

Figure 2-8. *Selecting the Amazon EC2 role*

You can skip the Tags screen by clicking **Next: Review**. On the last screen, name the role **AdminRole** and click the **Create role** button. (See Figure 2-9.)

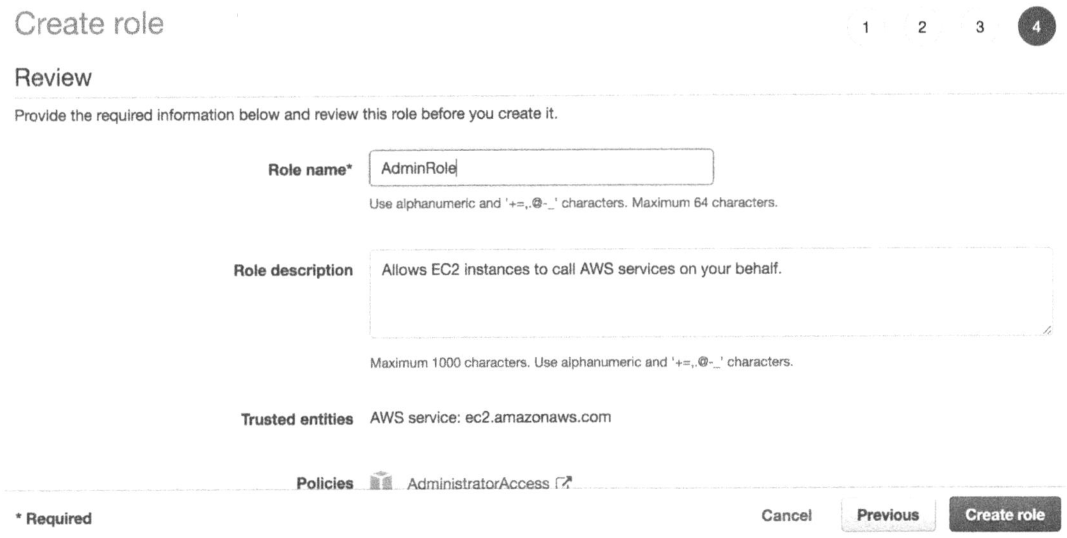

Figure 2-9. *Naming the EC2 role*

We will use this role in the second exercise of Chapter 3.

Summary

In this chapter, we created an AWS account and IAM user. Then we installed the AWS Tools for PowerShell and configured our PowerShell scripting environment with a default region and credentials. Finally, we created an EC2 key pair and an IAM role. We now have everything in place to begin using the cloud. In the next chapter, we will launch a few basic instances.

CHAPTER 3

Basic Instance Management

Now that we're done configuring our environment, we'll jump right in and get started by creating an instance. An EC2 instance is, simply, a server running in the cloud. With a few quick clicks, we will have our first server up and running.

In this chapter, we will learn to create new instances and connect them. Then we will discuss how to start, stop, and terminate instances. We will learn various ways to access metadata and add custom metadata tags. In the exercises at the end of the chapter, we will build a PowerShell script to automate the launch process and customize the configuration of an instance.

Creating Instances

Let's get started by creating a new instance. In this section we'll launch a Windows Server 2019 instance. I'll begin by using AWS Management Console. The console will give us a good overview of all the options available. Then, we will see how to do the same thing with a single line using PowerShell.

Launching an Instance with the Web Console

For this first exercise – launching an instance with the Web Console – we are going to include step-by-step instructions with figures. The Web Console changes often so don't be surprised if the console screens look a bit different from the following figures.

We will sign in using the URL and IAM account we created in Chapter 2. Do not use the e-mail address we used to create the account. When we sign in, we will be taken to the AWS Management Console home page. The home page lists all of the AWS services available. Under the All services drop-down and Compute group, click the EC2 link (see Figure 3-1). Elastic Compute Cloud (EC2) is Amazon's service for creating servers in the cloud.

© Brian Beach, Steven Armentrout, Rodney Bozo, Emmanuel Tsouris 2019
B. Beach et al., *Pro PowerShell for Amazon Web Services*, https://doi.org/10.1007/978-1-4842-4850-8_3

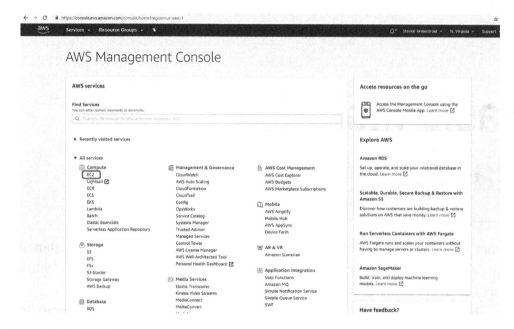

Figure 3-1. *The home page*

On the EC2 dashboard, make sure the region in the top right corner is the same one we used to create our key pair in the last chapter (e.g., Northern Virginia), as shown in Figure 3-2. Then click the Launch Instance button to start the wizard.

Figure 3-2. *EC2 dashboard*

The first page of the wizard lists the Amazon Machine Images (AMI). An AMI is a template image used to create a new instance. The Quick Start tab includes some of these images created by Amazon Web Services for public use. There are additional images available from the other tabs, currently more than 115,000. For now, we just need a basic version of Windows to get our feet wet. Find Microsoft Windows Server 2019 Base and click the Select button (see Figure 3-3).

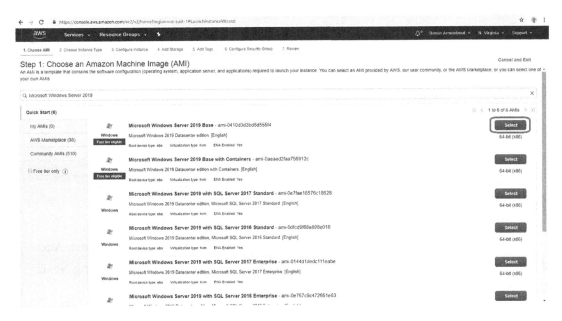

Figure 3-3. *Choosing an AMI*

On the instance details page, ensure that the instance type is set to t2 micro and click the button Next: Configure Instance Details (see Figure 3-4). The instance type is the virtual hardware we want to use. There are numerous combinations of processors, memory, network, and so on.

Only the micro instance is eligible for the free tier and will be labeled as such in the console. Read more about the free tier on the AWS web site. (An up-to-date description of the instance types are available at `http://docs.aws.amazon.com/AWSEC2/latest/UserGuide/instance-types.html`.)

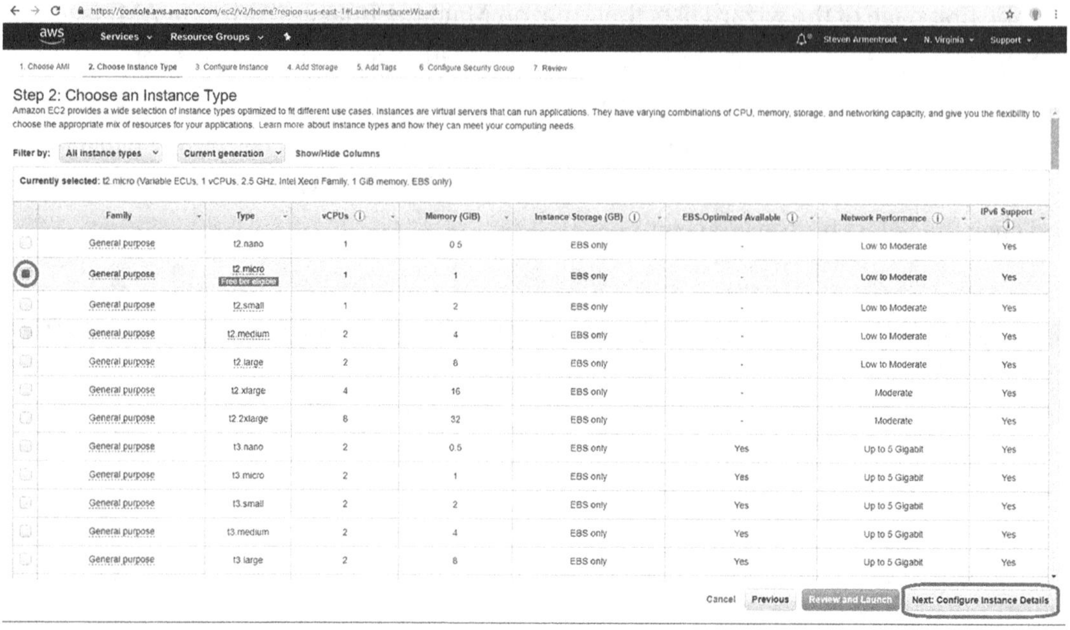

Figure 3-4. *Choosing an Instance Type*

Skip the page labeled as "Step 3: Configure Instance Details" by clicking Next: Add Storage. Skip the page labeled as "Step 4: Configure Instance Details" by clicking Next: Add Tags. We will review all of these advanced options in future chapters.

On the Tag Instance page, select the Add Tag button, and for Key field enter "Name" and for the Value field enter "My First Instance" and click Next: Configure Security Group (see Figure 3-5).

Figure 3-5. *Tagging the Instance*

On the Configure Security Group screen, select the default group from the list of existing security groups (see Figure 3-6) and click the button that says Review and Launch. Security groups act like a firewall within AWS. We can use security groups to control what traffic is allowed to flow to and from the instance. (We will spend time looking at security groups in Chapter 6).

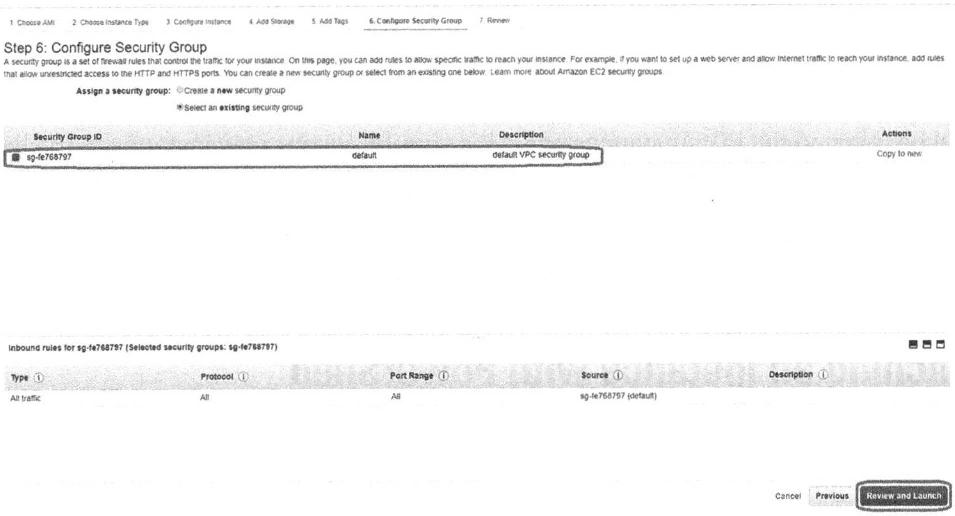

Figure 3-6. *Configure Security Group*

Take a minute to review the options we selected on the next page and click Launch. This will load the key pair dialog box. Select the key pair we created in the previous chapter (see Figure 3-7). Remember that AWS uses this key to encrypt the Windows administrator password. Select the confirmation box and then click Launch Instances.

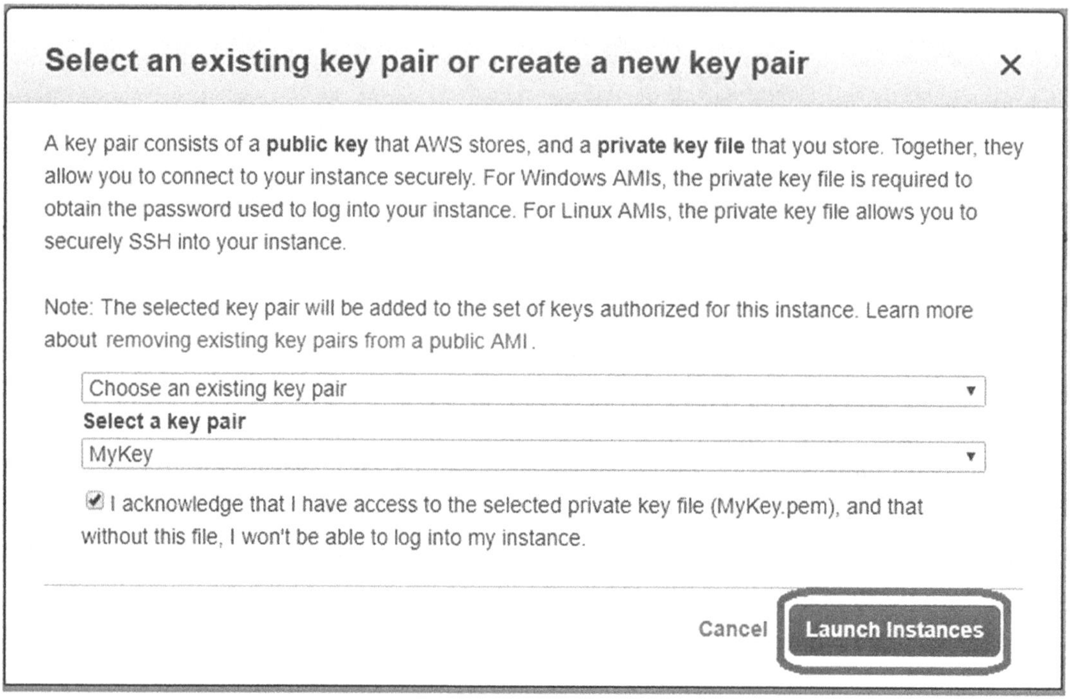

Figure 3-7. *Choosing our key pair*

We just launched our first server in the cloud. Click the View Instances button, and we will be taken to the EC2 Instances page. We should see our new instance in the list with a state of pending.

It will take about 10 minutes for the instance to launch. While we are waiting, let's discuss how we can do the same thing in PowerShell using a single line of code.

Launching an Instance with PowerShell

In PowerShell, we use the New-EC2Instance command to create instances. This is a really rich command that can do everything the wizard can do. For now we will focus on the basics of the New-EC2Instance command.

In the following example, we specify only the required parameters to successfully launch an instance.

```
$AMI = Get-EC2ImageByName -Name 'WINDOWS_2016_BASE'

New-EC2Instance -ImageId $AMI[0].ImageId -KeyName 'MyKey' -InstanceType
't2.micro' -MinCount 1 -MaxCount 1
```

Let's look at each parameter in turn, most of which are the same ones we saw when using the wizard in the preceding section:

- An AMI is uniquely identified by an image ID value. The image IDs are different in each region. The ImageId parameter specifies which AMI we want to launch; therefore, the examples will use Get-EC2ImageByName to look up the correct ID in our currently defined default region. (We will discuss the Get-EC2ImageByName command in Chapter 7).

- MinCount and MaxCount specify how many instances to launch. See the sidebar on reservations for details.

- KeyName is the name of the key pair we created in the last chapter. It is used to encrypt the administrator password. Technically, this parameter is optional, but without it we will not be able to retrieve the administrator password.

- InstanceType describes the hardware we wish to use, and again we will use the t2.micro.

RESERVATIONS

Let's spend a minute talking about the MinCount and MaxCount parameters. New-EC2Instance always creates instances in batches called reservations. We are going to be using the reservation object in many of the scripts later in this chapter.

A reservation is a batch of instances launched at the same time. Even if we only want a single instance, we create a batch of size one. Every account has a limit on the number of runnable instances for each instance type per region. Some instance types support many dozens of launches by default, while some very powerful instance types may only allow one or two launches. Even Amazon has a finite number of instances available.

AWS will try to launch the number of instances specified in MaxCount. If it cannot launch the MaxCount due to account or regional capacity limits, Amazon will launch the largest possible number above MinCount. If the MinCount is more than Amazon EC2 will permit, no instances are launched and there will be a capacity or limit error.

Despite the name, New-EC2Instance actually returns a reservation object rather than an instance. If we want to check the individual instances, the reservation includes a list called RunningInstance.

```
$AMI = Get-EC2ImageByName -Name 'WINDOWS_2016_BASE'
```

```
$Reservation = New-EC2Instance –ImageId $AMI[0].ImageId -KeyName 'MyKey'
-InstanceType 't2.micro' -MinCount 2 -MaxCount 2
```

```
$Reservation.Instances
```

We can use a zero-based array syntax to read the individual instances. For example:

```
$Reservation.RunningInstance[0].InstanceId
```

```
$Reservation.RunningInstance[1].InstanceId
```

This will produce output similar to the following instance IDs:

```
i-05ebc32ffa7c0ed38
i-072bf9d8756b8c17d
```

By the way, although the attribute is called RunningInstance, it also contains instances that are in a stopped state.

Notice that we did not specify the security group (i.e., firewall). Unlike the Web Console wizard, the API will use the default group if we don't specify one. There are numerous additional parameters to the New-EC2Instance command. These correspond to the options we skipped in the wizard. Don't worry. We will talk about them all in later chapters.

Windows instances take about 10 minutes to launch regardless of how we create them. The instance(s) we launched with PowerShell are probably still launching, but the one we launched with the AWS Management Console is probably ready; let's go check it now.

Checking the Instance Console Screenshot

Returning to the Web Console, let's check on that instance we launched earlier. To view the running instances, select the services drop-down in the AWS Web Console. Either find and locate EC2 under the Compute group or use the find tool using EC2 as our search string and select EC2. When the EC2 dashboard console loads, select the Running Instances link.

We will now check on the instance using the Get Instance Screenshot tool. This tool will take a snapshot of our instances display output in its current state and show it to us. This can be a very useful for diagnosing instances that are not responding or are failing to launch. If a bug check occurred or service failed to start, we can usually find details by reviewing the instance screenshot.

On the instances page, select the instance, and right-click the instance and we will be presented with a drop-down menu. Alternatively, after selecting our instance we can select the Actions button at the top. In the drop-down menu, highlight Instance Settings and click Get Instance Screenshot (see Figure 3-8).

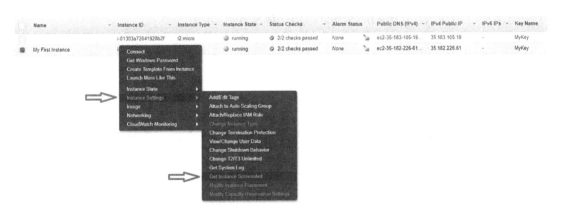

Figure 3-8. *Selecting the Instance Console Screenshot*

A new page will load displaying a screenshot of our new instance. In our example we should see the login prompt (see Figure 3-9).

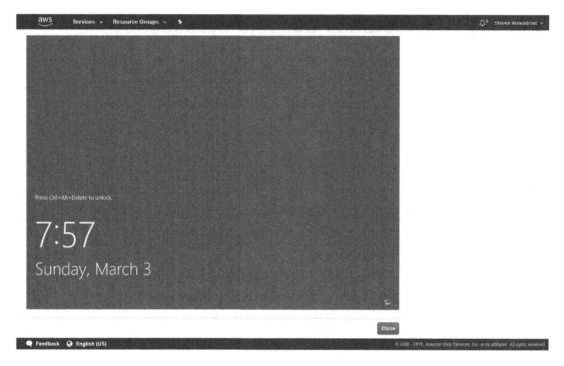

Figure 3-9. *Displaying the Instance Console Screenshot*

Select Close on the bottom right corner of instance screenshot window to return back to the Instance Web Console.

Checking the Instance Console System Log

When an AWS provided image is launched, it performs some configurations and customizations at boot to prepare it for use. A summary log of these activities can be seen using the Get System Log tool.

To review our instance log, on the instances page, select the instance and right-click it and we will be presented with a drop-down menu. Alternatively, after selecting our instance we can select the Actions button at the top. In the drop-down menu, highlight Instance Settings and click Get System Log (see Figure 3-10).

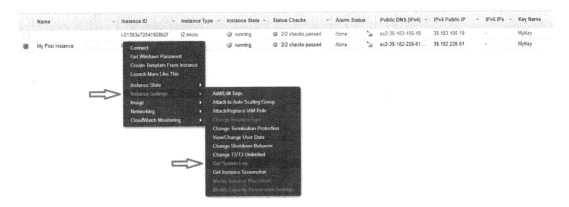

Figure 3-10. *Selecting the Get System Log*

A pop-up screen will load displaying the log output. If the instance was successfully configured at launch, we should see a "Windows is Ready to Use" message near the end of the System Log (see Figure 3-11).

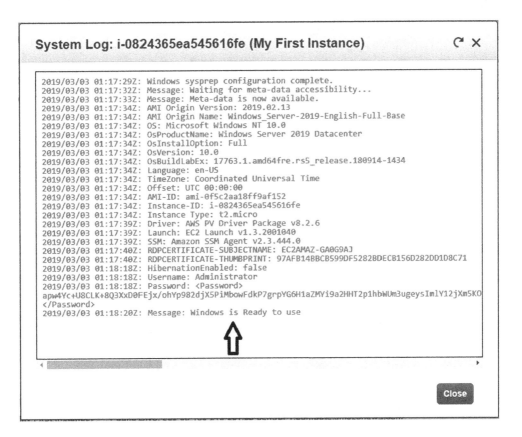

Figure 3-11. *Displaying the System Log*

Select Close on the bottom right corner of System Log window to return back to the Instance Web Console.

Connecting to an Instance

Remember, from the last chapter, that AWS will generate a new administrator password and encrypt it using our key pair. On the instances page, select the instance, and click the Connect button at the top of the screen. Then click the Get Password button (see Figure 3-12).

Figure 3-12. *Connect to Your Instance*

Now, click the Choose File button (see Figure 3-13) and locate the private key we created in Chapter 2. Then click the Decrypt Password button.

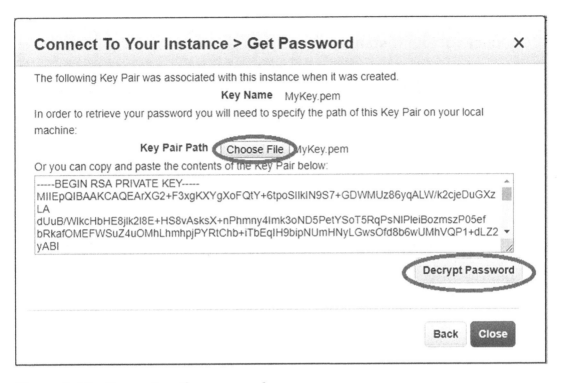

Figure 3-13. *Decrypting the password*

The dialog will now show the temporary password. Select the password and copy it to our clipboard and then click the Download Remote Desktop File link and run it (see Figure 3-14). This will launch a Remote Desktop session and prompt us for the password we just decrypted and copied to our clipboard. Paste the password in and click the Connect button.

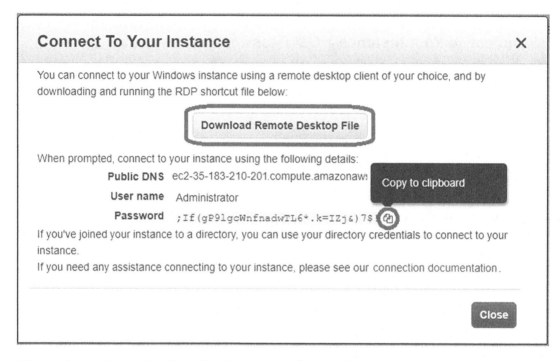

Connect To Your Instance   ✕

You can connect to your Windows instance using a remote desktop client of your choice, and by downloading and running the RDP shortcut file below:

> **Download Remote Desktop File**

When prompted, connect to your instance using the following details:

Public DNS   ec2-35-183-210-201.compute.amazonaws

User name   Administrator   Copy to clipboard

Password   ;If(gP9lgcWnfnadwTL6ᵛ.k=IZjᵃ)7$

If you've joined your instance to a directory, you can use your directory credentials to connect to your instance.

If you need any assistance connecting to your instance, please see our connection documentation.

> **Close**

Figure 3-14. *Downloading the Remote Desktop File*

Great! Now we know how to create and connect to an instance using the Web Console.

Note   If the RDP connection fails, we may need to add a rule to the security group to allow Remote Desktop Protocol (RDP) access from our IP. Follow the following instructions. We will discuss security groups in detail in Chapter 6.

1. From the EC2 Web Console selections on the left under Network & Security, choose Security Groups.

2. Select the group named Default and choose the Inbound tab and select the Edit button.

3. In the Edit inbound rules window, choose the Add Rule button.

4. Under Type, select the drop-down and choose RDP.

5. Under Source, select the drop-down and choose My IP.

6. Finally, click the Save button.

We can, of course, retrieve the password using PowerShell. The PowerShell command is Get-EC2PasswordData command. Get-EC2PasswordData takes an instance ID and the path to the private key and returns the password.

Note that the instance ID will be different from these examples. Each instance has a different ID. We can get the ID from the instances page of the AWS Management Console.

```
Get-EC2PasswordData -InstanceId 'i-0824365ea545616fe' –PemFile 'c:\aws\
MyKey.pem'
```

The preceding code will return an error if the password is not available yet. Remember, it takes about 10 minutes to launch a new instance. We will discuss how to test for password availability in the first exercise at the end of this chapter.

Now that we know how to launch and connect to an instance, let's talk about starting, stopping, rebooting, and terminating instances.

Managing the Instance Life Cycle

Now that we have a few instances created, we will want to manage them. We can Start, Stop, Reboot, and Terminate (i.e., Delete) an instance by right-clicking it in the AWS Management Console and highlighting Instance State. Figure 3-15 shows the context menu.

Note   Stop - Hibernate is a new AWS feature that allows instances to be stopped in a powered down hibernation state instead of using a full shutdown. This can be helpful for customers who need scale their servers up and down quickly. As of this writing, Windows Servers are not yet supported and will not be selectable. The latest information and configuration requirements can be found at `https://docs.aws.amazon.com/AWSEC2/latest/UserGuide/Hibernate.html`.

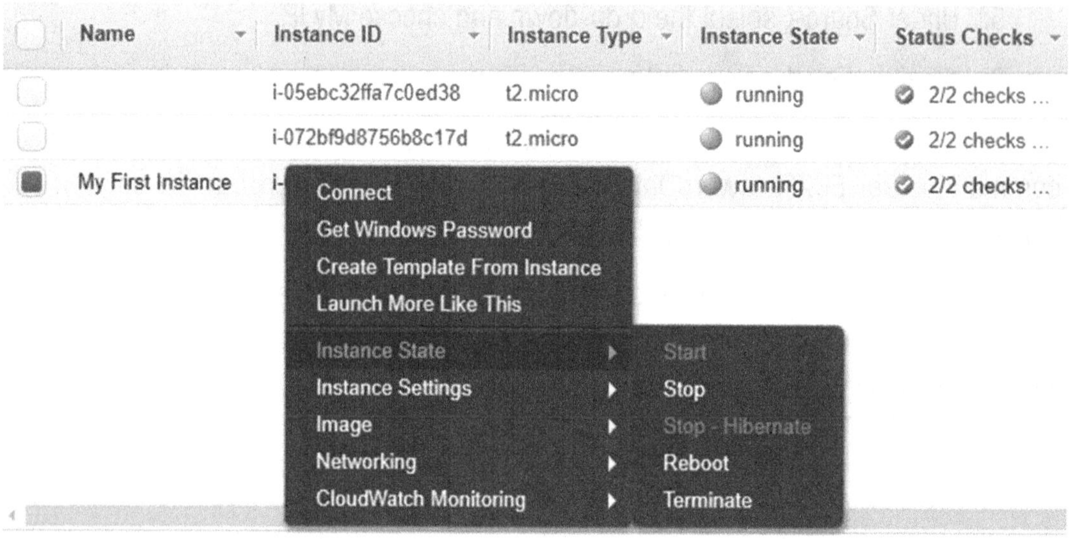

	Name		Instance ID		Instance Type	Instance State	Status Checks
☐		▾	i-05ebc32ffa7c0ed38	▾	t2.micro	● running	✓ 2/2 checks ...
☐			i-072bf9d8756b8c17d		t2.micro	● running	✓ 2/2 checks ...
■	My First Instance		i-			● running	✓ 2/2 checks ...

```
Connect
Get Windows Password
Create Template From Instance
Launch More Like This

Instance State          ▶    Start
Instance Settings       ▶    Stop
Image                   ▶    Stop - Hibernate
Networking              ▶    Reboot
CloudWatch Monitoring   ▶    Terminate
```

Figure 3-15. *Instance Life-Cycle Menu Options*

The equivalent PowerShell commands are pretty simple. They each have a parameter called Instance, which is the ID of the instance we want to start, stop, and so on.

To stop an instance, we use Stop-EC2Instance:

```
Stop-Ec2Instance -Instance i-0824365ea545616fe
```

To start an instance, we use Start-EC2Instance:

```
Start-Ec2Instance -Instance i-0824365ea545616fe
```

To reboot an instance, we use Restart-EC2Instance:

```
Restart-Ec2Instance -Instance i-0824365ea545616fe
```

To terminate an instance, we use Remove-EC2Instance. We will be asked to confirm the termination. We can add the force attribute to suppress the prompt.

```
Remove-EC2Instance -Instance i-0824365ea545616fe -Force
```

Listing Instances and Metadata

We have already seen the list of instances in the Web Console. We can use the Get-EC2Instance to list instances in PowerShell. The primary purpose of Get-EC2Instance is to return a list of all the instances in our account. In addition, we will use the Get-EC2Instance command to get metadata about the instance. Metadata includes information such as the IP address, drive configuration, and type of instance.

```
Get-EC2Instance
```

The preceding command returns the following results:

```
GroupNames    : {}
Groups        : {}
Instances     : {MyKey}
OwnerId       : 123456789012
RequesterId   :
ReservationId : r-0a585598e4c8ab8c4

GroupNames    : {}
Groups        : {}
Instances     : {MyKey, MyKey}
OwnerId       : 123456789012
RequesterId   :
ReservationId : r-0182baba42744a323
```

If we want a specific instance, use the Instance parameter, for example, reading the

```
Get-EC2Instance -Instance i-0824365ea545616fe
```

This command returns the following results:

```
GroupNames    : {}
Groups        : {}
Instances     : {MyKey}
OwnerId       : 123456789012
RequesterId   :
ReservationId : r-0a585598e4c8ab8c4
```

41

Note that Get-EC2Instance returns a reservation object. Remember that New-EC2Instance always creates a batch called a reservation. When we call Get-EC2Instance, AWS returns the reservation that includes its collection of instances.

The instances attribute contains the metadata of the instances we requested. Of course, we can dot source the AWS commands using PowerShell to get details of the instances object, for example, to get a list of all instances as a table.

```
(Get-EC2Instance).Instances
```

The preceding command returns the following results:

InstanceId	InstanceType	Platform	PrivateIpAddress
PublicIpAddress	SecurityGroups	SubnetId	VpcId
----------	------------	--------	----------------
---------------	--------------	--------	-----
i-0824365ea545616fe	t2.micro	Windows	172.31.23.186
35.182.226.61	{default}	subnet-0433d96d	vpc-dd608bb4
i-072bf9d8756b8c17d	t2.micro	Windows	172.31.1.36
99.79.67.159	{default}	subnet-bed9d3c6	vpc-dd608bb4
i-05ebc32ffa7c0ed38	t2.micro	Windows	172.31.4.75
35.183.48.244	{default}	subnet-bed9d3c6	vpc-dd608bb4

To access the instance metadata of a specific instance, we use the Instance parameter and dot source the instances output object. For example:

```
(Get-EC2Instance -Instance i-0824365ea545616fe).Instances
```

This command returns the following results:

InstanceId	InstanceType	Platform	PrivateIpAddress
PublicIpAddress	SecurityGroups	SubnetId	VpcId
----------	------------	--------	----------------
---------------	--------------	--------	-----
i-0824365ea545616fe	t2.micro	Windows	172.31.23.186
35.182.226.61	{default}	subnet-0433d96d	vpc-dd608bb4

To see all the properties of a specific instance, we can pipe the output to either use format-list or select-object. For example:

```
(Get-EC2Instance -Instance i-0824365ea545616fe).Instances | Select-Object *
```

This results in

```
Tag                    : {Name}
AmiLaunchIndex         : 0
Architecture           : x86_64
BlockDeviceMappings    : {/dev/sda1}
ClientToken            :
CpuOptions             : Amazon.EC2.Model.CpuOptions
EbsOptimized           : False
ElasticGpuAssociations : {}
EnaSupport             : True
Hypervisor             : xen
IamInstanceProfile     :
ImageId                : ami-0f5c2aa18ff9af152
InstanceId             : i-0824365ea545616fe
InstanceLifecycle      :
InstanceType           : t2.micro
KernelId               :
KeyName                : MyKey
LaunchTime             : 3/3/2019 11:03:22 PM
Monitoring             : Amazon.EC2.Model.Monitoring
NetworkInterfaces      : {ip-172-31-23-186..compute.internal}
Placement              : Amazon.EC2.Model.Placement
Platform               : Windows
PrivateDnsName         : ip-172-31-23-186.compute.internal
PrivateIpAddress       : 172.31.23.186
ProductCodes           : {}
PublicDnsName          : ec2-35-182-226-61.compute.amazonaws.com
PublicIpAddress        : 35.182.226.61
RamdiskId              :
RootDeviceName         : /dev/sda1
RootDeviceType         : ebs
SecurityGroups         : {default}
SourceDestCheck        : True
SpotInstanceRequestId  :
SriovNetSupport        :
```

```
State                  : Amazon.EC2.Model.InstanceState
StateReason            :
StateTransitionReason  :
SubnetId               : subnet-0433d96d
Tags                   : {Name}
VirtualizationType     : hvm
VpcId                  : vpc-dd608bb4
```

This will give us a great deal of information about the instance including storage, network, and other details. We will use this information throughout the rest of the book. Before we get into that, let's look at one other way to access some instance metadata using the metadata URL.

Using the Metadata URL

Get-EC2Instance is a great way to get information about an instance, but there is another way. The metadata URL returns much of the same information as Get-EC2Instance, but always returns information about the current instance.

The metadata URL is a web service that runs under each instance that returns metadata about the current instance. The URL is `http://169.254.169.254/latest/meta-data`.

Note the metadata service is only available from executing queries and scripts directly on the EC2 instance. We cannot use the API from a machine outside AWS, nor can we use the metadata service to get information about another instance.

Opening the metadata URL in Internet Explorer on an instance lists all of the options available (see Figure 3-16).

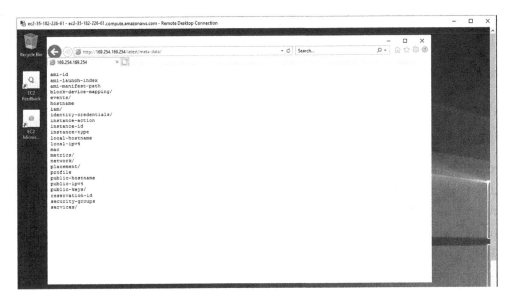

Figure 3-16. *Metadata URL*

Navigating to any of the sub-URLs will return useful information about the instance. For example, navigating to http://169.254.169.254/latest/meta-data/instance-type will return the type of hardware we are running on (see Figure 3-17).

Figure 3-17. *Using the metadata URL*

Of course, we can also access metadata from PowerShell using the Invoke-RestMethod command and passing the metadata URL.

```
Invoke-RestMethod 'http://169.254.169.254/latest/meta-data/instance-type'
```

This results in

```
t2.micro
```

A common use of the metadata URL is to discover the ID of the current instance and then use it to make calls to the AWS API. This way, we can write a generic script that will run on any EC2 instance.

The following script uses the metadata API to discover the instance ID and then calls Get-EC2Instance on it. Note that the instance ID was not known ahead of time. Instead, it was discovered by the script.

```
$InstanceID = Invoke-RestMethod 'http://169.254.169.254/latest/meta-data/
instance-id'
Get-EC2Instance $InstanceID
```

Using User Data

One of the options we skipped over in the section on launching new instances was user data. User data is similar to metadata, but it allows us to include any custom data we want. The user data is available via a web service call, just like the metadata in the prior section.

One common use of user data is to include information needed to bootstrap the instance, or configure it after launch. We will do this in the second exercise at the end of this chapter.

To include user data, simply type whatever we want into the text box at the bottom of the third page under Advanced Details of the Launch Instance wizard (see Figure 3-18).

It is common, but not required, to use XML in the user data section. Using XML makes it easier to parse the data later. In the example in Figure 3-18, we are using a combination of free-form text and XML-formatted data.

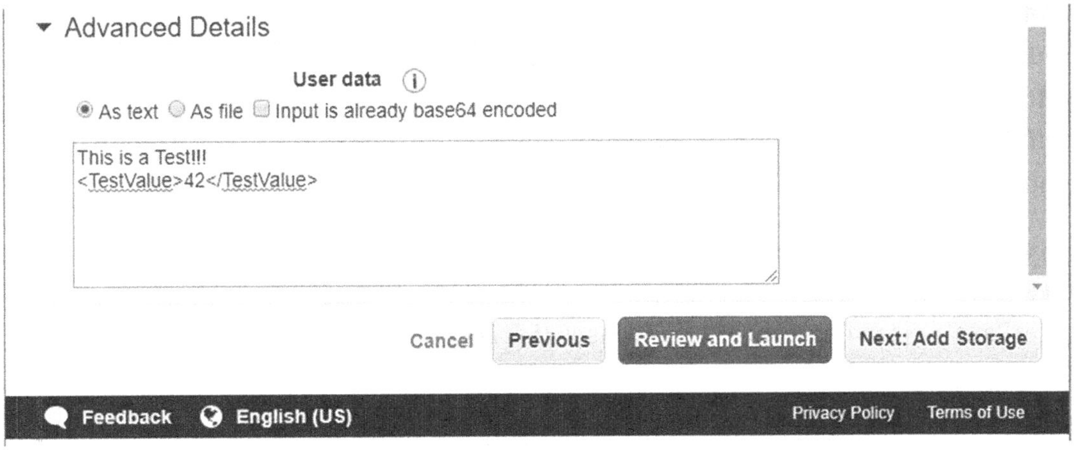

Figure 3-18. *Setting User Data*

Once the instance launches and we Remote Desktop in, we can retrieve the data using the user data URL `http://169.254.169.254/latest/user-data` (see Figure 3-19).

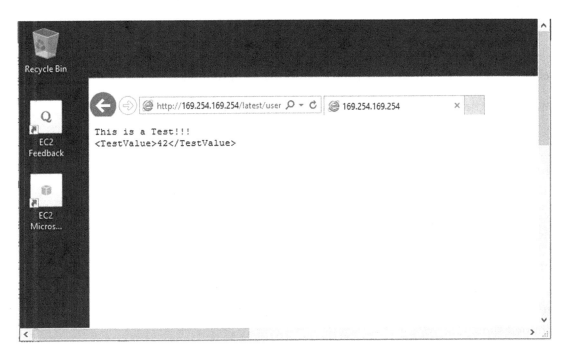

Figure 3-19. *Retrieving User Data*

Similar to the metadata URL, this URL will always return the user data for the running instance. Each instance has its own unique user data.

We can also include user data when calling New-EC2Instance from PowerShell using the UserData parameter. AWS anticipates that the user data will include XML. Remember that the API call is also a web service that may be formatted as XML. Therefore, to avoid confusion, we must base 64 encode the user data section. For example, the following code is equivalent to the console example shown earlier:

```
$UserData = @' This is a Test!!!
<TestValue>42</TestValue> '@
$UserData = [System.Convert]::ToBase64String([System.Text.Encoding]::ASCII.
GetBytes($UserData))
$AMI = Get-EC2ImageByName -Name 'WINDOWS_2016_BASE'
$Reservation = New-EC2Instance -ImageId $AMI[0].ImageId -KeyName 'MyKey'
-InstanceType 't2.micro' -MinCount 1 -MaxCount 1 -UserData $UserData
```

Note the @'...'@ syntax, this is just a convenient way to include a multiline string in PowerShell.

We can also use the Invoke-RestMethod command that we used in the previous section to retrieve the user data from PowerShell. For example:

```
Invoke-RestMethod 'http://169.254.169.254/latest/user-data'
```

This results in

```
This is a Test!!!
<TestValue>42</TestValue>
```

We can change the user data after launching an instance, but the instance must be in a stopped state. Let's stop our instance and try replacing the user data with well-formed XML.

From the EC2 Instances Web Console, right-click our instance and highlight Instance State then select Stop. After a couple minutes, the instance should be in the stopped state.

Again, right-click the instance and highlight Instance Settings then select View/Change User Data. Clear the current user data and input the following XML into the user data box and save it. Start the instance again.

```
<documentation>
<document>
<name>GettingStarted</name> <url>http://awsdocs.s3.amazonaws.com/EC2/
latest/ec2-gsg.pdf</url> </document> <document>
<name>UserGuide</name> <url>http://awsdocs.s3.amazonaws.com/EC2/latest/ec2-
ug.pdf</url> </document> <document>
<name>APIReference</name> <url>http://awsdocs.s3.amazonaws.com/EC2/latest/
ec2-api.pdf</url> </document> </documentation>
```

The benefit of using XML is that the Invoke-RestMethod command will parse the response. This means that we can interact with the response like any other object in PowerShell and we get IntelliSense in the IDE as well. Note how we can navigate the object hierarchy and format the response:

```
$Response = Invoke-RestMethod 'http://169.254.169.254/latest/user-data'
$Response.documentation.document | Format-Table
```

The preceding code results in the following output:

```
name            url
----            ---
GettingStarted http://awsdocs.s3.amazonaws.com/EC2/latest/ec2-gsg.pdf
UserGuide      http://awsdocs.s3.amazonaws.com/EC2/latest/ec2-ug.pdf
APIReference   http://awsdocs.s3.amazonaws.com/EC2/latest/ec2-api.pdf
```

There is one other really cool feature of user data. We can include scripts that we want to run when the instance boots the first time. We can include Windows command shell scripts inside <script>...</script> or PowerShell scripts inside <powershell>... </powershell> tags. We will do this in the second exercise at the end of this chapter.

Working with Tags

Every object in AWS supports tags. Tags are a great way to keep track of all our instances and other objects. A tag is simply a key/value pair used to describe the object. For example, we can use a tag to record the name of an instance or which department owns it. We can use tags to record any additional information we need.

Each object can have up to 50 tags. The key can be up to 128 characters, and the value can be up to 256 characters long. Note how we can access tags on the EC2 Web Console using the Tags tab when selecting an instance (see Figure 3-20). We can edit the tags using the Add/Edit Tags button.

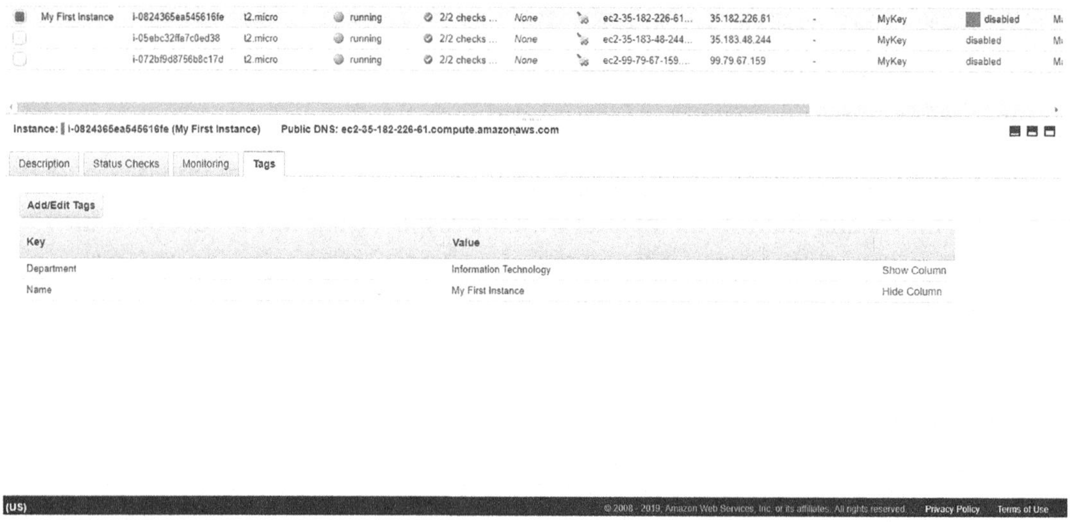

Figure 3-20. *The Tags tab*

In PowerShell we can read the tags from the tag collection of any object. To get the tags for an instance, just get a reference to the instance and read the Tag property:

```
$Reservation = Get-EC2Instance -Instance i-0824365ea545616fe
$Instance = $Reservation.Instances
$Instance.Tag
```

Here is the result:

```
Key        Value
---        -----
Department Information Technology
Name       My First Instance
```

If we want to retrieve a specific tag, use the where-object command to find it:

```
$Tag = $Instance.Tag | Where-Object {$_.Key -eq "Name"}
$Tag.Value
```

Creating tags is a bit harder. A tag is a .Net object so there is no PowerShell command to create an EC2 tag. Instead, we use the generic new-object command to create a .Net object of type Amazon.EC2.Model.Tag. Once we have the new tag object, we can use the New-EC2Tag PowerShell command to set the Key and Value properties.

Let's add another descriptive tag to our instance:

```
$Tag = New-Object Amazon.EC2.Model.Tag
$Tag.Key ='Role'
$Tag.Value = 'File Server'
New-EC2Tag -ResourceId i-0824365ea545616fe -Tag $Tag
```

When there is only a few instances, it is relatively simple to keep track of everything. Once we launch ten or more, it quickly gets very confusing.

One trick is to tag everything. Each instance has at least one volume and one network interface attached. Whenever a new instance is created, tag the instance and all of the attached resources.

AWS makes it easy to tag multiple objects at once. We simply pass all the IDs to New-EC2Tag as an array. There is no need to tell AWS what type of object each is. It can figure that out on its own. In this example we will launch a new instance and tag the instance and its resources.

```
$AMI = Get-EC2ImageByName -Name 'WINDOWS_2016_BASE'
$Reservation = New-EC2Instance -ImageId $AMI[0].ImageId -KeyName 'MyKey'
-InstanceType 't2.micro' -MinCount 1 -MaxCount 1
$InstanceId = $Reservation.Instances.InstanceId
Start-Sleep -s 60 #Wait for drives to be created and mounted, etc.
$Reservation = Get-EC2Instance -Instance $InstanceId
$VolumeId = $Reservation.Instances.Blockdevicemappings.EBS.VolumeId
$NetworkInterfaceId = $Reservation.Instances.NetworkInterfaces.
NetworkInterfaceId
$Tag = New-Object Amazon.EC2.Model.Tag
$Tag.Key = 'Name'
$Tag.Value = 'Multi Tagged Server'
New-EC2Tag -ResourceId $InstanceId, $VolumeId, $NetworkInterfaceId -Tag $Tag
```

Notice that Start-Sleep in the previous command. When we create a new instance, the command may return before all of the resources have been allocated. Therefore, we may find that a volume or network interface is null if we move too quickly.

To get around this, we have the script sleep for a few seconds. Then we query AWS for an updated copy of the instance metadata. This gives AWS enough time to allocate resources.

Working with Filters

In the previous section, we used the Where-Object command to filter a collection and find a specific tag. This same method could be applied to other objects – for example, to find all of the instances owned by a given department.

AWS provides a better solution: filters. A filter allows us to specify search criteria to be executed on the server side. This way we don't have to download metadata from hundreds of instances and sort through them when we are only interested in a handful.

The Get methods usually include a filter parameter. The filter allows us to return only those resources with a specific value for a given attribute. For example, if we want to return a list of instances that are currently in a running state, we can use the instance-state-code filter. A value of 16 indicates an instance is running.

The filter names and values are not always intuitive. They use the AWS CLI syntax, which may be foreign to a user of the PowerShell API. Included is a list of filters and values with each Get command in Appendix C.

Once again, we use the generic New-Object to create the filter. For example:

```
$Filter = New-Object Amazon.EC2.Model.Filter
$Filter.Name = 'instance-state-code'
$Filter.Value = 16
Get-EC2Instance -Filter $Filter
```

Optionally we can just use a hashtable using the name and value key pair. In this example we will use the friendlier 'instance-state-name' filter of 'running'.

```
$Filter = @{name='instance-state-name';value='running'}
Get-EC2Instance -Filter $Filter
```

We can also use filters to search for custom tags. For example, assume we record the department that owns each instance. If we wanted to retrieve all instances that belong to the Information Technology department, we could use

```
$Filter = @{name='tag:Department';value='Information Technology'}
Get-EC2Instance -Filter $filter
```

When we filter on tags, we use the format tag, followed by the key name. Remember that keys and their values are case sensitive. When creating keys manually using the Web Console, be consistent.

If we wanted to retrieve all of the running and pending instances that belong to the Information Technology department, we could use multiple filters that specify the tag of "Department" with the value of "Information Technology" and an instance-state-name with a value of "running" or "pending". To do that we can add multiple comma-separated values for a given name and pass multiple hashtables as an array.

```
$Filter = @(@{name='instance-state-name';value='running','pending'};
@{name='tag:Department';value='Information Technology'})
Get-EC2Instance -Filter $filter
```

EXERCISE 3.1: WAITING FOR AN INSTANCE TO LAUNCH

For this exercise let's assume that we often receive requests to create new instances from developers in our organization and those developers don't have access to the AWS Web Console. As AWS adoption has grown, this has become very time-consuming. It would be nice to script the build in PowerShell.

We can create a new instance and get the password with a few lines of code, and it would be great if a script could wait for the build to finish and then automatically e-mail the password to the requestor. But, how do we know when the server is finished?

One way to determine whether the server is finished is to poll the instance to check if the password is available. We can call the Get-EC2PasswordData command to check if a password exists. This provides a convenient way to check for password availability.

Let's start by creating a new method, called GetPasswordWhenReady. This method checks once every minute until the password is ready and then returns it. The method takes three parameters. The first is the ID of the instance to wait on. The second is the location of the private key used to decrypt the password. The third is the number of minutes to wait for the password, after which the script will give up.

Note that the script writes periods to the screen each minute to let the user know that it is still working. Also note that we had the set WarningAction to stop as the cmdlet Get-EC2Password Data throws a warning to our catch statement when the password has yet to be generated.

```
Function GetPasswordWhenReady
{
    Param(
        [string][Parameter(Mandatory=$True)] $InstanceId,
        [string][Parameter(Mandatory=$True)] $PemFile,
        [Int] $TimeOut = 35
    )
    $RetryCount = $TimeOut
    Write-Host "Waiting for password..." -NoNewline
    While($RetryCount -gt 1)
    {
        Try {
            $Password = Get-EC2PasswordData -InstanceId $InstanceId -PemFile
            $PemFile -WarningAction stop
            Write-Host ""
            Return $Password
        }
        Catch {
            $RetryCount--
            Start-Sleep -s 60 #It's not ready. Let's wait for it.
            Write-Host "..." -NoNewline #It's nice to give a little feedback
            now and then
        }
    }
    throw "Failed to get password from $InstanceId after waiting $Timeout minutes."
}
```

All we need now is a method that sends e-mails. This method will take three parameters: recipient, instance address, and password. Note that we have hard-coded the from address and SMTP server name in my script. We will need to change them to our own SMTP server settings if one is configured.

```
Function SendInstanceReadyEmail {
    Param(
        [string][Parameter(Mandatory=$True)] $Recipient,
```

```
        [string][Parameter(Mandatory=$True)] $InstanceAddress,
        [string][Parameter(Mandatory=$True)] $Password
    )
    $Message = "Access the instance at $InstanceAddress. The administrator
    password is $Password."
    #Create the message
    $Email = New-Object Net.Mail.MailMessage
    $Email.From = "admin@brianbeach.com"
    $Email.ReplyTo = "admin@brianbeach.com"
    $Email.To.Add($Recipient)
    $Email.Subject = "Instance is Ready"
    $Email.Body = $Message
    #Send the message
    $SMTP = New-Object Net.Mail.SmtpClient('smtp.brianbeach.com')
    $SMTP.Send($Email)
}
```

Now we can test it. Here we are creating a new instance and retrieving the ID. Then we wait for the password to become available. This usually takes about 5–10 minutes. Once the password is ready, we refresh the metadata. Remember that some attributes are not available when New-EC2Instance returns. By refreshing the metadata after the build completes, we know that all variables are present. Now we can send an e-mail to the requestor.

```
Param(
    [string][Parameter(Mandatory=$false)] $ImageID,
    [string][Parameter(Mandatory=$false)] $KeyName = 'MyKey',
    [string][Parameter(Mandatory=$false)] $PemFile = 'c:\aws\MyKey.pem',
    [string][Parameter(Mandatory=$false)] $InstanceType = 't2.micro',
    [string][Parameter(Mandatory=$true)] $EmailRecipient
)
#Create a new instance
If([System.String]::IsNullOrEmpty($ImageID))
{
    $ImageID = (Get-EC2ImageByName -Name "WINDOWS_2016_BASE")[0].ImageId
}
$Reservation = New-EC2Instance -ImageId $ImageID -KeyName $KeyName
-InstanceType $InstanceType -MinCount 1 -MaxCount 1
$InstanceId = $Reservation.Instances[0].InstanceId
#Get the password to the new instance
```

```
$Password = GetPasswordWhenReady -Instance $InstanceId -PemFile $PemFile
#Get the latest meta-data including the DNS name
$Reservation = Get-EC2Instance -Instance $InstanceId
$InstanceAddress = $Reservation.RunningInstance[0].PrivateIPAddress
#Send an email with connection info
SendInstanceReadyEmail -Recipient $EmailRecipient -InstanceAddress
$InstanceAddress -Password $Password
```

EXERCISE 3.2: BOOTSTRAPPING WITH USER DATA

At this point we know how to launch and manage instances. Before we close this chapter, let's spend a minute talking about how we can customize instances. We could, of course, just log in and configure each instance manually, but the cloud is all about automation and standardization.

If we script the configuration of our server, the results will be more consistent and reproducible.

Amazon thought of this, and it included the capability to run configuration scripts when a server boots. In this exercise, we are going to configure our instance for remote administration. We will use a PowerShell script in the user data to complete the configuration.

Amazon includes the EC2Config or EC2Launch service agent (depending on the OS version) in every Windows AMI they provide. The first time an instance boots, this agent service will check the user data for <script>...</script> or <powershell>...</powershell> tags and then execute them at the command prompt or PowerShell prompt, respectively. By default, scripts are run only the first time an instance boots, but we can configure it to run every time the instance starts (we will look at this in Chapter 7).

We talked in the last chapter about specifying default credentials and a default region. We will use a server role to provide credentials, but remember that we still need to set the default region and we can use PowerShell in the user data to accomplish this. When a new AWS instance launches, it will be ready to run scripts without further configuration.

On our next instance launch, let's make a few more changes with a user data script to enable PowerShell remoting for administration and Windows Management Instrumentation (WMI) for monitoring and management.

PowerShell remoting is really easy. The command is simply Enable-PSRemoting. WMI is a bit more complicated. WMI is already running, but Windows Firewall will block external access. Fortunately, the firewall rules are already configured. They just need to be enabled. All we need to do is use the PowerShell command Enable-NetFirewallRule. Here we enable PSRemoting and then find and enable all of the WMI firewall rules:

```
Enable-PSRemoting
Get-NetFirewallRule | Where { $_.DisplayName -like "Windows Management
Instrumentation *" } |
Enable-NetFirewallRule
```

The complete script is available with the accompanying code in a file called Bootstrap.ps1. For information on downloading the sample code, see Chapter 1. We could use the "As file" option under advanced details in the Configure Instance page of the Launch Instance Wizard to open this file, but we are going to generate the user data and launch the instance using only PowerShell.

The following script will open the bootstrap script from disk. Then it will format the script for use with the AWS API. Finally, it will launch the instance, passing the script as user data.

```
param(
    [parameter(mandatory=$false)][string]$KeyName = 'MyKey',
    [parameter(mandatory=$false)][string]$RoleName = 'AdminRole',
    [parameter(mandatory=$false)][string]$UserDataFile = 'C:\AWS\Chapter3\
    Exercise2\Bootstrap.ps1',
    [parameter(mandatory=$false)][string]$ImageId,
    [parameter(mandatory=$false)][string]$InstanceType = 't2.micro'
)
#If no image was specified, assume 2016 base
If([System.String]::IsNullOrEmpty($ImageID)){$ImageID = (Get-EC2ImageByName
-Name "WINDOWS_2016_BASE")[0].ImageId}
#Read the bootstrap script from the file specified
#Get-Content returns an array of strings. Raw converts the array to a single
string
$BootstrapScript = Get-Content -Raw $UserDataFile
#Add the PowerShell tags to the script
$BootstrapScript = @"
<powershell>
$BootstrapScript
</powershell>
```

```
"@
#Base 64 encode the script
$UserData = [System.Convert]::ToBase64String([System.Text.Encoding]::ASCII.
GetBytes($BootstrapScript))
#Get the IAM Role to apply to the new instance
$Profile = Get-IAMInstanceProfile -InstanceProfileName $RoleName
#Launch the new instance with bootstrap script
$Reservation = New-EC2Instance -ImageId $ImageId -KeyName $KeyName
-InstanceType $InstanceType -MinCount 1 -MaxCount 1 -UserData $UserData
-InstanceProfile_Arn $Profile.Arn
$InstanceId = $Reservation.Instances[0].InstanceId
Write-Host "Launched new instance with ID $InstanceId"
```

User data is a really powerful option. We can use this to make just about any customizations we need without ever logging into a server. As our adoption of AWS matures, we will likely begin to use features such as Auto Scaling, which deploys instances automatically in response to load. Obviously, it is critical that we can auto configure these instances at launch. (We will talk more about Auto Scaling in Chapter 8).

Summary

In this chapter, we got a good introduction to instances. We learned to launch and verify instances using both Web Console and PowerShell. We learned how to start, stop, and terminate instances. We also learned how to discover information about our instance using both PowerShell and the metadata URL. Next, we learned how to include custom data with user data and tags. Then we discussed how to use filters to find specific instances. In the examples we created a complete script to manage launching instances. Then we learned how to customize our instance at launch using user data.

In the next chapter, we will discuss storage including volumes and snapshots. Volumes are the disks that are attached to an instance, and snapshots are point-in-time backups of our volumes.

CHAPTER 4

Elastic Block Storage

In the last chapter, we learned how to launch and manage instances. In this chapter, we will focus on the volumes, or disks, attached to the instance. We will learn how to customize and add additional volumes at launch. Then we will look at modifying the volumes after launch. This chapter will also cover snapshots. Snapshots are a point-in-time copy of a volume, often used for backups. Snapshots can be used to create copies of volumes or to recover from a disaster. We will talk about using snapshots to create a backup of a volume and how to restore a volume when a disaster occurs.

Let's start with a little background. Volumes are based on a technology Amazon calls Elastic Block Storage (EBS). EBS is network-attached storage used by EC2 instances. Like iSCSI in a traditional data center, EBS shares bandwidth with other network-attached storage traffic. This means performance is affected by network load. We will see how to configure quality of service to guarantee the minimum performance of our volumes.

EBS volumes are redundant within an availability zone. Therefore, there is no need to create RAID arrays of EBS disks within the operating system. Remember that an availability zone is a single data center. Despite the redundancy EBS provides, it is possible to lose an entire availability zone in a disaster. Therefore, we still need to back up our volumes using snapshots. Snapshots are backups of volumes stored in the Simple Storage Service (S3). (We will talk about S3 in detail in Chapter 11.) Each snapshot is stored in multiple availability zones within a region to provide very high durability. In addition, we will see how to copy snapshots from one region to another.

Let's get started by building on our experience in Chapter 3. In the next section, we will extend our launch scripts to control volumes at launch.

© Brian Beach, Steven Armentrout, Rodney Bozo, Emmanuel Tsouris 2019
B. Beach et al., *Pro PowerShell for Amazon Web Services*, https://doi.org/10.1007/978-1-4842-4850-8_4

Managing Volumes at Launch

In the last chapter, we discussed launching a new EC2 instance. Remember when we skipped over a few of the screens in the wizard. Let's return to the wizard and look at the Add Storage configuration screen. This screen allows us to specify the number, size, and performance characteristics of the volumes that will be attached to the instance.

Open the AWS EC2 Management Console and click the Launch Instance button on the EC2 dashboard. Navigate through the wizard and stop on the Add Storage screen (see Figure 4-1). This screen lists the default volumes that come with the Amazon Machine Image (AMI) we choose. Remember that an AMI is the template that describes an instance as well as snapshots of its volume data. Most Windows images include a 30GB root volume. SQL images are larger, and most Linux distributions are significantly smaller.

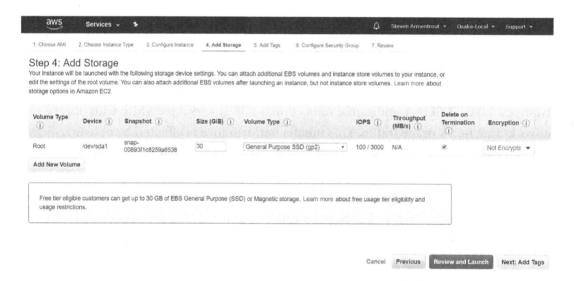

Figure 4-1. *Add Storage configuration*

We can change the size of the root volume by simply typing into the text box under the heading Size (GiB). The initial size is the minimum size the AMI snapshot requires and cannot be reduced. Thirty GB is good enough for most Windows applications, but some applications, such as SQL Server, require more storage and will start at a higher value. A single volume can be set between 1GB and 16TB. In addition, we can configure the IO operations per second (IOPS) for a volume. (We will talk about provisioned IOPS later in this chapter).

We can also choose to delete the volume on termination. If we check this box, the volume will be automatically deleted when we terminate the instance. In general, the root volume is configured to auto delete by default, and any additional volumes we attach are not.

WHAT'S A GIBIBYTE (GIB)?

If we look closely at Figure 4-2, we may notice the Volume size is measured in GiB, which is the abbreviation for gibibyte. A gibibyte (GiB) is closely related to, but not equal to, a gigabyte (GB).

We know that 1KB = 1024 bytes but in other scientific disciplines 1K = 1000. Computer scientists prefer 1024 because it is a power of 2 ($2^{10} = 1024$).

Amazon is using the unambiguous gibibyte. In these examples we will use the old GB but really mean GiB.

Manipulating the root volume in PowerShell is verbose, but straightforward. PowerShell uses .NET objects to describe the drive configuration. We simply pass the .NET object to the New-EC2Instance we used in Chapter 3.

First, we use the Amazon.EC2.Model.EbsBlockDevice object to describe the volume. Here we want a 55GB GP2 volume, which does not use provisioned IOPS. In addition, we want the volume to be deleted when we terminate the instance.

```
$Volume = New-Object Amazon.EC2.Model.EbsBlockDevice
$Volume.VolumeSize = 55
$Volume.VolumeType = 'GP2'
$Volume.DeleteOnTermination = $True
```

Next, we use the Amazon.EC2.Model.BlockDeviceMapping object to describe how the volume should be attached to the instance. The root volume is always attached to "/dev/sda1". Notice that we are passing the EbsBlockDevice object created by the preceding code.

```
$Mapping = New-Object Amazon.EC2.Model.BlockDeviceMapping
$Mapping.DeviceName = '/dev/sda1'
$Mapping.Ebs = $Volume
```

Finally, we call New-EC2Instance and include the BlockDeviceMapping parameter describing how we want the volume configured.

```
$AMI = Get-EC2ImageByName -Name 'WINDOWS_2016_BASE'
$Reservation = New-EC2Instance -ImageId $AMI[0].ImageId -KeyName 'MyKey'
-InstanceType 't2.micro' -MinCount 1 -MaxCount 1 -BlockDeviceMapping
$Mapping
$Instance = $Reservation.RunningInstance[0]
Write-output $Instance.InstanceId
```

We can also add additional volumes to the instance at launch. See Figure 4-2. Windows instances will support up to 26 total volumes. The New Instance Wizard allows us to add additional volumes using the Add New Volume button in the Add Storage Configuration page. Most of these options are the same as the root volume with a couple of differences, described next.

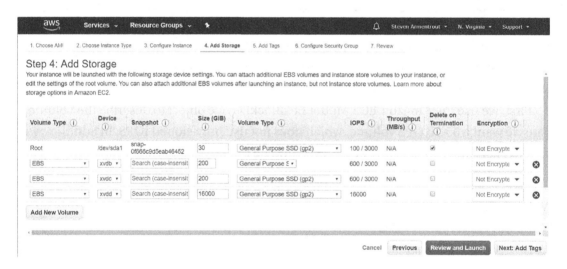

Figure 4-2. *EBS volumes*

We can choose to use a snapshot to initialize our disk. Recall that a snapshot is a copy of a volume at a specific point in time. The root volume always uses the snapshot specified for the AMI we selected, but additional volumes can use any snapshot. We can choose our own snapshot, or there are numerous interesting datasets available for public use. Leaving the snapshot entry field blank results in a new empty volume.

We must set a device name. The device name describes how the EBS volume is attached to the instance. This is like describing which port the disk is plugged into on a physical machine. For EBS volumes we should use xvd[b-z]. Just use them in order: xvdb, xvde, xvdf, and so on. These device names are auto-filled in using the console for Windows AMIs but need to be specified when using PowerShell.

Additional volumes are handled just like the root volume when using PowerShell. For each additional volume, we create another EbsBlockDevice and BlockDeviceMapping objects. Note that the root volume is always attached at device name "/dev/sda1" and the second EBS disk is attached at "xvdb".

In the following example, note that we have chosen to delete the root volume when the instance is terminated, but we will keep the second volume by setting DeleteOnTermination attribute to false. We separate the mapping objects by commas when calling New-EC2Instance to create an array of mappings.

```
$Volume1 = New-Object Amazon.EC2.Model.EbsBlockDevice
$Volume1.DeleteOnTermination = $True
$Volume1.VolumeSize = 30
$Volume1.VolumeType = 'gp2'
$Mapping1 = New-Object Amazon.EC2.Model.BlockDeviceMapping
$Mapping1.DeviceName = '/dev/sda1'
$Mapping1.Ebs = $Volume1
$Volume2 = New-Object Amazon.EC2.Model.EbsBlockDevice
$Volume2.DeleteOnTermination = $False
$Volume2.VolumeSize = 100
$Volume2.VolumeType = 'gp2'
$Mapping2 = New-Object Amazon.EC2.Model.BlockDeviceMapping
$Mapping2.DeviceName = 'xvdf'
$Mapping2.Ebs = $Volume2
$AMI = Get-EC2ImageByName -Name 'WINDOWS_2016_BASE'
$Reservation = New-EC2Instance -ImageId $AMI[0].ImageId -KeyName 'MyKey'
-InstanceType 't2.micro' -MinCount 1 -MaxCount 1 -BlockDeviceMapping
$Mapping1, $Mapping2
$Instance = $Reservation.RunningInstance[0]
Write-output $Instance.InstanceId
```

If we want to use a snapshot to initialize the second volume, we can use the SnapshotId parameter. We can use a snapshot we created or use one of the many already available. For example, the following partial code will generate a 100GB volume containing the Windows 2016 installation media from a snapshot found in Northern Virginia. Note that there are no CD/DVD drives in EC2 instances. (Later in this chapter, we will talk more about discovering the numerous snapshots available with AWS).

```
$MediaSnapshot = Get-EC2Snapshot -Filter @(@{name='description';value="Wind
ows 2016 English Installation Media"},@{name='owner-alias';value="amazon"})
$Volume2 = New-Object Amazon.EC2.Model.EbsBlockDevice
$Volume2.DeleteOnTermination = $False
$Volume2.VolumeSize = 100
$Volume2.VolumeType = 'gp2'
$Volume2.SnapshotId = $MediaSnapshot[0].SnapshotId
```

When launching some instance types in the console such as m5d or i2, we will see additional volume types. In the Add Storage launch step, they will appear with Volume Type names like "Instance Store 0" or "ephemeral0". These are what is known as ephemeral volumes. Ephemeral volumes allow us to access disks local to the host server. While EBS volumes are network-attached storage, ephemeral (instance store) volumes are directly attached storage.

There can be significant performance gains using the directly attached ephemeral volumes, but this approach comes with some limitations. The ephemeral drives are not persisted when the instance is stopped. If an instance is stopped or placed into a shutdown state, the data is simply deleted. Therefore, ephemeral drives are good only for temporary storage such as a cache or when used in a high availability or clustering architecture to preserve the data. Note however this data loss does not happen during a reboot since the instance never reaches a stopped state.

If we selected a micro instance, there are no ephemeral volumes. In Figure 4-3, we have chosen an i2.xlarge that includes an 800GB ephemeral SSD. We also added a second 100GB EBS volume. Note that the ephemeral drives are attached by default. Some ephemeral drives can be removed if we want, but we don't pay anything extra by leaving them attached. Just be careful that we're not using the ephemeral drives when we expect to be using an EBS volume.

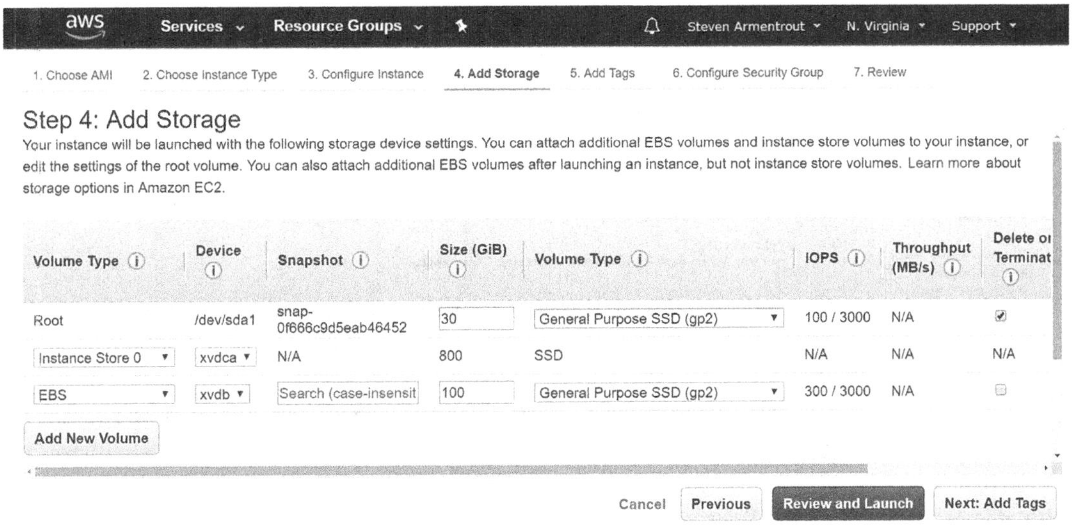

Figure 4-3. *Ephemeral volumes*

When we create an instance using PowerShell, the ephemeral drives are also attached automatically. There is no reason to remove them, but we can do so by creating a BlockDeviceMapping with NoDevice set to true. Note in the following partial code example that there is no EbsBlockDevice object in this case.

```
$Mapping = New-Object Amazon.EC2.Model.BlockDeviceMapping
$Mapping.DeviceName = 'xvdca'
$Mapping.NoDevice = $true
```

Figure 4-4 shows the disk configuration of a Windows Server 2016 instance with all three volume types: a 30GB root volume, one additional 100GB EBS volume, and an 800GB ephemeral volume. Not all instance types have 800GB ephemeral volumes. Some, such as the t2.micro, have no ephemeral volumes. Other instance types can have as much as 48TB total of ephemeral storage.

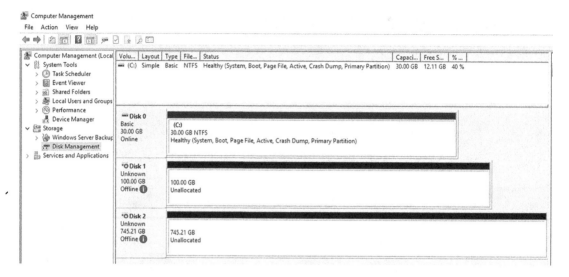

Figure 4-4. *EBS and ephemeral volumes as seen by Windows*

As we have seen, Amazon makes it easy to manage volumes when launching an instance. Unfortunately, we don't always know exactly what the volumes should look like. We do our best to estimate how big each volume needs to be, but requirements change. New software is installed, usage patterns change, and so on.

Encrypting Volumes at Launch

When configuring and adding volumes in the Add Storage step, an encrypted selection exists. Enabling this setting will enable data at reset security by encrypting our volume and resultant snapshots with keys defined in the AWS Key Management Service (KMS). This will enable an extra layer of defense to protect our data and to meet regulatory or compliance needs. Enabling encryption does result in some changes to be aware of:

- Encrypts data at rest inside the volume.

- Encrypts all data moving between the volume and the instance.

- Encrypts all snapshots created from the volume.

- Encrypts all volumes created from those snapshots.

- Once encrypted, a volume cannot be unencrypted.

- Not all instance types support encrypted volumes.

- Only new empty volumes can be encrypted.

- Encrypted volumes and snapshots have sharing restrictions.

- Encryption is limited to EBS volumes only and requires an encryption key from the AWS Key Management Service (KMS).

Key Management Service is outside the scope of this chapter so more information about using KMS for EBS encryption can be found at https://docs.aws.amazon.com/ AWSEC2/latest/UserGuide/EBSEncryption.html.

To encrypt a volume using PowerShell, we first need to find the KMS KeyId. We will use the default EBS key by searching KMS for the key with alias "alias/aws/ebs" and getting its TargetKeyId property. We then will create a secondary 100GB EBS volume with encryption enabled using this key ID.

This default EBS encryption key gets created the first time we launch an instance from the console and have encryption enabled set on a volume. If the key cannot be found, try launching an instance with an encrypted volume from the console first.

```
$KMSKeyId = (Get-KMSAliasList | Where-Object {$_.AliasName -eq "alias/aws/
ebs"}).TargetKeyId
$Volume1 = New-Object Amazon.EC2.Model.EbsBlockDevice
$Volume1.DeleteOnTermination = $True
$Volume1.VolumeSize = 30
$Volume1.VolumeType = 'gp2'
$Mapping1 = New-Object Amazon.EC2.Model.BlockDeviceMapping
$Mapping1.DeviceName = '/dev/sda1'
$Mapping1.Ebs = $Volume1
$Volume2 = New-Object Amazon.EC2.Model.EbsBlockDevice
$Volume2.DeleteOnTermination = $False
$Volume2.VolumeSize = 100
$Volume2.VolumeType = 'gp2'
$Volume2.Encrypted = $true
$Volume2.KmsKeyId = $KMSKeyId
$Mapping2 = New-Object Amazon.EC2.Model.BlockDeviceMapping
$Mapping2.DeviceName = 'xvda'
$Mapping2.Ebs = $Volume2
$AMI = Get-EC2ImageByName -Name 'WINDOWS_2016_BASE'
```

```
$Reservation = New-EC2Instance -ImageId $AMI[0].ImageId -KeyName 'MyKey'
-InstanceType 't2.micro' -MinCount 1 -MaxCount 1 -BlockDeviceMapping
$Mapping1,$Mapping2
$Instance = $Reservation.RunningInstance[0]
```

In the next section, we will discuss how to add volumes to a running instance, and in Exercise 4.1 we will resize a volume.

Adding a Volume to a Running Instance

Often, we want to add a volume after the instance is already running. We can create a new volume and attach it to a running instance at any time.

To create a volume from the EC2 Web Console, on the left side click the plus sign next to ELASTIC BLOCK STORE field to expand it and select Volumes. Click the Create Volume button on the Volumes page that opens. The Create Volume page will open, and we will need to specify all the options we discussed earlier, plus the Availability Zone (see Figure 4-5). Remember from Chapter 1 that an availability zone is one of many data centers in a region, so we can only attach a volume to an instance in the same availability zone.

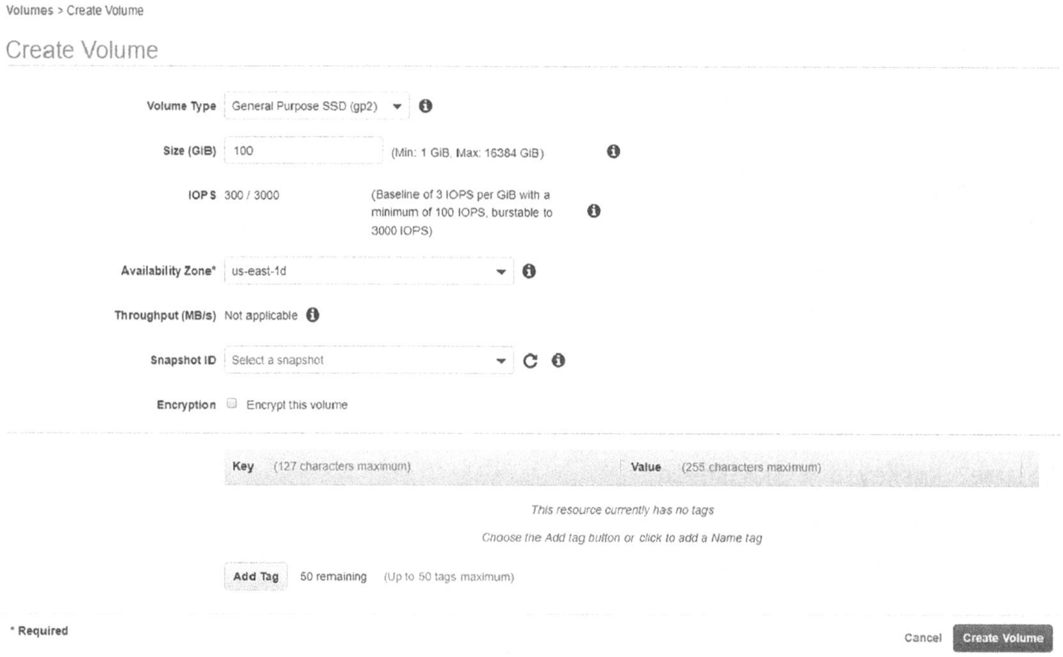

Figure 4-5. *Creating a new volume*

Creating a volume in PowerShell is simple. But before we attach volumes, let's create a new Windows Server 2016 instance:

```
$AMI = Get-EC2ImageByName -Name 'WINDOWS_2016_BASE'
$Reservation = New-EC2Instance -ImageId $AMI[0].ImageId -KeyName 'MyKey'
-InstanceType 't2.micro' -MinCount 1 -MaxCount 1
$Instance = $Reservation.RunningInstance[0]
```

Now we find the availability zone of our new instance by getting the AvailabilityZone property of the subnet we launched in.

```
$AvailZone = (Get-EC2Subnet -SubnetId $Instance.SubnetId).AvailabilityZone
```

The following example creates a new 100GB empty volume:

```
$LargeVolume = New-EC2Volume -Size 100 -AvailabilityZone $AvailZone
-VolumeType gp2
```

If we want to use a snapshot to initialize our volume, just specify the snapshot ID. This example creates a new volume with the public Windows 2016 install media:

```
$MediaSnapshot = Get-EC2Snapshot -Filter @(@{name='description';value="Wind
ows 2016 English Installation Media"},@{name='owner-alias';value="amazon"})
$SnapshotVolume = New-EC2Volume -SnapshotId $MediaSnapshot[0].SnapshotId
-AvailabilityZone $AvailZone -VolumeType gp2
```

Once the volumes are created, we can attach them to an instance using the Add-EC2Volume command. In the following example, we use a while loop to wait for the volumes to become available. Then we attach them to an instance using Add-EC2Volume and wait for them to become in use.

```
While ($addvolumes.status -ne "available") {Start-Sleep -Seconds
10; $addvolumes = Get-EC2Volume -VolumeIds $LargeVolume.
VolumeId,$SnapshotVolume.VolumeId }

Add-EC2Volume -VolumeId $LargeVolume.VolumeId -InstanceId $Instance.
InstanceId -Device 'xvdg'
Add-EC2Volume -VolumeId $SnapshotVolume.VolumeId -InstanceId $Instance.
InstanceId -Device 'xvdh'
```

```
While ($usedvolumes.status -ne "in-use") {Start-Sleep -Seconds
10; $usedvolumes = Get-EC2Volume -VolumeIds $LargeVolume.
VolumeId,$SnapshotVolume.VolumeId}
```

Once we are done with the volumes, we can detach them from the instance using
Dismount-EC2Volume. We can also delete them using Remove-EC2Volume. We will
again use a while loop to check that the volumes are in an available state before deleting
them. If the volumes fail to reach an available state after a minute, they may be locked
by the OS on the instance. It's best practice to offline volumes in the instance before
running the EC2 dismount. Ensure the volumes are offline in the instance and restart the
following code again:

```
Dismount-EC2Volume -VolumeId $LargeVolume.VolumeId
Dismount-EC2Volume -VolumeId $SnapshotVolume.VolumeId
While ($detachvolumes.status -ne "available") {Start-Sleep -Seconds
10; $detachvolumes = Get-EC2Volume -VolumeIds $LargeVolume.
VolumeId,$SnapshotVolume.VolumeId }

Remove-EC2Volume -VolumeId $LargeVolume.VolumeId –Force
Remove-EC2Volume -VolumeId $SnapshotVolume.VolumeId –Force
```

Managing Quality of Service

Some instances – database servers, for example – are more IO intensive and some
instance workloads are more throughput intensive, while others still just need low-cost
storage for long-term data archiving. AWS offers several options for EBS storage types,
and they each have unique benefits:

- General Purpose SSD (GP2) is the default general purpose storage
  type recommended for most workloads. It's a SSD-based storage with
  a balance between price and performance. We get three IOPS per GB
  for minimum baseline performance and many thousands of burst
  IOPS per volume.

- Throughput Optimized HDD (st1) are low-cost volumes suited for
  throughput intensive workloads.

- Cold HDD (sc1) is the lowest-cost storage option recommended for infrequently accessed large volumes of data.

- Provisioned IOPS SSD (io1) is designed for mission critical high-throughput and low-latency workloads. Like GP2, io1 is SSD based but allows for much higher baseline performance that's explicitly defined for the volume.

- Io1 volumes allow for up to 50 IOPS per GB sustained performance with a maximum of 64,000 IOPS per volume on Nitro-based instance types.

Aside from choosing the proper storage type for our workload, we also need to consider that EBS volumes are shared network storage. Obviously, there are many AWS tenants competing for the same resources. In addition, the EBS traffic is typically competing for bandwidth with the other traffic to and from our own instance. EBS-optimized instances get guaranteed network bandwidth between the instance and the EBS volumes. This ensures that we get the expected performance regardless of how congested the network gets.

To create an EBS-optimized instance, we can launch our instance on an instance type that is EBS Optimized by default or we can enable the EbsOptimized flag on a new or existing instance. Note that most current generation instance types enable EBS Optimization by default and not all instance types support EBS optimization. In the following example, we are launching an EBS-optimized instance on m1.large that does support it but is not enabled by default.

```
$AMI = Get-EC2ImageByName -Name 'WINDOWS_2016_BASE'
$Reservation = New-EC2Instance -ImageId $AMI[0].ImageId -KeyName 'MyKey' -
InstanceType 'm1.large' -MinCount 1 -MaxCount 1 -EbsOptimized:$true
$Instance = $Reservation.RunningInstance[0]
```

In the following example, we are going to launch a new instance with a Provisioned IOPS SSD (io1) root volume. To specify IOPS at launch time, use the EbsBlockDevice object. Simply, set the volume type to "io1" and specify the IOPS desired. In the following example, we are launching a new EBS-optimized instance with a root volume of 30GB provisioned at 1000 IOPS.

```
$Volume = New-Object Amazon.EC2.Model.EbsBlockDevice
$Volume.DeleteOnTermination = $True
```

```
$Volume.VolumeSize = 30
$Volume.VolumeType = 'io1'
$volume.IOPS = 1000
$Mapping = New-Object Amazon.EC2.Model.BlockDeviceMapping
$Mapping.DeviceName = '/dev/sda1'
$Mapping.Ebs = $Volume
$AMI = Get-EC2ImageByName -Name 'WINDOWS_2016_BASE'
$Reservation = New-EC2Instance -ImageId $AMI[0].ImageId -KeyName 'MyKey'
-InstanceType 'm1.large' -MinCount 1 -MaxCount 1 -BlockDeviceMapping
$Mapping -EbsOptimized:$true
$Instance = $Reservation.RunningInstance[0]
```

We can also create a new volume with provisioned IOPS and attach it to an existing instance:

```
$AvailZone = (Get-EC2Subnet -SubnetId $Instance.SubnetId).AvailabilityZone
$Volume = New-EC2Volume -Size 100 -AvailabilityZone $AvailZone -VolumeType
io1 -IOPS 2000
```

We could attach this volume to an instance the same way we did in the previous section:

```
Add-EC2Volume -VolumeId $Volume.VolumeId -InstanceId $Instance.InstanceId
-Device 'xvdf'
```

Now we know how to create and manage volumes. We can add volumes when launching a new instance or add a volume to a running instance. We can also manage the quality of service to guarantee performance. Next, we will talk about snapshots. Snapshots allow us to take a point-in-time copy of a volume.

Working with Snapshots

Snapshots are used to create a point-in-time copy of a volume often used for backup and recovery. Creating a new snapshot is simple. Just call New-EC2Snapshot and pass the ID of the volume. We can also add an optional description. For example, let's assume we are about to do a risky upgrade and we want to take a snapshot of an instance. First, stop the instance and create the snapshot of its root volume. Note that our instance and volumes will have different IDs than the ones explicitly defined in the following examples:

```
$Snapshot = New-EC2Snapshot -VolumeId vol-0b8daf5e53c94fd69 -Description
'Before upgrade to version 3.22'
```

Now, let's assume that our suspicions were correct, and we need to roll back the change. We already know how to restore a snapshot. We did it in the last section. We just create a new volume using the snapshot and verify that the volume is in the same availability zone as the instance we want to restore.

```
$Volume = New-EC2Volume  -AvailabilityZone us-east-1b -VolumeType gp2
-SnapshotId $Snapshot.SnapshotId
```

Note that we did not define a volume size here. When specifying a snapshot in a new volume creation, if the volume size is not set, then the new volume is automatically set to the snapshot size.

We cannot overwrite the contents of an existing volume. A restore always creates a new volume. Therefore, to replace the volume of an existing instance, we must detach the current volume and replace it with the one restored from the snapshot. Let's replace it with the restored volume. Note that this is the root volume and the instance should be stopped first.

```
Dismount-EC2Volume -VolumeId vol-0b8daf5e53c94fd69
While($BadVolume.Status -ne 'available') {Start-Sleep -Seconds 10;
$BadVolume = Get-EC2Volume  -VolumeId vol-0b8daf5e53c94fd69}
Add-EC2Volume -VolumeId $Volume.VolumeId -InstanceId i-0af9c78cd49747e08
-Device '/dev/sda1'
While($Volume.Status -ne 'in-use') {Start-Sleep -Seconds 10; $Volume =
Get-EC2Volume  -VolumeId $Volume.VolumeId }
Remove-EC2Volume -VolumeId vol-0b8daf5e53c94fd69 -Force
```

Now, boot the instance, and we are back where we were before the upgrade. Let's assume the upgrade works the second time, and we want to delete the snapshot. Just use Remove-EC2Snapshot:

```
Remove-EC2Snapshot -SnapshotId $Snapshot.SnapshotId –Force
```

Before we move on, let's talk about backup strategy. Many firms are accustomed to taking tape backups each night and storing them offsite. Can a snapshot replace offsite tape backups? Absolutely! Snapshots are stored in the AWS S3. S3 data is replicated three times across multiple availability zones within a region. This provides 99.999999999% durability. But, let's say we have a truly critical application that cannot stand an outage. It is possible that an entire region will suffer a power outage or other catastrophe that could bring our application down temporarily.

We can optionally copy the snapshot to another region using snapshot copy.

Let's assume we have an application running in Northern Virginia (us-east-1) and want to copy it to Northern California (us-west-1). The copy is always initiated from the destination region.

```
Copy-EC2Snapshot -SourceRegion 'us-east-1' -SourceSnapshotId 'snap-
0f390256dde249d88' -Region 'us-west-1' -Description 'Copied from Northern
Virginia'
```

Now, in the unlikely case that all the data in the Northern Virginia region was destroyed, we could recover our application in Northern California. While the previous examples are an effective strategy as a backup solution, there are some more advanced strategies using AWS Systems Manager that we will learn about in Chapter 16. To learn how Systems Manager Run command can manage backups, see `https://docs.aws.amazon.com/systems-manager/latest/userguide/integration-vss.html`.

Managing Public Snapshots

At the beginning of this chapter, we created a volume that included the Windows 2016 install media from a public snapshot. There are numerous snapshots available for our use. We can get a list by running Get-EC2Snapshot, but be warned that there are a lot of snapshots to sift through, and not all of them are from trustworthy sources.

To get a list of snapshots provided by Amazon, filter on the owner-alias property. This will narrow the list considerably. In the following example, we use two filters when looking for Windows 2016 media.

```
Get-EC2Snapshot -Filter @(@{name='description';value="Windows
2016*Installation Media"},@{name='owner-alias';value="amazon"})
```

In addition to software, Amazon has numerous datasets that can be used for testing. For example, the following command will return US Census snapshot data located in the us-east-1 region:

```
Get-EC2Snapshot -Filter @(@{name='description';value="* US Census
(Windows)"},@{name='owner-alias';value="amazon"}) -Region us-east-1
```

If we have an interesting dataset to make available to others, we can share our snapshots. We can choose to share with a specific AWS account or with all AWS accounts. If we want to share our snapshot with everyone, we call Edit-EC2SnapshotAttribute with the UserGroup attribute set to all. The following examples will also use a sample snapshot ID. To try these examples, we just need to replace the snapshot ID with our own but keep in mind that this snapshot will be usable by anyone within AWS. Share the snapshot and check the permissions using the Get-EC2SnapshotAttribute cmdlet.

```
Edit-EC2SnapshotAttribute -SnapshotId 'snap-0f390256dde249d88' -Attribute
'createVolumePermission' -OperationType 'add' -UserGroup 'all'
(Get-EC2SnapshotAttribute -Attribute 'createVolumePermission' -SnapshotId
snap-0f390256dde249d88).CreateVolumePermissions
```

Note that changes to permissions can take some time to propagate. Some upstream services and the EC2 Console may take several minutes before the snapshot can be accessed in other accounts. A direct describe call using the snapshot ID is the best way to get the most accurate permission settings. To remove the public access, rerun the command but change the OperationType value to remove.

```
Edit-EC2SnapshotAttribute -SnapshotId 'snap-0f390256dde249d88' -Attribute
'createVolumePermission' -OperationType 'remove' -UserGroup 'all'
```

If we prefer to share with a specific account, use the UserId attribute and supply the account number. We will again read back the snapshot CreateVolumePermissions attribute to validate our change. Note that we must remove the dashes from the account number, for example, if the account number is 1234-1234-1234.

```
Edit-EC2SnapshotAttribute -SnapshotId 'snap-0f390256dde249d88' -Attribute
'createVolumePermission' -OperationType 'add' -UserId '123412341234'
(Get-EC2SnapshotAttribute -Attribute 'createVolumePermission' -SnapshotId
snap-0f390256dde249d88).CreateVolumePermissions
```

If we want to remove a user's permission, once again set the OperationType to "remove". For example:

```
Edit-EC2SnapshotAttribute -SnapshotId 'snap-0f390256dde249d88' -Attribute
'createVolumePermission' -OperationType 'remove' -UserId '123412341234'
```

And, if we want to remove all permissions to a snapshot, use the Reset-EC2SnapshotAttribute cmdlet. For example:

```
Reset-EC2SnapshotAttribute -SnapshotId 'snap-0f390256dde249d88' -Attribute
'createVolumePermission'
```

In this chapter, we learned about volumes and snapshots. We learned how to add volumes to an instance and make copies of a volume using snapshots. In the first exercise, we will build a script to resize a volume. In the second exercise, we will build a script to back up all the volumes in an account.

EXERCISE 4.1: RESIZING A VOLUME

Over time, we may find that a volume is not big enough, and we need to resize it. In this example we will build a script that automates the process. The exercise script takes two parameters, the volume ID we want to resize and the incremental size in Gigabytes we want to add.

```
Param(
    [string][Parameter(Mandatory=$True)] $VolumeId,
    [int][Parameter(Mandatory=$True)] $GBIncrement
)
```

Before we start, let's get a reference to the volume so we know how it is attached and what instance it is attached to.

```
$TargetVolume = Get-EC2Volume -Volume $VolumeId
$Attachment = $TargetVolume.Attachment[0]
```

Note that we cannot make the volume smaller as there would not be room for the partition or snapshot data.

```
[int]$NewSize = $TargetVolume.Size + $GBIncrement
If ($Attachment.InstanceId -ne $null)
{
    If ((Get-EC2InstanceStatus $Attachment.InstanceId).InstanceState -ne
    "stopped")
    {
        Write-Warning "Instance not in a stopped state. File system integrity
        errors may be exist in the snapshot." -WarningAction Continue
    }
}
```

Now, we can create a new snapshot backup of the volume before we resize it. Let's also give the new snapshot a description. Remember to wait until the snapshot completes before we try to resize it.

```
$Snapshot = New-EC2Snapshot -VolumeId $TargetVolume.VolumeId -Description
"$(get-date -f o). Snapshot before extending volume: $($TargetVolume.
VolumeId) on Instance:$($Attachment.InstanceId)"
While ($Snapshot.Status -ne 'completed')
{
$Snapshot = Get-EC2Snapshot -SnapshotId $Snapshot.SnapshotId; Start-Sleep
-Seconds 15
}
```

Next, we extend the current volume.

```
 Edit-EC2Volume -VolumeId $TargetVolume.VolumeId  -Size $NewSize
```

The script is complete, but we are not quite done yet. The EBS volume has been resized, but the Windows partition has not. See Figure 4-6 for a visualization. To extend the partition, log into Windows and start the Computer Management MMC. On the Disk Management page, right-click the partition and select Extend Volume. Accept the defaults to extend it to its maximum size.

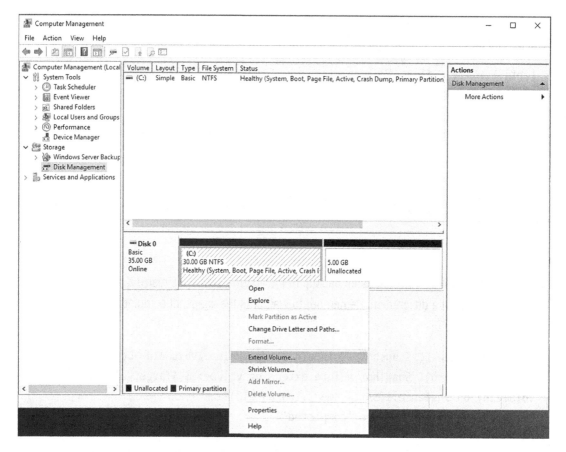

Figure 4-6. *Extending the partition*

Optionally we can run the following script on the instance to scan for a volume partition that has a drive letter. It extends the first matching partition with all available unused space.

```
Foreach ($Partition in $(Get-Partition | Where-Object {$_.Driveletter -ne
$Null}))
{Update-Disk -Number $Partition.Disknumber
$maxSize = $((Get-PartitionSupportedSize -DiskNumber $Partition.Disknumber
-PartitionNumber $Partition.PartitionNumber).sizeMax)
If ($Partition.Size -lt $maxSize){Resize-Partition -DiskNumber $Partition.
Disknumber -PartitionNumber $Partition.PartitionNumber -Size $maxSize;break}}
```

Finally, we can delete the snapshot if all goes well.

```
Remove-EC2Snapshot -SnapshotId $Snapshot.SnapshotId -Force
```

In this exercise we resized a volume while taking a snapshot as a backup for safety. In the next exercise, we will create a script to back up all the volumes in our account on a schedule.

EXERCISE 4.2: CREATING A BACKUP AGENT

AWS gives us the tools to back up and recover a volume on demand, but we really need scheduled backups and the ability to delete snapshots after a specified retention period. Let's create a script that will back up every volume in a region for our AWS account.

Note that this backup agent script will run from an instance. To perform the activities in this exercise, the instance must be configured with the AdminRole IAM role we created in Chapter 2.

Our script will take three parameters: a type parameter used to differentiate backup sets, RetentionDays for the number of days to keep the backups, and the region to perform the backups. These parameters allow us to run multiple instances of the script with different configurations. For example, the following parameters indicate to run a daily backup retained for two weeks and a weekly backup retained for 90 days.

```
param(
    [parameter(mandatory=$false)][string]$Type = 'Daily',
    [parameter(mandatory=$false)][string]$RetentionDays = 14,
    [parameter(mandatory=$false)][string]$Region = "us-east-1"
)
```

The first thing we need to do is determine which volumes to back up. We may not want every volume backed up. For example, we don't want to back up our SQL data files. We only want to create a snapshot of the volume that contains the SQL backup files.

Let's use a tag to determine which volumes should be backed up. We will create a new tag, named "BackupEnabled". We prefer to back up all volumes by default; therefore, the first part of the script will look for any volumes that have not been tagged. If it finds any, it will assume they should be backed up, and set the BackupEnabled tag to true. If we don't want a volume backed up, just change the tag value to "false".

Unfortunately, we can only use a filter to find items that have been tagged. We cannot use a filter to find items that have not been tagged. Therefore, we need to get all instances and loop over them and check for the tag. If it does not exist, we add it using the New-EC2Tag we learned about in the last chapter.

```
# First, find any new volumes that have not been marked for backup
Set-DefaultAWSRegion -region $Region
Get-EC2Volume | ForEach-Object {
    $HasKey = $False
    $_.Tag | ForEach-Object { If ($_.Key -eq 'BackupEnabled')
    { $HasKey = $True } }
    If ($HasKey -eq $False) {
        # Add Tag to this volume
        $VolumeId = $_.VolumeId
        $Tag = New-Object amazon.EC2.Model.Tag
        $Tag.Key='BackupEnabled'
        $Tag.Value='true'
        Write-Host "Found new volume: $VolumeId"
        New-EC2Tag -ResourceId $VolumeId -Tag $Tag }
}
```

Now that our volumes are tagged, we can use a filter to find all the volumes that need to be backed up. We can then loop over the volumes and take a snapshot.

```
$Filter = New-Object Amazon.EC2.Model.Filter
$Filter.Name = 'tag:BackupEnabled'
$Filter.Value = 'True'
Get-EC2Volume -Filter $Filter | ForEach-Object {
#Backup routine goes here
}
```

If there is a disaster, we may not be able to access the metadata about which snapshot came from which instance. Therefore, if the volume is currently attached to an instance, we should record the name and attachment information in the snapshot description. The following code uses the Get-EC2Instance command we learned about in the last chapter to get information about the instance.

```
# Backup Routine
If ($_.state -eq "in-use"){
$Device = $_.Attachment[0].Device
```

```
$InstanceId = $_.Attachment[0].InstanceId
$Reservation = Get-EC2Instance $InstanceId
$Instance = $Reservation.RunningInstance | Where-Object {$_.InstanceId -eq
$InstanceId}
$Name = ($Instance.Tag | Where-Object { $_.Key -eq 'Name' }).Value
$Description = "Attached to InstanceID $InstanceId with Name '$Name' as
$Device;" }
Else{$Description = "Unattached to Instance"}
$Volume = $_.VolumeId
Write-Host "Creating snapshot of volume: $Volume; $Description"
$Snapshot = New-EC2Snapshot $Volume -Description "$Type backup of volume
$Volume; $Description"
```

We should also tag the snapshots, so we know which were created by our script. We don't want our script to delete snapshots it didn't create. For example, if a developer takes a snapshot before rolling out a new version of an application, they may not want that to be deleted after two weeks. Let's add a tag called "BackupType" used to differentiate scheduled backups from any others.

```
# Add a tag so we can distinguish this snapshot from all the others
$Tag = New-Object amazon.EC2.Model.Tag
$Tag.Key='BackupType'
$Tag.Value=$Type
New-EC2Tag -ResourceId $Snapshot.SnapshotID -Tag $Tag
```

Great! The routine to create a snapshot is done. Now we just have to create a routine to delete old backups after the retention period expires. In this routine, we find all of the snapshots that were created by the backup agent, using the BackupType tag. Then, check how old it is. If it is older than the retention period, the snapshot is deleted.

```
# Retention routine. Delete any snapshots created by this tool that are older
than the specified number of days
$Filter = New-Object Amazon.EC2.Model.Filter
$Filter.Name = 'tag:BackupType'
$Filter.Value = $Type
$RetentionDate = ([DateTime]::Now).AddDays(-$RetentionDays)
Get-EC2Snapshot -Filter $filter |
Where-Object { [datetime]::Parse($_.StartTime) -lt $RetentionDate} |
```

```
ForEach-Object { $SnapshotId = $_.SnapshotId
Write-Host "Removing snapshot: $SnapshotId"
Remove-EC2Snapshot -SnapshotId $SnapshotId -Force }
```

At this point all we must do is schedule the script to run once a day. We have this script deployed on an AWS instance, and it's saved as C:\AWS\DailyBackup.ps1.

To schedule the job, log into the instance that is going to run the script and open task scheduler. Then follow these steps:

1. Click the Create a Basic Task link.

2. Name the task "DailyBackup" and click Next.

3. Choose Daily and click Next.

4. Pick a time of day for the script to run and click Next.

5. Choose Start a Program and click Next.

6. Fill in the next screen, as shown in Figure 4-7, and click Next.

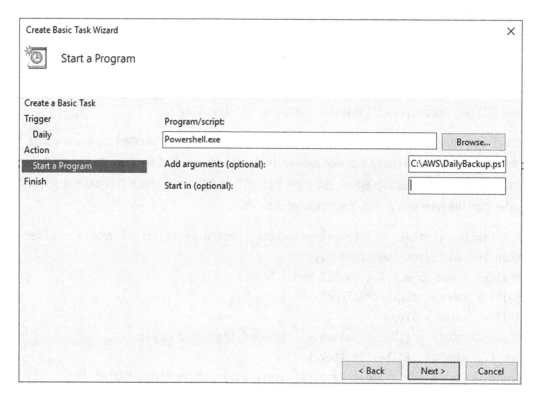

Figure 4-7. *Configure a scheduled task*

7. Check the "open the properties dialog for this task when I click Finish" option and click Finish.

8. Click the Change User or Group... button.

9. Change the user to NETWORK SERVICE, as shown in Figure 4-8, and click OK.

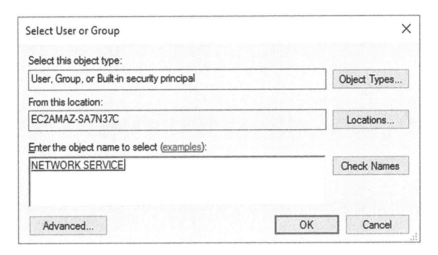

Figure 4-8. *Configure User or Group*

10. Click OK to close the wizard.

In this exercise we created a scheduled task that uses snapshots to create a backup of all volumes in a region. Let's stop and reflect on how easy that was. A few lines of code just replaced backup tapes forever. We don't need an operator on staff after hours to put tapes in servers. We don't need to manage tape storage and rotation. If we added a call to Copy-EC2Snapshot targeting another region, we would never have to ship tapes to an offsite storage location again.

Summary

In this chapter, we examined volumes and snapshots. We learned how to customize and add additional volumes at launch as well as modify volumes after launch. We learned how to back up and restore a volume using highly durable snapshots and copy snapshots to another region for even greater durability. In the first example, we created a script to resize a volume. We can use this script anytime we are running out of space in an existing instance. In the second example, we created a scheduled task that backs up all the volumes for a region in our account. We can use this script to replace tape backups.

In the next chapter, we will learn how to configure a Virtual Private Cloud (VPC). VPC allows us to create your own private network configuration in the cloud. We will discuss subnets, routing, and security.

CHAPTER 5

Virtual Private Cloud

In this chapter we are going to discuss Virtual Private Cloud (VPC). VPC allows you to configure a custom network topology, as well as manage IP routing and security. A network topology is the structure of the network and controls how data flows between nodes.

This chapter will be a bit different from the prior ones. On one hand, the commands are relatively simple. Most only have one or two parameters. On the other hand, these primitive commands can be woven together in countless ways to create a seemingly endless combination of network topologies.

Throughout this chapter, we will continue to explore the Web Console and the individual PowerShell commands. In previous chapters, each section stood alone. All the sections in this chapter will build upon each other and come together at the end to produce a single solution, pictured in Figure 5-1.

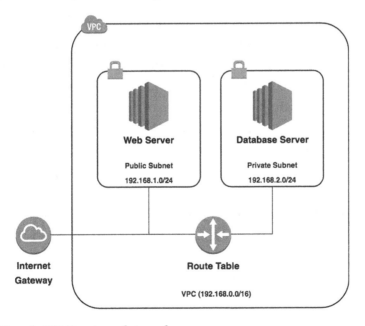

Figure 5-1. *Simple VPC network topology*

Figure 5-1 shows a simple network with two subnets. The public subnet is Internet accessible. We would use the public subnet to host our web servers. The private subnet is not connected to the Internet and is used to host our database. This is a common pattern in IT. Typically we put the web servers in the "DMZ" and keep the database behind a firewall with more stringent policies.

Note   This chapter often takes a roundabout solution in order to show you each command. For example, I could have created a new route table for the public subnet rather than altering the Main route table and then creating a new main table. But then I would not have reason to talk about deleting route tables and altering associations. If you want a streamlined script, Exercise 5.1 includes a complete script that will build the network pictured in Figure 5-1 in a much more direct manner than I followed throughout the chapter.

Let's get started with the first step in this process: creating a VPC.

Creating a VPC

VPC allows you to create one or more networks of EC2 instances. Note that by default, each account can have up to five VPCs per region. For example, you can implement a layered security approach or span multiple availability zones for high availability. This chapter and Chapter 6 focus on security, while Chapter 8 focuses on high availability.

As usual, let's start in the Web Console and then move to PowerShell. In the Web Console, from the Services drop-down at the top of the screen, choose VPC. We will build up our VPC in stages so we can discuss each piece. Note that AWS offers a VPC wizard, which we are not going to use. The second option in the VPC wizard, "VPC with Public and Private Subnets," is similar to the network we are going to create in this chapter.

To create a new VPC, navigate to the Your VPCs page and click the Create VPC button. The Create VPC dialog has only one tab (see Figure 5-2). Enter the CIDR range you wish to use.

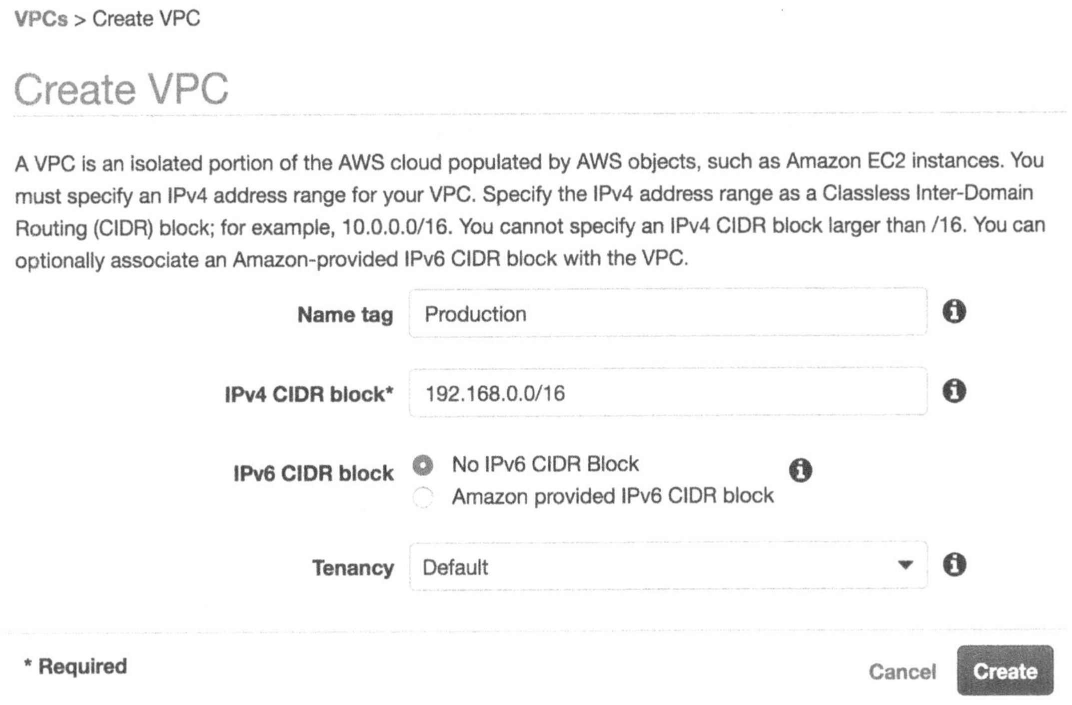

Create VPC

A VPC is an isolated portion of the AWS cloud populated by AWS objects, such as Amazon EC2 instances. You must specify an IPv4 address range for your VPC. Specify the IPv4 address range as a Classless Inter-Domain Routing (CIDR) block; for example, 10.0.0.0/16. You cannot specify an IPv4 CIDR block larger than /16. You can optionally associate an Amazon-provided IPv6 CIDR block with the VPC.

Name tag	Production	ⓘ
IPv4 CIDR block*	192.168.0.0/16	ⓘ
IPv6 CIDR block	⦿ No IPv6 CIDR Block ⓘ ○ Amazon provided IPv6 CIDR block	
Tenancy	Default ▼	ⓘ

* Required   Cancel   **Create**

Figure 5-2. *The Create VPC dialog box*

You can provision an IPv4 CIDR block up to a "/16." A "/16" network will give you about 65,535 hosts. You can use any network, but note that VPC addresses are not Internet accessible. Your hosts will access the Internet using Network Address Translation (NAT). Therefore, you should use a private (non-routable) segment such as 10.0.0.0/8, 172.16.0.0/12, or 192.168.0.0/16. VPC also supports associating IPv6 CIDR block addresses to your VPC and also subnets, which use IPv6 addresses that are public and Internet accessible. In this chapter, we won't go into detail on IPv6, what we will say is that it is supported and there is a migration path from IPv4.

Most organizations are already using the 10.0.0.0 network. Therefore, I tend to use 10.0.0.0 for any VPC that will be attached to the corporate network. AWS uses 172.16.0.0 for the default VPC; support for new deployments of EC2-Classic has been deprecated. That leaves 192.168.0.0. I like to use 192.168.0.0 for VPCs that are neither attached to the corporate network nor the default VPC. This makes it easy to tell which VPC is which later.

The Tenancy option allows you to provision a dedicated VPC. If you choose a dedicated VPC, you can only launch dedicated instances into that VPC. A dedicated instance runs on dedicated hardware that is not shared with other AWS clients. This is an expensive option and not one I have used often.

The equivalent PowerShell is equally simple.

```
$VPC = New-EC2Vpc -CidrBlock '192.168.0.0/16'
$VPC.VpcId
```

As you can see, creating a VPC is really easy. Before we can launch a machine into the VPC, we need to carve it up into multiple subnets. In the next section, we will create a subnet.

Creating a Subnet

Now that we have our VPC created, we want to carve it up into multiple subnets to host our instances. (We will add hosts to the subnet in Chapter 6.)

Each subnet is assigned to an availability zone. Remember from Chapter 1 that an availability zone is one of multiple data centers that comprise a region. We can use multiple availability zones to ensure high availability. (I will cover high availability in Chapter 8.)

Each subnet is also assigned a subset of the VPC's address space, again using CIDR notation. Here I am using a "/24." This will divide the VPC into 256 subnets of about 256 hosts each.

RESERVED IPS

In reality, we will not get 256 hosts per subnet when using "/24." The first four and last addresses are reserved. The reserved addresses are used as follows:

First - Network ID

Second - Gateway

Third - DHCP and DNS services

Fourth - Reserved for future use

Last - Network Broadcast

Creating a subnet using the Web Console is relatively easy. You simply identify the availability zone and CIDR range (see Figure 5-3).

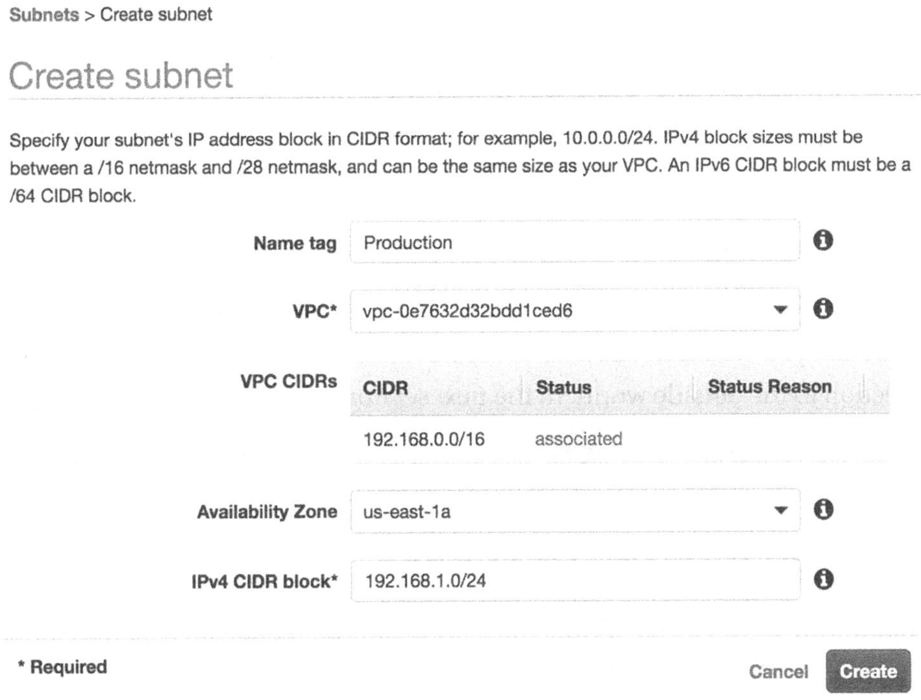

Subnets > Create subnet

Create subnet

Specify your subnet's IP address block in CIDR format; for example, 10.0.0.0/24. IPv4 block sizes must be between a /16 netmask and /28 netmask, and can be the same size as your VPC. An IPv6 CIDR block must be a /64 CIDR block.

Name tag	Production
VPC*	vpc-0e7632d32bdd1ced6

VPC CIDRs	CIDR	Status	Status Reason
	192.168.0.0/16	associated	

Availability Zone	us-east-1a
IPv4 CIDR block*	192.168.1.0/24

* Required   Cancel   **Create**

Figure 5-3. *The Create subnet dialog box*

Creating a subnet with PowerShell is equally easy. Just use New-EC2Subnet. This command takes the same parameters as the Web Console: the VPC, availability zone, and CIDR block. In this example, we will store the newly created VPC in the "Subnet1a" variable, so we can reference the object later.

```
$Subnet1a = New-EC2Subnet -VpcId $VPC.VpcId -CidrBlock '192.168.2.0/24'
-AvailabilityZone 'us-east-1a'
```

You can list the subnets with the Get-EC2Subnet command. Unfortunately, Get-EC2Subnet does not have a VPC parameter. This is true of all the VPC-related commands. If you want to list the subnets in a given VPC, you have to use a filter. For example:

```
$VPCFilter = New-Object Amazon.EC2.Model.Filter
$VPCFilter.Name = 'vpc-id'
$VPCFilter.Value = $VPC.VpcId
Get-EC2Subnet -Filter $VPCFilter
```

Of course you can delete a subnet using the `Remove-EC2Subnet` command. Note that if the subnet has instances assigned, the remove command will fail. `$Subnet1a` is a variable that was instantiated when we created our subnet. In the preceding example, we created a filter based on this variable. Alternatively, we can manually create a filter by replacing `$VPCFilter.Value = $VPC.VpcId` with `$VPCFilter.Value = 'vpc-xxxxxx'`.

```
Remove-EC2Subnet -SubnetId $Subnet1a -Force
```

At this point we have a VPC with a single subnet. We could launch an instance into this subnet, but you would not be able to connect to the instance because our VPC has no connection to the outside world. In the next section, we will add an Internet gateway, which is a connection to the Internet.

Creating an Internet Gateway

At this point your VPC is isolated from the world. You can launch an instance, but it cannot connect to the Internet. More importantly, you cannot connect to it either. To create a connection to the Internet, you need an Internet gateway.

Think of the Internet gateway like your router at home. It connects all of the instances in your VPC to the Internet using Network Address Translation (NAT). While your home network probably only has only one public IP address, the EC2 Internet gateway allows you to assign a public IP address to each instance. These public IP addresses are known as elastic IP addresses. (We will be assigning elastic IP addresses in Chapter 6.)

The process of creating an Internet gateway is the same using the Web Console or PowerShell. First you create a new gateway and then you connect it to a VPC. In PowerShell it looks like this (`$InternetGateway` is a variable containing the unique identifier of the Internet gateway you just created):

```
$InternetGateway = New-EC2InternetGateway
Add-EC2InternetGateway -InternetGatewayId
$InternetGateway.InternetGatewayId -VpcId
    $VPC.VpcId
```

Despite the two-step process, you can only connect the gateway to one VPC at a time. If necessary, you can disconnect the gateway from VPC and connect it to another. Alternatively, you can create additional Internet gateways to connect other VPCs to the Internet.

At this point you have a VPC with a subnet and Internet connection. In the next section, we will configure routing within the VPC.

Managing Route Tables

Now that we have an Internet connection, we need to tell instances how to find that connection. We use routes to do this. Every subnet is associated with a route table that tells an instance the best way to reach a given destination.

Note   Routing is a fairly complicated topic. If you are not familiar with IP routing, I recommend reading up on the basics.

When we create the VPC, AWS created a default route table (see Figure 5-4). Notice that the route table is associated with 0 subnets; this is deceiving. The route table is not explicitly associated with any subnets, but it is identified as the Main route table in the VPC. Subnets will use the Main route table unless you explicitly configure them to use another route table. Therefore, all of the subnets in our VPC are using this route table.

Figure 5-4. *Sample route table displayed in the Web Console*

The Main route table has only one route by default. This route says that all traffic destined for 192.168.0.0/16 should stay local. Remember that our VPC is using the range 192.168.0.0/16. In other words, only local traffic is configured by default; there is no route to the Internet.

To list route tables in PowerShell, use Get-EC2RouteTable. If you have more than one VPC, use a filter to display only those route tables in a given VPC. In this scenario, the previously created filter can be used or a new filter can be created, as shown in the following. Previously, we used a filter based on the VPC we created. Here, we will manually set the filter by replacing $VPCFilter.Value = $VPC.VpcId with $VPCFilter.Value = 'vpc-xxxxxx'.

```
$VPCFilter = New-Object Amazon.EC2.Model.Filter
$VPCFilter.Name = 'vpc-id'
$VPCFilter.Value = 'vpc-57074739'
Get-EC2RouteTable -Filter $VPCFilter
```

Each route table has a Routes property that contains a list of the individual routes. It is easier to read if you pipe the list to Format-Table:

```
$VPCFilter = New-Object Amazon.EC2.Model.Filter
$VPCFilter.Name = 'vpc-id'
$VPCFilter.Value = 'vpc-57074739'
 (Get-EC2RouteTable -Filter $VPCFilter).Routes | Format-Table
```

If you want to get a reference to the Main route table, use the association.main filter with a value of true. Note that true will be passed as a string and must be specified in lowercase. We will use the manually created filter (i.e., $VPCFilter.Value = 'vpc-xxxxxx') in this example.

```
$VPCFilter = New-Object Amazon.EC2.Model.Filter
$VPCFilter.Name = 'vpc-id'
$VPCFilter.Value = 'vpc-57074739'
$IsDefaultFilter = New-Object Amazon.EC2.Model.Filter
$IsDefaultFilter.Name = 'association.main'
$IsDefaultFilter.Value = 'true'
$DefaultRouteTable = Get-EC2RouteTable -Filter $VPCFilter, $IsDefaultFilter
$DefaultRouteTable.Routes | Format-Table
```

Now we want to tell our instances about the Internet gateway. To do this, we add a new route to the route table. In Figure 5-5, I am adding a route to 0.0.0.0/0 to the Internet gateway we created.

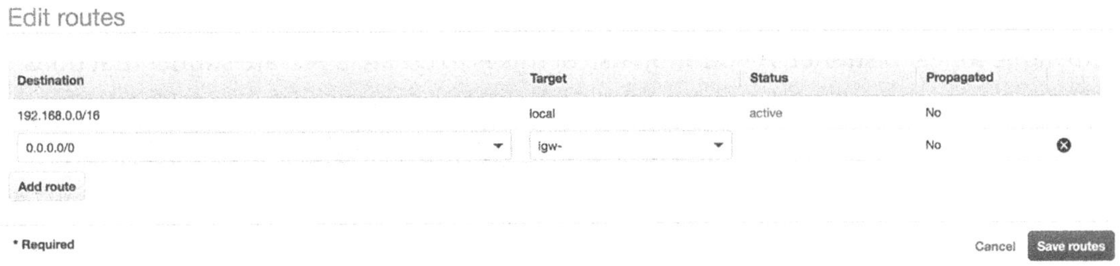

Edit routes

Destination		Target		Status	Propagated	
192.168.0.0/16		local		active	No	
0.0.0.0/0	▼	igw-	▼		No	⊗

Add route

* Required   Cancel   Save routes

Figure 5-5. *Adding a new route to a route table*

The route table works like this. Whenever a request is received, AWS looks at the route table to determine what to do with it. It tries to match the request with the most specific route. The larger the number after the forward slash, the more specific the route. Since the rule we just added has a zero after the slash, this rule will be evaluated last.

For example, assume a request is destined for www.google.com at 173.194.43.2. AWS will first check it against the most specific rule. In this case the 192.168.0.0/16 is the most specific. The rule says to check if the first 16 bits of the destination (e.g., 173.194) match the route (192.168). Since they do not match, AWS tries the next route. The next route has a zero after the slash. Since there are zero bits to match, this rule always matches (this is called the default route). Therefore, AWS routes the request to the Internet gateway.

To add a new route to the route table using PowerShell, use the New-EC2Route command. We will use previously created variables for this command. For simplicity reasons, we will be using the $InternetGateway.InternetGatewayId variable previously created.

```
New-EC2Route -RouteTableId $DefaultRouteTable.RouteTableId -DestinationCidrBlock
'0.0.0.0/0'
     -GatewayId $InternetGateway.InternetGatewayId
```

You can also create a route that points to a specific instance. You might do this if you want to take specific actions on the traffic. For example, you might want to run a software firewall or web proxy on an EC2 instance. AWS offers many such virtual appliances in the marketplace. There is an example of this in the exercises at the end of Chapter 6.

To route traffic to a specific instance in PowerShell, use InstanceId rather than GatewayId.

```
New-EC2Route -RouteTableId 'rtb-52007473c'  -DestinationCidrBlock
'0.0.0.0/0' -InstanceId
     'i-12345678'
```

93

Not all subnets in a VPC need to use the same route table. You can create a custom route table for each subnet. A common use of this is to create a private subnet that does not have Internet connectivity and a public subnet that does. Security standards often require that databases be hosted in a private subnet without Internet connectivity.

Let's create a new route table that does not have Internet connectivity.

```
$CustomRoute = New-EC2RouteTable -VpcId $VPC.VpcId
```

Now that we have more than one route table, we need to associate the subnet with a route table. To this we use a route table association.

```
Register-EC2RouteTable -RouteTableId $CustomRoute.RouteTableId -SubnetId
$Subnet1a.SubnetId
```

At this point, we have two route tables in our VPC. Remember that we added Internet connectivity to our Main route. This is the route that will be used by default. It would be better security practice to have our Main route table be private. This way, if we create a new subnet, it defaults to the subnet without Internet access and only gets it if we explicitly assign it to the public subnet.

Changing the Main route table is less than intuitive because there is no command to change the Main route table. First, you have to find the Main route table using filters. Then, you find the Main route table association. Typically, an association maps a route table to a subnet, but the main association is special in that the subnet is blank.

```
$VPCFilter = New-Object Amazon.EC2.Model.Filter
$VPCFilter.Name = 'vpc-id'
$VPCFilter.Value = 'vpc-57074739'
$IsDefaultFilter = New-Object Amazon.EC2.Model.Filter
$IsDefaultFilter.Name = 'association.main'
$IsDefaultFilter.Value = 'true'
$MainRouteTable = Get-EC2RouteTable -Filter $VPCFilter, $IsDefaultFilter
$Association = $MainRouteTable.Associations | Where-Object {$_.Main -eq $True}
$Association
```

This command returns

```
RouteTableAssociationId  RouteTableId   SubnetId   Main
-----------------------  ------------   --------   ----
rtbassoc-5307473d        rtb-5207473c              True
```

Since there is no command to change the Main route table, we have to reassign the existing association to a new route table using the Set-EC2RouteTableAssociation command.

```
Set-EC2RouteTableAssociation -AssociationId 'rtbassoc-5307473d'
    -RouteTableId 'rtb-d65006b8'
```

I know that was a lot of material very quickly. I used as many variables as possible to make things more consumable. In any case, I strongly recommend that you work through the examples at the end of this chapter to better understand EC2 routing. Let's review our progress so far. We created a VPC, added a subnet and Internet gateway, and configured routing. In the next section, we will configure network security.

Managing Network ACLs

Network access control lists (ACLs) allow you to control what types of traffic can enter and leave a subnet. Each ACL contains an ordered list of inbound and outbound rules. If you have worked with EC2 Classic in the past, you are likely familiar with security groups. ACLs and security groups are similar in that they allow you to filter traffic on the network. (We will cover security groups in Chapter 6.) The main differences are the following:

1. ACLs are applied to a network segment, while security groups are applied to individual instances.

2. Security groups are stateful, while ACLs are stateless. This means ACLs require a rule for both the request and response, while security groups only require a request rule.

AWS creates a default ACL for each new VPC. As you can see in Figure 5-6, the default ACL contains two rules. The first allows all traffic to anywhere and second denies all traffic to anywhere. Rules are executed in order. Therefore, the first rule is always applied, and the default behavior is to allow all traffic to and from anywhere. Obviously it is a good idea to create more conservative rules.

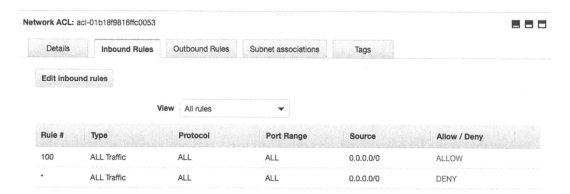

Figure 5-6. *Network ACLs*

To get the same list using PowerShell, use the `Get-EC2NetworkACL` command. Again, I am using a filter to only return the ACLs from one VPC because you may have more than one VPC in a given region. Notice that there are both inbound (egress=false) and outbound (egress=true) rules. Figure 5-6 was displaying the inbound rules only.

```
$VPCFilter = New-Object Amazon.EC2.Model.Filter
$VPCFilter.Name = 'vpc-id'
$VPCFilter.Value = 'vpc-57074739'
$ACL = Get-EC2NetworkAcl -Filter $VPCFilter
$ACL.Entries | Format-Table
```

This code returns the following output:

```
RuleNumber Protocol RuleAction Egress CidrBlock Icmp PortRange
---------- -------- ---------- ------ --------- ---- ---------
100         -1       allow      True   0.0.0.0/0
32767       -1       deny       True   0.0.0.0/0
100         -1       allow      False  0.0.0.0/0
32767       -1       deny       False  0.0.0.0/0
```

As you can see from the two rules numbered 100, the default ACL allows all traffic into and out of the subnet. Now let's learn how to modify the default rules.

Securing the Public Subnet

It is bad practice to allow all traffic into our network. Let's assume that we are running a web site. The public subnet hosts a web server and the private subnet hosts a database. We want to allow the minimum set of traffic possible into each subnet.

First let's remove the rule 100 that allows all traffic. Note that I am removing both the inbound and outbound rules. To get the ACL ID, we will return the value of the previously created variable, that is, $ACL.NetworkAclId. For ease of use, the variable will be used for the subsequent examples.

```
Remove-EC2NetworkAclEntry -NetworkAclId acl-5507473b -RuleNumber 100 -Egress
$true -Force
Remove-EC2NetworkAclEntry -NetworkAclId acl-5507473b -RuleNumber 100 -Egress
$false -Force
```

Now let's add rules for the public subnet. First, we need to allow HTTP traffic from the Internet. Remember that 0.0.0.0/0 means traffic from anywhere. Also, HTTP uses port 80 and TCP is protocol 6.

```
New-EC2NetworkAclEntry -NetworkAclId acl-5507473b -RuleNumber 100 -CidrBlock
'0.0.0.0/0'
    -Egress $False -PortRange_From 80 -PortRange_To 80 -Protocol 6
    -RuleAction 'Allow'
```

Remember that ACLs are stateless. This means that we need to create separate rules for the request and response. Security groups on the other hand are stateful. You only need to create a rule for the request, and AWS takes care of the response.

When the browser makes a request to our web server, the destination port is 80. But, there is also a source port, called the ephemeral port. The ephemeral port is chosen at random in the range 49152 to 65535. The web server sends its reply back to the ephemeral port the request was received from. Therefore, we need a corresponding egress rule for the reply:

```
New-EC2NetworkAclEntry -NetworkAclId 'acl-5507473b' -RuleNumber 100
-CidrBlock '0.0.0.0/0'
    -Egress $True -PortRange_From 49152 -PortRange_To 65535 -Protocol 6
    -RuleAction 'Allow'
```

The web server also needs to talk to the database. Let's assume the database server is running Microsoft SQL Server and is located in the private subnet. SQL Server uses port 1433 and the CIDR range for the private subnet is 192.168.2.0/24. Therefore, we need to allow the request on port 1433 and the response in the ephemeral range.

```
New-EC2NetworkAclEntry -NetworkAclId 'acl-5507473b' -RuleNumber 200
-CidrBlock '192.168.2.0/24'
    -Egress $True -PortRange_From 1433 -PortRange_To 1433 -Protocol 6
    -RuleAction 'Allow'

New-EC2NetworkAclEntry -NetworkAclId 'acl-5507473b' -RuleNumber 200
-CidrBlock '192.168.2.0/24'
    -Egress $False -PortRange_From 49152 -PortRange_To 65535 -Protocol 6
    -RuleAction 'Allow'
```

Notice that I have incremented the rule number by 100. It is common to increment by 100 to allow room to insert additional rules later. Remember that the rules are always executed in order, until a rule is found that either allows or denies the traffic. Before moving on to the private subnet, let's spend a minute looking at deny rules.

You may have noticed that we allow HTTP traffic from any source (i.e., 0.0.0.0/0). This includes the private subnet. This is not really what we intended. We wanted to allow traffic from the Internet, but not within the VPC. We can block this by adding a deny rule that fires before rule 100.

```
New-EC2NetworkAclEntry -NetworkAclId 'acl-5507473b' -RuleNumber 50
-CidrBlock '192.168.0.0/16'
    -Egress $False -PortRange_From 80 -PortRange_To 80 -Protocol 6
    -RuleAction 'Deny'

New-EC2NetworkAclEntry -NetworkAclId 'acl-5507473b' -RuleNumber 50
-CidrBlock '192.168.0.0/16'
    -Egress $True -PortRange_From 49152 -PortRange_To 65535 -Protocol 6
    -RuleAction 'Deny'
```

In the preceding example, I have added a new rule with rule number 50. This rule will fire first. If a request is received from within the VPC, the request will be denied and processing will stop. If the request is received from outside the VPC, this rule will not match and rule 100 will fire next. Rule 100 will then allow the request and processing will stop.

Now let's look at what would happen if we received a request we didn't anticipate. We didn't plan for HTTPS requests. If we received a request on port 443, rules 50, 100, and 200 would again fire in order, but none would match because none of the existing rules are for port 443. Next, rule 32767 would fire and deny the request. Rule 32767 is the max rule number. It is always present and cannot be deleted. In other words, if none of the rules that we create match, the traffic is always denied.

FINDING THE NEXT ACL RULE NUMBER

When you create new rules, you often need to know the largest rule number in the list so you can use the next number. Here is a quick script to find the largest egress rule in PowerShell. The first portion of the script will gather the largest ACL rule entry and store it in the $MaxAcl variable.

```
$MaxAcl = ((Get-EC2NetworkAcl -NetworkAclId acl-5507473b).Entries | Where-
Object
        {$_.Egress -and $_.RuleNumber -lt 32767 } | Measure-Object RuleNumber
        -Maximum).Maximum
```

Next we will add 100 to the $MaxAcl entry.

```
$NextAcl = $MaxAcl + 100
```

Finally, we will view the next largest egress rule number.

```
$NextAcl
```

Now that we have the public subnet configured, let's look at the private subnet.

Securing the Private Subnet

At this point we have our public subnet locked down, but we have ignored our private subnet. Even worse, we have been applying the rules to the only access control list in the VPC. This means that the rules we applied to the public subnet have also been applied to the private one that is going to host our database server. Let's fix this.

First, let's create a new access control list for the private subnet. In PowerShell, we use the New-EC2NetworkAcl command.

```
$ACL = New-EC2NetworkAcl -VpcId 'vpc-57074739'
$ACL.Entries | Format-Table
```

This code returns the following output:

```
RuleNumber Protocol RuleAction Egress CidrBlock Icmp PortRange
---------- -------- ---------- ------ --------- ---- ---------
32767      -1       deny       True   0.0.0.0/0
32767      -1       deny       False  0.0.0.0/0
```

Notice that the list is effectively empty. The only entries are the default deny rules. This is different from the ACL that was created when we created the VPC. That ACL allowed all traffic, and this one denies all traffic.

Let's add rules to allow all traffic in and out of our private subnet. This may seem like we are cutting corners. Why don't we create specific rules like we did for the public subnet? We could, and we probably should, but remember that the public subnet is Internet accessible. The public subnet is much more likely to be attacked. It is common to put much stronger controls on the public subnets and leave the private subnets free to communicate among one another. Think of this like your house. You likely have a much better lock on your front door than you do on your bedroom. For now let's keep it simple and allow all traffic.

```
New-EC2NetworkAclEntry -NetworkAclId $ACL.NetworkAclId -RuleNumber 100
-CidrBlock '0.0.0.0/0'
    -Egress $True -Protocol '-1' -RuleAction 'Allow'
New-EC2NetworkAclEntry -NetworkAclId $ACL.NetworkAclId -RuleNumber 100
-CidrBlock '0.0.0.0/0'
    -Egress $False -Protocol '-1' -RuleAction 'Allow'
```

Now, all we have to do is attach this ACL to the private subnet, which was created at the beginning of this chapter. The process is similar to changing the Main route table. First, we use a filter to find the ACL associated with the subnet. Then, we get a reference to the association for the ACL. Next, we get a reference to the new ACL we want to assign to the subnet. Finally, we use the Set-EC2NetworkAclAssociation to point the association to the new ACL.

```
$SubnetFilter = New-Object Amazon.EC2.Model.Filter
$SubnetFilter.Name = 'association.subnet-id'
$SubnetFilter.Value = 'subnet-334e185d'
$OldACL = Get-EC2NetworkAcl -Filter $SubnetFilter
$OldAssociation = $OldACL.Associations | Where-Object { $_.SubnetId -eq
$SubnetFilter.Value}
Set-EC2NetworkAclAssociation -AssociationId $OldAssociation.
NetworkAclAssociationId
     -NetworkAclId $ACL.NetworkAclID
```

Working with ACLs can be very tedious. You must very careful to identify the traffic in both directions. In Chapter 6 we will discuss security groups, which offer a much easier solution to filter traffic to and from individual instances. Before we end this chapter, let's have a quick look at configuring DHCP.

Managing DHCP

VPC uses Dynamic Host Configuration Protocol (DHCP) to configure the instances in the VPC. Although you are likely familiar with DHCP, it works a bit differently at AWS.

First, IP addresses are assigned to the instance for life. Once a primary IP address is assigned, it cannot be changed and cannot be assigned to another instance until the instance is terminated. (Note that you can add and remove secondary IP addresses, which we will do in Chapter 6.)

Second, you cannot change the network configuration from within the instance. AWS does not use layer two broadcasts to discover network configuration changes. Rather it depends on the instance metadata to make forwarding decisions. If you change an IP address from within Windows, AWS will not learn of the change, and traffic will not be forwarded to the server.

In addition to managing IP addresses, DHCP is also used to configure DNS, NetBIOS, and Network Time Protocol (NTP). AWS offers DNS and NTP services, but if you prefer, you can choose to override the default settings to use another service.

Let's imagine that we are going to launch an Active Directory (AD) server into our private subnet. Our AD instance will be assigned the IP address 192.168.2.10. The domain name is brianbeach.com. We want AD to be the primary DNS, NetBIOS, and NTP server. Using the Web Console, you simply create a new option set and then associate it with a VPC (see Figure 5-7).

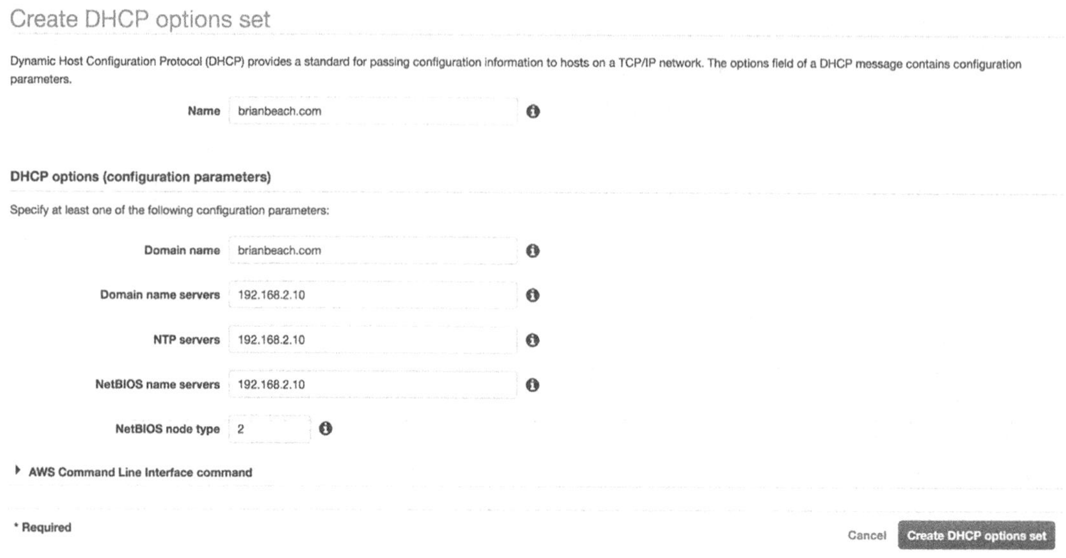

Create DHCP options set

Dynamic Host Configuration Protocol (DHCP) provides a standard for passing configuration information to hosts on a TCP/IP network. The options field of a DHCP message contains configuration parameters.

Name	brianbeach.com ⓘ

DHCP options (configuration parameters)

Specify at least one of the following configuration parameters:

Domain name	brianbeach.com ⓘ
Domain name servers	192.168.2.10 ⓘ
NTP servers	192.168.2.10 ⓘ
NetBIOS name servers	192.168.2.10 ⓘ
NetBIOS node type	2 ⓘ

▶ AWS Command Line Interface command

* Required   Cancel   **Create DHCP options set**

Figure 5-7. *Creating a new DHCP option set*

To change the DHCP configuration using PowerShell, we first create an array of configuration options. Then, we use New-EC2DHCPOption to create a new option set. Finally, we associate to the new option set with our VPC using Register-EC2DhcpOption:

```
$Domain = New-Object Amazon.EC2.Model.DhcpConfiguration
$Domain.Key = 'domain-name'
$Domain.Value = 'brianbeach.com'
$DNS = New-Object Amazon.EC2.Model.DhcpConfiguration
$DNS.Key = 'domain-name-servers'
$DNS.Value = '192.168.2.10'
$NTP = New-Object Amazon.EC2.Model.DhcpConfiguration
$NTP.Key = 'ntp-servers'
$NTP.Value = '192.168.2.10'
$NetBios= New-Object Amazon.EC2.Model.DhcpConfiguration
$NetBios.Key = 'netbios-name-servers'
$NetBios.Value = '192.168.2.10'
$NetBiosType = New-Object Amazon.EC2.Model.DhcpConfiguration
$NetBiosType.Key = 'netbios-node-type'
$NetBiosType.Value = '2'
```

```
$DHCP = New-EC2DHCPOption -DhcpConfiguration $Domain, $DNS, $NTP, $NetBios,
$NetBiosType
Register-EC2DhcpOption -DhcpOptionsId $DHCP.DhcpOptionsId -VpcId 'vpc-
57074739'
```

Note that the DHCP configuration is associated with a VPC rather than a subnet. You cannot have a different configuration in each subnet. If you choose to use your own DNS or other service, it is a good idea to launch more than one of each service for high availability. For instance, you might have two AD servers. One uses IP 192.168.2.10, and one uses 192.168.12.10. To configure this, just include both in the Options array. For example:

```
$Domain = New-Object Amazon.EC2.Model.DhcpConfiguration
$Domain.Key = 'domain-name'
$Domain.Value = 'brianbeach.com'
$DNS1 = New-Object Amazon.EC2.Model.DhcpConfiguration
$DNS1.Key = 'domain-name-servers'
$DNS1.Value = '192.168.2.10'
$DNS2 = New-Object Amazon.EC2.Model.DhcpConfiguration
$DNS2.Key = 'domain-name-servers'
$DNS2.Value = '192.168.12.10'
$DHCP = New-EC2DHCPOption -DhcpConfiguration $Domain, $DNS1, $DNS2
```

In the preceding example, note that not all options are required. You can choose to configure only some options. If you choose to omit DNS, be sure to include a reference to AmazonProvidedDNS or you will not be able to resolve any DNS names. Here is an example if you want to change the default domain name, but use Amazon's DNS:

```
$Domain = New-Object Amazon.EC2.Model.DhcpConfiguration
$Domain.Key = 'domain-name'
$Domain.Value = 'brianbeach.com'
$DNS = New-Object Amazon.EC2.Model.DhcpConfiguration
$DNS.Key = 'domain-name-servers'
$DNS.Value = 'AmazonProvidedDNS'
$DHCP = New-EC2DHCPOption -DhcpConfiguration $Domain, $DNS
```

In the next section, we will cover one of the most popular VPC features, as it allows connectivity of multiple VPCs, either within region or across regions.

VPC Peering

Since the first book was written, there have been a lot of VPC service features and enhancements released. One of such features is the support for VPC Peering, which allows two VPCs to communicate as if they were part of the same network. These peering connections can be within the same AWS region or AWS accounts, different regions or accounts. One benefit for using a VPC Peering connection is that the connectivity does not use a customer managed component; instead, all network traffic uses the AWS networking backbone which eliminates a single point of failure or bandwidth bottlenecks.

To get started with creating a VPC Peering connection between two VPCs, we first need to make sure the prerequisites for setting up the connection are met. These are some of the most important prerequisites, although these may change depending on your network configuration and requirements:

- Ensure you don't have overlapping CIDR blocks, as they are not supported.

- IAM user with the privileges to create a VPC Peering connection.

In order to provide an example and visualize the creation of a VPC Peering connection, we will create two new simple VPCs which will be used for the peering.

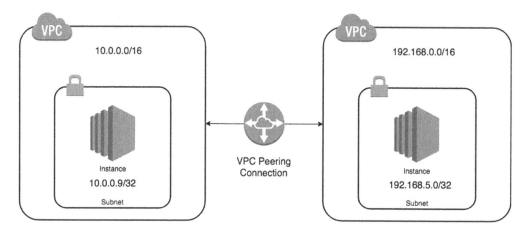

Figure 5-8. *VPC Peering*

The first set of commands will create a new VPC in the US-EAST-2 region and create a new VPC within this region. We will store the newly created variable object of the VPC into the $VPC2 variable.

```
Set-DefaultAWSRegion -Region us-east-2
$VPC2 = New-EC2Vpc -CidrBlock '10.0.0.0/16'
$VPC2.VpcId
```

Once we get the VPC ID and confirm that the new VPC got created successfully, we can create a subnet within this VPC. As usual, we will store the object of the newly created subnet in a variable.

```
$Subnet2a = New-EC2Subnet -VpcId $VPC2.VpcId -CidrBlock '10.0.0.0/24'
-AvailabilityZone 'us-east-2a'
```

Once this is completed, we will follow the same process to create another VPC and subnet in the US-WEST-1. As examples, we will use both $VPC3.VpcId and VpcId directly.

```
Set-DefaultAWSRegion -Region us-west-1
$VPC3 = New-EC2Vpc -CidrBlock '192.168.0.0/24'
$VPC3.VpcId
$Subnet3a = New-EC2Subnet -VpcId 'vpc-xxxxxxx' -CidrBlock '192.168.0.0/24'
-AvailabilityZone 'us-west-1a'
```

After both VPCs are created, we can then proceed with configuring the peering connection. The first step to make this happen is to submit a peering request to the owner of the destination VPC. Once the request has been made, we will locate the owner of the target VPC and ask him/her to accept the request.

```
Set-DefaultAWSRegion -Region us-east-2
New-EC2VpcPeeringConnection -VpcId $VPC3.VpcId -PeerVpcId $VPC2.VpcId
-PeerOwnerId XXXXXXX
```

Note   The PeerOwnerId is for the account ID of the owner of the target VPC. If the peering connection performed is within the same account, then the account name for the source VPC must be included. This is also the account that must approve the peering connection, which is outlined in next section. In the previous section, ensure the VPC IDs for VPC2 and VPC3 are different and that they reference each other when creating the peering connection.

If you encounter any issues creating the peering request from PowerShell, go to the AWS Console and make the request.

Once the request has been submitted, it must be approved from the target VPC account, from the target region. The approval can either be done from the AWS Console as shown in Figure 5-9 or by using the following command. Replace the appropriate VPC Peering connection ID prior to running the following command:

```
Set-DefaultAWSRegion -Region us-west-1
Approve-EC2VpcPeeringConnection -VpcPeeringConnectionId pcx-XXXXXXXXXX
```

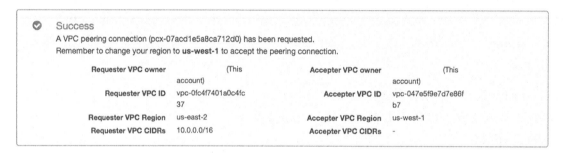

Figure 5-9. *VPC peering request*

Accepting the peering request will be equivalent to setting up physical connectivity between these two networks. After it has been set up, the routing must be configured to ensure nodes in these networks know how to find the right path for connectivity. In the following example, I will set up the route from US-WEST-1 to US-EAST-2. The reverse must also be done, so that both networks can communicate with each other. Reference the appropriate route table and gateway IDs prior to executing the following command:

```
New-EC2Route -RouteTableId rtb-XXXXXXXXXX -DestinationCidrBlock 10.0.0.0/24
-GatewayId pcx-XXXXXXXXXX
```

Note   Network access control lists and security groups must be configured to allow traffic between these two networks. Please reference either prior section of this chapter or Chapter 6 for additional guidance.

One very important thing to remember about VPC Peering connections is that they are not transitive, meaning, if there are three VPCs, VPC1, VPC2, and VPC3. The fact that VPC1 and VPC2, and VPC2 and VPC3 are peered does not mean that VPC1 will be able to communicate with VPC3; all VPCs must be peered individually.

That was a lot of content to get through. I'm glad you made it! At this point your VPC is complete. In the next chapter, we will launch a few instances into the new VPC. But, before we do, let's look at this chapter's exercises. In the first exercise, we will build a streamlined script that creates a new VPC identical to the one described in this chapter. In the second example, we will use a virtual private gateway to connect the VPC to a local office.

EXERCISE 5.1: CREATING A VIRTUAL PRIVATE CLOUD

In this exercise, we will create an end-to-end script to provision a Virtual Private Cloud (see Figure 5-8). The VPC wizard, available in the Web Console, does a good job of creating a VPC, but you want more control. In addition, you want the process to run unattended. Therefore, you decide to script the build in PowerShell.

In continuous integration, you want to start fresh to ensure that manual changes made the day before do not impact the results of testing. In the cloud, we can truly start from the ground up every day. Imagine how difficult this would be with physical switches and routers. AWS makes continuous integration really easy.

This exercise will create and configure the VPC shown in Figure 5-10. I assume our application is a simple web application with a SQL Server database. The script will create a public subnet for the web server and a private subnet for the SQL Server. Note that the script will not launch the instances. We will build on this recipe in later chapters. Here are the main components of our script:

- Create a VPC

- Create a DHCP option set

- Create subnets

- Add an Internet gateway

- Configure a routing table

- Configure ACLs

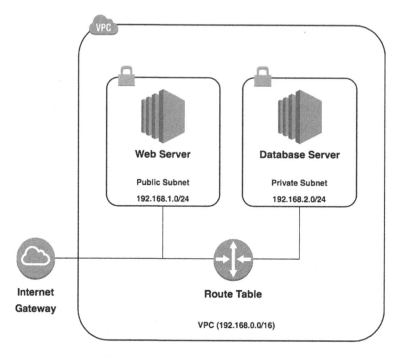

Figure 5-10. *Simple VPC (Note: Our script will not add instances.)*

Our script takes a few parameters. First, it requires a domain name (e.g., `brianbeach.com`). Second, it takes the CIDR range of the VPC and two subnets.

```
param
(
    [string][parameter(mandatory=$true)]$DomainName,
    [string][parameter(mandatory=$false)]$VPCCIDR = '192.168.0.0/16',
    [string][parameter(mandatory=$false)]$PublicSubnetCIDR = '192.168.1.0/24',
    [string][parameter(mandatory=$false)]$PrivateSubnetCIDR = '192.168.2.0/24'
)
```

Next, we create a new VPC. I wait a few seconds to avoid errors. The following Create Subnet command will fail if the VPC has not been created.

```
$VPC = New-EC2Vpc -CidrBlock $VPCCIDR
Start-Sleep -s 15 #This can take a few seconds
```

Then, we configure the DHCP options. Here I am using the default DNS provider.

```
#Configure the DHCP Options
$Domain = New-Object Amazon.EC2.Model.DhcpConfiguration
$Domain.Key = 'domain-name'
$Domain.Value = $DomainName
$DNS = New-Object Amazon.EC2.Model.DhcpConfiguration
$DNS.Key = 'domain-name-servers'
$DNS.Value = 'AmazonProvidedDNS'
$DHCP = New-EC2DHCPOption -DhcpConfiguration $Domain, $DNS
Register-EC2DhcpOption -DhcpOptionsId $DHCP.DhcpOptionsId -VpcId $VPC.VpcId
```

Now we can create our two subnets. The web servers will be hosted in the public subnet and have Internet access. The SQL Server will be hosted in the private subnet and will not have Internet access.

```
#Pick the first availability zone in the region.
$AvailabilityZones = Get-EC2AvailabilityZone
$AvailabilityZone = $AvailabilityZones[0].ZoneName

#Create and tag the Public subnet.
$PublicSubnet = New-EC2Subnet -VpcId $VPC.VpcId
    -CidrBlock $PublicSubnetCIDR -AvailabilityZone $AvailabilityZone
Start-Sleep -s 15 #This can take a few seconds
$Tag = New-Object Amazon.EC2.Model.Tag
$Tag.Key = 'Name'
$Tag.Value = 'Public'
New-EC2Tag -ResourceId $PublicSubnet.SubnetId  -Tag $Tag

#Create and tag the Private subnet.
$PrivateSubnet = New-EC2Subnet -VpcId $VPC.VpcId
    -CidrBlock $PrivateSubnetCIDR -AvailabilityZone $AvailabilityZone
Start-Sleep -s 15 #This can take a few seconds
$Tag = New-Object Amazon.EC2.Model.Tag
$Tag.Key = 'Name'
$Tag.Value = 'Private'
New-EC2Tag -ResourceId $PrivateSubnet.SubnetId  -Tag $Tag
```

Now, we add an Internet gateway and configure the route table.

```
#Add an Internet Gateway and attach it to the VPC.
$InternetGateway = New-EC2InternetGateway
Add-EC2InternetGateway -InternetGatewayId $InternetGateway.InternetGatewayId
-VpcId $VPC.VpcId

#Create a new routeTable and associate it with the public subnet
$PublicRouteTable = New-EC2RouteTable -VpcId $VPC.VpcId
New-EC2Route -RouteTableId $PublicRouteTable.RouteTableId
-DestinationCidrBlock '0.0.0.0/0'
    -GatewayId $InternetGateway.InternetGatewayId
$NoEcho = Register-EC2RouteTable -RouteTableId $PublicRouteTable.RouteTableId
    -SubnetId $PublicSubnet.SubnetId
```

Finally, we configure the ACLs.

```
#Create a new Access Control List for the public subnet
$PublicACL = New-EC2NetworkAcl -VpcId $VPC.VpcId
New-EC2NetworkAclEntry -NetworkAclId $PublicACL.NetworkAclId -RuleNumber 50
    -CidrBlock $VPCCIDR -Egress $false -PortRange_From 80
    -PortRange_To 80 -Protocol 6 -RuleAction 'Deny'
New-EC2NetworkAclEntry -NetworkAclId $PublicACL.NetworkAclId -RuleNumber 50
    -CidrBlock $VPCCIDR -Egress $true -PortRange_From 49152
    -PortRange_To 65535 -Protocol 6 -RuleAction 'Deny'
New-EC2NetworkAclEntry -NetworkAclId $PublicACL.NetworkAclId -RuleNumber 100
    -CidrBlock '0.0.0.0/0' -Egress $false -PortRange_From 80
    -PortRange_To 80 -Protocol 6 -RuleAction 'Allow'
New-EC2NetworkAclEntry -NetworkAclId $PublicACL.NetworkAclId -RuleNumber 100
    -CidrBlock '0.0.0.0/0' -Egress $true -PortRange_From 49152
    -PortRange_To 65535 -Protocol 6 -RuleAction 'Allow'
New-EC2NetworkAclEntry -NetworkAclId $PublicACL.NetworkAclId -RuleNumber 200
    -CidrBlock $PrivateSubnetCIDR -Egress $true -PortRange_From 1433
    -PortRange_To 1433 -Protocol 6 -RuleAction 'Allow'
New-EC2NetworkAclEntry -NetworkAclId $PublicACL.NetworkAclId -RuleNumber 200
    -CidrBlock $PrivateSubnetCIDR -Egress $false -PortRange_From 49152
    -PortRange_To 65535 -Protocol 6 -RuleAction 'Allow'
New-EC2NetworkAclEntry -NetworkAclId $PublicACL.NetworkAclId -RuleNumber 300
    -CidrBlock '0.0.0.0/0' -Egress $false -PortRange_From 3389
    -PortRange_To 3389 -Protocol 6 -RuleAction 'Allow'
```

```
#Associate the ACL to the public subnet
$VPCFilter = New-Object Amazon.EC2.Model.Filter
$VPCFilter.Name = 'vpc-id'
$VPCFilter.Value = $VPC.VpcId
$DefaultFilter = New-Object Amazon.EC2.Model.Filter
$DefaultFilter.Name = 'default'
$DefaultFilter.Value = 'true'
$OldACL = (Get-EC2NetworkAcl -Filter $VPCFilter, $DefaultFilter )
$OldAssociation = $OldACL.Associations | Where-Object { $_.SubnetId -eq
$PublicSubnet.SubnetId }
$NoEcho = Set-EC2NetworkAclAssociation -AssociationId $OldAssociation.
NetworkAclAssociationId
    -NetworkAclId $PublicACL.NetworkAclId

#Log the most common IDs
Write-Host "The VPC ID is" $VPC.VpcId
Write-Host "The public subnet ID is" $PublicSubnet.SubnetId
Write-Host "The private subnet ID is" $PrivateSubnet.SubnetId
```

As you can see, it is easy to create and re-create a VPC. The examples in the next chapter will build on this VPC. Feel free to use the script to create a new VPC for each exercise in Chapter 6. In the next example, we will build a new VPC that is attached to our corporate network.

EXERCISE 5.2: CREATING A VIRTUAL PRIVATE GATEWAY

In this exercise, we will use a VPN connection to extend a company's private network directly to the VPC. This will allow you to connect to the private instance in your VPC and allow VPC instances to access resources on your local network. We will create a virtual private gateway and connect our offices to Amazon using an IPSec tunnel.

Figure 5-11 provides an overview of the configuration. Our corporate LAN is using the private IP range 10.0.0.0/0. We have decided to allocate a section of this, 10.200.0.0/16, for use at AWS.

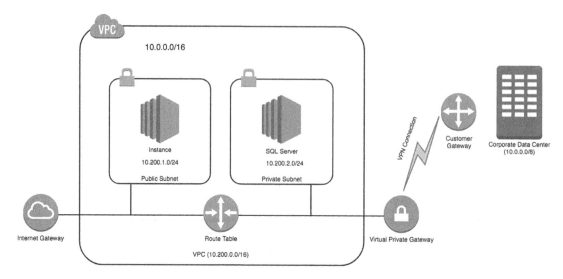

Figure 5-11. *VPC with a virtual private gateway*

I'm going to assume that you know how to create the VPC, subnets, and so on. Let's get right to configuring the VPN connection. Note that you will be charged for the VPN connection as soon as you create the virtual private gateway, even if you never connect the local side of the VPN connection.

The first step is describing your customer gateway to AWS. The customer gateway is your side of the tunnel. If you have multiple office locations, you can connect up to five customer gateways to each VPC. You need to tell AWS your public IP address to connect to and the type of tunnel you want to create. At this time, IPSec is the only type of tunnel supported. The PowerShell command is New-EC2CustomerGateway.

```
$CustomerGateway = New-EC2CustomerGateway -Type 'ipsec.1' -IpAddress
'198.51.100.12'
```

The next thing you need to do is to create the virtual private gateway. This is Amazon's side of the tunnel. You simply tell AWS which availability zone to use and the type of tunnel you want to create. Then you attach it to an existing VPC.

```
$VpnGateway = New-EC2VpnGateway -Type 'ipsec.1' -AvailabilityZone
$AvailabilityZone
Add-EC2VpnGateway -VpnGatewayId $VpnGateway.VpnGatewayId  -VpcId $VpcId
```

Now that we have both sides of the tunnel established, we create a new connection between them by calling New-EC2VpnConnection. You need to pass the ID of the customer gateway and the virtual private gateway as well as passing the type of tunnel one more time.

```
$VPNConnection = New-EC2VpnConnection -Type 'ipsec.1' -CustomerGatewayId
    $CustomerGateway.CustomerGatewayId -VpnGatewayId $VpnGateway.
    VpnGatewayId
    -StaticRoutesOnly $true
```

Note that I have configured this tunnel to use static routes. This means that you need to tell AWS what networks are available on your side of the tunnel. You could also use dynamic routing and allow Border Gateway Protocol (BGP) to learn the routes. BGP is beyond the scope of this book.

Before we can add static routes, we need to wait for the configuration to complete. I am using the following loop to wait for the VPN connection to come online.

```
While ($VPNConnection.VpnConnectionState -eq 'pending') {
    #Wait for the VPN connection to become available
    Start-Sleep -s 15
    $VPNConnection = Get-EC2VpnConnection
        -VpnConnectionId  $VPNConnection.VpnConnectionId
}
```

Now that the tunnel is up, we have to configure the static routing. We need to tell AWS that the rest of the private network is available on the other side of the tunnel. The following rule tells AWS that it can find the 10.0.0.0/8 network by sending traffic over the tunnel. Note that AWS already knows that 10.200.0.0/16 is the local network. Remember that the most specific route (the one with the largest number after the slash) is chosen first.

```
New-EC2VpnConnectionRoute -VpnConnectionId $VPNConnection.VpnConnectionId
    -DestinationCidrBlock '10.0.0.0/8'
```

We could also choose to have traffic from our private instances bound for the Internet go over the tunnel rather than using a NAT gateway from the prior section. The benefit of this is that we can configure the traffic to use all of existing network appliances such as black lists, data loss prevention, and so on. The downside is that we introduce a lot of latency, specifically when accessing an Internet address hosted in the Amazon data center such as S3.

```
New-EC2VpnConnectionRoute -VpnConnectionId $VPNConnection.VpnConnectionId
    -DestinationCidrBlock '0.0.0.0/0'
```

The last thing we need to do is configure the route tables for the individual subnets in our VPC. Let's assume that we want our private instances to access the public Internet over the VPN tunnel and our public instances to use the Internet gateway. Both subnets will have access to the rest of the private network over the VPN tunnel.

My private route table looks like this. Note that the default route (0.0.0.0/0) is pointed to the virtual gateway.

```
(Get-EC2RouteTable -RouteTableId $PrivateRouteTableID)[0].routes | Format-Table
===
DestinationCidrBlock GatewayId      InstanceId State
-------------------- ---------      ---------- ------
10.200.0.0/16        local                     active
10.0.0.0/8           vgw-e424c48d              active
0.0.0.0/0            vgw-e424c48d              active
```

And, my public route table looks like this. Note that the default route (0.0.0.0/0) is pointed to the Internet gateway.

```
(Get-EC2RouteTable -RouteTableId $PublicRouteTableID)[0].routes | Format-Table
===
DestinationCidrBlock GatewayId      InstanceId State
-------------------- ---------      ---------- ------
10.200.0.0/16        local                     active
10.0.0.0/8           vgw-e424c48d              active
0.0.0.0/0            igw-79095f17              active
```

Of course, you would want to configure your ACLs as well, but I think we have spent enough time on ACLs in the chapter. I'll leave that up to you.

Please note that the preceding VPN configuration is for Amazon. You will also need to configure your side of the tunnel on whatever device you are using. The process is different on each device type, but Amazon will help you by autogenerating a script for common hardware types.

From the Web Console, go to the VPN service, click VPN connection from the left navigation, and click the Download Configuration button. Now choose your hardware configuration (see Figure 5-12) and click "Yes, Download" to download a script for your device.

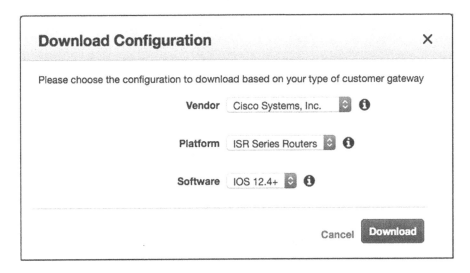

Figure 5-12. *Downloading a VPN configuration for your local device*

Once the VPN tunnel is established, you will be able to communicate with the AWS instances as if they were on the local network.

Summary

In this chapter, we learned about networking with AWS. We learned to create a VPC, add subnets, control how traffic is routed and filtered, and even how to connect two VPCs in different regions. As you can see, VPC is very powerful and very simple. You can quickly build network topologies that would take weeks to implement with physical equipment.

In addition, we saw how easy it was to script the build. When used with continuous integration, a scripted VPC can be used to wipe and rebuild the entire environment on a daily basis.

In the next chapter, I will show you how to launch instances into our new VPC and manage their behavior. We will learn how to configure IP addresses and network interfaces and security groups. Grab a cup of coffee and keep reading!

CHAPTER 6

Advanced Instance Management

In the last chapter, we learned how to create a Virtual Private Cloud (VPC) and specify our network topology. In this chapter, we are going to build on the VPC concepts by discussing how we can configure our instances in a VPC.

Before launching our instances, we first need to understand and configure the appropriate security groups. Security groups protect the Elastic Network Interface (ENI) attached to each of our instances, which is how they differ from the network access control lists (ACLs) discussed in Chapter 5.

In this chapter, we are going to learn how to create and manage rules, discuss the differences between security groups and traditional firewalls, and walk through the process of adding servers to a security group.

Once we have our security groups configured, we can launch our instances into one of our VPCs. We will discuss managing private IP addresses and assigning public IP addresses. Finally, we will wrap up the chapter with a look at creating, attaching, and managing Elastic Network Interfaces (ENIs).

Managing Security Groups

A security group is a stateful virtual firewall that protects the ENI attached to our instance. Traditionally, firewalls protect trusted networks from untrusted ones, creating security zones. For example, a firewall protects our private network from the Internet, but the machines on the private network may have no restrictions when communicating with others on that same private network.

© Brian Beach, Steven Armentrout, Rodney Bozo, Emmanuel Tsouris 2019
B. Beach et al., *Pro PowerShell for Amazon Web Services*, https://doi.org/10.1007/978-1-4842-4850-8_6

In recent years, firewall costs have decreased dramatically, and we have begun to use them to protect much smaller segments of our networks. For example, we may use a firewall to separate the finance department from the rest of the organization or to protect a single application that hosts sensitive data.

Amazon EC2 security groups take this idea to the next level. An EC2 security group is similar to having a firewall in front of each network interface attached to our instances. No two instances can communicate without traversing that firewall, not even if they are in the same subnet or security group. In other words, the security group is part of our instances network interface, rather than part of the network itself. We can even attach multiple ENIs to our instances, each with multiple security groups associated with it!

Our security group allows us to control the flow of traffic to and from our instances. This includes controlling the type of traffic (e.g., TCP, UDP, or ICMP) allowed, port ranges to allow, and the source and destination addresses permitted to communicate.

We refer to the rules controlling traffic flow into our instances as ingress (inbound) rules, while the rules controlling the traffic flowing away from our instances are called egress (outbound) rules. When we define our security group rules later, we will see the terms ingress and egress used to describe these inbound and outbound rules, respectively.

Note   While there were security groups in EC2 Classic, you could only filter inbound traffic. With VPC, security groups filter both inbound and outbound traffic.

When we launch a new instance using PowerShell and do not specify a security group, the instance will be associated with our default security group. The default group allows an instance to communicate freely with any other instance in the same default security group. It does this because the security group itself is included in the inbound rules for all protocols over any port. In order to connect to our new instance using RDP, we will need to add an inbound (or ingress) rule allowing incoming connections over the RDP port (3389).

Caution   If you use the Create EC2 Instance Wizard in the AWS Management Console, it will give you an option to create a new security group for each instance or select an existing group. When choosing the default option to create a new group, the wizard sets an ingress rule allowing the port to be open to the world (0.0.0.0/0). You should change this rule before proceeding with the wizard, unless you truly want it open to the world. It is a good idea to only allow RDP or SSH connections from trusted IP addresses or network address ranges. So, be sure and restrict the inbound security group rules when using the wizard.

Displaying Security Groups

We can find our security groups by opening up the AWS Management Console, finding the EC2 service, and then looking for the Network & Security heading in the left pane. We will go ahead and start by looking at our default security group. In Figure 6-1 you can see that there is only one inbound rule.

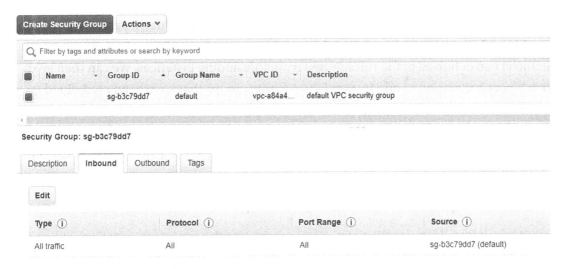

Figure 6-1. *Inbound security group rules*

Notice that this inbound rule allows all traffic, for all protocols, on any port from the security group sg-b3c79dd7, the same security group we are already looking at. In other words, this rule allows any instance in the security group to communicate with any other instance in the group. The security group blocks other inbound traffic by default.

Now we will look at the outbound rules in Figure 6-2. Again, there is only a single rule. This rule allows outbound traffic for any protocol, on any port, to any destination. Specifically, the security group allows all outbound traffic by default.

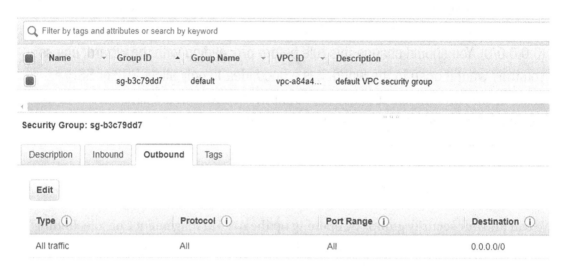

Figure 6-2. *Outbound security group rules*

Unlike traditional firewall rules, we are not specifying individual instances by IP address. In fact, we might not even have an instance in our VPC yet. The security architect can define all of the rules necessary before adding instances. We can then give developers permission to add instances to security groups that have been predefined, and our developers will not have to wait for a change request approval to open the firewall ports later.

Returning to PowerShell, we can list the security groups using the Get-EC2Security Group command.

```
Get-EC2SecurityGroup | Select-Object Description, GroupId | Format-Table
```

This command returns a list of security groups for all our VPCs.

```
Description                     GroupId
-----------                     -------
default VPC security group      sg-b3c79dd7
```

Now, take note of your specific GroupID for the default VPC. In the next section, we will use that GroupID to modify the security group.

Adding and Removing Rules

We are now going to add an inbound rule to our default VPC security group, allowing us to access our Windows instances with Remote Desktop Protocol (RDP).

To add inbound rules to the group, we use the now-common pattern of creating a .Net object to describe the rule and then call `Grant-EC2SecurityGroupIngress`.

Tip   The `IpRanges` property expects IP ranges specified with CIDR notation. While the `FromPort` and `ToPort` properties specify a range of destination ports, not the source and destination port.

RDP runs on TCP port 3389; therefore, the PowerShell command is the following:

```
$RDPRule = New-Object Amazon.EC2.Model.IpPermission
$RDPRule.IpProtocol='tcp'
$RDPRule.FromPort = 3389
$RDPRule.ToPort = 3389
```

We could use `'0.0.0.0/0'` and open up traffic to the whole world, but we should take a more secure and least access approach by narrowing down the range needed for our environment. To do this, we would use a specific IP address or subnet range for `IpRanges`.

For this next example, use your IP address to set the IP range. Replace the IP address in the following CIDR with your specific IP address:

```
$RDPRule.IpRanges = '99.86.37.184/32'
```

Tip   If you do not know your IP address, you can try searching Google for "My IP Address," and Google will display your outbound IP address.

However, if we really needed to open up this rule to the whole world (or entire Internet), then we could use that special `'0.0.0.0/0'` value.

```
$RDPRule.IpRanges = '0.0.0.0/0'
```

Caution   Using '0.0.0.0/0' for the IpRanges property goes against numerous best practices since you are enabling all IP addresses on the Internet to access that port on your instance. For RDP and SSH, the recommendation is always to limit the exposure of these ports to only those who need the access. While opening up these ports may be needed for a short time during testing, troubleshooting, or development, when it comes to your production configuration, you will want to authorize only trusted IP addresses or subnet ranges to access these ports on your instances.

Now that we have defined our IpPermission object, we can create our ingress rule:

Note   Replace the security group ID in the following examples with your own specific security group ID.

```
Grant-EC2SecurityGroupIngress -GroupId 'sg-b3c79dd7' -IpPermissions $RDPRule
```

The process to add an outbound rule is almost identical, but we would use the Grant-EC2SecurityGroupEgress command. Note that there is no need to add outbound rules because the default group already allows all traffic outbound.

```
Grant-EC2SecurityGroupEgress -GroupId 'sg-b3c79dd7' -IpPermissions $RDPRule
```

We can easily create a security group using the New-EC2SecurityGroup command. For example, if we were developing a web application, we might create a security group allowing HTTP and HTTPS requests from the Internet.

Note   Replace the VPC ID in the following example with your own specific VPC ID.

```
$GroupId = New-EC2SecurityGroup -VpcId 'vpc-881acde9' -GroupName 'Web'
-GroupDescription
    "Allows HTTP/S traffic from the internet."
```

New security groups allow all outbound traffic by default, but do not allow any inbound traffic. With this rule, we will allow any IP address to reach our instance using TCP over ports 80 (HTTP) and 443 (HTTPS):

```
$HTTPRule = New-Object Amazon.EC2.Model.IpPermission
$HTTPRule.IpProtocol='tcp'
$HTTPRule.FromPort = 80
$HTTPRule.ToPort = 80
$HTTPRule.IpRanges = '0.0.0.0/0'

$HTTPSRule = New-Object Amazon.EC2.Model.IpPermission
$HTTPSRule.IpProtocol='tcp'
$HTTPSRule.FromPort = 443
$HTTPSRule.ToPort = 443
$HTTPSRule.IpRanges = '0.0.0.0/0'

Grant-EC2SecurityGroupIngress -GroupId $GroupId -IpPermissions $HTTPRule,
$HTTPSRule
```

We can also remove inbound and outbound rules using Revoke-EC2Security GroupIngress and Revoke-EC2SecurityGroupEgress, respectively. For example, we might want to remove the default rule that allows all outbound traffic from our web group.

Unlike ACLs, security groups are stateful, so we do not need rules explicitly allowing return traffic. Our security group knows that the originating HTTP request is going to have a corresponding response and will automatically allow it. We only need the outbound rule when the instance is acting as the client, surfing the Web, or downloading software. For our new group, we want to prevent any unauthorized outbound traffic from our instance. Therefore, we will not need the default outbound rule and will remove it.

```
$Rule = New-Object Amazon.EC2.Model.IpPermission
$Rule.IpProtocol='-1'
$Rule.IpRanges = '0.0.0.0/0'

Revoke-EC2SecurityGroupEgress -GroupId $GroupId -IpPermissions $Rule
```

Note We used an `IpProtocol` of `"-1"`, which means all protocols. We can create security group rules by either specifying the name or IP protocol number, for example, ICMP (protocol 1), TCP (protocol 6), and UDP (protocol 17). For convenience, we can use the name or the number for these common protocols. However, for less common protocols, we must specify the protocol number.

As we saw in Figure 6-1, we can create rules based on other security groups. For example, imagine our web application has an SQL database. The web servers must be able to access the SQL Server. However, the number of web servers will change throughout the day depending on the load.

For this scenario, we will create a new SQL group for our SQL Servers.

Note Replace the VPC and Security Group IDs in the following example with your own specific IDs.

```
$GroupId = New-EC2SecurityGroup -VpcId vpc-881acde9 -GroupName SQL
-GroupDescription

  "Allows SQL Queries from the web server."
```

Next, we need to create a UserIdGroupPair object to hold our security group ID.

```
$WebGroup = New-Object Amazon.EC2.Model.UserIdGroupPair
$WebGroup.GroupId = 'sg-0c3b9863'
```

Then we will grant access to any instance in the web security group we created. Since we are using Microsoft SQL Server, we will specify TCP port 1433.

```
$SQLRule = New-Object Amazon.EC2.Model.IpPermission
$SQLRule.IpProtocol='tcp'
$SQLRule.FromPort = 1433
$SQLRule.ToPort = 1433
$SQLRule.UserIdGroupPair = $WebGroup
```

Finally, we pass the GroupId and `$SQLRule` to `Grant-EC2SecurityGroupIngress` in order to apply the rule to the security group.

```
Grant-EC2SecurityGroupIngress -GroupId $GroupId -IpPermissions $SQLRule
```

With this new security group in place, all we have to do is add new web servers to our web security group and AWS will allow our instances to communicate with the SQL Server. When launching new instances, there is no need to update the security group rules.

Before we close this section, we should look at a scenario where we might want to create an ICMP rule, for example, being able to ping all of our instances from outside of our VPC.

Caution   Allowing ping from outside a VPC is not recommended and poses a security risk, but is covered here to illustrate how ICMP rules work.

Say we like throwing caution to the wind and decide to add a new rule to our default security group allowing ICMP Echo Request messages from anywhere. ICMP uses message types rather than ports. To enable an ICMP message, you use an `IpProtocol` of `"icmp"` and then put the message type in `FromPort`. For example, an ICMP Echo Request is message type 8. Note that the `ToPort` is not used and should be set to `-1`.

In this section, we discussed security groups and security group rules. We learned how a security group is similar in concept to a firewall, but in reality, the rules apply to an instances network interface rather than the network segment. Finally, we looked at how we can add or remove various security group rules to fit the needs of our applications. Now, we will move on to launching an instance into our VPC.

Launching Instances into a VPC

VPC gives us considerable control over network configuration of our EC2 instances. We are going to start by launching a new instance into the VPC we created in Chapter 5. If you have not created a VPC, use the script from Exercise 5.1.

We are going to begin by looking at the Launch Instance Wizard. From the Amazon EC2 Console, when we click the Launch Instance button, it takes us into the Launch Instance Wizard. On the third step, Configure Instance Details, if we select a specific subnet, a new Network Interfaces section appears. Notice the network configuration options shown in Figure 6-3. This section allows us add additional network interfaces to our instance. It also allows us to choose a subnet and specify an IP address. In addition, we can add secondary IP addresses to our instance.

Figure 6-3. *Network options in the Launch Instances Wizard*

Launching an instance into our VPC with PowerShell is almost how we launched an instance in Chapter 3. Once again, we will use the New-EC2Instance command, but this time we add one new parameter: the ID of the subnet to launch our instance in. Note that we can only connect with RDP to instances in a public subnet, so we will use a public subnet here.

Note   Key pair names are case sensitive.

```
$AMI = Get-EC2ImageByName -Name 'WINDOWS_2016_BASE'

New-EC2Instance -ImageId $AMI[0].ImageId -KeyName 'MyKey' -InstanceType
't2.micro' -SubnetId subnet-7922ea18
```

That is all it takes to launch an instance into our VPC. The instance we just launched has a random public IP address assigned by EC2, along with a randomly assigned private IP address for use within our VPC. This private IP falls within the CIDR range of the subnet we specified and is assigned using DHCP.

If we need to control the private IP address of the instance, we can specify an IP address to set at launch, using the `PrivateIPAddress` parameter. This is similar to setting a static DHCP address (or DHCP reservation).

Note   Your private IP range might be different.

```
$AMI = Get-EC2ImageByName -Name 'WINDOWS_2016_BASE'

New-EC2Instance -ImageId $AMI[0].ImageId -KeyName 'MyKey' -InstanceType
't2.micro' -SubnetId subnet-7922ea18 -PrivateIpAddress 192.168.1.5
```

Note that the IP address must fall within the CIDR range configured within the subnet and is immutable. We can set it when launching a new instance, but cannot change it once the instance is running. Also, remember that the first four IP addresses and the last IP address of each subnet are reserved.

Of course, we can also select existing security groups when launching an instance. As we can see in Figure 6-4, when we choose to select an existing security group, we have the option of selecting more than one group. For example, we can associate our new instance to the web and default groups that we discussed earlier. Our web group allows HTTP traffic and our default group allows RDP.

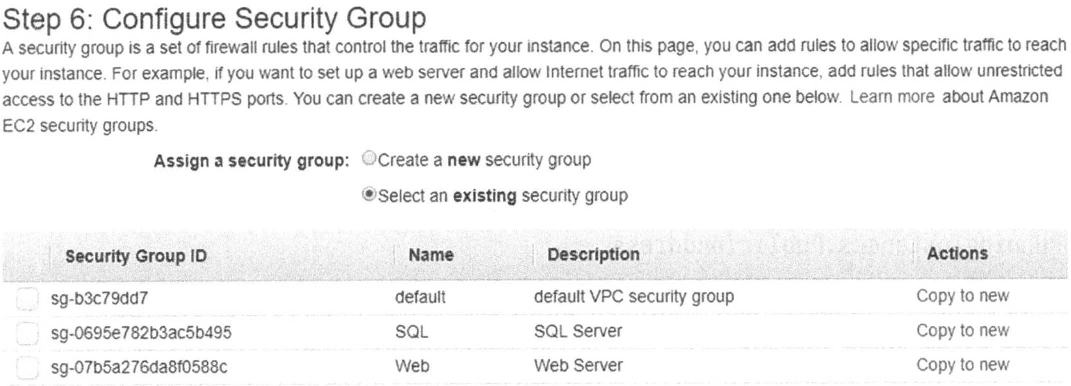

Step 6: Configure Security Group
A security group is a set of firewall rules that control the traffic for your instance. On this page, you can add rules to allow specific traffic to reach your instance. For example, if you want to set up a web server and allow Internet traffic to reach your instance, add rules that allow unrestricted access to the HTTP and HTTPS ports. You can create a new security group or select from an existing one below. Learn more about Amazon EC2 security groups.

Assign a security group: ○ Create a **new** security group

⦿ Select an **existing** security group

	Security Group ID	Name	Description	Actions
☐	sg-b3c79dd7	default	default VPC security group	Copy to new
☐	sg-0695e782b3ac5b495	SQL	SQL Server	Copy to new
☐	sg-07b5a276da8f0588c	Web	Web Server	Copy to new

Figure 6-4. *Security groups in the Launch Instance Wizard*

To add an instance to a security group using PowerShell, we use the
SecurityGroupId parameter and pass an array of security group IDs.

```
$AMI = Get-EC2ImageByName -Name 'WINDOWS_2016_BASE'

New-EC2Instance -ImageId $AMI[0].ImageId -KeyName 'MyKey' -InstanceType
't2.micro' -SubnetId subnet-7922ea18 -SecurityGroupId sg-b3c79dd7,
sg-07b5a276da8f0588c
```

As we have just seen, launching instances into a specific VPC gives us the ability to
control the private network configuration of our instances. We launched an instance into
our public subnet and enabled HTTP and RDP traffic from the Internet using security
groups.

Subnets and Public IP Addresses

For instances to be public, we launch them in a public subnet (one with a route to the
Internet gateway), and it must have a public IP address associated with it. Our default
VPC already has both an Internet gateway and subnets that automatically map a public
IP address to our EC2 instance when we launch it.

We can use this public IP address to connect to our instances with RDP. However,
when we stop our instance and restart it, this auto-assigned public IP address will
change. The public IP address changes because EC2 randomly assigns it when
we start our instance. We can look at any of our running EC2 instances and their
PublicIpAddress by examining the RunningInstance property of the Get-EC2Instance
cmdlet:

```
$RunningInstances = (Get-EC2Instance).RunningInstance
$RunningInstances.PublicIpAddress
```

EC2 knows when to assign a public IP address because subnets have a property,
MapPublicOnLaunch. This property tells EC2 if it should auto-assign a public IP address
to instances when launched in this subnet. We can also create subnets with this property
set to false, which would result in our instances not getting a public IP address assigned.
This is useful for our database servers, which only need to talk to our frontend web
servers. However, keep in mind, to RDP (or SSH) to instances with only private IP
addresses, we must use a bastion host (or jump box) that has a public IP and can talk to
our instance via subnet, VPC, and security group configuration.

To view our subnets and see which ones have this property assigned, we can use Get-EC2Subnet and look at the MapPublicOnLaunch property:

```
Get-EC2Subnet | Select-Object SubnetId, MapPublicIpOnLaunch
```

We can see from the output which subnets have the MapPublicIpOnLaunch property set to true.

```
SubnetId                MapPublicIpOnLaunch
--------                -------------------
subnet-600e232a             True
subnet-842dcded             True
subnet-59858621             True
```

When launching a new instance, even if our subnet has the MapPublicOnLaunch property set to true, we can still choose whether to auto-assign it a public IP or not. We do that by calling New-EC2Instance and specify $true or $false for the AssociatePublicIp property:

```
$AMI = Get-EC2ImageByName -Name 'WINDOWS_2016_BASE'

New-EC2Instance -ImageId $AMI[0].ImageId -KeyName 'MyKey' -InstanceType
't2.micro' -SubnetId subnet-7922ea18 -AssociatePublicIp $false
```

As we talked about before, the public IP address will change when our instance stops and starts again. There will be times when we need a public IP address that does not change, for example, when we want to be able to stop and start an instance, but ensure it always uses the same IP address for RDP, or is associated with a domain name. For these scenarios, we can use an elastic IP address.

Managing Elastic IP Addresses

For cases when a random public IP address is not what we need, but would like to associate a fixed public IP address with our instance, we have the ability to create an Elastic IP (EIP) address.

AWS uses Network Address Translation (NAT) to map traffic between the private IP and the EIP. The NAT is implemented in the Internet gateway.

To create an EIP address, we use New-EC2Address and specify VPC for the Domain property, which tells EC2 that we are going to use the EIP in a VPC rather than with EC2 Classic. For example:

```
$EIP = New-EC2Address -Domain vpc
```

EC2 will randomly assign an EIP. In order to associate the EIP to our instance, we use the Register-EC2PrivateIpAddress cmdlet.

Note   Replace InstanceId with your own Instance ID.

```
Register-EC2Address -InstanceId i-1234567890 -AllocationId $EIP.
AllocationId
```

LOGGING INTO A VPC INSTANCE

At this point, we have learned that we can open the AWS Web Console, decrypt our password using our key pair, and click the connect link to log into our instance using Remote Desktop. If this does not sound familiar, jump back to Chapter 3 and review.

If you have any issues, walk through these troubleshooting steps:

1.   Check your VPC, and make sure it has an Internet gateway.

2.   The public subnet has a route to the Internet gateway.

3.   The subnet has an ACL allowing RDP in from the Internet.

4.   The subnet has an ACL allowing a reply in from the ephemeral ports.

5.   The instance is in a public subnet.

6.   The default security group allows RDP in from your computer or the Internet.

7.   The instance is a member of the default security group.

8.   The instance has either a public IP or an EIP address assigned.

VPC is a powerful feature that gives you a lot of control over your environment, but as a result, it can also be complicated. If you run into trouble seting up new VPCs initially, don't worry, you will get very good at diagnosing issues as you learn more about VPCs.

It is common to reassign an EIP as part of a disaster recovery plan. If the EIP is already associated with another instance, EC2 returns an error when we try to reassign it. We can avoid this error by passing $true to the AllowReassign attribute, which allows us to reassign an EIP that is assigned to another instance.

```
Register-EC2Address -InstanceId i-1234567890 -AllocationId $EIP.
AllocationId
    -AllowReassociation:$true
```

We can remove the EIP address from an instance using the Unregister-EC2Address command. First, we get a reference to the EIP using Get-EC2Address. Then, we call Unregister-EC2Instance and pass the association ID.

Note   Specify the public IP for your specific EIP.

```
$EIP = Get-EC2Address -PublicIp '54.208.194.131'
Unregister-EC2Address -AssociationId $EIP.AssociationId
```

Caution   AWS charges a small hourly fee for any EIP that is not associated with a running instance.

If you no longer need an EIP or intend to stop your instance for a while, consider disassociating the EIP by using the Remove-EC2Address command to avoid paying any extra fees.

```
$EIP = Get-EC2Address -PublicIp '54.208.194.131'
Remove-EC2Address -AllocationId $EIP.AllocationId -Force
```

Now that we know how to manage our IP addresses, we will look more closely at private IP addresses. As you will see in the next section, spending a little extra time planning can make your application easier to manage.

Managing Private IPs

In the previous sections, we referred to the private IP as an attribute of an instance. This was oversimplification. In reality, an instance can have many network interfaces and each interface can have many IP addresses. We will look at adding network interfaces in the next section. For now, we will focus on IP addresses.

When AWS displays the private IP address of an instance, we see the first IP address of the first network interface. Earlier, we discussed we could not change the private IP address of an instance. Specifically, this means we can not change the first IP address of a network interface. What we can do, however, is add additional IP addresses to an interface.

One common use is for disaster recovery. We could easily move a secondary IP between instances. If we have a critical application that relies on a single instance, we might want to keep a second instance on standby. If we detect a failure on our primary instance, we could then move the IP address to a secondary instance.

To add a secondary IP address to an instance, first we must find the network interface. All of the network interfaces are available from the NetworkInterfaces property of the Instance object.

```
$Reservation = Get-EC2Instance -Instance i-b67722cd
$Instance = $Reservation.RunningInstance[0]
$ENI = $Instance.NetworkInterfaces[0]
```

Now that we have the network interface, we can use the Register-EC2PrivateIpAddress method to add a secondary IP address. For example:

Note   When specifying a private IP address, you must use a valid IP address within the subnet range associated with your ENI.

```
Register-EC2PrivateIpAddress -NetworkInterfaceId $ENI.NetworkInterfaceId
    -PrivateIpAddresses '192.168.1.6'
```

Unfortunately, DHCP will not configure secondary IP addresses. In order to use secondary IPs, you must disable DHCP and configure the network interface manually. Luckily, there are PowerShell commands for this. The following example will configure an instance with a static network configuration.

Note   Log in to the instance to configure and execute these commands locally.

```
#Disable DHCP
Set-NetIPInterface -InterfaceAlias 'Ethernet' -Dhcp Disabled

#Configure the primary IP
New-NetIPAddress -InterfaceAlias 'Ethernet' -IPAddress '192.168.1.5'
-PrefixLength 24
    -DefaultGateway '192.168.1.1'

#Configure DNS
Set-DnsClientServerAddress -InterfaceAlias 'Ethernet' -ServerAddresses
'192.168.0.2'

#Add the secondary IP address
New-NetIPAddress -InterfaceAlias 'Ethernet' -IPAddress '192.168.1.6'
-PrefixLength 24
```

Caution   Static network configurations can be dangerous. You must be careful to ensure that the IP addresses assigned within Windows match those assigned in AWS. Remember that EC2 implements security groups at the network interface attached to the instance. This means that if you assign a different IP address, the security groups may not allow traffic to flow to the instance. Taking a snapshot before manually configuring the security groups is highly recommended to give yourself a way to back out any breaking changes.

Now that we know how to manage IP addresses, let's take a closer look at the network interfaces.

Managing Elastic Network Interfaces

As we have covered so far, an EC2 instance can have multiple network interfaces. Amazon calls these interfaces Elastic Network Interfaces (ENIs). The maximum number of interfaces varies with the instance type. Unlike secondary IP addresses, we can assign different subnets to each network interface. See Figure 6-5.

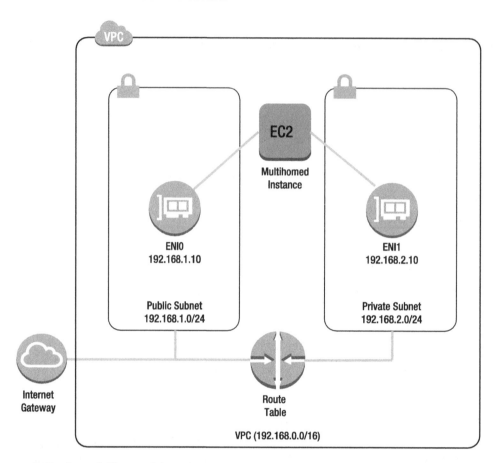

Figure 6-5. *A multihomed instance*

Every instance has at least one ENI, but we can add additional interfaces when launching an instance. Remember that the SubnetId, PrivateIpAddress, and SecurityGroupId attributes of the New-EC2Instance command act on the default ENI. We cannot use these parameters to launch instances with multiple interfaces.

If we want to add multiple interfaces to an instance, we would use a .Net object to describe them. Then, we pass an array of interfaces to the New-EC2Instance command using the NetworkInterfaces attribute. Each ENI has its own IP address and can be in a different subnet. In addition, each ENI can be in a different set of security groups. To launch the instance pictured in Figure 6-5, I used the following PowerShell script:

```
$ENI0 = New-Object Amazon.EC2.Model.InstanceNetworkInterfaceSpecification
$ENI0.PrivateIpAddress = '192.168.1.10'
$ENI0.SubnetId = 'subnet-7922ea18'
```

```
$ENI0.DeviceIndex = 0
$ENI0.Groups.Add('sg-e775d688')

$ENI1 = New-Object Amazon.EC2.Model.InstanceNetworkInterfaceSpecification
$ENI1.PrivateIpAddress = '192.168.2.10'
$ENI1.SubnetId = 'subnet-2f22ea4e'
$ENI1.DeviceIndex = 1
$ENI1.Groups.Add('sg-e775d688')

$AMI = Get-EC2ImageByName -Name 'WINDOWS_2016_BASE'
New-EC2Instance -ImageId $AMI[0].ImageId -KeyName 'MyKey' -InstanceType
't2.micro' -NetworkInterfaces $ENI0, $ENI1
```

Unfortunately, the reservation returned from New-EC2Instance does not include the network interfaces. The command returns asynchronously, and it takes a few seconds for the interfaces to attach. To see the details, we will have to wait a few seconds and then run Get-EC2Instance to refresh our copy of the metadata. For example:

```
$Reservation = Get-EC2Instance -Instance i-b67722cd
$Instance = $Reservation.RunningInstance[0]
$Instance.NetworkInterfaces | Format-Table
```

This command returns

```
NetworkInterfaceId SubnetId         MacAddress        PrivateIpAddress
------------------ ---------------- ----------------- ----------------
eni-cc478fad       subnet-7922ea18 2a:5b:de:70:8... 192.168.1.10
eni-cf478fae       subnet-2f22ea4e 2a:5b:de:7b:8... 192.168.2.10
```

If we would like to add an interface to an existing instance, we can. First, we create a new ENI using the New-EC2NetworkInterface command. Then, attach it to an instance using the Add-EC2NetworkInterface command. For example:

```
$NIC = New-EC2NetworkInterface -SubnetId subnet-1619ce77 -PrivateIpAddress
192.168.1.15
    -GroupId sg-d23596bd
Add-EC2NetworkInterface -NetworkInterfaceId $NIC.NetworkInterfaceId
-InstanceId i-c829b8b3
    -DeviceIndex 1
```

If we want to remove an ENI, we detach it using `Dismount-EC2NetworkInterface`. First, we get the attachment ID and then pass that to the `Dismount-EC2NetworkInterface` command.

```
$NIC = Get-EC2NetworkInterface eni-c00ad7a1
Dismount-EC2NetworkInterface -AttachmentId $NIC.Attachment.AttachmentId
```

There are a few reasons that we might choose to add multiple interfaces to a server. On physical machines, we often include multiple interfaces to increase reliability and bandwidth. In EC2, and all virtual machine environments, the interfaces all share the same physical interface in the hypervisor. Therefore, there is no real reliability or bandwidth gain.

Another reason for multiple interfaces is to allow a machine to span multiple subnets. Again, there are multiple reasons we may choose this. One common practice is to have a management subnet used for administration and backup that is separate from the primary subnet. Again, this is likely not valuable with EC2. Security groups allow us to control administrative traffic, and backups do not use our private network.

We might choose to span subnets to allow our instance to route traffic from one subnet to another. We could launch an application firewall that does traffic inspection or data loss prevention. The instance would have an interface in the private and public subnets, and we would configure the route table to route all Internet traffic through the application firewall.

Note that if we want use an instance to route traffic, we first must disable the source/ destination check. Typically, AWS will discard any traffic sent to an instance where the instance's IP address is not the source or destination. In order for the instance to forward traffic, we must disable this check. (We will do this in Exercise 6-1.)

```
Edit-EC2NetworkInterfaceAttribute -NetworkInterfaceId eni-c00ad7a1
-SourceDestCheck:$false
```

One other reason to use multiple interfaces is disaster recovery. Just as you might move a secondary IP from the primary to standby instance, you could move the ENI. There are two advantages of moving an ENI rather than a secondary IP. First, route tables refer to the interface rather than IP. If your disaster recovery plan involves an instance that is routing traffic, you should use an ENI. Second, we can use DHCP to configure multiple ENIs, but not multiple IP addresses on the same interface.

At this point, we know how to manage security groups, private IPs, EIPs, and ENIs. Finally, let us test our knowledge with a couple of examples.

EXERCISE 6.1: MANAGING PRIVATE INSTANCES

In Chapter 5, we created a private subnet. Remember that instances in a private subnet are not accessible from the Internet. While this is a good security practice, it introduces some new challenges.

The obvious issue is how we administer the private instances. How do we log in to a private instance to configure it, debug issues, and so on? One way to address this is to launch a Remote Desktop Gateway (RDGW) server in the public subnet and use it as a proxy to access the private instances.

In addition, the private instances are not able to access the Internet. This means that they cannot connect to the Internet resources to get patches, antivirus definitions, and so on. A common solution to this problem is to launch a proxy server in the public subnet and configure the route table to route traffic from the private subnet through this proxy.

Figure 6-6 describes the complete solution. We will launch two new instances in a new subnet. Administrative traffic comes in through the RDP gateway, and outbound web traffic goes out through the NAT gateway.

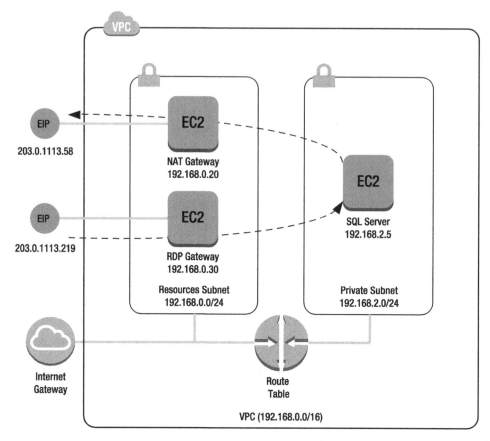

Figure 6-6. *VPC with a NAT gateway and RDP gateway*

This example is, by far, the most complicated example in the book. Don't worry if you have to read through it more than once. We could have simply put all the instances in a public subnet or left the ACLs and security groups open to all traffic. However, this is a common pattern for a real-world enterprise VPC architecture. These security controls are very likely to please any enterprise security architect.

Let's begin by altering our network configuration. This exercise assumes you already have a VPC that we can use. If you would like to create a new VPC, and leave your existing ones alone, use Exercise 5.1 to create one. We are going to add a new public subnet to host our resources (the NAT and RDP gateways) with the CIDR block 192.168.0.0/24.

First, we define a few variables including the VPCID, CIDR block, and the AMIs to use.

```
param
(
    [string][parameter(mandatory=$true)]$VPCID,
    [string][parameter(mandatory=$false)]$ResourcesSubnetCIDR =
    '192.168.0.0/24',
    [string][parameter(mandatory=$false)]$NAT_AMI,
    [string][parameter(mandatory=$false)]$RDP_AMI
)
```

If the user does not provide an AMI, let's assume they want the default NAT and Windows Server 2016.

```
If([System.String]::IsNullOrEmpty($NAT_AMI)){ $NAT_AMI = (Get-EC2ImageByName
-Name 'VPC_NAT')[0].ImageId}
```

```
If([System.String]::IsNullOrEmpty($RDP_AMI)){ $RDP_AMI = (Get-EC2ImageByName
-Name 'WINDOWS_2016_BASE')[0].ImageId}
```

Next, we choose an availability zone. We can simply get the first availability zone in the region.

```
$VPC = Get-EC2VPC -VpcID $VPCID
$AvailabilityZones = Get-EC2AvailabilityZone
$AvailabilityZone = $AvailabilityZones[0].ZoneName
```

Now we create the resources subnet, which will use a route table configured just like the public subnet that we created in Chapter 5.

```
$ResourcesSubnet = New-EC2Subnet -VpcId $VPCID -CidrBlock
$ResourcesSubnetCIDR
    -AvailabilityZone $AvailabilityZone
$ResourcesRouteTable = New-EC2RouteTable -VpcId $VPC.VpcId
$VPCFilter = New-Object Amazon.EC2.Model.Filter
$VPCFilter.Name = 'attachment.vpc-id'
$VPCFilter.Value = $VPCID
$InternetGateway = Get-EC2InternetGateway -Filter $VPCID
New-EC2Route -RouteTableId $ResourcesRouteTable.RouteTableId
-DestinationCidrBlock
    '0.0.0.0/0' -GatewayId $InternetGateway.InternetGatewayId
Register-EC2RouteTable -RouteTableId $ResourcesRouteTable.RouteTableId
-SubnetId
    $ResourcesSubnet.SubnetId
```

Next, we need to configure the ACLs for our new subnet. First, we will allow traffic in to configure the NAT and RDP gateway servers. The NAT instance is running Linux and requires SSH port 22. The RDP instance is running Windows and requires RDP port 3389. In addition, we need to remember to open the ephemeral ports to allow the return traffic.

```
$ACL = New-EC2NetworkAcl -VpcId $VPCID
New-EC2NetworkAclEntry -NetworkAclId $ACL.NetworkAclId -RuleNumber 100
-CidrBlock
     '0.0.0.0/0' -Egress $false -PortRange_From 22 -PortRange_To 22 -Protocol 6
     -RuleAction Allow
New-EC2NetworkAclEntry -NetworkAclId $ACL.NetworkAclId -RuleNumber 110
-CidrBlock
     '0.0.0.0/0' -Egress $false -PortRange_From 3389 -PortRange_To 3389
     -Protocol 6
     -RuleAction Allow
New-EC2NetworkAclEntry -NetworkAclId $ACL.NetworkAclId -RuleNumber 120
-CidrBlock
     '0.0.0.0/0' -Egress $true  -PortRange_From 49152 -PortRange_To 65535
     -Protocol 6
     -RuleAction Allow
```

Now, we need to pass through the NAT gateway to download patches over HTTP and HTTPS. Therefore, we need to allow traffic on 80 and 443 from our private subnets, through the resources subnet, and out to the Internet.

```
New-EC2NetworkAclEntry -NetworkAclId $ACL.NetworkAclId -RuleNumber 200
-CidrBlock
     $VPC.CidrBlock -Egress $false -PortRange_From 80 -PortRange_To 80
     -Protocol 6
     -RuleAction Allow
New-EC2NetworkAclEntry -NetworkAclId $ACL.NetworkAclId -RuleNumber 210
-CidrBlock
     $VPC.CidrBlock -Egress $false -PortRange_From 443 -PortRange_To 443
     -Protocol 6
     -RuleAction Allow
New-EC2NetworkAclEntry -NetworkAclId $ACL.NetworkAclId -RuleNumber 230
-CidrBlock
     $VPC.CidrBlock -Egress $true -PortRange_From 49152 -PortRange_To 65535
     -Protocol 6
     -RuleAction Allow
```

```
New-EC2NetworkAclEntry -NetworkAclId $ACL.NetworkAclId -RuleNumber 240
-CidrBlock
    '0.0.0.0/0' -Egress $true -PortRange_From 80 -PortRange_To 80 -Protocol 6
    -RuleAction Allow
New-EC2NetworkAclEntry -NetworkAclId $ACL.NetworkAclId -RuleNumber 250
-CidrBlock
    '0.0.0.0/0' -Egress $true -PortRange_From 443 -PortRange_To 443
    -Protocol 6
    -RuleAction Allow
New-EC2NetworkAclEntry -NetworkAclId $ACL.NetworkAclId -RuleNumber 260
-CidrBlock
    '0.0.0.0/0' -Egress $false -PortRange_From 49152 -PortRange_To 65535
    -Protocol 6
    -RuleAction Allow
```

We will also need to allow RDP traffic in through our RDP gateway. The RDP gateway creates an SSL tunnel (port 443) from the client to the gateway. Then it uses RDP (port 3389) from the gateway to the server. Again, we need to remember the ephemeral ports.

```
New-EC2NetworkAclEntry -NetworkAclId $ACL.NetworkAclId -RuleNumber 300
-CidrBlock
    '0.0.0.0/0' -Egress $false -PortRange_From 443 -PortRange_To 443
    -Protocol 6
    -RuleAction Allow
New-EC2NetworkAclEntry -NetworkAclId $ACL.NetworkAclId -RuleNumber 310
-CidrBlock
    '0.0.0.0/0' -Egress $true -PortRange_From 49152 -PortRange_To 65535
    -Protocol 6
    -RuleAction Allow
New-EC2NetworkAclEntry -NetworkAclId $ACL.NetworkAclId -RuleNumber 320
-CidrBlock
    $VPC.CidrBlock -Egress $true -PortRange_From 3389 -PortRange_To 3389
    -Protocol 6
    -RuleAction Allow
New-EC2NetworkAclEntry -NetworkAclId $ACL.NetworkAclId -RuleNumber 330
-CidrBlock
    $VPC.CidrBlock -Egress $false -PortRange_From 49152 -PortRange_To 65535
    -Protocol 6
    -RuleAction Allow
```

Next, we have to create security groups to protect the instances we are going to launch in the resources subnet. First, we will create a security group for administration. This will allow SSH port 22 and RDP port 3389 to configure the servers.

```
$RDPRule = New-Object Amazon.EC2.Model.IpPermission
$RDPRule.IpProtocol='tcp'
$RDPRule.FromPort = 3389
$RDPRule.ToPort = 3389
$RDPRule.IpRanges = '0.0.0.0/0'
$SSHRule = New-Object Amazon.EC2.Model.IpPermission
$SSHRule.IpProtocol='tcp'
$SSHRule.FromPort = 22
$SSHRule.ToPort = 22
$SSHRule.IpRanges = '0.0.0.0/0'
$AdminGroupId = New-EC2SecurityGroup -VpcId $VPCID -GroupName 'Admin'
-GroupDescription
    "Allows RDP and SSH for configuration."
Grant-EC2SecurityGroupIngress -GroupId $AdminGroupId -IpPermissions $RDPRule,
$SSHRule
```

Second, we will create a security group to allow HTTP and HTTPS traffic from anywhere in the VPC to the NAT gateway.

```
$HTTPRule = New-Object Amazon.EC2.Model.IpPermission
$HTTPRule.IpProtocol='tcp'
$HTTPRule.FromPort = 80
$HTTPRule.ToPort = 80
$HTTPRule.IpRanges = $VPC.CidrBlock
$HTTPSRule = New-Object Amazon.EC2.Model.IpPermission
$HTTPSRule.IpProtocol='tcp'
$HTTPSRule.FromPort = 443
$HTTPSRule.ToPort = 443
$HTTPSRule.IpRanges = $VPC.CidrBlock
$NatGroupId = New-EC2SecurityGroup -VpcId $VPCID -GroupName 'NATGateway'
    -GroupDescription "Allows HTTP/S from the VPC to the internet."
Grant-EC2SecurityGroupIngress -GroupId $NatGroupId -IpPermissions $HTTPRule,
$HTTPSRule
```

Third, we will create a security group to allow RDP over SSL from the Internet to the RDP gateway.

```
$RDPRule = New-Object Amazon.EC2.Model.IpPermission
$RDPRule.IpProtocol='tcp'
$RDPRule.FromPort = 443
$RDPRule.ToPort = 443
$RDPRule.IpRanges = '0.0.0.0/0'
$RdpGroupId = New-EC2SecurityGroup -VpcId $VPCID -GroupName 'RDPGateway'
    -GroupDescription "Allows RDP over HTTPS from the internet."
Grant-EC2SecurityGroupIngress -GroupId $RdpGroupId -IpPermissions $RDPRule
```

Fourth, we must allow RDP traffic from the RDP gateway to the instances in the default subnet.

```
$VPCFilter = New-Object Amazon.EC2.Model.Filter
$VPCFilter.Name = 'vpc-id'
$VPCFilter.Value = $VPCID
$GroupFilter = New-Object Amazon.EC2.Model.Filter
$GroupFilter.Name = 'group-name'
$GroupFilter.Value = 'default'
$DefaultGroup = Get-EC2SecurityGroup -Filter $VPCFilter, $GroupFilter
$RDPGatewayGroup = New-Object Amazon.EC2.Model.UserIdGroupPair
$RDPGatewayGroup.GroupId = $RdpGroupId
$RDPRule = New-Object Amazon.EC2.Model.IpPermission
$RDPRule.IpProtocol='tcp'
$RDPRule.FromPort = 3389
$RDPRule.ToPort = 3389
$RDPRule.UserIdGroupPair = $RDPGatewayGroup
Grant-EC2SecurityGroupIngress -GroupId $DefaultGroup.GroupId -IpPermissions
$RDPRule
```

Now we associate the resource subnet we created with the new ACL.

```
$VPCFilter = New-Object Amazon.EC2.Model.Filter
$VPCFilter.Name = 'vpc-id'
$VPCFilter.Value = $VPCID
$DefaultFilter = New-Object Amazon.EC2.Model.Filter
$DefaultFilter.Name = 'default'
$DefaultFilter.Value = 'true'
$OldACL = (Get-EC2NetworkAcl -Filter $VPCFilter, $DefaultFilter )
```

```
$OldAssociation = $OldACL.Associations | Where-Object { $_.SubnetId -eq
    $ResourcesSubnet.SubnetId }
$NoEcho = Set-EC2NetworkAclAssociation -AssociationId $
    OldAssociation.NetworkAclAssociationId -NetworkAclId $ACL.NetworkAclId
```

Next, we launch a NAT gateway to serve as an outbound proxy. A NAT gateway is simply a Red Hat Linux instance that forwards traffic to the Internet. There are numerous other proxies available in the AWS marketplace that can do advanced inspection, but they are all relatively expensive. The NAT gateway is offered by Amazon as an inexpensive (you pay only for the instance) solution.

```
$Reservation = New-EC2Instance -ImageId $NAT_AMI -KeyName 'MyKey'
-InstanceType
    't2.micro' -SubnetId $ResourcesSubnet.SubnetId
$NATInstance = $Reservation.RunningInstance[0]
$Tag = New-Object Amazon.EC2.Model.Tag
$Tag.Key = 'Name'
$Tag.Value = 'NATGateway'
New-EC2Tag -ResourceId $NATInstance.InstanceID  -Tag $tag
```

We must wait for the instance to boot before moving on. This is different from the exercise in Chapter 3. Here we are just waiting for the instance to boot. We do not have to wait for the initialization to complete and the password to be available.

```
Start-Sleep -s 60
While ((Get-EC2InstanceStatus -InstanceId $NATInstance.InstanceID).
InstanceState.name
    -ne 'running')
{
    Start-Sleep -s 60
    $NATInstance = (Get-EC2Instance -Instance $NATInstance.InstanceID).
    RunningInstance[0]
}
```

In order for the NAT instance to route traffic, we need to disable the source/destination check on the network interface. Usually an instance must be either the source or destination of any traffic that it sends or receives. To disable the check, we use the Edit-EC2NetworkInterfaceAttribute command.

```
$NIC = $NATInstance.NetworkInterfaces[0]
Edit-EC2NetworkInterfaceAttribute -NetworkInterfaceId $NIC.NetworkInterfaceId
    -SourceDestCheck:$false
```

Next, we assign the instance an EIP. Remember that the Internet gateway uses NAT to translate private IP addresses to Internet IP addresses. Therefore, traffic from an instance in a private subnet to the Internet gets translated twice. First, the NAT gateway translates the private IP of the sender to its own private IP. Second, the Internet gateway translates from the private IP of the NAT gateway to its corresponding EIP.

```
$EIP = New-EC2Address -Domain 'vpc'
Register-EC2Address -InstanceId $NATInstance.InstanceID -AllocationId $EIP.
AllocationId
```

Finally, we find the Main route table for the VPC and set the default route to the NAT gateway. I assume here that all of your private subnets are using the Main route table.

```
#Find the Main Route Table for this VPC
$VPCFilter = New-Object Amazon.EC2.Model.Filter
$VPCFilter.Name = 'vpc-id'
$VPCFilter.Value = $VPC.VpcId
$IsDefaultFilter = New-Object Amazon.EC2.Model.Filter
$IsDefaultFilter.Name = 'association.main'
$IsDefaultFilter.Value = 'true'
$MainRouteTable = (Get-EC2RouteTable -Filter $VPCFilter, $IsDefaultFilter)

#Replace the default route with reference to the NAT gateway
$MainRouteTable.Routes | Where-Object { $_.DestinationCidrBlock -eq
'0.0.0.0/0'} | %
    {Remove-EC2Route -RouteTableId $MainRouteTable.RouteTableId
    -DestinationCidrBlock $_.DestinationCidrBlock -Force}
New-EC2Route -RouteTableId $MainRouteTable.
RouteTableId  -DestinationCidrBlock
    '0.0.0.0/0' -InstanceId $NATInstance.InstanceId
```

That takes care of the outbound traffic. Instances on the private subnets will route their traffic out through the NAT gateway, which will, in turn, route it through the Internet gateway. Now let's move on to the RDP gateway.

Remote Desktop Gateway is a Windows feature available beginning with Windows Server 2008 R2 and above which allows the RDP client to connect securely over the public Internet using HTTPS to instances on a remote private network. The complete configuration of Remote Desktop Gateway requires SSL certificates and is beyond the scope of this book. (For more details about the configuration of RDP gateway, see `http://technet.microsoft.com/en-us/library/dd983941(v=ws.10).aspx`.)

For now, let's use the user data section we learned about in Chapter 3 to enable the RDP gateway feature after the instance launches.

```
#Create a user data script to configure the RDP Gateway
$UserData = @'
<powershell>
Add-WindowsFeature -Name RDS-Gateway -IncludeAllSubFeature
</powershell>
'@
$UserData =
    [System.Convert]::ToBase64String([System.Text.Encoding]::ASCII.
    GetBytes($UserData))
```

Next, we will launch the instance, remembering to include the subnet and pass the user data script to execute after launch.

```
$Reservation = New-EC2Instance -ImageId $RDP_AMI -KeyName 'MyKey'
-InstanceType
    't2.micro' -SubnetId $ResourcesSubnet.SubnetId -UserData
    $UserData
$RDPInstance = $Reservation.RunningInstance[0]
$Tag = New-Object Amazon.EC2.Model.Tag
$Tag.Key = 'Name'
$Tag.Value = 'RDPGateway'
New-EC2Tag -ResourceId $RDPInstance.InstanceID  -Tag $tag
```

Now, we wait for the instance to boot and allocate an additional EIP for the NAT instance and we are done.

```
Start-Sleep -s 60
While ((Get-EC2InstanceStatus -InstanceId $RDPInstance.InstanceID).
InstanceState.name
    -ne 'running')
```

```
{
    Start-Sleep -s 60
    $RDPInstance = (Get-EC2Instance -Instance $RDPInstance.InstanceID).
    RunningInstance[0]
}
$EIP = New-EC2Address -Domain 'vpc'
Register-EC2Address -InstanceId $RDPInstance.InstanceID -AllocationId $EIP.
AllocationId
```

If you have completed the configuration of the RDP gateway, you should be able to connect to
a private instance and attempt to run Windows update. In order to connect to an instance in
the private network, you need to tell your remote desktop client about the gateway server. See
Figure 6-7. From the Advanced tab, click the Settings button, and enter the name of the server
gateway. Now you can connect to the VPC instances as if they were publicly accessible.

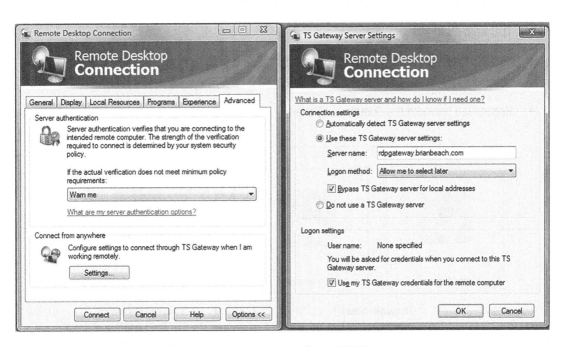

Figure 6-7. *Remote Desktop Connection with an RDP gateway*

EXERCISE 6.2: LEAST PRIVILEGE SECURITY GROUPS

So far, we have been placing all of our private instances in the default group. The default group allows unrestricted communications between all the group members. While this makes configuration easy, it is not as secure as it could be.

In information security, the principle of least privilege requires that a system only have access to the resources it requires to do its job. In this example, we will build a set of security groups that allows the minimum set of permissions required for a simple application. Our simple application, shown in Figure 6-8, consists of a web server and SQL Server, both of which are members of an Active Directory domain.

At a high level, our application requires the following traffic flows:

- HTTP/HTTPS from the Internet to the IIS server

- TDS from IIS to SQL

- Multiple protocols from the domain members (IIS and SQL) to the domain controllers

- Replication between the domain controllers

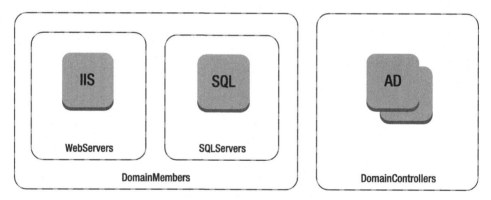

Figure 6-8. *Least privilege security groups*

Note that the IIS and SQL Servers are members of two groups. Rather than adding the domain member rules to the WebServer and SQLServer groups, it is better to have a group of each distinct role a server can hold. This will make it easier to maintain the rules over time.

First, we have to create the four groups pictured in Figure 6-8.

```
$DomainMembersGroupId = New-EC2SecurityGroup -GroupName 'DomainMembers'
-GroupDescription
     "Domain Members" -VpcId $VPCID
$DomainControllersGroupId = New-EC2SecurityGroup -GroupName
'DomainControllers'
     -GroupDescription "Domain controllers" -VpcId $VPCID
$WebServersGroupId = New-EC2SecurityGroup -GroupName 'WebServers'
-GroupDescription "Web
     servers" -VpcId $VPCID
$SQLServersGroupId = New-EC2SecurityGroup -GroupName 'SQLServers'
-GroupDescription "SQL
     Servers" -VpcId $VPCID
```

Next, we add rules to the web group. The web group will allow HTTP (port 80) and HTTPS (port 443) from anywhere on the Internet.

```
#First, the Web instances must allow HTTP/S from the internet
$HTTPRule = New-Object Amazon.EC2.Model.IpPermission
$HTTPRule.IpProtocol='tcp'
$HTTPRule.FromPort = 80
$HTTPRule.ToPort = 80
$HTTPRule.IpRanges = '0.0.0.0/0'
$HTTPSRule = New-Object Amazon.EC2.Model.IpPermission
$HTTPSRule.IpProtocol='tcp'
$HTTPSRule.FromPort = 443
$HTTPSRule.ToPort = 443
$HTTPSRule.IpRanges = '0.0.0.0/0'
Grant-EC2SecurityGroupIngress -GroupId $WebServersGroupId
     -IpPermissions $HTTPRule, $HTTPSRule
```

Then, we add rules to the SQL group. The SQL Server should only be accessed from the web server. SQL uses a protocol called Tabular Data Stream (TDS) that runs on port 1433. In addition, applications are increasingly using SQL FileStream to store attachments. FileStream requires NetBIOS (port 139) and SMB (port 445) to stream the attachments to and from the SQL Server.

```
$WebGroup = New-Object Amazon.EC2.Model.UserIdGroupPair
$WebGroup.GroupId = $WebServersGroupId
$SQLRule = New-Object Amazon.EC2.Model.IpPermission
$SQLRule.IpProtocol='tcp'
$SQLRule.FromPort = 1433
$SQLRule.ToPort = 1433
$SQLRule.UserIdGroupPair = $WebGroup
$NetBIOSRule = New-Object Amazon.EC2.Model.IpPermission
$NetBIOSRule.IpProtocol='tcp'
$NetBIOSRule.FromPort = 139
$NetBIOSRule.ToPort = 139
$NetBIOSRule.UserIdGroupPair = $WebGroup
$SMBRule = New-Object Amazon.EC2.Model.IpPermission
$SMBRule.IpProtocol='tcp'
$SMBRule.FromPort = 445
$SMBRule.ToPort = 445
$SMBRule.UserIdGroupPair = $WebGroup
Grant-EC2SecurityGroupIngress -GroupId $SQLServersGroupId -IpPermissions
$SQLRule, $NetBIOSRule, $SMBRule
```

Now, we add rules to the DomainMembers group. The DomainMembers group is simple,
allowing only ping from the domain controllers. The domain controllers will occasionally ping
the domain members to check that they are still running. In addition, the DomainMembers
group is the source of all the rules in the DomainControllers group.

```
$DCGroup = New-Object Amazon.EC2.Model.UserIdGroupPair
$DCGroup.GroupId = $DomainControllersGroupId
$PingRule = New-Object Amazon.EC2.Model.IpPermission
$PingRule.IpProtocol='icmp'
$PingRule.FromPort = 8
$PingRule.ToPort = -1
$PingRule.UserIdGroupPair = $DCGroup
Grant-EC2SecurityGroupIngress -GroupId $DomainMembersGroupId -IpPermissions
$PingRule
```

Finally, we add rules to the DomainControllers group. This group has several rules. We will
break them down by IP protocol.

First, assuming we have more than one domain controller, they must be able to replicate data between each other. Therefore, we are allowing unrestricted communications between the controllers.

```
$AllRule = New-Object Amazon.EC2.Model.IpPermission
$AllRule.IpProtocol='-1'
$AllRule.UserIdGroupPair = $DCGroup
Grant-EC2SecurityGroupIngress -GroupId $DomainControllersGroupId
-IpPermissions $AllRule
```

Second, the domain controllers allow ping from any of the domain members:

```
$DMGroup = New-Object Amazon.EC2.Model.UserIdGroupPair
$DMGroup.GroupId = $DomainMembersGroupId
$PingRule = New-Object Amazon.EC2.Model.IpPermission
$PingRule.IpProtocol='icmp'
$PingRule.FromPort = 8
$PingRule.ToPort = -1
$PingRule.UserIdGroupPair = $DMGroup
Grant-EC2SecurityGroupIngress -GroupId $DomainControllersGroupId
-IpPermissions $PingRule
```

Third, the domain controller must allow an array of TCP communication types from the domain members. These include

- 53 – DNS queries. Note DNS uses both TCP and UDP.

- 88 – Kerberos authentication. Note Kerberos uses both TCP and UDP.

- 135 – Remote procedure calls. Note: RPC will also use a port in the range 49152-65535.

- 137–139 – NetBIOS. Note Kerberos uses both TCP and UDP.

- 389 and 636 – Lightweight Directory Access Protocol (LDAP).

- 445 – Server Message Block (SMB).

- 464 – Password reset. Note that it uses both TCP and UDP.

- 3268 – Microsoft global catalog.

```
#Domain controllers must allow numerous TCP protocols from domain members
$DNSRule = New-Object Amazon.EC2.Model.IpPermission
$DNSRule.IpProtocol='tcp'
$DNSRule.FromPort = 53
$DNSRule.ToPort = 53
$DNSRule.UserIdGroupPair = $DMGroup
$KerberosRule = New-Object Amazon.EC2.Model.IpPermission
$KerberosRule.IpProtocol='tcp'
$KerberosRule.FromPort = 88
$KerberosRule.ToPort = 88
$KerberosRule.UserIdGroupPair = $DMGroup
$NetBIOSRule = New-Object Amazon.EC2.Model.IpPermission
$NetBIOSRule.IpProtocol='tcp'
$NetBIOSRule.FromPort = 137
$NetBIOSRule.ToPort = 139
$NetBIOSRule.UserIdGroupPair = $DMGroup
$RPCRule = New-Object Amazon.EC2.Model.IpPermission
$RPCRule.IpProtocol='tcp'
$RPCRule.FromPort = 135
$RPCRule.ToPort = 135
$RPCRule.UserIdGroupPair = $DMGroup
$LDAPRule = New-Object Amazon.EC2.Model.IpPermission
$LDAPRule.IpProtocol='tcp'
$LDAPRule.FromPort = 389
$LDAPRule.ToPort = 389
$LDAPRule.UserIdGroupPair = $DMGroup
$SMBRule = New-Object Amazon.EC2.Model.IpPermission
$SMBRule.IpProtocol='tcp'
$SMBRule.FromPort = 445
$SMBRule.ToPort = 445
$SMBRule.UserIdGroupPair = $DMGroup
$PasswordRule = New-Object Amazon.EC2.Model.IpPermission
$PasswordRule.IpProtocol='tcp'
$PasswordRule.FromPort = 464
$PasswordRule.ToPort = 464
$PasswordRule.UserIdGroupPair = $DMGroup
$LDAPSRule = New-Object Amazon.EC2.Model.IpPermission
$LDAPSRule.IpProtocol='tcp'
```

```
$LDAPSRule.FromPort = 636
$LDAPSRule.ToPort = 636
$LDAPSRule.UserIdGroupPair = $DMGroup
$ADRule = New-Object Amazon.EC2.Model.IpPermission
$ADRule.IpProtocol='tcp'
$ADRule.FromPort = 3268
$ADRule.ToPort = 3269
$ADRule.UserIdGroupPair = $DMGroup
$RpcHpRule = New-Object Amazon.EC2.Model.IpPermission
$RpcHpRule.IpProtocol='tcp'
$RpcHpRule.FromPort = 49152
$RpcHpRule.ToPort = 65535
$RpcHpRule.UserIdGroupPair = $DMGroup
Grant-EC2SecurityGroupIngress -GroupId $DomainControllersGroupId
-IpPermissions $DNSRule,
    $KerberosRule, $RPCRule, $LDAPRule, $PasswordRule, $LDAPSRule, $ADRule,
    $RpcHpRule
```

Fourth, the domain controller must allow an array of UDP communication types from the domain members. These include

- 53 – DNS queries. Note DNS uses both TCP and UDP.

- 88 – Kerberos authentication. Note Kerberos uses both TCP and UDP.

- 123 – Network Time Protocol.

- 137–139 – NetBIOS. Note Kerberos uses both TCP and UDP.

- 389 – Lightweight Directory Access Protocol (LDAP).

- 464 – Password reset. Note that it uses both TCP and UDP.

```
#Domain controllers must allow numerous TCP protocols from domain members
$DNSRule = New-Object Amazon.EC2.Model.IpPermission
$DNSRule.IpProtocol='udp'
$DNSRule.FromPort = 53
$DNSRule.ToPort = 53
$DNSRule.UserIdGroupPair = $DMGroup
$KerberosRule = New-Object Amazon.EC2.Model.IpPermission
$KerberosRule.IpProtocol='udp'
```

```
$KerberosRule.FromPort = 88
$KerberosRule.ToPort = 88
$KerberosRule.UserIdGroupPair = $DMGroup
$NTPRule = New-Object Amazon.EC2.Model.IpPermission
$NTPRule.IpProtocol='udp'
$NTPRule.FromPort = 123
$NTPRule.ToPort = 123
$NTPRule.UserIdGroupPair = $DMGroup
$NetBIOSRule = New-Object Amazon.EC2.Model.IpPermission
$NetBIOSRule.IpProtocol='udp'
$NetBIOSRule.FromPort = 137
$NetBIOSRule.ToPort = 139
$NetBIOSRule.UserIdGroupPair = $DMGroup
$LDAPRule = New-Object Amazon.EC2.Model.IpPermission
$LDAPRule.IpProtocol='udp'
$LDAPRule.FromPort = 389
$LDAPRule.ToPort = 389
$LDAPRule.UserIdGroupPair = $DMGroup
$PasswordRule = New-Object Amazon.EC2.Model.IpPermission
$PasswordRule.IpProtocol='udp'
$PasswordRule.FromPort = 464
$PasswordRule.ToPort = 464
$PasswordRule.UserIdGroupPair = $DMGroup
Grant-EC2SecurityGroupIngress -GroupId $DomainControllersGroupId
-IpPermissions $DNSRule,
    $KerberosRule, $NTPRule, $NetBIOSRule, $LDAPRule, $SMBRule,
    $PasswordRule
```

As we have seen, security groups allow us to create very specific rules to secure our resources. By writing rules that are based on other security groups, we define our security policy before launching instances. This gives us the benefit of not needing to change the rules as we launch each instance. The rules in this example are just a starting point. You will need to add additional groups and rules as your infrastructure grows.

Summary

Amazon VPC gives us numerous capabilities to build our ultimate virtual network, with the isolation and security we need for our applications, all without the headaches of managing traditional networking equipment.

We can define outbound rules in our security groups. We can control the network configuration at launch including subnet, security group, and private IP address. We can assign publicly addressable EIPs. We can even add multiple IP addresses and multiple network interfaces.

All of these features allow us to create network configurations that are as simple or complex as we need them to be. In the examples, we explored advanced patterns for managing enterprise networks. First, we discussed how to manage and patch private instances using an RDP and NAT gateway. Second, we created a series of security groups to implement least privileged access for Windows instances in an Active Directory domain.

While VPC brings us numerous capabilities, it can also involve complexity. We will keep things relatively simple in the remaining chapters on EC2, by using a VPC configuration that allows us to focus on features without the complexity discussed in Chapters 5 and 6. In the next chapter, we discuss creating our own Amazon Machine Images.

CHAPTER 7

Amazon Machine Images

In the last few chapters, we have focused on creating and managing instances. This chapter is about the templates we use to create those instances. Amazon refers to these templates as Amazon Machine Images (AMIs). In this chapter we will explore the AMIs that already exist, and we will discuss how to create your own AMI and share it with others. Finally, we learn how to import a VM from VMware or Hyper-V into AWS.

Many users will never have occasion to create a custom AMI. Most users will be happy with the countless images that Amazon and its partners make available. But some users will want to have complete control over their environment. For example, you may have a corporate server image that you want to make available to your companies' employees that are using AWS.

As your experience progresses, you will likely find that you want to automate instance builds. Configuration management tools are all about scripting server builds to minimize build time and ensure consistency between builds. Assuming you want to automate the build, there are many options. Most fall on a spectrum somewhere between scripted builds and prepared images.

Working with Scripted Builds and Prepared Images

At one end of the spectrum is the scripted build. With a scripted build, you start with a generic image and use a series of scripts to configure the server as needed. For example, to create a Web Server, you might start with the Amazon Windows Server 2019 Base image. Then you could use the user data to include a custom PowerShell script that enables the Web Server role and downloads the application from source control.

At the other end of the spectrum is the prepared image. With a prepared image, you configure the server, usually manually, and then create an image. When a user needs a new server, he or she selects your server image and creates a new instance. If you choose a prepared image, be sure to update the image periodically with the latest security patches and virus definitions.

157

© Brian Beach, Steven Armentrout, Rodney Bozo, Emmanuel Tsouris 2019
B. Beach et al., *Pro PowerShell for Amazon Web Services*, https://doi.org/10.1007/978-1-4842-4850-8_7

Both options have benefits and drawbacks. The scripted build is best when the application is changing often. You always get the latest code and can change the script as requirements change. The prepared image, on the other hand, is best when the application is stable. There are fewer external dependencies that can cause errors and the build is usually faster.

Of course, there are many options on the spectrum between scripted build and prepared image. The Amazon Windows AMIs provide a good example. Amazon offers a base image as well as SQL Server images. By using the SQL Server image, you do not have to script the configuration of SQL Server. You simply focus on scripting the deployment of your application.

Most of this chapter is focused on preparing images, but don't overlook scripting as an option. There are many AWS Services that will help you script instance configuration such as CloudFormation and OpsWorks. Chapters 15–17 will cover Systems Manager which can be used to script instance configuration with Ansible, Salt, or PowerShell Desired State Configuration (DSC).

Listing AMIs

Before we create our own AMI, or simply an image, let's take a deeper look at the images that are already available. We don't want to spend time creating and maintaining an image if an identical image already exists.

Caution   There are over 100,000 images available giving you a ton of options to choose from, but be careful! You should only launch images from publishers you trust. As you will see later in this chapter, anyone can publish an image.

You can find images using the `Get-EC2Image` command, but this command will return the complete list of over 100,000 images. Obviously, this is far too many to look through one at a time.

Limiting the Number of Instance Results

As you might expect, you can use filters to limit the number of instances. For example, if you are interested in a Windows image, you can use the platform filter. The following example will return about 15,000 Windows images in the Northern Virginia region.

```
$Filter = New-Object Amazon.EC2.Model.Filter
$Filter.Name = "platform"
$Filter.Value = "windows"
Get-EC2Image -Filter $Filter | Select-Object Name
```

We can also filter by publisher using owner-alias. For example, you might list only those images that Amazon publishes. Again, it is a really good idea to only use images published by an owner you trust, such as Amazon. The following example will return about 5000 images:

```
$Filter = New-Object Amazon.EC2.Model.Filter
$Filter.Name = "owner-alias"
$Filter.Value = "amazon"
Get-EC2Image -Filter $Filter | Select-Object Name
```

This is still too many images to comb through one by one. Of course, you can combine two or more filters. If we combine the platform and owner alias, we get a more reasonable list of about 1800 images.

```
$Filter1 = New-Object Amazon.EC2.Model.Filter
$Filter1.Name = "platform"
$Filter1.Value = "windows"
$Filter2 = New-Object Amazon.EC2.Model.Filter
$Filter2.Name = "owner-alias"
$Filter2.Value = "amazon"
Get-EC2Image -Filter $Filter1, $Filter2 | Select-Object Name
```

Finding an Instance by Name

The prior examples assume you do not yet know which image you are looking for. If you know the name of the image you want to find, you can use the name filter. For example, to find the Windows Server 2019 Base image, use

```
$Filter = New-Object Amazon.EC2.Model.Filter
$Filter.Name = "name"
$Filter.Value = "Windows_Server-2019-English-Full-Base-2019.01.10"
Get-EC2Image -Filter $Filter
```

Note that that command is going to fail. Amazon updates most of its images periodically with the latest patches and updates. By the time you read this, that image will likely no longer exist. Luckily, filters support the wildcard character (*). For example:

```
$Filter = New-Object Amazon.EC2.Model.Filter
$Filter.Name = "name"
$Filter.Value = "Windows_Server-2019-English-Full-Base*"
Get-EC2Image -Filter $Filter
```

So, let's review. We can use a combination of the platform and owner-alias filters to discover new images from a trusted source. Then, once we know the name, we can search by name. If all of this seems cumbersome to you, I agree. Wouldn't it be great if we had a short list of the most common images?

Locating the Most Common Images

Luckily Amazon thought of the idea of getting a short list of the most common images and included another command, Get-EC2ImageByName. This command will return most of the images that you find on the Quick Start tab of the New Instance Wizard in the AWS Management Console. Note that the command may return an array with multiple versions of a given instance. The most recent version will be listed first in the array. For example:

```
Get-EC2ImageByName -Name "WINDOWS_2016_BASE"
```

You can run Get-EC2ImageByName without any parameters to get a list of available names.

Finally, if you have launched your own images, as described later in this chapter, you can find them by using the Owner parameter of the Get-EC2Image command. For example:

```
Get-EC2Image -Owner self
```

Now that we know how to find images, we can decide whether we need to create our own. Let's assume that none of the existing images meet our needs and we have decided to create our own image. Images are created using SysPrep and the EC2Config Service. Before we get started creating an image, let's look at EC2Launch.

Introducing EC2Launch

Before we move on to creating an image, I want to introduce EC2Launch. Note that EC2Launch runs on Windows 2016 or newer images. It replaces the EC2Config Service that was installed on Windows images through 2012 R2. We have mentioned these tools a few times in prior chapters, but now is a good time to look at it in detail.

EC2Launch is used to configure Windows instances. It plays a critical role in configuring an instance when it boots for the first time. For example, the EC2Launch is responsible for encrypting the administrator password and executing scripts in the user data.

When an instance boots for the first time, the EC2Config Service performs the following tasks:

1. Renames the computer. This is disabled by default.

2. Sets the administrator password. By default, a new, random password will be generated and encrypted with the specified key pair.

3. Creates RDP certificate. A new self-signed host certificate is created for Remote Desktop connection. You cannot use RDP without a certificate.

4. Extends the OS partition. Remember that you can change the size of the OS volume at launch. Therefore, the service extends the partition to fill the volume.

5. Activates Windows if necessary.

6. Writes event log entries to the AWS System Log. This can help debug errors that occur before RDP is available in the boot sequence.

7. Creates a new wallpaper image. This includes useful information (name, type, memory, etc.) about the image.

8. Configures a few custom routes. For example, 169.254.169.250 and 169.254.169.251 are the default KMS servers and 169.254.169.254 is the metadata URL we used in Chapter 3.

Most of these actions are enabled by default, but you can customize them as needed by editing the file:

```
C:\ProgramData\Amazon\EC2-Windows\Launch\Config\LaunchConfig.json
```

There is also a GUI tool available for editing the JSON. It is located at

```
C:\ProgramData\Amazon\EC2-Windows\Launch\Settings\Ec2LaunchSettings.exe
```

The GUI looks like Figure 7-1.

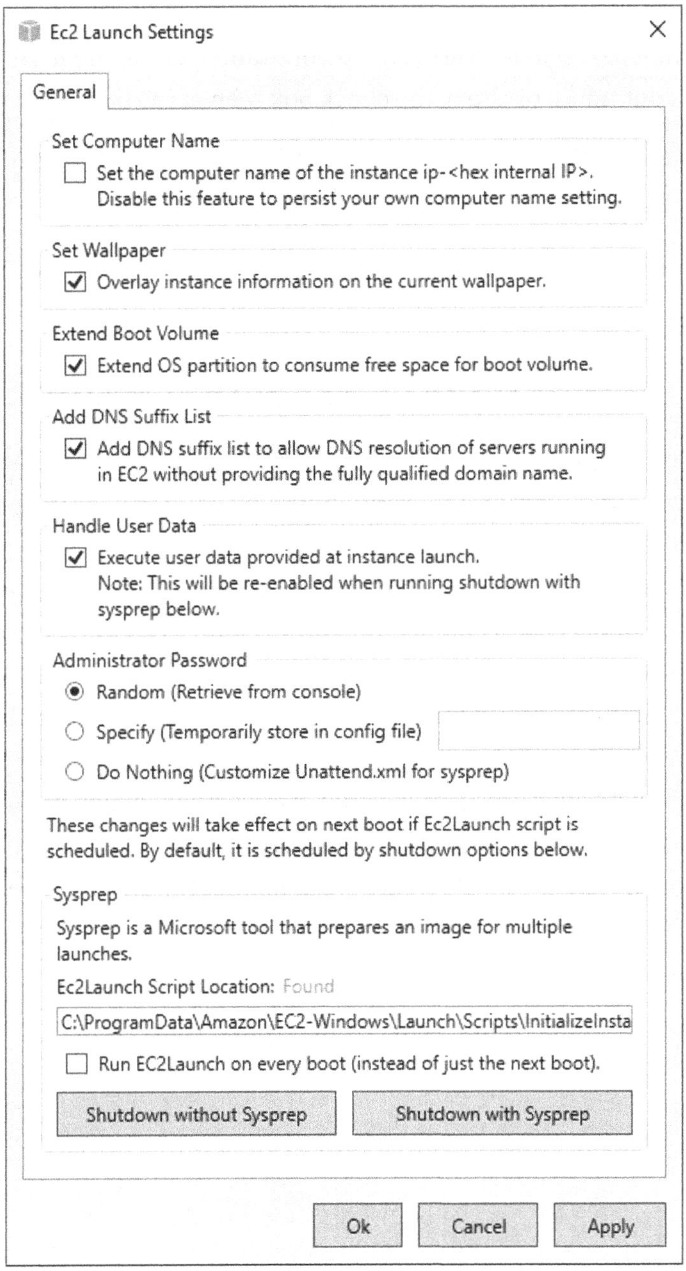

Figure 7-1. *EC2 Launch Settings*

The default behavior is to run EC2Launch on the first launch. However, there may be times when you want to run it on every boot. If you want to configure it, run on every boot, run the following command, or check the check box seen at the bottom of Figure 7-1.

```
C:\ProgramData\Amazon\EC2-Windows\Launch\Scripts\InitializeInstance.ps1
-SchedulePerBoot
```

Now that we understand EC2Launch, let's look at the EC2LaunchSettings tool.

Preparing an AMI Using EC2LaunchSettings

In the prior section, we learned about EC2Launch. In this section we will prepare an image of our own. To start, launch a new Windows Server 2019 Base instance that will serve as our template. You remember how to do that right?

Once the instance boots, you can log in and make whatever changes you want. Let's assume we are developing a web application and we want to create a server to test it on. Our application requires that we enable a few unique features of IIS.

In Figure 7-2 I have configured the required roles and services. First, I enabled the Web Server (IIS) role (see the Select server roles dialog in Figure 7-2). Next, I enabled the Windows Identity Foundation feature (see the Select features dialog in Figure 7-2). Finally, I enabled six of the nine Web Server Security Role Services (see the Select role services dialog in Figure 7-2). Obviously your configuration will depend on the applications you intend to run on the instance.

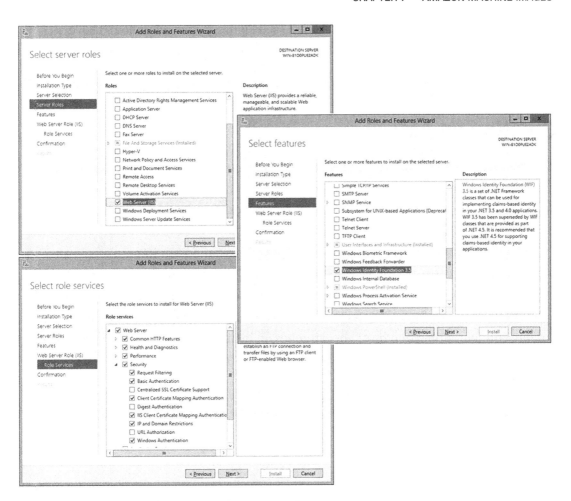

Figure 7-2. *Configuring the Web Server role*

Once you have configured your server and installed any software you want in the template, it is time to prepare the image. As I mentioned in the prior section, you use EC2LaunchSettings to create an image. Behind the scenes, EC2LaunchSettings uses SysPrep to do the heavy lifting.

Caution   Before continuing, you should take a snapshot of the instance. Once we SysPrep the image, there is no going back. If the instance fails to boot, you will have to start over from scratch.

Open the Ec2LaunchSettings application (see Figure 7-1 for reference). Leave the defaults and simply click the Shutdown with SysPrep button. This will take a few minutes. Once it's done, we can finally create the AMI.

Creating an AMI

The instance is now configured and waiting to run setup. We want to clone the instance in this state, so that each copy runs setup when it first boots. It's finally time to create an image. Let's look at the AWS Administration Console first and then discuss the PowerShell commands.

In the AWS Management Console, right-click the instance you want to create an image of and select Create Image (EBS AMI). Figure 7-3 shows the Create Image dialog box. From here you can give your image a name and description and configure the volumes. Remember, from Chapter 4, that the user will have the option of modifying the volume configuration when he or she launches an instance of your image. If the image requires multiple volumes, you can set default values here.

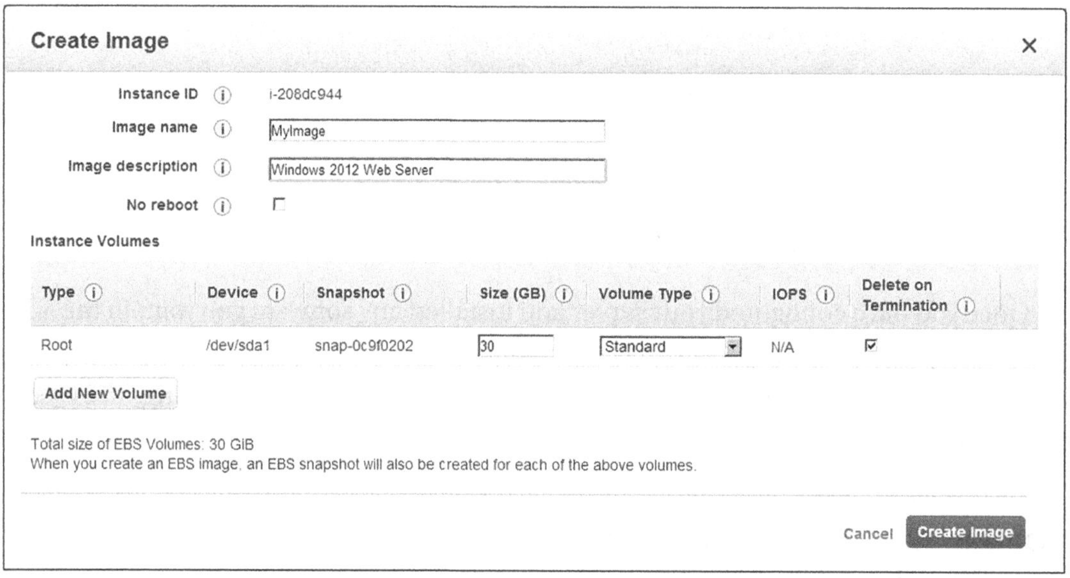

Figure 7-3. *Create Image dialog box*

The equivalent PowerShell command is New-EC2Image. The command takes the ID of the instance you want to make a template from, as well as a name and description, and returns the ID of the new image. For example:

```
$AMIID = New-EC2Image -InstanceId i-99999999 -Name "WIN2019WEB"
-Description "Windows Web Server"
```

Note that you must replace the instance ID with the instance you want to create an image of. As you might expect, it takes a few minutes to create the image. You can check the ImageState to see if the image is ready. To wait for an image, you can use a while loop similar to the following example:

```
$AMI = Get-EC2Image $AMIID
While($AMI.ImageState -ne "available") {
        $AMI = Get-EC2Image $AMIID
        Start-Sleep -Seconds 15
}
```

Modifying the drive configuration works just like it did when we used the New-EC2Instance command in Chapter 4. Let's add another 100GB volume to our image to store IIS log files. Remember that the EC2Config Service is configured to automatically mount and format any additional volumes that we attach. All we need to do is create a block device and mapping descriptor and pass it to the New-EC2Image command using the BlockDeviceMapping attribute. For example:

```
$Volume1 = New-Object Amazon.EC2.Model.EbsBlockDevice
$Volume1.DeleteOnTermination = $True
$Volume1.VolumeSize = 30
$Volume1.VolumeType = "standard"

$Mapping1 = New-Object Amazon.EC2.Model.BlockDeviceMapping
$Mapping1.DeviceName = "/dev/sda1"
$Mapping1.Ebs = $Volume1

$Volume2 = New-Object Amazon.EC2.Model.EbsBlockDevice
$Volume2.DeleteOnTermination = $False
$Volume2.VolumeSize = 100
$Volume2.VolumeType = "standard"
```

```
$Mapping2 = New-Object Amazon.EC2.Model.BlockDeviceMapping
$Mapping2.DeviceName = "xvdf"
$Mapping2.Ebs = $Volume2

$AMIID = New-EC2Image -InstanceId i-9999999
    -Name "WIN2019WEB2" -Description "Windows Web Server 2"
    -BlockDeviceMapping $Mapping1, $Mapping2
```

At this point you have your own custom AMI and you can create instances. This same process can be used to make as many variations as you need. If you find that an image is particularly useful, you may want to share it with others. In the next section, I will show you how to share your image.

Sharing an AMI

You may find that you want to share an image with other accounts. Maybe your company has multiple accounts and you want to use a single corporate image across all accounts. Or maybe you have an image that includes a trial version of your company's software and you want to share it with the world.

To share an image with another account, you use the Edit-EC2ImageAttribute command. In the following example, I am granting permission to launch an instance of an image to users of the account 1234-1234-1234. Obviously your image ID and account ID will be different.

```
Edit-EC2ImageAttribute -ImageId 'ami-71ebba18' -Attribute 'launchPermission'
    -OperationType 'add' -UserId '123412341234'
```

To share an image with all accounts, you grant permission to the group "all." For example:

```
Edit-EC2ImageAttribute -ImageId 'ami-71ebba18' -Attribute
'launchPermission'
    -OperationType "add" -UserGroup "all"
```

You can check which accounts and groups have access by using the Get-EC2ImageAttribute command.

```
Get-EC2ImageAttribute -ImageId 'ami-71ebba18' -Attribute 'launchPermission'
```

To revoke the launch permission from an account, use the remove operation type. For example:

```
Edit-EC2ImageAttribute -ImageId 'ami-71ebba18' -Attribute
'launchPermission'
    -OperationType 'remove' -UserId '123412341234'
```

You can revoke the launch permission from the group the same way. For example:

```
Edit-EC2ImageAttribute -ImageId 'ami-71ebba18' -Attribute 'launchPermission'
    -OperationType 'remove' -UserGroup 'all'
```

If you want to revoke the launch permission from all users and groups, you can use the Reset-EC2ImageAttribute command. For example:

```
Reset-EC2ImageAttribute  -ImageId 'ami-71ebba18' -Attribute
'launchPermission'
```

Finally, if you are sharing images between accounts, you can list the images owned by a specific account by supplying the account number to the Get-EC2Image command. For example:

```
Get-EC2Image -Owner 123412341234
```

As you can see, AMIs are a powerful tool. You can leverage the tens of thousands of existing images, create your own images, and even share your images with others.

Although it is easy to customize an Amazon AMI, it would be great if we could leverage the library of images we already have onsite. In Exercise 7.1, I will show you how to import an existing VM image from an onsite hypervisor like VMware or Hyper-V.

EXERCISE 7.1: UPLOADING A VM

Many of us already have a library of images that we have built for our VMware or Hyper-V environments. Luckily Amazon allows you to upload an existing image into EC2.

There are a few ways to do this. If you have a lot of instances to import, you should look at the Server Migration Service (SMS). SMS is easiest way to import VMs into AWS. However, this is a book on PowerShell, so let's import an image using PowerShell.

Before you export the image, you should prepare the VM by checking the following:

1. Check that remote desktop is enabled.

2. Check that Windows Firewall allows public RDP traffic.

3. Ensure that DHCP is enabled.

4. Disable antivirus and intrusion detection systems.

5. Remove any virtualization tools such as the VMware Tools.

6. Disconnect any DVD (or other removable media) devices.

7. Stop the VM before importing it.

Now, it is time to export the image from your hypervisor. The import process supports VMDK, VHD, and OVF file formats. Let's assume that our file is called GoldenImage.vmdk.

Next we upload the file to an S3 bucket. We are going to do this in two parts: first, upload the file to S3 and, second, import the image. Splitting it into two parts is really ingenious. It means that we could bulk import a bunch on VMs using an AWS Snowball. Snowball is a hardware appliance for importing (or exporting) large volumes of data through the mail.

We will cover S3 in detail in Chapter 11. For now, I will assume you have an S3 bucket called mybucket. You can upload the file like this:

Write-S3Object -File GoldenImage.vmdk -BucketName mybucket

Once the file is uploaded, we can import it. First we need to create a .Net object to describe our image, called an ImageDiskContainer. The DiskImageContainer tells the API the type of image and where to find the file in S3. For example:

```
$container = New-Object Amazon.EC2.Model.ImageDiskContainer
$container.Format="VMDK"
$container.UserBucket = New-Object Amazon.EC2.Model.UserBucket
```

```
$container.UserBucket.S3Bucket = "mybucket"
$container.UserBucket.S3Key = "GoldenImage.vmdk"
```

Now we can import the image using the Import-EC2Image command like this:

```
Import-EC2Image -DiskContainer $container -ClientToken GoldenImage
-Description "Golden Image" -Platform Windows -LicenseType AWS
```

As you might expect, the import operation takes a while. Import-EC2Image will return an ImportTaskId that you can use to check on the status. For example:

```
ec2-resume-import "c:\aws\MyImage.vhd" -t import-i-fh37272p
    -o %AWS_ACCESS_KEY% -w %AWS_SECRET_KEY%
```

Once the upload completes, Amazon will begin the conversion behind the scenes. There is no progress bar for this, but you can check on the conversion progress using `ec2-describe-conversion-tasks` command and passing your TaskId. For example:

```
ec2-describe-conversion-tasks import-i-fh37272p
```

Once the conversion completes, you will have an instance running in EC2 Classic. The import command does not clean up the temporary data stored in S3. You can delete it manually or use the `ec2-delete-disk-image` command.

Once your instance is imported, you can either use it as is or follow the instructions in this chapter to create derivative images. As you can see, the Import-EC2Image command will allow you to leverage your existing image library in the cloud and ensure that you have the same bits running on site and in the cloud.

Summary

In this chapter, we learned about Amazon Machine Images. We saw how to find and leverage the over 100,000 images already available. Then we discussed how to create our own custom images. We discussed how to prepare a Windows instance using SysPrep. Finally, we learned how to share our images with others and import images from our on-prem infrastructure.

Then, in the first exercise, we saw an alternative to rolling a custom image: scripted builds. In the second exercise, we saw how to import an existing image from VMware or Hyper-V. In the next chapter, we will talk about scalability and high availability.

CHAPTER 8

Monitoring and High Availability

This chapter is about architecting your application for high availability. We have covered almost all of the PowerShell commands for EC2, but EC2 is only one of many services that AWS offers. In this chapter, we will examine a few of the services that you can use in concert with EC2 to build a highly available application. These services include Elastic Load Balancers (ELBs), Simple Notification Service (SNS), CloudWatch, Auto Scaling, and Route 53.

We will start by creating a new VPC focused on high availability. This will be a great opportunity to review the material in the prior chapters. Next, we will create an ELB to balance HTTP and HTTPS web traffic across multiple instances. We will configure the ELB to automatically detect errors and remove unhealthy instances. Then, we will use SNS and CloudWatch to create an early warning system that can email us when the application is under stress.

Once that detection system is running, we will use Auto Scaling to automatically scale the application by monitoring load. Auto Scaling will leverage scripted builds to launch and terminate instances throughout the day without human involvement. Finally, we will discuss how Route 53 can be used to extend our application across multiple regions, serving each user from the location nearest them.

This chapter has two exercises. In the first, we consolidate everything we learned in the chapter into one streamlined script. In the second, we create a script to scale up (or resize) an instance. Let's get started.

© Brian Beach, Steven Armentrout, Rodney Bozo, Emmanuel Tsouris 2019
B. Beach et al., *Pro PowerShell for Amazon Web Services*, https://doi.org/10.1007/978-1-4842-4850-8_8

Architecting for High Availability

In Chapters 5 and 6, we spent a lot of time discussing VPC with a focus on security. This section focuses on availability. This is not to suggest that we must trade security for high availability. AWS gives you everything you need to achieve both.

We have also discussed regions and availability zones on multiple occasions. Remember that each region includes multiple availability zones connected by high-speed, low-latency links. Each availability zone is a stand-alone data center with distinct power, cooling, and resources. By designing an application to span availability zones, you can build redundancy into your application.

A VPC is limited to a single region, but as shown in Figure 8-1, it can span multiple availability zones. As you already know, a VPC can contain multiple subnets, and each subnet can be in its own availability zone. By spreading our application across availability zones, we can achieve high availability. If once the data centers were to fail, the application could continue running in the other.

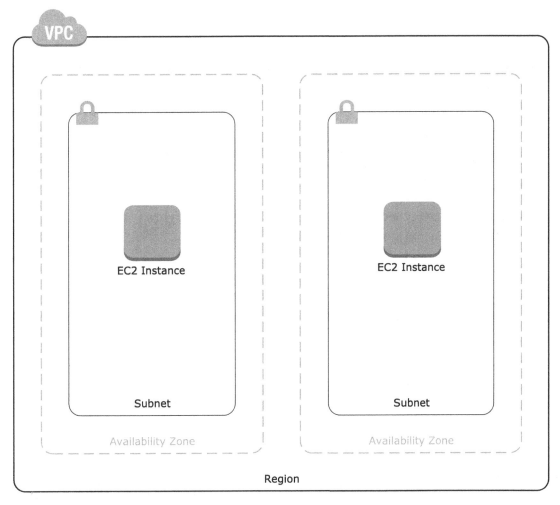

Figure 8-1. *High availability VPC*

Let's get started by creating the VPC in Figure 8-1. This will be a great opportunity to review much of what we learned in prior chapters.

Let's assume our application is a simple, single-tier web application with no database. First, we create a new VPC and pick two availability zones in the same region. For example, I am using a private 192.168.0.0 network and the Northern Virginia region. You may have to change the script to use availability zones in your region.

```
$VPC = New-EC2Vpc -CidrBlock '192.168.0.0/16'
$AvailabilityZone1 = 'us-east-1a'
$AvailabilityZone2 = 'us-east-1b'
```

Next, we create two subnets in our VPC. Notice that each subnet is using a different availability zone. (If any of this is unfamiliar, go back and review Chapter 5.)

```
$WebSubnet1 = New-EC2Subnet -VpcId $VPC.VpcId -CidrBlock '192.168.3.0/24'
    -AvailabilityZone $AvailabilityZone1
$WebSubnet2 = New-EC2Subnet -VpcId $VPC.VpcId -CidrBlock '192.168.4.0/24'
    -AvailabilityZone $AvailabilityZone2
```

We also need to configure security groups. Let's assume our servers will accept HTTP and HTTPS requests on ports 80 and 443.

```
$ElbGroupId = New-EC2SecurityGroup -GroupName 'NLBTargets'
-GroupDescription "NLB Target"
    -VpcId $VPC.VpcId
$HTTPRule = New-Object Amazon.EC2.Model.IpPermission
$HTTPRule.IpProtocol='tcp'
$HTTPRule.FromPort = 80
$HTTPRule.ToPort = 80
$HTTPRule.IpRanges = '0.0.0.0/0'
$HTTPSRule = New-Object Amazon.EC2.Model.IpPermission
$HTTPSRule.IpProtocol='tcp'
$HTTPSRule.FromPort = 443
$HTTPSRule.ToPort = 443
$HTTPSRule.IpRanges = '0.0.0.0/0'
$NoEcho = Grant-EC2SecurityGroupIngress -GroupId $ElbGroupId -IpPermissions
$HTTPRule,  $HTTPSRule
```

We need to launch at least two instances. This is going to be a web application, so I am using the user data parameter to install and configure IIS. You could use the same method to install your application. (If you have forgotten how to do this, return to Chapter 3.)

```
$UserData = [System.Convert]::ToBase64String([System.Text.Encoding]::ASCII.
GetBytes(@'
<powershell>
Install-WindowsFeature Web-Server -IncludeManagementTools
-IncludeAllSubFeature3
</powershell>
'@))
```

Finally, we launch the two instances being careful to specify different subnets. (We covered this in Chapter 6 if you want to review.)

```
$AMI = Get-EC2ImageByName 'WINDOWS_2012_BASE'
$Reservation1 = New-EC2Instance -ImageId $AMI[0].ImageId -KeyName 'MyKey'
    -InstanceType 't2.micro' -MinCount 1 -SecurityGroupId $ElbGroupId
    -MaxCount 1 -SubnetId $WebSubnet1.SubnetId -UserData $UserData
$Instance1 = $Reservation1.RunningInstance[0]
$Reservation2 = New-EC2Instance -ImageId $AMI[0].ImageId -KeyName 'MyKey'
    -InstanceType 't2.micro' -MinCount 1 -SecurityGroupId $ElbGroupId
    -MaxCount 1 -SubnetId $WebSubnet2.SubnetId -UserData $UserData
$Instance2 = $Reservation2.RunningInstance[0]
```

At this point we have new VPC with two subnets each in a different availability zone. In addition, we have launched two identical instances. If one of the instances fails, the other will keep running. In fact, even if the entire availability zone failed, the instance in the other zone will keep running. In the next section, we create a load balancer to distribute the load between our two instances.

Managing Elastic Load Balancers

Now that we have multiple instances deployed in multiple data centers, we need a way to distribute requests between them. This is the role of a load balancer. A load balancer receives requests and forwards them to instances in our VPC. The load balancer also monitors the health of the instances and stops sending requests to unhealthy instances automatically. In addition, the load balancer can be configured to terminate SSL and offload the encryption/decryption from the instances acting as web servers.

Elastic Load Balancing (ELB) is actually a family of load balancers including the Classic Load Balancer, Network Load Balancer (NLB), and Application Load Balancer (ALB). I am only going to cover the NLB here, but I want you to be aware that the other variations exist. The functionality of the Classic Load Balancer has been replaced by the ALB and NLB so you can mostly ignore the Classic Load Balancer. The ALB adds support for content-based routing and other enterprise features. You can route traffic to different targets based on host header or URI path.

Figure 8-2 shows our VPC from the prior section with an NLB added. Notice that the NLB is configured in both availability zones. Obviously we need the NLB to be highly available just like the instances we created in the last section. Luckily Amazon does a lot of the heavy lifting for us when we use an NLB. Let's create one now.

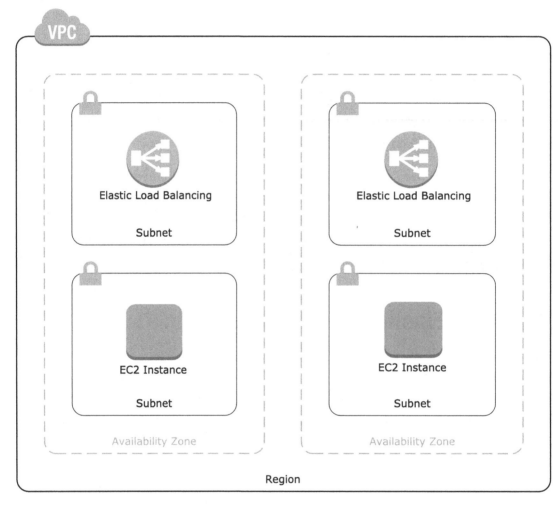

Figure 8-2. *VPC with ELB*

Preparing the VPC for an ELB

First, we need to create a subnet in each availability zone for the NLB to live in. When we configure the NLB, we tell Amazon to use these subnets. Initially, Amazon will launch an NLB into either one of the subnets. If that availability zone fails, Amazon routes all traffic to the other availability zone. Let's create two more subnets.

```
$ElbSubnet1 = New-EC2Subnet -VpcId $VPC.VpcId -CidrBlock '192.168.1.0/24'
    -AvailabilityZone $AvailabilityZone1
$ElbSubnet2 = New-EC2Subnet -VpcId $VPC.VpcId -CidrBlock '192.168.2.0/24'
    -AvailabilityZone $AvailabilityZone2
```

This NLB is going to accept requests from the Internet; therefore, we need to add an Internet gateway to our VPC.

```
$InternetGateway = New-EC2InternetGateway
Add-EC2InternetGateway -InternetGatewayId $InternetGateway.
InternetGatewayId -VpcId $VPC.VpcId
```

Note   Not all ELBs are Internet facing. You can create an internal ELB that balances traffic between tiers of your application. You can also use PrivateLink to share your application with other AWS accounts.

Now that we have an Internet gateway, we are going to need to configure the route table to use it. One great side effect of using an ELB is that only the ELB needs to be exposed to the Internet. Our instances can live on the private network with no connection to the Internet. Let's configure a new route table so that only our NLB subnets are public. (If you need to review Internet gateways and route tables, see Chapter 5.)

```
$PublicRouteTable = New-EC2RouteTable -VpcId $VPC.VpcId
New-EC2Route -RouteTableId $PublicRouteTable.RouteTableId
-DestinationCidrBlock '0.0.0.0/0'
    -GatewayId $InternetGateway.InternetGatewayId
$NoEcho = Register-EC2RouteTable -RouteTableId $PublicRouteTable.RouteTableId
    -SubnetId $ElbSubnet1.SubnetId
$NoEcho = Register-EC2RouteTable -RouteTableId $PublicRouteTable.RouteTableId
    -SubnetId $ElbSubnet2.SubnetId
```

Now that we have our VPC configured, let's create an NLB.

Configuring an NLB

Let's get started by configuring an NLB for HTTP. We will configure HTTPS in the next section. First we create the load balancer. In the following example, I am specifying that I want a Network Load Balancer (as opposed to an Application Load Balancer). I also tell it which subnets the load balancer should run it.

```
$LoadBalancer = New-ELB2LoadBalancer -Type network -Name 'WebLoadBalancer'
-Subnets $ElbSubnet1.SubnetId, $ElbSubnet2.SubnetId
```

Next, we need to create a target group. A target group is simply a list of instances behind the load balancer. The NLB will balance traffic among the instances in this group. The target group also tracks the health of the instances and takes them out of service if they fail. In the following code, I create a new target group and add our two instances.

```
$TargetGroup = New-ELB2TargetGroup -Name 'WebTargetGroup' -Protocol TCP
-Port 80 -VpcId $VPC.VpcId
Register-ELB2Target -TargetGroupArn $TargetGroup.TargetGroupArn -Target
@{id=$Instance1.InstanceId}
Register-ELB2Target -TargetGroupArn $TargetGroup.TargetGroupArn -Target
@{id=$Instance2.InstanceId}
```

Now we just need to connect the NLB to the target group. We do this by defining a listener. In the following example, I use a .Net object to create a listener that forwards all traffic it receives to the target group we created earlier. Note that the ALB supports other actions not covered here including redirection, static responses, and authentication.

```
$Action = New-Object 'Amazon.ElasticLoadBalancingV2.Model.Action'
$Action.Type = 'forward'
$Action.TargetGroupArn = $TargetGroup.TargetGroupArn
$Listner = New-ELB2Listener -Protocol TCP -Port 80 -LoadBalancerArn
$LoadBalancer.LoadBalancerArn -DefaultAction $Action
```

It will take a few minutes for the load balancer to launch and complete the initial health checks on the instances to ensure they are healthy. Once it's ready, you can get the DNS name of the load balancer using the DNSName parameter. You can copy this and paste it into your browser to test the configuration. You can also use a DNS CNAME to map this address to a friendly name (e.g., www.example.com).

```
$LoadBalancer.DNSName
```

Now that we have an NLB up and running, let's look how we can control health checks.

Configuring a Health Check

When we created the preceding target group, we used the default health check configuration. Let's describe our target group to see that configuration.

```
Get-ELB2TargetGroup -Name WebTargetGroup
```

The previous command returns the following results:

```
TargetGroupName                   : WebTargetGroup
HealthCheckEnabled                : True
HealthCheckIntervalSeconds        : 30
HealthCheckPath                   :
HealthCheckPort                   : traffic-port
HealthCheckProtocol               : TCP
HealthCheckTimeoutSeconds         : 10
HealthyThresholdCount             : 3
UnhealthyThresholdCount           : 3
LoadBalancerArns                  : {...}
Port                              : 80
Protocol                          : TCP
TargetType                        : instance
VpcId                             : vpc-123456789012
```

This is the default health check and it works as follows. Every 30 seconds (HealthCheckInterval) the ELB will attempt to create a TCP (protocol) connection on port 80 (port). If it succeeds three times (HealthyThresholdCount), the instance is healthy. If the connection is not completed within 10 seconds (HealthCheckTimeoutSeconds), the instance is unhealthy. If the instance fails to respond three times (UnhealthyThresholdCount), the ELB will stop forwarding traffic. At this point, the ELB will continue to monitor the instance. If the instance recovers, the ELB will continue to monitor it until it succeeds three times (the HealthyThresholdCount), at which point the ELB will begin forwarding traffic to it again.

Note that the NLB we are using only supports checking the TCP connection. The ALB can do additional checks. For example, you can configure the ALB to request a specific page (e.g., default.htm) using HTTP on port 80 and ensure the web server responds with a 200 status.

If you want, you can check the health of the instances behind the load balancer using Get-ELB2TargetHealth. This command will return a list of instances along with the health of each instance.

```
(Get-ELB2TargetHealth -TargetGroupArn $TargetGroup.TargetGroupArn).
TargetHealth
```

At this point our NLB is running and forwarding HTTP requests to our instances. In the next section, we add support for HTTPS.

Configuring an ELB for HTTPS

Most applications today require TLS for at least some portion of the site. As I mentioned earlier, an ELB can be configured to terminate HTTPS. Note that the ELB can also receive an HTTPS request and forward it to the instance without decrypting it, but I did not include an example. Let's add a new listener to our NLB that terminates HTTPS.

The first step is to create a TLS certificate. You could also import a certificate you already own, but AWS Certificate Manager (ACM) will allow you to easily create free certificates. In the following example, I am creating a certificate for www.example.com. Of course you need to change example.com to a domain that you own.

```
$CertificateArn = New-ACMCertificate -DomainName www.example.com
-ValidationMethod EMAIL
```

ACM will validate the certificate by sending an email to the address in the domain registrar (i.e., the email address returned by a whois command). You can also choose to use DNS validation. In this case you will need to prove control over the authoritative DNS for the domain by adding a few CNAME records to the database. Either way, the New-ACMCertificate command will return the ARN of the certificate.

After you have approved your certificate, it will take a few minutes before it is issued. You can check the status with the Get-ACMCertificateDetail command.

```
(Get-ACMCertificateDetail -CertificateArn $CertificateArn).Status
```

Once the certificate is issued, you can create a new listener for HTTPS. This command is similar to the HTTP listener we created earlier. However, we need an additional .Net object to describe the certificate. Also note that I have changed the protocol to TLS and the port to 443.

```
$Action = New-Object 'Amazon.ElasticLoadBalancingV2.Model.Action'
$Action.Type = 'forward'
$Action.TargetGroupArn = $TargetGroup.TargetGroupArn

$Certificate = New-Object 'Amazon.ElasticLoadBalancingV2.Model.Certificate'
$Certificate.CertificateArn = $CertificateArn

$Listner = New-ELB2Listener -Protocol TLS -Port 443 -LoadBalancerArn
$LoadBalancer.LoadBalancerArn -DefaultAction $Action -Certificate $Certificate
```

Obviously you are going to have to create a CNAME record to map your domain (e.g., www.example.com) to the ALB. Now that our load balancer is up and running, let's spend a minute on CloudWatch.

Monitoring with CloudWatch

Our application is now highly available. If one of the instances becomes unhealthy, the load balancer will remove it from service and send all the traffic to the other instance. While automatic issue resolution is desirable, we still want to know what is happening with our application in the cloud. We need monitoring to alert us when something goes wrong. In this section we will use CloudWatch to create an alert that will email us when CPU utilization exceeds 75% for an extended period of time.

CloudWatch is Amazon's monitoring solution. CloudWatch can be used to monitor most of the AWS services. In addition, you can create custom metrics using the CloudWatch API. You can configure CloudWatch to take multiple actions when it detects an issue, including sending an email, terminating the instance, launching additional instances, executing a Lambda function, and many other actions.

The first step in creating an email alert is to create a topic with Simple Notification Service (SNS). SNS is a service for sending notifications. It uses a publish-subscribe architecture where many receivers subscribe to notifications that are published using the SNS API. Let's begin by creating a new topic using the New-SNSTopic command.

```
$Topic = New-SNSTopic -Name 'MyTopic'
```

Now that our topic is defined, we want to subscribe to it using email. To create a subscription, use the `Connect-SNSNotification` command. You will get an email asking you to confirm your email address, and you must accept it before you can receive notifications.

```
Connect-SNSNotification -TopicArn $Topic -Protocol 'email' -Endpoint
'alerts@example.com'
```

Now that our notification is configured, let's test it. Remember that SNS is a generic notification service. CloudWatch uses it to send alerts, but you can also use it to send custom notifications. To publish a new message, use the `Publish-SNSMessage` command. You should receive an email notification with the custom message. For example:

```
Publish-SNSMessage -TopicArn $Topic -Message "This is a test!"
```

Now that our notification is configured, we can create an alert. We want to monitor our two instances and receive a notification when CPU utilization exceeds 75% for an extended period of time. The first thing we need to do is define the CloudWatch dimension. A dimension is used to group alerts. In this case we want to group our alerts by instance. Without this dimension we would be measuring the average CPU utilization of all instances in our account. We use a .Net object to create a dimension for the first instance.

```
$Dimension = New-Object 'Amazon.CloudWatch.Model.Dimension'
$Dimension.Name = 'InstanceId'
$Dimension.Value = $Instance1.InstanceId
```

Now we can create the alarm using the `Write-CWMetricAlarm` command. This command has a ton of parameters. Here is a description of each:

- `AlarmName` is just a name unique within the account.

- `AlarmDescription` is anything that will help you remember what the alarm does.

- `Namespace` defines which AWS service is being monitored.

- `MetricName` is what we want to monitor, for example, CPU Utilization (see appendix E for a list).

- `Statistic` describes how to aggregate the metric, for example, average, minimum, maximum, and so on.

- `Threshold` is the value to compare the metric to.

- `Unit` is the unit the metric is measured in, for example, MB, GB, and so on.

- `ComparisonOperator` can be greater than, less than, and so on.

- `EvaluationPeriods` is the number of periods the condition must be true before the alarm is raised.

- `Period` is the length of the evaluation period. In my example, we are waiting for two periods of 5-minute before raising the alarm.

- `Dimensions` are the dimensions we created earlier.

- `AlarmActions` is the action to take when the alarm is raised. In my example, send a notification.

The following example will create an alarm when the average CPU utilization exceeds 75% for two consecutive 5-minute monitoring periods.

```
Write-CWMetricAlarm -AlarmName 'CPU75' -AlarmDescription 'Alarm when CPU
exceeds 75%'
    -Namespace 'AWS/EC2' -MetricName 'CPUUtilization' -Statistic
    'Average'  -Threshold 75
    -ComparisonOperator 'GreaterThanThreshold' -EvaluationPeriods 2
    -Period (60*5)
    -Dimensions $Dimension -AlarmActions $Topic -Unit 'Percent'
```

CloudWatch is now monitoring our instance. You could create another alarm to monitor the other instance if you want, but I will show an easier way to monitor an entire group of instances in the next section. It will take at least 10 minutes (two periods of 5 minutes) to gather enough data to determine the current state. In the meantime, let's test our notification by explicitly setting the alarm using the `Set-CWAlarmState` command.

```
Set-CWAlarmState -AlarmName 'CPU75' -StateValue 'ALARM' -StateReason 'Testing'
```

You should receive an email alarm just like the one you would receive if an instance were in distress. This section has hardly scratched the surface of SNS and CloudWatch. Spend some time reading the documentation about these powerful services. In the next section, we will use Auto Scaling to automatically add and remove instances depending on load.

Using Auto Scaling

Notifications are a great start, but depending on an administrator to respond to alarms is slow. The cloud brings infinite elasticity and with it a whole new way of thinking. Auto Scaling allows us to build an application that automatically responds to changes in demand. Our application can scale out when demand is high and scale in when demand is low. In addition, Auto Scaling can detect issues and replace unhealthy instances.

Figure 8-3 shows the same web application we have been working on throughout this chapter, but the two web instances have been replaced by an Auto Scaling group. The Auto Scaling group is responsible for measuring current load and launching the appropriate number of instances to serve our users.

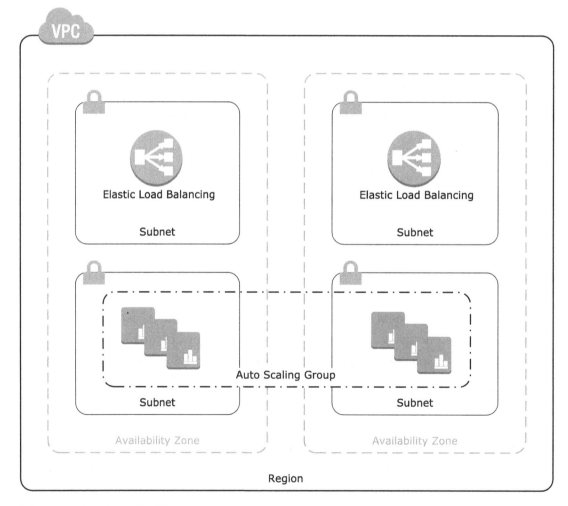

Figure 8-3. *Auto Scaling*

The first thing we need to do is terminate the two instances we launched earlier. Going forward, we are going to let the Auto Scaling group launch all of our instances. We don't want to confuse things by launching instances manually.

```
Remove-EC2Instance -Instance $Instance1.InstanceId
Remove-EC2Instance -Instance $Instance2.InstanceId
```

Rather than launching instances one at a time, we are going to define a launch configuration and save it for later. The launch configuration is simply a template that the Auto Scaling group will use whenever it needs to launch an instance. Creating a launch configuration is very similar to launching an instance. First, we define the user data script.

```
$UserData = [System.Convert]::ToBase64String([System.Text.Encoding]::ASCII.
GetBytes(@'
<powershell>
Install-WindowsFeature Web-Server -IncludeManagementTools
-IncludeAllSubFeature
</powershell>
'@))
```

Then, we call the New-ASLaunchConfiguration command. New-ASLaunchConfiguration takes all the same parameters as New-EC2Instance and a name used to save the configuration.

```
$AMI = Get-EC2ImageByName 'WINDOWS_2012_BASE'
New-ASLaunchConfiguration -LaunchConfigurationName 'MyLaunchConfig'
-ImageId $AMI[0].ImageId
    -KeyName 'MyKey' -SecurityGroups $ElbGroupId -UserData $UserData
    -InstanceType 't2.micro'
```

With our launch configuration defined, we can create an Auto Scaling group using New-ASAutoScalingGroup. The Auto Scaling group defines how many instances can be launched. DesiredCapacity is the number of instances we think we need, but we also define a min and max that Auto Scaling can work within depending on load. Auto Scaling will ensure that we always have at least the minimum number of instances, but not more than the max.

In addition, we tell the group what subnets to launch instances into, and optionally, which load balancer target group to register with when they start. Note that not all applications will require a load balancer. Some applications will get work from a queue or database table. If you are using a load balancer, you should set HealthCheckType=ELB to adopt the same health check the load balancer is using. By default, Auto Scaling will use instance health – as reported by the hypervisor – to ensure the instance is healthy. You don't want to end up in a situation where the load balancer has marked all the instances as unhealthy, but the Auto Scaling group is keeping them in service because it thinks they are healthy.

Finally, we can define a HealthCheckGracePeriod and DefaultCoolDown. These last two parameters are really important. HealthCheckGracePeriod defines how long, in seconds, to wait before evaluating the health of a new instance. The default value is 5 minutes, but it can sometimes take longer for a Windows instance to launch and configure itself. If we do not override the defaults, the Auto Scaling group will think the instance is unhealthy and replace it before it finishes configuration. Similarly, DefaultCoolDown defines how long to wait between each Auto Scaling action. Again the default is 5 minutes. If we don't change this, Auto Scaling will keep launching more and more instances while it waits for the first instance to boot up.

```
$VPCZoneIdentifier = $WebSubnet1.SubnetId + "," + $WebSubnet2.SubnetId
New-ASAutoScalingGroup -AutoScalingGroupName 'MyAutoScalingGroup'
    -LaunchConfigurationName 'MyLaunchConfig'
    -MinSize 2 -MaxSize 8 -DesiredCapacity 2
    -VPCZoneIdentifier  $VPCZoneIdentifier
    -TargetGroupARNs $TargetGroup.TargetGroupArn
    -HealthCheckType 'ELB' -HealthCheckGracePeriod (10*60)
    -DefaultCooldown (15*60)
```

As soon as we run New-ASAutoScalingGroup, the group will begin to launch new instances. You can use the Get-ELBInstanceHealth command to monitor the instances that the group is managing and determine the status of each. You will use this command often while you tune your Auto Scaling rules.

```
(Get-ELB2TargetHealth -TargetGroupArn $TargetGroup.TargetGroupArn).TargetHealth
```

At this point, the Auto Scaling group will launch the desired number of instances and monitor health. If an instance fails, it will be replaced, but we have not defined any Auto Scaling rules so it will not yet respond to changes in load. We use CloudWatch to define the rules just like we did before, but rather than sending a notification, the rule will trigger an Auto Scaling policy.

The first thing we need to do is define a new CloudWatch dimension. In the previous example, we measured the load of an individual instance. In this example, we want to measure the average load of all the instances in our Auto Scaling group. The following dimension will calculate the aggregate over the entire group.

```
$Dimension = New-Object 'Amazon.CloudWatch.Model.Dimension'
$Dimension.Name = 'AutoScalingGroupName'
$Dimension.Value = 'MyAutoScalingGroup'
```

Now we can define a policy to scale up using Write-ASScalingPolicy. This policy simply says to increase the capacity by two instances. Note that you can also override the default cool down to ensure the instance has time to boot before the next scaling occurs.

```
$ScaleUpPolicy = Write-ASScalingPolicy -PolicyName 'MyScaleOutPolicy'
    -AutoScalingGroupName 'MyAutoScalingGroup'
    -ScalingAdjustment 2 -AdjustmentType 'ChangeInCapacity' -Cooldown (15*60)
```

You can also define a percentage change rather than a specific count.

```
$ScaleUpPolicy = Write-ASScalingPolicy -PolicyName 'MyScaleOutPolicy'
    -AutoScalingGroupName 'MyAutoScalingGroup'
    -ScalingAdjustment 20 -AdjustmentType 'PercentChangeInCapacity'
    -Cooldown (30*60)
```

With the scaling policy defined, we can create a cloud watch alarm to trigger it. This is almost identical to the alarm we created for notification except that the action invokes the scaling policy rather than sending an email.

```
Write-CWMetricAlarm -AlarmName 'AS75'
    -AlarmDescription 'Add capacity when average CPU within the auto
    scaling group is more than 75%' -Threshold 75
    -MetricName 'CPUUtilization' -Namespace 'AWS/EC2' -Statistic 'Average'
    -Period (60*5)
```

```
    -ComparisonOperator 'GreaterThanThreshold' -EvaluationPeriods 2
    -AlarmActions $ScaleUpPolicy.PolicyArn -Unit 'Percent' -Dimensions
    $Dimension
```

Of course, we also need a policy to remove instances when load diminishes. Otherwise our application will grow and never contract. The policy and alarm are almost identical with a few exceptions. First, the ScalingAdjustment is a negative number to indicate we are removing instances. Second, our alarm is defined as less than 25%.

```
$ScaleInPolicy = Write-ASScalingPolicy -PolicyName 'MyScaleInPolicy'
    -AutoScalingGroupName 'MyAutoScalingGroup'
    -ScalingAdjustment -2 -AdjustmentType 'ChangeInCapacity' -Cooldown (30*60)

Write-CWMetricAlarm -AlarmName 'AS25'
    -AlarmDescription 'Remove capacity when average CPU within the auto
    scaling group is less than 25%' -Threshold 25
    -MetricName 'CPUUtilization' -Namespace 'AWS/EC2' -Statistic 'Average'
    -Period (60*5)
    -ComparisonOperator 'LessThanThreshold' -EvaluationPeriods 2
    -AlarmActions $ScaleInPolicy.PolicyArn -Unit 'Percent' -Dimensions
    $Dimension
```

Once your Auto Scaling group is running, it will work continuously to keep the application properly scaled. In fact, if you manually terminate an instance, it will be replaced within a few minutes. We have launched a lot of infrastructure in the chapter. Let's delete the Auto Scaling group and load balancer before moving on. First, we set the desired capacity of Auto Scaling group to zero to terminate all the instances.

```
Update-ASAutoScalingGroup -AutoScalingGroupName 'MyAutoScalingGroup'
-MinSize 0 -DesiredCapacity 0
```

Once that is complete, you can delete the Auto Scaling group.

```
Remove-ASAutoScalingGroup -AutoScalingGroupName 'MyAutoScalingGroup'
```

Then you can delete the load balancer and target group.

```
Remove-ELB2LoadBalancer -LoadBalancerArn $LoadBalancer.LoadBalancerArn
Remove-ELB2TargetGroup -TargetGroupArn $TargetGroup.TargetGroupArn
```

At this point, we have created a self-healing, Auto Scaling application, but we can go a step further. In the next section, we will look at how Route 53 distribute load across the globe.

Using Route 53

Our application is now architected for high availability, but we could go even further. At the moment, we have achieved high availability by launching redundant instances across availability zones in Northern Virginia. We could also launch a redundant stack in another region. This way the application would continue to work even if an entire region failed. This is where Route 53 comes in.

As seen in Figure 8-4, Route 53 can be used to balance traffic between regions, similar to how an ELB routes traffic between instances. Route 53 is a DNS service and requires that you make AWS your DNS provider. This is a significant commitment you are not likely willing to make to run a few samples from a book. As a result, I have not included any examples in this section, but I wanted you to be aware of Route 53 and how it can help you scale.

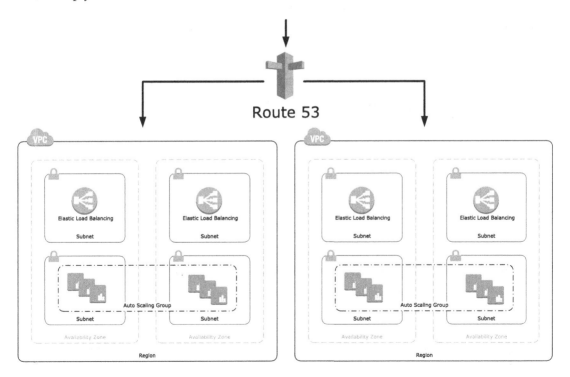

Figure 8-4. *Route 53*

There is another advantage to this architecture beyond high availability. As you know, AWS offers multiple regions around the world. If we deploy our application in many regions, we can serve users from the region closest to them, minimizing latency. This will give the user the best experience.

The advantage of using Amazon's DNS service is that it offers latency-based routing. Latency-based routing uses geolocation to determine which region is closest to the user and will therefore give them the best experience. In addition, Route 53 can monitor the health of each region and will not route users to a region that is unhealthy.

As we have seen throughout this chapter, AWS offers many services that can be used to monitor and scale an application. In the first exercise, we will pull together everything we learned in this chapter into a single script.

EXERCISE 8.1: SCALING OUT

In this chapter, we learned how to use EC2, VPC, SNS, CloudWatch, Auto Scaling, and Route 53 to create a self-healing application that automatically responds to changes in load. In the process, we took a roundabout approach focused more on exploring each technology than the final solution. In this exercise, we will pull together everything we learned into a single provisioning script that will add an Auto Scaling group to an existing VPC.

First, we need to define the input parameters. This script will add to an existing VPC; therefore, we expect the VPC, subnets (two for the ELBs and two for the application instances), and security groups to be defined already. In addition, the script takes the instance type, AMI, and user data configuration script.

```
param
(
    [string][parameter(mandatory=$true)]$VpcId,
    [string][parameter(mandatory=$true)]$ElbSubnet1Id,
    [string][parameter(mandatory=$true)]$ElbSubnet2Id,
    [string][parameter(mandatory=$true)]$WebSubnet1Id,
    [string][parameter(mandatory=$true)]$WebSubnet2Id,
    [string][parameter(mandatory=$true)]$SecurityGroupId,
    [string][parameter(mandatory=$false)]$InstanceType = 't2.micro',
    [string][parameter(mandatory=$false)]$AmiId,
```

```
    [string][parameter(mandatory=$true)]$UserData,
    [string][parameter(mandatory=$false)]$KeyName = 'MyKey'
)
```

Note that the instance type and AMI are optional. If the AMI is missing, we will look up the 2012 Base image for the current region.

```
If([System.String]::IsNullOrEmpty($AmiId)){ $AmiId = (Get-EC2ImageByName -Name
    'WINDOWS_2012_BASE')[0].ImageId}
```

Next, we launch the new load balancer for our application. In this exercise I am only configuring HTTP, but you could easily adapt the script to support HTTPS as described in the chapter.

```
$LoadBalancer = New-ELB2LoadBalancer -Type network -Name 'WebLoadBalancer'
-Subnets $ElbSubnet1Id, $ElbSubnet2Id

$TargetGroup = New-ELB2TargetGroup -Name 'WebTargetGroup' -Protocol TCP -Port
80 -VpcId $VpcId

$Action = New-Object 'Amazon.ElasticLoadBalancingV2.Model.Action'
$Action.Type = 'forward'
$Action.TargetGroupArn = $TargetGroup.TargetGroupArn
$Listner = New-ELB2Listener -Protocol TCP -Port 80 -LoadBalancerArn
$LoadBalancer.LoadBalancerArn -DefaultAction $Action
```

Now, we create a launch configuration based on the instance type, AMI, and user data passed in.

```
$UserData = [System.Convert]::ToBase64String([System.Text.Encoding]::ASCII.
GetBytes($UserData))

New-ASLaunchConfiguration -LaunchConfigurationName 'MyLaunchConfig'
    -ImageId $AmiId -KeyName $KeyName  -InstanceType $InstanceType
    -SecurityGroups $SecurityGroupId -UserData $UserData
```

Then, we create the Auto Scaling group. Here I am specifying two to eight instances with a 10-minute grace period and cool down. This is probably too high, but again we don't know what the application is; therefore, it is better to err on the high side. If the instance is not up and running within the cool-down period, it will be killed and replaced. This will result in thrashing, where the Auto Scaling continuously kills and replaces instances without giving them time to become effective.

```
New-ASAutoScalingGroup -AutoScalingGroupName 'MyAutoScalingGroup'
    -LaunchConfigurationName 'MyLaunchConfig'
    -MinSize 2 -MaxSize 8 -DesiredCapacity 2 -TargetGroupARNs $TargetGroup.
    TargetGroupArn
    -VPCZoneIdentifier "$WebSubnet1Id, $WebSubnet2Id" -HealthCheckType 'ELB'
    -HealthCheckGracePeriod (10*60) -DefaultCooldown (15*60)
```

Now we can configure CloudWatch to monitor our application. First, we create a new dimension that aggregates metrics across the entire Auto Scaling group.

```
$Dimension = New-Object 'Amazon.CloudWatch.Model.Dimension'
$Dimension.Name = 'AutoScalingGroupName'
$Dimension.Value = 'MyAutoScalingGroup'
```

Next, we create a policy and alarm to add two instances when CPU utilization exceeds 75%.

```
$ScaleUpArn = Write-ASScalingPolicy -PolicyName 'MyScaleOutPolicy'
    -AutoScalingGroupName 'MyAutoScalingGroup'
    -ScalingAdjustment 2 -AdjustmentType 'ChangeInCapacity' -Cooldown (15*60)
Write-CWMetricAlarm -AlarmName 'AS75'
    -AlarmDescription 'Add capacity when average CPU within the auto scaling
    group is more than 75%'
    -MetricName 'CPUUtilization' -Namespace 'AWS/EC2' -Statistic 'Average'
    -Period (60*5) -Threshold 75
    -ComparisonOperator 'GreaterThanThreshold' -EvaluationPeriods 2
    -AlarmActions $ScaleUpArn.PolicyArn
    -Unit 'Percent' -Dimensions $Dimension
```

Finally, we create a policy and alarm to remove two instances when CPU utilization is below 25%.

```
$ScaleInArn = Write-ASScalingPolicy -PolicyName 'MyScaleInPolicy'
    -AutoScalingGroupName 'MyAutoScalingGroup'
    -ScalingAdjustment -2 -AdjustmentType 'ChangeInCapacity' -Cooldown (15*60)
    Write-CWMetricAlarm -AlarmName 'AS25'
    -AlarmDescription 'Remove capacity when average CPU within the auto
    scaling group is less than 25%'
    -MetricName 'CPUUtilization' -Namespace 'AWS/EC2' -Statistic 'Average'
    -Period (60*5) -Threshold 25
```

```
-ComparisonOperator 'LessThanThreshold' -EvaluationPeriods 2
-AlarmActions $ScaleInArn.PolicyArn
-Unit 'Percent' -Dimensions $Dimension
```

That's all you need to build a self-healing application that automatically responds to changes in load. Auto Scaling is a great solution, but the application must be built with scaling in mind. Some applications are simply not built to scale out. For these applications, you must scale up. In the next section, we create a script to scale up, or move from one instance type to another.

EXERCISE 8.2: SCALING UP

In this chapter, we created a solution to scale out in response to load. Scaling out refers to adding additional instances in response to demand. Another option is to scale up, or increase the size of an instance. Some systems, such as relational databases, do not scale out easily. These applications must be scaled up.

Luckily AWS has a command for this named Edit-EC2InstanceAttribute. Edit-EC2InstanceAttribute allows you to change many of instance's attributes including

- BlockDeviceMappings

- DisableApiTermination

- EbsOptimized

- Groups

- InstanceInitiatedShutdownBehavior

- InstanceType

- Kernel

- Ramdisk

- SourceDestCheck

- UserData

We are interested in changing the InstanceType. Let's create a quick script to resize an instance. Our script will take two simple parameters, the instance ID you want to modify and the new instance type.

```
Param(
    [string][Parameter(Mandatory=$false)] $InstanceId,
    [string][Parameter(Mandatory=$false)] $NewInstanceType
)
```

Now all we need to do is call `Edit-EC2Instance` specifying the `InstanceType` attribute.

```
Edit-EC2InstanceAttribute -InstanceId $InstanceId -InstanceType
$NewInstanceType
```

That's all there is to it. Once again AWS makes it easy to do something that would be really hard with physical servers in a traditional data center.

Before we wrap up, I want to point out a few limitations of this script:

1.   Your instance must be stopped before you can resize it.

2.   Be really careful with ephemeral storage. Ephemeral disk configurations depend on the instance type and are not always compatible across systems. Be really careful with Elastic Network Interfaces (ENIs) and secondary IP addresses. Again, ENIs and secondary IP configurations differ among instance types.

3.   Be careful with marketplace instances. Marketplace instances cannot be resized as you are licensed for a specific size.

In this exercise we created a script that can be used to resize an instance. In general, scaling out is preferred, but when the application does not support it, we can always scale up.

Summary

In this chapter, we saw the true power of the cloud and AWS. We used VPC to build a highly available application served from two or more active-active data centers. We developed a notification system using SNS and CloudWatch to provide an early warning system that informs the administrator before the application fails.

We also used an ELB to balance traffic across multiple instances and monitor the health of the individual instances. In addition, we used Auto Scaling to monitor load in real time to dynamically resize the application by launching and terminating instances in response to load. Finally, we deployed our application in multiple regions and used Route 53 to automatically route users to the nearest region, minimizing latency.

In the exercises we created scripts to scale out and scale up depending on the application.

It is very easy to overlook the power of what we just did. Very few traditional enterprises can achieve web scale using their own data centers and enterprise solution. But, using the cloud, a single person can build a world-class application from their favorite coffee shop.

This chapter wraps up our discussion on Elastic Compute Cloud (EC2). In the remaining three chapters, we will examine Relational Database Service (RDS), Simple Storage Service (S3), and Identity and Access Management (IAM).

CHAPTER 9

Identity and Access Management

If you have been following along from the beginning, we have completed all of the examples in this book while signed in as a user with administrator privileges. While this is a convenient way to learn a new technology, you should never run a production system with administrator privileges. If part of the system were compromised, you want to ensure you limit access as much as possible.

This chapter is all about Identity and Access Management (IAM). IAM is how you manage users, groups, and permissions. In this chapter, I show you how to create users and groups. I also explain how IAM policies work and how to create them. IAM policies describe which resources a user can access and the operations they can perform on those resources. You will see that IAM gives you unprecedented control over access.

Finally, in the two exercises at the end of the chapter, we will create a framework for least privileged access and grant access to billing and support. Let's get started.

Managing Users

Let's begin by adding a few users to our AWS account. We added a single user back in Chapter 2 using the AWS Management Console. Now let's add a few using PowerShell.

To add users, you use the New-IAMUser command. The following script will add six users:

```
New-IAMUser -UserName 'alice'
New-IAMUser -UserName 'bob'
New-IAMUser -UserName 'chris'
New-IAMUser -UserName 'dan'
New-IAMUser -UserName 'eve'
New-IAMUser -UserName 'frank'
```

© Brian Beach, Steven Armentrout, Rodney Bozo, Emmanuel Tsouris 2019
B. Beach et al., *Pro PowerShell for Amazon Web Services*, https://doi.org/10.1007/978-1-4842-4850-8_9

As you might expect, there is also a `Get-IAMUser` command that can be used to get information about a user, such as the username and date the account was created.

```
Get-IAMUser -UserName 'alice'
```

`Get-IAMUser` works a bit differently from other commands. Most "get" methods return a list of all objects when you call them without parameters. If you call `Get-IAMUser` without the `UserName` parameter, it returns the currently logged in user. This is useful when writing a generic script that needs to discover who is currently logged in. For example, you might want to tag an instance with the name of the current user.

```
$User = Get-IAMUser
$Tag = New-Object Amazon.EC2.Model.Tag
$Tag.Key ='Owner'
$Tag.Value = $User.UserName
```

Note that Get-IAMUser only works for users. Toward the end of this chapter, we will talk about IAM roles. If you are writing code to get the current user, I suggest using Get-STSCallerIdentity. Get-STSCallerIdentity will work for both users and roles.

If you want to list all of the users in the account, use the `Get-IAMUsers` command.

```
Get-IAMUsers | Format-Table
```

You may remember from Chapter 2 that there are multiple types of credentials. We discussed that users need a password to access the AWS Management Console and access keys to use the REST API and PowerShell. But not all users require both types of credentials. To allow a user to access the AWS Management Console, you must assign a password using the `New-IAMLoginProfile` command.

```
New-IAMLoginProfile -UserName 'alice' -Password 'PASSWORD'
-PasswordResetRequired:$True
```

Note that PasswordResetRequired is optional. If you omit PasswordResetRequired, the user will *not* be forced to reset their password on the next console login. There are two commands for changing a user's password. The first, Edit-IAMPassword, allows a user to change their own password. It always acts on the current user and requires the old password.

```
Edit-IAMPassword -OldPassword 'PASSWORD' -NewPassword 'Du2[/uiCq8LKjW'
```

The second, `Update-IAMLoginProfile`, is an administrative action. `Update-IAMLoginProfile` can change any user's password and does not require the original password.

```
Update-IAMLoginProfile -UserName alice -Password 'Du2[/uiCq8LKjW'
```

If you want to remove a login profile, and deny access to the AWS Management Console, use the `Remove-IAMLoginProfile` command.

```
Remove-IAMLoginProfile -UserName 'alice' -Force
```

If you want the user to be able to use the REST API, you must create an access key using the `New-IAMAccessKey` command. Remember that we are using the REST API with PowerShell. Therefore, a user needs an access key to use PowerShell for AWS. The `New-IAMAccessKey` command returns an object that includes both the `AccessKeyId` and `SecretAccessKey`.

```
$Keys = New-IAMAccessKey -UserName 'alice'
$Keys.AccessKeyId
$Keys.SecretAccessKey
```

Remember to save the secret key because you cannot get it again. To store a copy in your PowerShell session, you can use the `Set-AWSCredentials` command discussed in Chapter 2. For example:

```
$Keys = New-IAMAccessKey -UserName 'alice'
Set-AWSCredentials -AccessKey $Keys.AccessKeyId -SecretKey $Keys.SecretAccessKey -StoreAs 'alice'
```

If you want to delete a user's access keys, you can use `Remove-IAMAccessKey`. A user can have more than one Access Key; therefore, you must specify which Access Key to remove.

```
Remove-IAMAccessKey -UserName 'alice' -AccessKeyId 'AKIAJV64XS4XLRAJIBAQ' -Force
```

You may find that you need to check if a user has either a password or access keys. You can use `Get-IAMLoginProfile` and `Get-IAMAccessKey` to check if they exist.

```
Get-IAMLoginProfile -UserName 'alice'
Get-IAMAccessKey -UserName 'alice'
```

Both of these methods return a create date for the credential. Given that each user can have two sets of access keys, the security conscious user will rotate these keys on a regular basis. For example, you might replace the older set of keys every 30 days. The following script will find the oldest set of keys for a user, delete them, and create a new set.

```
$Key = Get-IAMAccessKey -UserName 'alice' | Sort-Object CreateDate
-Descending | Select AccessKeyId -First 1
Remove-IAMAccessKey -UserName 'alice' -AccessKeyId $Key.AccessKeyId-Force
$Keys = New-IAMAccessKey -UserName 'alice'
$Keys.AccessKeyId
$Keys.SecretAccessKey
```

Now that we have a user created, we need to assign the user permissions. Before we do, let's look at groups. Groups allow you to group related users together and assign them permissions as a unit. This process is usually less time-consuming and less error prone.

Managing Groups

When you apply permissions to individual users, it is very difficult to keep track of who has access to which resources. Grouping related users makes managing permissions much easier. Groups reduce the number of unique permissions sets you need to keep track of. (In the first exercise at the end of this chapter, we build a set of common groups as a starting point.)

To create a new group, use the New-IAMGroup command and assign a name.

```
New-IAMGroup -GroupName 'AWS_USERS'
```

Initially the group is empty. To add a user to a group, use the Add-IAMUserToGroup command and pass the name of the user and the group to add him or her to.

```
Add-IAMUserToGroup -UserName 'alice' -GroupName 'AWS_USERS'
```

If you want to remove a user from a group, use the Remove-IAMUserFromGroup command passing the name of the user and the group to remove him or her from.

```
Remove-IAMUserFromGroup -UserName 'alice' -GroupName 'AWS_USERS' -Force
```

Listing groups is similar to listing users. You use the `Get-IAMGroups` (plural) command to list all the groups in your account.

```
Get-IAMGroups
```

You use the `Get-IAMGroup` (singular) command to get a specific group.

```
Get-IAMGroup -GroupName 'AWS_USERS'
```

Note that these two commands return different information. The `Get-IAMGroups` (plural) command returns a group object that does not include the group members. The `Get-IAMGroup` (singular) command returns a `GetGroupResult` object that includes the group and a collection of users.

Therefore, to list the members of a group, use `Get-IAMGroup` and then read the users property.

```
(Get-IAMGroup -GroupName 'AWS_USERS').Users
```

To get the opposite – a list of groups a user is a member of – you can use the `Get-IAMGroupForUser` command. For example:

```
Get-IAMGroupForUser 'alice'
```

Unlike the `Get-IAMUser` command, `Get-IAMGroupForUser` cannot be called without a group parameter. It would be nice if calling `Get-IAMGroupForUser` would list the groups the current user is a member of. We can use a little PowerShell magic to combine `Get-IAMUser` and `Get-IAMGroupForUser` to get the list. For example:

```
Get-IAMUser | Get-IAMGroupForUser
```

At this point we have created a few users and groups and have added users to groups. But, our users still don't have permission to do anything. In the next section, we will grant permission to our users.

Managing Policies

We use policies to grant permissions to users and groups. Policies are JSON statements that describe what API calls a user or group is allowed to call. You can grant or deny access to every API call. Before we get started, let's do a quick review of JSON.

JSON PRIMER

JavaScript Object Notation (JSON) was first used to send objects from a web server to a browser. JSON uses key/value pairs to represent attributes. Here are a few examples of attributes in JSON:

```
"Name": "Joe"
"Age": 35
"Male": true
```

An array can be represented by a single key and multiple values in square brackets. For example:

```
"Children": ["Mary", "Charles", "Sam"]
```

An object is simply a list of key/value pairs separated by commas and enclosed in curly braces. For example, we might represent a person as

```
{
    "Name": "Joe",
    "Age": 35,
    "Male": true,
    "Children": ["Mary", "Charles", "Sam"]
}
```

We can also nest objects inside other objects. For example:

```
{
    "Name": "Joe",
    "Age": 35,
    "Male": true,
    "Children": [
        {
            "Name": "Mary",
            "Age": 3,
            "Male": false
        },
        {
            "Name": "Charles",
            "Age": 5,
```

```
            "Male": true
        },
        {

            "Name": "Sam",
            "Age": 7,
            "Male": true
        }
    ]
}
```

This is a very brief introduction, but you can see that JSON can be used to represent very complex structures. I could write a whole book on JSON – and others have – but this is all we need to understand IAM policy statements.

Policy statements are written in JSON. The statement must include three sections: effect, action, and resource. The effect of the statement is to either allow access or deny access. The action is a list of API calls that are allowed. The resource section lists the objects the user is allowed to act on. For example, the following statement will allow a user to call any method on any object. In other words, this is an administrator policy.

```
{
  "Statement": [
    {
      "Effect": "Allow",
      "Action": "*",
      "Resource": "*"
    }
  ]
}
```

Policy Actions

Actions determine which API calls are allowed or denied by a policy. Remember that PowerShell commands call API WebMethods. In other words, you can grant or deny access to each individual PowerShell command.

Before we can write a policy, we need to know the API method name. There is a helper cmdlet, Get-AWSCmdletName, which you can use to map cmdlets to API methods. For example:

```
PS C:\>  Get-AWSCmdletName | Where CmdletName -eq New-Ec2Instance

CmdletName        ServiceOperation ServiceName
----------        ---------------- -----------
New-EC2Instance RunInstances      Amazon Elastic Compute Cloud
```

Now that we know the API names, let's write a custom policy. We use an array to list multiple methods in a single policy. Note that the method name is preceded by the service type (i.e., "iam:") The following example allows access to all the read methods in IAM. In other words, this policy grants read-only access to IAM.

```
{
  "Statement": [
    {
      "Effect": "Allow",
      "Action": [
          "iam:GetAccountPasswordPolicy",
          "iam:GetAccountSummary",
          "iam:GetGroup",
          "iam:GetGroupPolicy",
          "iam:GetInstanceProfile",
          "iam:GetLoginProfile",
          "iam:GetRole",
          "iam:GetRolePolicy",
          "iam:GetServerCertificate",
          "iam:GetUser",
          "iam:GetUserPolicy",
          "iam:ListAccessKeys",
          "iam:ListAccountAliases",
          "iam:ListGroupPolicies",
          "iam:ListGroups",
          "iam:ListGroupsForUser",
```

```
        "iam:ListInstanceProfiles",
        "iam:ListInstanceProfilesForRole",
        "iam:ListMFADevices",
        "iam:ListRolePolicies",
        "iam:ListRoles",
        "iam:ListServerCertificates",
        "iam:ListSigningCertificates",
        "iam:ListUserPolicies",
        "iam:ListUsers",
        "iam:ListVirtualMFADevices"
      ],
      "Resource": "*"
    }
  ]
}
```

You can also use a wildcard or "*" character to specify API methods that start with a specific pattern. For example, we could simplify the preceding policy using wildcards.

```
{
  "Statement": [
    {
      "Effect": "Allow",
      "Action": [
        "iam:Get*",
        "iam:List*"
      ],
      "Resource": "*"
    }
  ]
}
```

Often you want to grant access to an entire service such as EC2. We can also scope a wildcard to grant access to a specific service. The following example will grant access to EC2 and S3.

```
{
  "Statement": [
    {
      "Effect": "Allow",
      "Action": [
        "ec2:*",
        "s3:*"
        ],
      "Resource": "*"
    }
  ]
}
```

As you can see, IAM policies allow fine-grained control over access. In Exercise 9.1 we will develop a set of least privileged roles for EC2. Now let's look at resources.

Policy Resources

So far, the policies we have written apply to all resources. When we granted access to S3 in the following example, we allowed the user to act on all objects in all buckets. Some services allow you to scope the access. In S3, we might want to allow access to a specific bucket or folder.

For example, to scope access to the "MyBucket" bucket

```
{
  "Statement": [
    {
      "Effect": "Allow",
      "Action": *,
      "Resource": "arn:aws:s3:::MyBucket"
    }
  ]
}
```

The resource statement is always written using an Amazon Resource Name (ARN). An ARN is used to uniquely identify an AWS resource across accounts and regions. The ARN format is as follows:

```
arn:aws:service:region:account:resource
```

Note that S3 is a special case. The bucket name is already unique; therefore, the ARN does not include the account and region and follows the format

```
arn:aws:s3:::BUCKET/KEY
```

Many, but not all, services support resource-level permission that allows you to scope a policy to specific resources. For example, you could scope access to a specific object in S3 as follows:

```
{
  "Statement": [
    {
      "Effect": "Allow",
      "Action": *,
      "Resource": "arn:aws:s3:::MyBucket/MyFolder/MyFile.txt"
    }
  ]
}
```

Of course, you can use wildcards here as well. The following example will scope access to all objects in the MyFolder folder in the MyBucket bucket:

```
{
  "Statement": [
    {
      "Effect": "Allow",
      "Action": *,
      "Resource": "arn:aws:s3:::MyBucket/MyFolder/*"
    }
  ]
}
```

209

IAM also allows a few variables in the policy statements. (See the sidebar for a list of supported variables.) Variables make it easier to create a generic policy. For example, let's assume that every user has a personal folder in S3 that is named with the user's username. It would be really tedious to write a policy for each user in the following format:

```
{
  "Statement": [
    {
      "Effect": "Allow",
      "Action": *,
      "Resource": "arn:aws:s3:::MyBucket/alice/*"
    }
  ]
}
```

You can write a generic policy that grants each user access to his or her own folder as follows:

```
{
  "Statement": [
    {
      "Effect": "Allow",
      "Action": *,
      "Resource": "arn:aws:s3:::MyBucket/${aws:username}/*"
    }
  ]
}
```

POLICY VARIABLES

Here is a list of variables supported in IAM policy statements.

Name	Description
aws:CurrentTime	Date and time of the request
aws:EpochTime	Date and time in Unix time format
aws:TokenIssueTime	Date and time that temporary credentials were issued
aws:principaltype	A value that indicates whether the principal is an account, user, federated, or assumed role (see the explanation that follows)
aws:SecureTransport	Boolean representing whether the request was sent using SSL
aws:SourceIp	The requester's IP address, for use with IP address conditions
aws:UserAgent	Information about the requester's client application, for use with string conditions
aws:userid	Unique ID for the current user
aws:username	Username of the current user
s3:prefix	Prefix passed in some S3 commands
s3:max-keys	Max-Keys information passed in some S3 commands
sns:Endpoint	Endpoint passed in some SNS calls
sns:Protocol	Protocol passed in some SNS calls

Unfortunately, not all services support resources. For example, S3 and IAM do, but EC2 does not. Luckily we can use conditions to control access to EC2 objects by tag. But, before we talk about conditions, let's look at policy actions.

Policy Actions

All of the policy statements we have written so far allow access to a resource. You can also deny access to a resource by using the deny action. For example, I could keep a user from terminating instances by denying access to the ec2:TerminateInstances action.

```
{
  "Statement": [
    {
      "Effect": "Deny",
      "Action": "ec2:TerminateInstances",
      "Resource": "*"
    }
  ]
}
```

Effect, resource, and action are required components of every policy statement. There are also numerous optional components. I'm not going to cover all of the options here, but I do want to discuss conditions. Conditions are very useful for controlling access to EC2. Let's have a look.

Policy Conditions

Conditions allow you to write custom logic to determine if an action is allowed. This is a complex topic that could easily fill a chapter. I am only going to show you how to write conditions based on EC2 tags. You can read more about conditions in the IAM user guide.

Imagine you want to allow users to terminate instances tagged DEV but not those considered QA or PROD. You could grant access to the terminate action, but use a condition to limit access to those instances that have a tag called "environment" with the value "dev".

```
{
    "Version": "2012-10-17",
    "Statement": [{
        "Effect": "Allow",
        "Action": "ec2:TerminateInstances",
        "Resource": "arn:aws:ec2:us-east-1:123456789012:instance/*",
```

```
      "Condition": {
        "StringEquals": {
          "ec2:ResourceTag/environment": "dev"
        }
      }
    }
  ]
}
```

Notice that I have included the optional version to tell AWS this policy requires the latest version of the policy language. Also notice the format of the resource ARN. Remember to replace the 123456789012 with your account number.

Now that we know how to write a policy, let's associate it with a user and group using PowerShell.

Creating Policies with PowerShell

Creating an IAM policy in PowerShell is really easy. You simply create the JSON statement as a string and then associate it with a user or group. For example, to grant Alice full control, use the `Write-IAMUserPolicy` command.

```
$Policy = @"
{
  "Statement": [
    {
      "Effect": "Allow",
      "Action": "*",
      "Resource": "*"
    }
  ]
}
"@

Write-IAMUserPolicy -UserName "alice" -PolicyName "alice-FullControl"
-PolicyDocument $Policy
```

Assigning a policy to a group is just as easy. For example, to grant full control to the ADMINS group, use the `Write-IAMGroupPolicy` command.

```
Write-IAMGroupPolicy -GroupName "ADMINS" -PolicyName "ADMINS-FullControl"
-PolicyDocument $Policy
```

As you can see, IAM policies give you fine-grained control over access to AWS. You can be very specific about who has access to which resources. The details are all contained in the policy statement. In Exercise 9.1 we will create a common set of groups with least privileged policy defined. Before we end the section on policies, let's spend a moment on managed policies.

Managed Policies

Up to this point, we have been creating policies by hand. In practice, this can get tedious. In addition, it is easy to make mistakes that grant more permission than you intend and compromise security. As you might expect, there are many common patterns that emerge. For example, most organizations have a team of system administrators and they grant them access to EC2, ECS, and so on, or network administrators that need access to VPC, Route 53, and so on.

Luckily, AWS has created a collection of managed policies that solve common problems. It is often much easier to use these policies rather than writing your own policies. In addition, you can create your own managed policies.

Why would you want to create a managed policy when you can attach a policy directly to a user? You can define a policy once and use it across many users, groups, and roles. This promotes consistent permissions across your security principals. In addition, managed policies support versioning so you can maintain a history of changes. Policies attached directly to a user do not support versioning.

Let's begin by looking at the managed policies in your account.

```
Get-IAMPolicies
```

If you want to list only those managed policies defined by AWS, excluding any customer managed policies, you can add the Scope=AWS attribute.

```
Get-IAMPolicies -Scope AWS
```

Conversely, you can list only those customer managed policies by adding the scope equals local attribute.

```
Get-IAMPolicies -Scope local
```

You can get details about a specific policy using the Get-IAMPolicy cmdlet. This command requires the Arn of the policy you are interested in.

```
Get-IAMPolicy -PolicyArn arn:aws:iam::aws:policy/AmazonGlacierReadOnlyAccess
```

You may notice that this command does not return the actual policy. Why? Remember that managed policies support versions. Therefore, each managed policy may have many versions. You can list the policies with the Get-IAMPolicyVersions cmdlet.

```
Get-IAMPolicyVersions -PolicyArn arn:aws:iam::aws:policy/
AmazonGlacierReadOnlyAccess
```

And, you can get a specific version using the Get-IAMPolicyVersion cmdlet.

```
Get-IAMPolicyVersion -PolicyArn arn:aws:iam::aws:policy/
AmazonGlacierReadOnlyAccess -VersionId v1
```

As I mentioned earlier, you can create your own managed policies. This allows you define your policies once and maintain version history. For example, let's assume you want to create a managed policy for system administrators. Of course, there is already an AWS-defined policy for system administrators. In general, I recommend using the built-in policies rather than writing your own. However, let's assume we want to create our own. Here I am granting the system administrators full control over EC2. Note that the version attribute is required when creating a managed policy.

```
$Policy = @"
{
   "Version": "2012-10-17",
  "Statement": [
    {
      "Effect": "Allow",
      "Action": "ec2:*",
```

```
      "Resource": "*"
    }
  ]
}
"@
```

```
New-IAMPolicy -PolicyName MySysAdminPolicy -PolicyDocument $Policy
```

Now, let's assume that we have started using containers and want to also give you system administrators access to Elastic Container Service (ECS) in addition to EC2. Therefore, I update the policy with a new version. Notice that I am setting the new version as the default.

```
$Policy = @"
{
  "Version": "2012-10-17",
  "Statement": [
    {
      "Effect": "Allow",
      "Action": ["ec2:*", "ecs:*"],
      "Resource": "*"
    }
  ]
}
"@
```

```
New-IAMPolicyVersion -PolicyArn arn:aws:iam::123456789012:policy/
MySysAdminPolicy -PolicyDocument $Policy -SetAsDefault $true
```

Finally, let's assume we changed our mind and want to roll back to version 1. We can do this with the Set-IAMDefaultPolicyVersion cmdlet.

```
Set-IAMDefaultPolicyVersion -PolicyArn arn:aws:iam::123456789012:policy/
MySysAdminPolicy -VersionId v1
```

This command will update the policy of all the security principals (user, groups, and roles) that are using the policy. Of course, the astute reader realizes that there are no principals using the policy. At this point we have created a policy, but we have not assigned the policy to a principal. The last thing we need to do is add the policy to a user, group, or role. Note: We will talk more about roles in the next section. Let's add the managed policy to the user Alice we created earlier.

```
Register-IAMUserPolicy -UserName alice -PolicyArn
arn:aws:iam::123456789012:policy/MySysAdminPolicy
```

Managing Roles

Remember from Chapter 2 that an IAM role can be used to associate a policy with an instance, rather than a user. This is just one example of a much more powerful concept. Roles allow you assign permission to AWS services, AWS accounts, SAML identities, and other resources. Let's look a few examples.

To list the roles defined in your account, use the Get-IAMRoles command. If you run this command, you should see the "AdminRole" we created using the AWS Management Console in Chapter 2.

```
Get-IAMRoles
```

You can also get a specific role using the Get-IAMRole command.

```
Get-IAMRole -Rolename AdminRole
```

Let's define a few roles to understand how they work. Creating a new role is similar to the process we used to create a user or group, but we also need a second policy that defines what resources can assume the role. There are two policies required: the first describes who can use the role, and the second describes what the role can do.

Let's begin by defining who can use this role. The policy shown here allows the EC2 service to assume this role. In other words, this policy can be used by EC2 instances, but not ECS containers.

```
$AssumeRolePolicy = @"
{
  "Version":"2008-10-17",
  "Statement":[
    {
      "Sid":"",
      "Effect":"Allow",
```

```
        "Principal":{"Service":"ec2.amazonaws.com"},
        "Action":"sts:AssumeRole"
      }
    ]
}
"@
```

Next, we create an access policy just like we did in the prior section. This policy gives the role administrator access to all services. Note that I cannot think of any reason to create an EC2 role with administrator permissions. You should be creating a policy with much less permission than I am in the example.

```
$AccessPolicy = @"
{
  "Statement": [
    {
      "Effect": "Allow",
      "Action": "*",
      "Resource": "*"
    }
  ]
}
"@
```

Now we can create the role using the New-IAMRole command, passing in the access policy.

```
New-IAMRole -RoleName 'MyAdminRole' -AssumeRolePolicyDocument
$AssumeRolePolicy
```

Next, we use Write-IAMRolePolicy to associate the access policy to the role, just like we did with users and groups earlier.

```
Write-IAMRolePolicy -RoleName 'MyAdminRole' -PolicyName 'MyAdminRole-
FullControl' -PolicyDocument $AccessPolicy
```

For most roles this is all you need to do. However, roles that will be assigned to EC2 instances need one last step. Before you can associate a role with an EC2 instance, you must create a new instance profile and add the new role to it.

```
New-IAMInstanceProfile -InstanceProfileName 'MyAdminRoleInstanceProfile'
Add-IAMRoleToInstanceProfile -RoleName 'MyAdminRole'
-InstanceProfileName  'MyAdminRoleInstanceProfile'
```

Let's look at another example. This time we will create a cross-account role. A cross-account role is simply a role that can be assumed by users in another account. The process is identical to creating a service role. However, rather than specifying a service as the principal, we specify another AWS account.

```
$AssumeRolePolicy = @"
{
  "Version": "2012-10-17",
  "Statement": [
    {
      "Effect": "Allow",
      "Principal": {"AWS": "arn:aws:iam::987654321000:root"},
      "Action": "sts:AssumeRole"
    }
  ]
}
"@
```

Now we can create the new role just like we did in the prior example.

```
New-IAMRole -RoleName 'MyCrossAccountRole' -AssumeRolePolicyDocument
$AssumeRolePolicy
```

Rather than attaching a policy directly to this role, I will use a managed policy. Once again, I am using the admin policy in the example, but I want to stress that you should use a role with less privilege in real life.

```
Register-IAMRolePolicy -RoleName MyCrossAccountRole -PolicyArn
arn:aws:iam::aws:policy/AdministratorAccess
```

You can also use roles to grant permissions to other services. For example, Auto Scaling needs to launch and terminated instances as load changes. You need to create a role that grants the Auto Scaling service permission to make these changes in your account. Luckily, AWS offers service-linked roles. Service-linked roles automatically define all of the permissions needed for a given service so you don't have to create them manually. Let's create a service-linked role for Auto Scaling.

```
New-IAMServiceLinkedRole -AWSServiceName autoscaling.amazonaws.com
```

Note   that you have used Auto Scaling at some point in the past, you will likely get an error because this role already exists.

At this point it should be clear that AWS offers a robust permission model that gives you tremendous control over your identities. Of course, this can get confusing so let's look at options to audit your IAM policies with PowerShell.

Auditing IAM Access

IAM gives you fine-grained control over your users and groups. It also gives you tools to audit user access. Let's start with a high-level summary and drill down. At the highest level, Get-IAMAccountSummary will return a report of IAM entities and quotas. We can use this to get the total number of users, groups, and roles. We can also get the number of MFA devices in use and check if MFA is enabled on the root account, along with a lot of other useful data.

```
Get-IAMAccountSummary
```

Another useful tool is the credential report. This report includes a high-level summary of each IAM credential (user or group). It will tell you when the user last logged in, how long it's been since they changed their password, when they last rotated their keys, and so on. You create the report in two steps. First, you request the report. This will take a few seconds so I am going to call Start-Sleep. If you have thousands of users, you may need to wait longer. Then I get the report in CSV format and convert to a PowerShell object. Then I can query the data as usual.

```
# Request the report
Request-IAMCredentialReport
# Wait for report generation
Start-Sleep 30
```

```
# Get the report as CSV
$Report = Get-IAMCredentialReport -AsTextArray | ConvertFrom-Csv
# Print a high-level summary
$Report | Format-Table
# Get details about a specific user
$Report | Where user -eq alice
```

The credential report tells you about a user's activity. If you want to see a report of the permissions attached to a user, check out the Get-IAMAccountAuthorizationDetails. Get-IAMAccountAuthorizationDetails will tell you what groups, managed policies, inline policies, and so on are associated with a specific user or group. For example, the following example will get all their permissions for Alice.

```
(Get-IAMAccountAuthorizationDetails).UserDetailList | Where UserName -eq alice
```

Finally, you may want to test that a user has permission to complete an action without actually doing it. For example, you may want to test that Alice has permission to terminate an EC2 instance without actually terminating anything. You can use the Test-IAMPrincipalPolicy cmdlet to validate a user's permissions.

```
Test-IAMPrincipalPolicy -PolicySourceArn arn:aws:iam::123456789012:user/
alice -ActionName ec2:TerminateInstance
```

At this point you know how to manage permissions for user, groups, and roles. Before we close this chapter, I want to discuss a few miscellaneous IAM commands.

Miscellaneous IAM Commands

I want to discuss a few miscellaneous IAM commands that did not warrant their own section. Therefore, I included them all here.

Managing Password Policy

Users that have access to the AWS Management Console need to have a password. Many organizations require a specific password policy. You can control the IAM password policy using the Update-IAMAccountPasswordPolicy command.

```
Update-IAMAccountPasswordPolicy
    -MinimumPasswordLength 8
    -RequireSymbols $false
    -RequireNumbers $true
    -RequireUppercaseCharacters $true
    -RequireLowercaseCharacters $true
    -AllowUsersToChangePassword $true
```

You can also get the current policy using Get-IAMAccountPasswordPolicy and remove the policy using Remove-IAMAccountPasswordPolicy.

Setting the Account Alias

Finally, you can get and set the account alias. Remember from Chapter 2 that the account alias is used to create an easy-to-remember sign-in URL.

You can set the account alias using the New-IAMAccountAlias command.

```
New-IAMAccountAlias -AccountAlias 'brianbeach'
```

You can also get the current alias using Get-IAMAccountAlias and remove the alias using Remove-IAMAccountAlias.

That brings us to the exercises. As you have seen, IAM gives you fine-grained control over access to AWS resources. You can be very specific about who has access to which resources. In Exercise 9.1 we create a set of common groups that provide least privileged access. In Exercise 9.2 we will learn how to permit access to billing and support.

EXERCISE 9.1: CREATING LEAST PRIVILEGED GROUPS

Throughout this book we have been using a single account that has administrator access to all services. Obviously this is a bad idea in production. We only want to allow those permissions that each user needs. Let's create a few common groups as a starting point.

Note: AWS supplies a series of managed policies called **AWS Managed Policies for Job Functions**. These policies define roles for common job functions. You should consider using them rather than creating your own policies and groups as I am doing in this example.

Let's assume that our company is using AWS for development. The main users are software developers. We have a team of AWS experts who support the developers. In addition, the developers are supported by the traditional system administrators and network administrators. The system administrators support the operating system, and the network administrators are responsible for routing, load balancers, and network security.

First, all users require a few common permissions. At a minimum they all need the ability to change their own password. Let's start by creating a group that allows a user to see the password policy change his or her own password. All users should be a member of this group. Note that all of these examples are included with the source code for this chapter.

```
$Policy = @"
{
  "Statement": [
    {
      "Effect": "Allow",
      "Action": [
        "iam:ChangePassword",
        "iam:GetAccountPasswordPolicy"
        ],
      "Resource": "*"
    }
  ]
}
"@

New-IAMGroup -GroupName "USERS"
Write-IAMGroupPolicy -GroupName "USERS" -PolicyName "USERS-ChangePassword"
    -PolicyDocument $Policy
```

Second, the AWS administrators require full access. Let's create a group that has full control of all services. This should be a very small group of people.

```
$Policy = @"
{
  "Statement": [
    {
      "Effect": "Allow",
      "Action": "*",
      "Resource": "*"
    }
```

```
        ]
    }
"@
New-IAMGroup -GroupName "ADMINS"
Write-IAMGroupPolicy -GroupName "ADMINS" -PolicyName "ADMINS-FullControl"
        -PolicyDocument $Policy
```

Third, the developers are using continuous development. They need to be able to create, start, stop, and terminate instances. Let's create a group for the developers.

```
$Policy = @"
{
    "Statement": [
        {
            "Effect": "Allow",
            "Action": [
                "ec2:AttachVolume",
                "ec2:CopySnapshot",
                "ec2:CreateKeyPair",
                "ec2:CreateSnapshot",
                "ec2:CreateTags",
                "ec2:CreateVolume",
                "ec2:DeleteKeyPair",
                "ec2:DeleteSnapshot",
                "ec2:DeleteTags",
                "ec2:DeleteVolume",
                "ec2:DescribeAddresses",
                "ec2:DescribeAvailabilityZones",
                "ec2:DescribeBundleTasks",
                "ec2:DescribeConversionTasks",
                "ec2:DescribeCustomerGateways",
                "ec2:DescribeDhcpOptions",
                "ec2:DescribeExportTasks",
                "ec2:DescribeImageAttribute",
                "ec2:DescribeImages",
                "ec2:DescribeInstanceAttribute",
                "ec2:DescribeInstances",
                "ec2:DescribeInstanceStatus",
```

```
"ec2:DescribeInternetGateways",
"ec2:DescribeKeyPairs",
"ec2:DescribeLicenses",
"ec2:DescribeNetworkAcls",
"ec2:DescribeNetworkInterfaceAttribute",
"ec2:DescribeNetworkInterfaces",
"ec2:DescribePlacementGroups",
"ec2:DescribeRegions",
"ec2:DescribeReservedInstances",
"ec2:DescribeReservedInstancesOfferings",
"ec2:DescribeRouteTables",
"ec2:DescribeSecurityGroups",
"ec2:DescribeSnapshotAttribute",
"ec2:DescribeSnapshots",
"ec2:DescribeSpotDatafeedSubscription",
"ec2:DescribeSpotInstanceRequests",
"ec2:DescribeSpotPriceHistory",
"ec2:DescribeSubnets",
"ec2:DescribeTags",
"ec2:DescribeVolumeAttribute",
"ec2:DescribeVolumes",
"ec2:DescribeVolumeStatus",
"ec2:DescribeVpcs",
"ec2:DescribeVpnConnections",
"ec2:DescribeVpnGateways",
"ec2:DetachVolume",
"ec2:EnableVolumeIO",
"ec2:GetConsoleOutput",
"ec2:GetPasswordData",
"ec2:ImportKeyPair",
"ec2:ModifyInstanceAttribute",
"ec2:ModifySnapshotAttribute",
"ec2:ModifyVolumeAttribute",
"ec2:MonitorInstances",
"ec2:RebootInstances",
"ec2:ReportInstanceStatus",
"ec2:ResetInstanceAttribute",
"ec2:ResetSnapshotAttribute",
```

```
          "ec2:RunInstances",
          "ec2:StartInstances",
          "ec2:StopInstances",
          "ec2:TerminateInstances",
          "ec2:UnmonitorInstances",
          "elasticloadbalancing:RegisterInstancesWithLoadBalancer"
       ],
       "Resource": "*"
    }
  ]
}
"@
New-IAMGroup -GroupName "DEVELOPERS"
Write-IAMGroupPolicy -GroupName "DEVELOPERS" -PolicyName "DEVELOPERS-
ManageInstances"
      -PolicyDocument $Policy
```

Fourth, the network administrators need full control over the VPC features. They also create
and configure load balancers and manage security groups. On the other hand, network
administrators do not need to create and destroy instances. Let's create a group for the
network administrators.

```
$Policy = @"
{
  "Statement": [
    {
      "Effect": "Allow",
      "Action": [
        "directconnect:*",
        "ec2:AllocateAddress",
        "ec2:AssociateAddress",
        "ec2:AssociateDhcpOptions",
        "ec2:AssociateRouteTable",
        "ec2:AttachInternetGateway",
        "ec2:AttachNetworkInterface",
        "ec2:AttachVpnGateway",
        "ec2:AuthorizeSecurityGroupEgress",
        "ec2:AuthorizeSecurityGroupIngress",
```

```
"ec2:CreateCustomerGateway",
"ec2:CreateDhcpOptions",
"ec2:CreateInternetGateway",
"ec2:CreateNetworkAcl",
"ec2:CreateNetworkAclEntry",
"ec2:CreateNetworkInterface",
"ec2:CreateRoute",
"ec2:CreateRouteTable",
"ec2:CreateSecurityGroup",
"ec2:CreateSubnet",
"ec2:CreateTags",
"ec2:CreateVpc",
"ec2:CreateVpnConnection",
"ec2:CreateVpnGateway",
"ec2:DeleteCustomerGateway",
"ec2:DeleteDhcpOptions",
"ec2:DeleteInternetGateway",
"ec2:DeleteNetworkAcl",
"ec2:DeleteNetworkAclEntry",
"ec2:DeleteNetworkInterface",
"ec2:DeleteRoute",
"ec2:DeleteRouteTable",
"ec2:DeleteSecurityGroup",
"ec2:DeleteSubnet",
"ec2:DeleteTags",
"ec2:DeleteVpc",
"ec2:DeleteVpnConnection",
"ec2:DeleteVpnGateway",
"ec2:DescribeAddresses",
"ec2:DescribeAvailabilityZones",
"ec2:DescribeBundleTasks",
"ec2:DescribeConversionTasks",
"ec2:DescribeCustomerGateways",
"ec2:DescribeDhcpOptions",
"ec2:DescribeExportTasks",
"ec2:DescribeImageAttribute",
"ec2:DescribeImages",
"ec2:DescribeInstanceAttribute",
```

```
"ec2:DescribeInstances",
"ec2:DescribeInstanceStatus",
"ec2:DescribeInternetGateways",
"ec2:DescribeKeyPairs",
"ec2:DescribeLicenses",
"ec2:DescribeNetworkAcls",
"ec2:DescribeNetworkInterfaceAttribute",
"ec2:DescribeNetworkInterfaces",
"ec2:DescribePlacementGroups",
"ec2:DescribeRegions",
"ec2:DescribeReservedInstances",
"ec2:DescribeReservedInstancesOfferings",
"ec2:DescribeRouteTables",
"ec2:DescribeSecurityGroups",
"ec2:DescribeSnapshotAttribute",
"ec2:DescribeSnapshots",
"ec2:DescribeSpotDatafeedSubscription",
"ec2:DescribeSpotInstanceRequests",
"ec2:DescribeSpotPriceHistory",
"ec2:DescribeSubnets",
"ec2:DescribeTags",
"ec2:DescribeVolumeAttribute",
"ec2:DescribeVolumes",
"ec2:DescribeVolumeStatus",
"ec2:DescribeVpcs",
"ec2:DescribeVpnConnections",
"ec2:DescribeVpnGateways",
"ec2:DetachInternetGateway",
"ec2:DetachNetworkInterface",
"ec2:DetachVpnGateway",
"ec2:DisassociateAddress",
"ec2:DisassociateRouteTable",
"ec2:GetConsoleOutput",
"ec2:GetPasswordData",
"ec2:ModifyNetworkInterfaceAttribute",
"ec2:MonitorInstances",
"ec2:ReleaseAddress",
"ec2:ReplaceNetworkAclAssociation",
```

```
        "ec2:ReplaceNetworkAclEntry",
        "ec2:ReplaceRoute",
        "ec2:ReplaceRouteTableAssociation",
        "ec2:ResetNetworkInterfaceAttribute",
        "ec2:RevokeSecurityGroupEgress",
        "ec2:RevokeSecurityGroupIngress",
        "ec2:UnmonitorInstances",
        "elasticloadbalancing:ConfigureHealthCheck",
        "elasticloadbalancing:CreateAppCookieStickinessPolicy",
        "elasticloadbalancing:CreateLBCookieStickinessPolicy",
        "elasticloadbalancing:CreateLoadBalancer",
        "elasticloadbalancing:CreateLoadBalancerListeners",
        "elasticloadbalancing:DeleteLoadBalancer",
        "elasticloadbalancing:DeleteLoadBalancerListeners",
        "elasticloadbalancing:DeleteLoadBalancerPolicy",
        "elasticloadbalancing:DeregisterInstancesFromLoadBalancer",
        "elasticloadbalancing:DescribeInstanceHealth",
        "elasticloadbalancing:DescribeLoadBalancers",
        "elasticloadbalancing:DisableAvailabilityZonesForLoadBalancer",
        "elasticloadbalancing:EnableAvailabilityZonesForLoadBalancer",
        "elasticloadbalancing:RegisterInstancesWithLoadBalancer",
        "elasticloadbalancing:SetLoadBalancerListenerSSLCertificate",
        "elasticloadbalancing:SetLoadBalancerPoliciesOfListener"
      ],
      "Resource": "*"
    }
  ]
}
"@
New-IAMGroup -GroupName "NETWORK_ADMINS"
Write-IAMGroupPolicy -GroupName "NETWORK_ADMINS" -PolicyName
     "NETWORK_ADMINS-ManageNetwork" -PolicyDocument $Policy
```

Fifth, system administrators need full control over the instances. They need all the access a developer has so they can support the developers. In addition they need to be able to create new Amazon Machine Images (AMIs). They do not need access to the networking features that are being supported by the network administrators. Let's create a group for the system administrators.

```
$Policy = @"
{
  "Statement": [
    {
      "Effect": "Allow",
      "Action": [
        "ec2:AttachVolume",
        "ec2:CancelConversionTask",
        "ec2:CancelExportTask",
        "ec2:CancelSpotInstanceRequests",
        "ec2:CopySnapshot",
        "ec2:CreateImage",
        "ec2:CreateInstanceExportTask",
        "ec2:CreateKeyPair",
        "ec2:CreatePlacementGroup",
        "ec2:CreateSnapshot",
        "ec2:CreateSpotDatafeedSubscription",
        "ec2:CreateTags",
        "ec2:CreateVolume",
        "ec2:DeleteKeyPair",
        "ec2:DeletePlacementGroup",
        "ec2:DeleteSnapshot",
        "ec2:DeleteSpotDatafeedSubscription",
        "ec2:DeleteTags",
        "ec2:DeleteVolume",
        "ec2:DeregisterImage",
        "ec2:DescribeAddresses",
        "ec2:DescribeAvailabilityZones",
        "ec2:DescribeBundleTasks",
        "ec2:DescribeConversionTasks",
        "ec2:DescribeCustomerGateways",
        "ec2:DescribeDhcpOptions",
        "ec2:DescribeExportTasks",
        "ec2:DescribeImageAttribute",
        "ec2:DescribeImages",
```

```
"ec2:DescribeInstanceAttribute",
"ec2:DescribeInstances",
"ec2:DescribeInstanceStatus",
"ec2:DescribeInternetGateways",
"ec2:DescribeKeyPairs",
"ec2:DescribeLicenses",
"ec2:DescribeNetworkAcls",
"ec2:DescribeNetworkInterfaceAttribute",
"ec2:DescribeNetworkInterfaces",
"ec2:DescribePlacementGroups",
"ec2:DescribeRegions",
"ec2:DescribeReservedInstances",
"ec2:DescribeReservedInstancesOfferings",
"ec2:DescribeRouteTables",
"ec2:DescribeSecurityGroups",
"ec2:DescribeSnapshotAttribute",
"ec2:DescribeSnapshots",
"ec2:DescribeSpotDatafeedSubscription",
"ec2:DescribeSpotInstanceRequests",
"ec2:DescribeSpotPriceHistory",
"ec2:DescribeSubnets",
"ec2:DescribeTags",
"ec2:DescribeVolumeAttribute",
"ec2:DescribeVolumes",
"ec2:DescribeVolumeStatus",
"ec2:DescribeVpcs",
"ec2:DescribeVpnConnections",
"ec2:DescribeVpnGateways",
"ec2:DetachVolume",
"ec2:EnableVolumeIO",
"ec2:GetConsoleOutput",
"ec2:GetPasswordData",
"ec2:ImportInstance",
"ec2:ImportKeyPair",
"ec2:ImportVolume",
```

```
            "ec2:ModifyImageAttribute",
            "ec2:ModifyInstanceAttribute",
            "ec2:ModifySnapshotAttribute",
            "ec2:ModifyVolumeAttribute",
            "ec2:MonitorInstances",
            "ec2:PurchaseReservedInstancesOffering",
            "ec2:RebootInstances",
            "ec2:RegisterImage",
            "ec2:ReportInstanceStatus",
            "ec2:RequestSpotInstances",
            "ec2:ResetImageAttribute",
            "ec2:ResetInstanceAttribute",
            "ec2:ResetSnapshotAttribute",
            "ec2:RunInstances",
            "ec2:StartInstances",
            "ec2:StopInstances",
            "ec2:TerminateInstances",
            "ec2:UnmonitorInstances"
        ],
        "Resource": "*"
    }
  ]
}
"@
New-IAMGroup -GroupName "SYS_ADMINS"
Write-IAMGroupPolicy -GroupName "SYS_ADMINS" -PolicyName "SYS_ADMINS-
ManageImages"
    -PolicyDocument $Policy
```

In this exercise we created a group for each of the teams that uses AWS at our fictitious company. Obviously you will need to tweak these groups to fit your company's needs, but I hope this will create a good framework to get you started. In the next exercise, we will grant access to billing and support to IAM users.

EXERCISE 9.2: DELEGATING ACCOUNT ACCESS TO IAM USERS

Back in Chapter 2, we discussed the difference between AWS account credentials and IAM users. Remember that the AWS account is the e-mail address you used to create your account. You almost never use this account, but there are a few times you need it. Two of these reasons are accessing your bill and getting support.

By default, you must log in using your AWS account credentials to see your bill or access support, but you can also grant access to IAM users. And, as you might expect, you can control exactly which users can access the billing and support features. Note that you have to pay extra for support.

You cannot enable IAM access to billing using PowerShell. You must sign into the AWS Management Console using your account credentials to enable it. The following steps show you how:

1. Sign into the console using the e-mail address and password you used to create your account.

2. Click your name on the menu bar at the top right of the screen.

3. Click My Account from the drop-down menu.

4. Scroll down until you see the section shown in Figure 9-1.

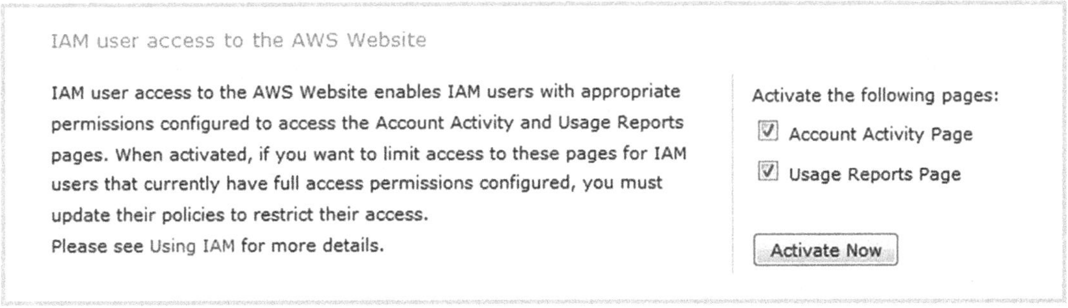

Figure 9-1. IAM access to the AWS web site

5. Select both the Account Activity Page check box and the Usage Reports Page check box. Click the Activate Now button.

Next we have to create an IAM policy granting access to IAM users. Interestingly, you cannot configure billing and support from the IAM wizard. You must create the policy manually. Luckily we know exactly how to do that. Let's create two groups: one for billing and one for support.

To create a group for billing, you allow access to `ViewBilling` and `ViewUsage`. Billing is the summary information and usage is the raw detail. Just like the last exercise, we will associate this policy with a new group called BILLING.

```
$Policy = @"
{
  "Statement": [
    {
      "Action": [
         "aws-portal:ViewBilling",
         "aws-portal:ViewUsage"
      ],
      "Effect": "Allow",
      "Resource": "*"
    }
  ]
}
"@

New-IAMGroup -GroupName "BILLING"
Write-IAMGroupPolicy -GroupName "BILLING"
      -PolicyName "BILLING-BillingAndUsage" -PolicyDocument $Policy
```

To create a group for support, we will create a policy that allows access to `support:*` and associate it with a new group called SUPPORT.

```
$Policy = @"
{
  "Statement": [
    {
      "Action": "support:*",
      "Effect": "Allow",
      "Resource": "*"
    }
  ]
}
"@
```

```
New-IAMGroup -GroupName "SUPPORT"
Write-IAMGroupPolicy -GroupName "SUPPORT"
    -PolicyName "SUPPORT-FullAccess" -PolicyDocument $Policy
```

Now, whenever you want to grant a user access to billing or support, you simply add the user to the appropriate group.

Summary

In this chapter, we saw how IAM provides unprecedented control over access. We learned to create users and manage their passwords and access keys. Then, we learned to create groups and manage membership. We also learned to create roles for EC2 instances.

Next we learned to create policies and saw that IAM offers the granularity to enable least privileged access control over all of the AWS services. In the exercises we created a collection of groups for common IT roles and enabled access to billing and support. This is a great start for creating an enterprise access policy.

In the next chapter, we will focus on Simple Storage Service (S3). S3 is a highly resilient data solution for storing files. This is the data store AWS uses to keep snapshots and RDS backups, but you can use it to store anything you want.

CHAPTER 10

Relational Database Service

Relational Database Service (RDS) is a service that makes it easy to create and manage a database in the cloud. RDS supports MySQL, MariaDB, PostgreSQL, Oracle, and SQL Server. While you could install and run any of these on an EC2 instance, RDS greatly simplifies the effort. RDS instances are managed by AWS, eliminating time-consuming activities, such as patching and backups, and allowing you to focus on your application.

In this chapter, we discuss the RDS architecture and learn to launch an SQL Server RDS instance. Next, we will learn to configure an RDS instance using parameters and options. Then, we will learn to manage backups and restores using both snapshots and point-in-time restores. We will also briefly cover Amazon Aurora in this chapter. Aurora is a MySQL- and PostgreSQL-compatible database optimized for the cloud.

In the exercises we will focus on securing an RDS instance running SQL Server. In the first exercise, we will enable SSL to encrypt the connection to SQL Server. In the second exercise, we will enable Transparent Database Encryption (TDE) to encrypt data and back up files stored on disk.

RDS Architecture

RDS is designed to be deployed in multiple availability zones for high availability. Therefore, your VPC must have subnets in at least two availability zones. Even if you choose to launch only a single stand-alone instance, you must have two subnets in different availability zones to use RDS.

AWS uses a DB Subnet Group to identify which subnets are reserved for RDS. You simply create two or more subnets in multiple availability zones and add them to the Subnet Group. In addition, we use VPC ACL and security groups to control access to the RDS instances.

© Brian Beach, Steven Armentrout, Rodney Bozo, Emmanuel Tsouris 2019
B. Beach et al., *Pro PowerShell for Amazon Web Services*, https://doi.org/10.1007/978-1-4842-4850-8_10

Figure 10-1 shows the basic configuration of a single instance RDS configuration. Later on we will deploy a highly available Multi-AZ configuration. Let's assume we have two web servers running on EC2 instances, and they will use an RDS SQL Server instance to store data. The RDS instance will be launched into one of the two subnets that make up the DB Subnet Group. Let's first configure the VPC.

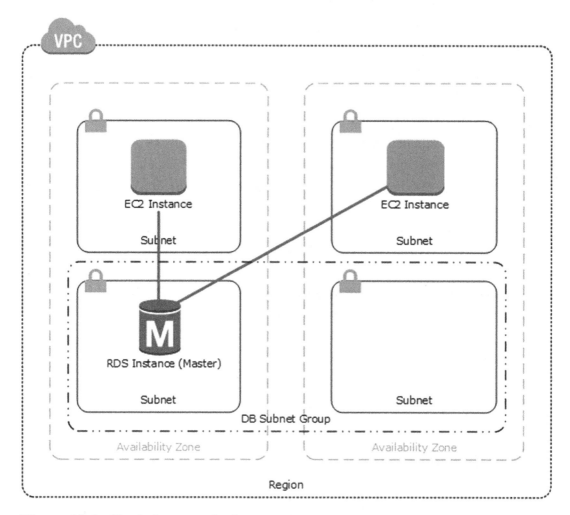

Figure 10-1. *Single instance deployment*

Creating a VPC

Before we can create a database instance, we need to configure a VPC for it to live in. Let's begin by creating a new VPC. If you prefer, you can add two new subnets to an existing VPC (e.g., the VPC created in Chapter 8). First, I create a new VPC using the 192.168.0.0 private IP range:

```
$VPC = New-EC2Vpc -CidrBlock '192.168.0.0/16'
```

Next, I create two subnets in our VPC. These are the subnets that the database instance will live in. Because we want to be able to support a multi-AZ deployment, I am using two different availability zones (this should all be familiar by now, but if you need to review, go back to Chapter 5); therefore

```
$AvailabilityZone1 = 'us-east-1a'
$AvailabilityZone2 = 'us-east-1b'
$PrimarySubnet = New-EC2Subnet -VpcId $VPC.VpcId -CidrBlock
'192.168.5.0/24' -AvailabilityZone $AvailabilityZone1
$StandbySubnet = New-EC2Subnet -VpcId $VPC.VpcId -CidrBlock
'192.168.6.0/24' -AvailabilityZone $AvailabilityZone2
```

Creating a Subnet Group

Now that we have our VPC configured, we need to describe how we plan to use it. We need to tell RDS which subnets to use for database instances. We do this using a subnet group. To create a subnet group, use the New-RDSSubnetGroup command. New-RDSSubnetGroup requires a name and description, along with a list of subnets to use. You will use the name rather than an ID to refer to this subnet group later. For example:

```
New-RDSDBSubnetGroup -DBSubnetGroupName 'MySubnetGroup'
-DBSubnetGroupDescription 'Pair of subnets for RDS' -SubnetIds
$PrimarySubnet.SubnetId, $StandbySubnet.SubnetId
```

Even if you do not plan to deploy a multi-AZ RDS instance, you must specify at least two subnets when creating a subnet group. In addition, the subnets must be in different availability zones.

Configuring Security Groups

The last thing we need is a security group. This security group is used to define which EC2 instances can connect to the RDS database instance. Let's create a new security group for the database and then allow traffic from EC2 instances in the default security group. First, we create a new security group for the RDS instance:

```
$RDSGroupId = New-EC2SecurityGroup –VpcId $VPC.VpcId -GroupName 'RDS'
-GroupDescription "RDS Instances"
```

Next, we get a reference to the default group. In this example I am going to allow any instance in the default group to access to our database instance. I am using filters to find the default group (if you need to review, see Chapter 6):

```
$VPCFilter = New-Object Amazon.EC2.Model.Filter
$VPCFilter.Name = 'vpc-id'
$VPCFilter.Value = $VPC.VpcId
$GroupFilter = New-Object Amazon.EC2.Model.Filter
$GroupFilter.Name = 'group-name'
$GroupFilter.Value = 'default'
$DefaultGroup = Get-EC2SecurityGroup -Filter $VPCFilter, $GroupFilter
$DefaultGroupPair = New-Object Amazon.EC2.Model.UserIdGroupPair
$DefaultGroupPair.GroupId = $DefaultGroup.GroupId
```

Then, we create a new rule allowing access on the default SQL Server port 1433 and specify the default group as the source:

```
$SQLServerRule = New-Object Amazon.EC2.Model.IpPermission
$SQLServerRule.IpProtocol='tcp'
$SQLServerRule.FromPort = 1433
$SQLServerRule.ToPort = 1433
$SQLServerRule.UserIdGroupPair = $DefaultGroupPair
Grant-EC2SecurityGroupIngress -GroupId $RDSGroupId -IpPermissions
$SQLServerRule
```

In addition, we are going to use MySQL in the Aurora example later in this chapter, so let's configure rules for MySQL as well:

```
$MySQLRule = New-Object Amazon.EC2.Model.IpPermission
$MySQLRule.IpProtocol='tcp'
$MySQLRule.FromPort = 3306
$MySQLRule.ToPort = 3306
$MySQLRule.UserIdGroupPair = $DefaultGroupPair
Grant-EC2SecurityGroupIngress -GroupId $RDSGroupId -IpPermissions
$MySQLRule
```

Now that we have our VPC configured, we are ready to launch a database instance. In the next section, we will create an SQL Server instance. We will start my launching a single-AZ database. Later in the chapter, we will examine a multi-AZ configuration for high availability.

Managing RDS Instances

Now that we have our VPC configured, we can begin working with RDS instances. Let's get started by launching a new SQL Server database on RDS.

Launching an Instance

To launch a new instance, we use the `New-RDSDBInstance` command. It takes a few minutes for a new instance to launch – especially using the micro instances – so let's jump right in and launch one. This is another one of those commands with a ton of options. While the new instance is launching, we can examine all of the optional parameters available.

Since you're reading a book on PowerShell, I assume you are most interested in SQL Server. Let's start with a stand-alone, single-AZ instance. This will not be highly available, but it will launch relatively quickly. To create a new stand-alone SQL Server instance, enter the following command:

```
New-RDSDBInstance -DBInstanceIdentifier 'SQLServer01' -Engine 'sqlserver-
ex' -AllocatedStorage 20 -DBInstanceClass 'db.t2.micro' -MasterUsername
'sa' -MasterUserPassword 'password' -DBSubnetGroupName 'MySubnetGroup'
-VpcSecurityGroupIds $GroupId
```

Note   Never use "password" as a password. Please choose something more
complex and novel.

The previous command includes the minimum set of the parameters required to
launch a database instance into a VPC, which are

- **DBInstanceIdentifier** is simply a unique name you will use to refer
  to the database instance later. Unlike the EC2 and VPC commands we
  have been using, RDS uses a name, called an identifier, rather than
  an ID.

- **Engine** defines which type of database you want to use. RDS supports
  multiple versions of MySQL, Oracle, and SQL Server. If you are not
  familiar with the various versions of each database, see the vendor's
  web site for details. The specific engine types are

  - **mysql** – There is only one version of MySQL that includes all
    options.

  - **mariadb** – There is only one version of MariaDB that includes all
    options.

  - **oracle-se1** – Oracle Standard Edition One.

  - **oracle-se2** – Oracle Standard Edition Two.

  - **oracle-se** – Oracle Standard Edition.

  - **oracle-ee** – Oracle Enterprise Edition.

  - **postgres** – There is only one version of PostgreSQL that includes
    all options.

  - **sqlserver-ex** – SQL Server Express.

  - **sqlserver-web** – SQL Server Web Express.

  - **sqlserver-se** – SQL Server Standard Edition.

  - **sqlserver-ee** – SQL Server Enterprise Edition.

- **AllocatedStorage** describes how much storage to allocate to the database. The maximum storage is 16TiB, and each engine type has a different minimum. See Table 10-1 for details of each database engine.

Table 10-1. *Storage by Engine Type*

Engine	Min Storage	Max Storage
mysql	5GB	16TiB
mariadb	5GB	16TiB
oracle-se1	10GB	16TiB
oracle-se2	10GB	16TiB
oracle-se	10GB	16TiB
oracle-ee	10GB	16TiB
postgres	5GB	16TiB
sqlserver-ee	200GB	16TiB
sqlserver-se	200GB	16TiB
sqlserver-ex	30GB	16TiB
sqlserver-web	30GB	16TiB

Note   The default storage type is magnetic disk which has a 1TiB storage limit and cannot be resized. I strongly suggest you override the default and use gp2 (SSD). See details under the Storage Type attribute later in this section.

- **DBInstanceClass** describes the hardware your database instance will use. This is similar to the EC2 instance types. SQL Server licensing limits which engines support instance types.

- **MasterUsername** and **MasterUserPassword** are used to log into the database. Note that the master user does not have system administrator rights to the database. Remember that you do not have access to the underlying operating system when using RDS.

Therefore, the master user has limited access. In addition, note that SQL Server only supports database accounts. Of course you can create additional database accounts after logging in.

- **DBSubnetGroupName** is the name of the subnet group we created earlier. RDS will launch the instance into one of the subnets in this group. If you want to specify which subnet to use, see the optional AvailabilityGroup parameter described later.

- **VpcSecurityGroupIds** is a list of security groups the RDS instance should be placed into.

In addition to the required parameters, New-RDSDBInstance also supports a bunch of optional parameters, which include

- **LicenseModel** allows you to choose from multiple software licensing models. Depending on the engine you are using, you can choose to bring your own license or have the cost of license included in with the hourly cost of the instance.

- **EngineVersion** defines the specific version of each database type. For example, RDS supports SQL Servers 2008, 2012, 2014, 2016, and 2017. If you omit this parameter, RDS will use the latest version. At the time I am writing this, the latest version of SQL Server is SQL Server 2017. If you want to list all of the supported engine versions, use the command Get-RDSDBEngineVersion | Format-Table.

- **AutoMinorVersionUpgrade** tells RDS to automatically apply minor updates. Updates are applied during the maintenance windows defined later. Major upgrades (e.g., SQL 2008 R2 to SQL 2012) are not supported. This option is enabled by default.

- **MultiAZ** specifies that you want to create both a primary and standby instance. The primary and standby will be launched into subnets in different availability zones as defined in the subnet group. (See the section on multi-AZ configuration later in this chapter.)

- **AvailabilityZone** specifies which availability zone to launch the instance into. In a VPC, RDS will use the subnet in the specified availability zone. You cannot specify availability zone if you are using the MultiAZ option.

- **StorageType** specifies the disk type to use. The options are standard, gp2, and io1. Note that standard (e.g., magnetic) is the default. I strongly suggest you use gp2.

- **IOPS** specifies the IO operations per second (IOPS) desired from the disk. This is similar to provisioned IOPS in EC2, and you pay a premium for this option just like EC2. RDS uses striping and can support 1000–30,000 IOPS.

- **StorageEncrypted** is a Boolean indicating the disk should be encrypted.

- **KmsKeyId** specifies which key to use for encryption.

- **PreferredMaintenanceWindow** defines a weekly outage window when Amazon can apply patches to the RDS instance. For example, you might specify sat:22:00-sat:23:00. If you omit this option, AWS will choose a random 30-minute window from an 8-hour block defined for each region. AWS will choose a time that is generally considered "off hours" for the region, but it is best to specify your own window.

- **PreferredBackupWindow** defines when the daily full backup is taken. For example, you might specify 23:00-24:00. The backup windows cannot overlap the maintenance window and must be a minimum of 30 minutes. (There is more detail on backup and recovery later in this chapter.)

- **BackupRetentionPeriod** defines how long to save backups. You can specify 0–8 days. The default is 1 day and specifying 0 days disables backup.

- **PubliclyAccessible** specifies that the instance will be assigned a public IP address and can be accessed from the Internet. In general this is a bad idea; I prefer to have a micro instance on the VPC that I can use for administration.

- **Port** allows you to change the default port for your database. Table 10-2 lists the default ports for each engine.

Table 10-2. *Default Port by Engine Type*

Engine	Default Port
MySQL/MariaDB	3306
Oracle	1521
PostgreSQL	5432
SQL Server	1433

- **DBParameterGroupName** allows you to alter engine parameters. For example, I will show you how to enable the Common Language Runtime (CLR) in the next section.

- **DBOptionGroupName** allows you to alter engine options. For example, I will show you how to enable Transparent Data Encryption (TDE) in the next section.

Wow, that was a lot of options to discuss. By now our instance should be running. You can use the Get-RDSDBInstance command to check on it. Check the DBInstanceStatus attribute. For example:

```
(Get-RDSDBInstance -DBInstanceIdentifier 'SQLServer01').DBInstanceStatus
```

It will take a while for the instance to start. Once it is running, you can get the endpoint address needed to connect to SQL Server. For example:

```
(Get-RDSDBInstance -DBInstanceIdentifier 'SQLServer01').Endpoint.Address
```

In my case this returned

```
sqlserver01.cz8cihropmwk.us-east-1.rds.amazonaws.com
```

You can now enter the address into SQL Server Management Studio to connect. Figure 10-2 shows an example.

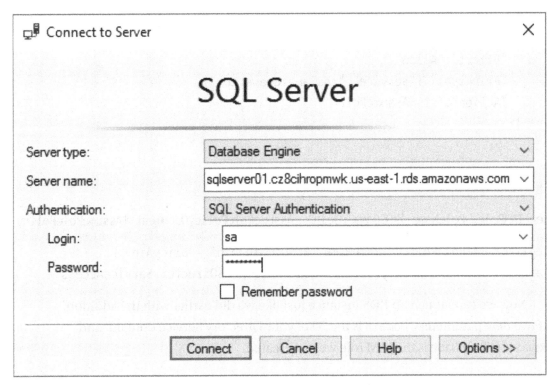

Figure 10-2. *Logging into an RDS with SQL Server Authentication*

Joining a Domain

You can optionally join your RDS instance to an Active Directory Domain using Directory Service. I'm not going to assume you already have Directory Service configured.

Note   RDS only supports the Microsoft Active Directory version of Directory Service. You cannot use Simple Active Directory or Active Directory Connector.

RDS is going to need permission to join the domain. There is a managed policy defined for RDS Directory Service Access, but you need to create an IAM role. Go back to Chapter 9 to review IAM roles.

```
$AssumeRolePolicy = @"
{
  "Version":"2008-10-17",
  "Statement":[
```

```
    {
      "Sid":"",
      "Effect":"Allow",
      "Principal":{"Service":"rds.amazonaws.com"},
      "Action":"sts:AssumeRole"
    }
  ]
}
"@
```

```
New-IAMRole -RoleName 'RDSDomainJoin' -AssumeRolePolicyDocument $AssumeRolePolicy
```

```
Register-IAMRolePolicy -RoleName 'RDSDomainJoin' -PolicyArn
'arn:aws:iam::aws:policy/service-role/AmazonRDSDirectoryServiceAccess'
```

Now we can launch an RDS instance just like we did earlier with the addition of two new parameters. Domain is the ID of your Directory Service domain, and DomainIAMRoleName is the IAM role we just created.

```
New-RDSDBInstance -DBInstanceIdentifier 'SQLServer02' -Engine 'sqlserver-
ex' -AllocatedStorage 20 -DBInstanceClass 'db.t2.micro' -MasterUsername
'sa' -MasterUserPassword 'password' -DBSubnetGroupName 'MySubnetGroup'
-VpcSecurityGroupIds $GroupId -Domain 'd-xxxxxxxxxx' -DomainIAMRoleName
'RDSDomainJoin'
```

Now you can log in with directory credentials, for example (Figure 10-3).

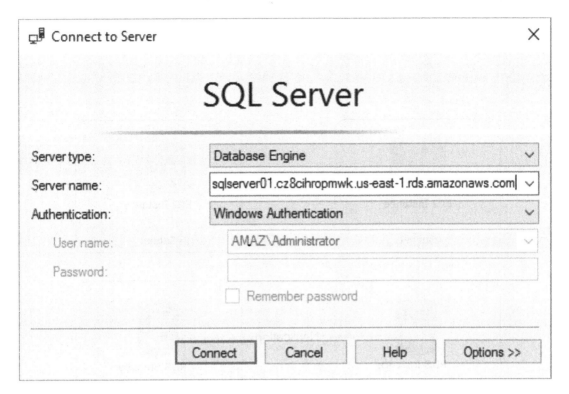

Figure 10-3. *Logging into an RDS with Windows Authentication*

All of the database we have launched so far have been single instance. Let's launch a highly available multi-AZ database next.

Multi-AZ Instances

RDS supports multi-AZ instances for high availability and durability. When you deploy a multi-AZ database, AWS deploys a primary instance in one AZ and a synchronous replica in another AZ (see Figure 10-4). All of the complexity is hidden from you, and the database appears to be one logical instance. If the primary database were to fail, RDS automatically fails over and updates the DNS entry so your application begins using the secondary without manual intervention.

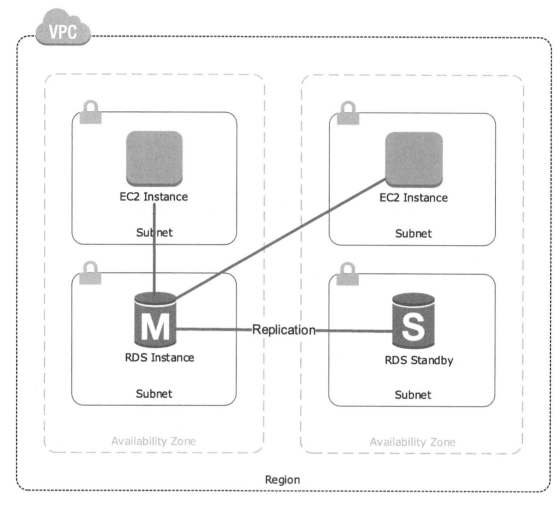

Figure 10-4. *Multi-AZ deployment*

Launching a multi-AZ instance is just like launching a stand-alone instance, except that we add the MultiAZ option. I am also going to override the default storage type to specify SSD disk. For example:

```
New-RDSDBInstance -DBInstanceIdentifier 'SQLServer03' -Engine 'sqlserver-
ex' -AllocatedStorage 20 -DBInstanceClass 'db.r4.large' -MasterUsername
'sa' -MasterUserPassword 'password' -DBSubnetGroupName 'MySubnetGroup'
-VpcSecurityGroupIds $GroupId -StorageType gp2 -MultiAZ $true
```

That is all there is to it! RDS takes care of the heavy lifting. All of the preceding options we discussed are supported, except for the `AvailabilityZone` parameter, on any of the commands that have it. You cannot choose which AZ the primary database runs in. RDS manages that behind the scenes.

Of course, we hope that we never need the standby instance, but we should plan for failure. It's also good to test your application and ensure if the failover works as expected. You can test the failover by running `Start-RDSDBClusterFailover`. For example:

```
Start-RDSDBClusterFailover -DBClusterIdentifier SQLServer03 -Force
```

In addition to replicating to a standby instance, RDS can also replicate to additional read replicas. Let's take a look in the next section.

Modifying an Instance

No sooner do you launch a new instance than you realize you need to change something. Many of the options we discussed in the last section can be modified after the RDS instance has been launched by using `Edit-RDSDBInstance`.

For example, let's assume we are running out of disk space and need to increase the volume size.

```
Edit-RDSDBInstance -DBInstanceIdentifier 'SQLServer03' -AllocatedStorage 30
-ApplyImmediately:$True
```

Notice that I have included the ApplyImmediately attribute. If I did not, the change would be applied during the next maintenance window. The following options can be altered using `Edit-RDSDBInstance`.

- `AllocatedStorage`
- `AllowMajorVersionUpgrade`
- `ApplyImmediately`
- `AutoMinorVersionUpgrade`
- `BackupRetentionPeriod`
- `DBInstanceClass`
- `DBParameterGroupName`

- DBSecurityGroups

- EngineVersion

- IOPS

- MasterUserPassword

- MultiAZ

- NewDBInstanceIdentifier

- OptionGroupName

- PreferredBackupWindow

- PreferredMaintenanceWindow

- VpcSecurityGroupIds

Notice that I can change the DBInstanceClass either scaling up or down. This allows me to resize my database when I need to. If you have a multi-AZ instance, RDS will perform this change without taking an outage. It will first resize the standby instance, then perform a failover, and finally resize the primary. Imagine we are approaching a busy period and want to scale up our db.r4.large to db.r4.xlarge.

```
Edit-RDSDBInstance -DBInstanceIdentifier 'SQLServer03' -DBInstanceClass
'db.r4.xlarge' -ApplyImmediately:$True
```

Note   Even with the graceful failover, active connections when the failover occurs will fail. Therefore, this is a modification best done without applying immediately.

As you can see, modifications are easy to make. You can also change database engine options. Will get to that shortly, but first let's look at how we delete a database.

Deleting an Instance

When you no longer need an instance, you can delete it using the
`Remove-RDSDBInstance` command. If you want to take a snapshot of the database before
deleting it, you can simply specify the identifier when you call remove. (I will explain
RDS snapshots later in the chapter.) The following command will delete the database we
created:

```
Remove-RDSDBInstance -DBInstanceIdentifier 'SQLServer03'
-FinalDBSnapshotIdentifier
    'SQLServer01-Final-Snapshot' -Force
```

If you don't need a backup of the instance, you can use the `SkipFinalSnapshot`
parameter to tell RDS not to back up the instance.

```
Remove-RDSDBInstance -DBInstanceIdentifier 'SQLServer03' -SkipFinalSnapshot
$true -Force
```

As you can see, RDS makes launching and managing a database instance really easy.
In the next section, we will discuss how to configure options specific to SQL Server.

Configuring a Database Engine

So far, all of the parameters we have configured are common to all of the database
engines. Obviously there are also engine-specific configuration options to choose from.
RDS breaks these into two categories: parameters and options. Let's spend a minute
looking at parameters and options specific to SQL Server.

Modifying Parameters

Parameters allow you to configure your database engine. RDS organizes parameters
into parameter groups for each engine type. For example, the default parameter group
for SQL Server Express is `default.sqlserver-ex-14.0`. You can get a list of parameter
groups using the `Get-RDSDBParameterGroup` command.

There are numerous parameters available for SQL Server, and not all parameters
are available on all SQL Server editions. For example, some options are only available
on the Enterprise Edition. To list the parameters available, use the `Get-RDSDBParameter`

command. For example, the following code will list the parameters specific to SQL Server Express:

```
Get-RDSDBParameter -DBParameterGroupName default.sqlserver-ex-14.0 |
    Format-Table ParameterName, Description, ParameterValue –AutoSize
```

If you want to customize the parameters, you can create your own parameter group using the New-RDSDBParameterGroup command. For example, let's assume you want to enable the Common Language Runtime (CLR) to support stored procedures written in .Net. Start by creating a new parameter group.

```
New-RDSDBParameterGroup -DBParameterGroupName 'SQL2017'
-DBParameterGroupFamily 'sqlserver-ex-14.0' -Description "SQL2017 with CLR
enabled"
```

Now you can configure the individual parameters in the group. Once again, we use a .Net object to describe the change and pass it to the EditRDSDBParameterGroup command. For example:

```
$Parameter = New-Object Amazon.RDS.Model.Parameter
$Parameter.ParameterName = 'clr enabled'
$Parameter.ParameterValue = 1
$Parameter.ApplyMethod = 'immediate'
Edit-RDSDBParameterGroup -DBParameterGroupName 'SQL2012' -Parameters
$Parameter
```

Note the ApplyMethod parameter. Some parameter changes can be applied immediately, while others require a reboot. You can check if a reboot is required by checking the apply type returned by Get-RDSDBParameter. If the apply type is static, then a reboot is required. If the apply type is dynamic, you can choose to apply the change immediately or after a reboot. To apply the change immediately, set the ApplyMethod parameter to immediate. To wait for the next reboot, set the ApplyMethod parameter to pending-reboot. You can force the reboot using the Restart-RDSDBInstance method.

Use the DBParameterGroupName of the New-RDSDBInstance or Edit-RDSDBInstance command to associate the new parameter group with an instance.

Modifying Options

Some database engines offer optional features that you can choose to enable. For example, SQL Server Enterprise Edition offers Transparent Data Encryption (TDE) or enabling backup and recovery to S3.

Option groups work a lot like parameter groups. First, you create a custom option group, and then you associate your instance with the custom group. Let's get started by creating a custom option group to enable S3 Backup on SQL 2017 Express Edition. This option allows RDS to read and write SQL backups (*.bac files) to S3. This is a great way to import data from an on-prem database to SQL Server. Let's begin by creating a new S3 bucket for our role.

```
New-S3Bucket -BucketName pwsh-book-rds-backup
```

RDS is going to need permission to S3 to read and write *.bac files. Therefore, we are going to need to create a new IAM role for RDS. If you need to review how IAM roles work go back to Chapter 9. Let's start by creating a new role and specifying the RDS service as the principal.

```
$AssumeRolePolicy = @"
{
  "Version":"2008-10-17",
  "Statement":[
    {
      "Sid":"",
      "Effect":"Allow",
      "Principal":{"Service":"rds.amazonaws.com"},
      "Action":"sts:AssumeRole"
    }
  ]
}
"@

$Role = New-IAMRole -RoleName 'RDSS3Backup' -AssumeRolePolicyDocument
$AssumeRolePolicy
```

Next we will define the permissions allowing RDS to access to the new S3 bucket we created earlier.

```
$AccessPolicy = @"
{
    "Version": "2012-10-17",
    "Statement":
    [
        {
        "Effect": "Allow",
        "Action":
            [
                "s3:ListBucket",
                "s3:GetBucketLocation"
            ],
        "Resource": "arn:aws:s3:::pwsh-book-rds-backup"
        },
        {
        "Effect": "Allow",
        "Action":
            [
                "s3:GetObjectMetaData",
                "s3:GetObject",
                "s3:PutObject",
                "s3:ListMultipartUploadParts",
                "s3:AbortMultipartUpload"
            ],
        "Resource": "arn:aws:s3:::pwsh-book-rds-backup/*"
        }
    ]
}
"@

Write-IAMRolePolicy -RoleName 'RDSS3Backup' -PolicyName 'RDSS3Backup-
S3Access' -PolicyDocument $AccessPolicy
```

Now we can create a new option group.

```
New-RDSOptionGroup -OptionGroupName 'SQL2017S3Backup'
-OptionGroupDescription "SQL2017 With S3 Backup Enabled" -EngineName
sqlserver-ex -MajorEngineVersion '14.00'
```

Similar to parameter groups, we use a .Net object to define the settings. In this case we enable the SQLSERVER_BACKUP_RESTORE option and specify the Arn of the new role we just created.

```
$OptionSetting = New-Object Amazon.RDS.Model.OptionSetting
$OptionSetting.Name = 'IAM_ROLE_ARN'
$OptionSetting.Value = $Role.Arn

$Option = New-Object Amazon.RDS.Model.OptionConfiguration
$Option.OptionName = 'SQLSERVER_BACKUP_RESTORE'
$Option.OptionSettings = $OptionSetting

Edit-RDSOptionGroup -OptionGroupName 'SQL2017S3Backup' -OptionsToInclude
$Option -ApplyImmediately $true
```

Now you can launch a new SQL Server instance and specify the option group.

```
New-RDSDBInstance -DBInstanceIdentifier 'SQLServer04' -Engine 'sqlserver-
ex' -AllocatedStorage 20 -DBInstanceClass 'db.t2.micro' -MasterUsername
'sa' -MasterUserPassword 'password' -DBSubnetGroupName 'MySubnetGroup'
-VpcSecurityGroupIds $GroupId -OptionGroupName 'SQL2017S3Backup'
```

Finally, we can restore a SQL Server backup from S3. Note that this command is run from SQL studio rather than the PowerShell command prompt.

```
exec msdb.dbo.rds_restore_database
        @restore_db_name='ledger',
        @s3_arn_to_restore_from='arn:aws:s3:::pwsh-book-rds-backup/ledger.
        bac';
```

Check out the exercises at the end of this chapter for an example of enabling Transparent Database Encryption (TDE). Next, let's look at native RDS backups using snapshots.

Working with Snapshots

RDS supports two types of backup: snapshots and point-in-time recovery. The backup windows and retention period we discussed earlier are related to point-in-time recovery and will be discussed in the next section. This section is about RDS snapshots, which are similar to EC2 snapshots.

A RDS snapshot creates a copy of the database just like an EC2 snapshot creates a copy of a volume. They are created manually using either the AWS Management Console or the API. You can create as many snapshots as you want, any time you want. Snapshots are retained until you manually delete them and are not affected by the retention period specified when you create the instance.

When you restore a RDS snapshot, AWS always creates a new instance. You cannot overwrite an existing database using a snapshot. This is just like restoring an EC2 snapshot, which, we already know, always creates a new volume rather than overwriting an existing one.

You can create a new snapshot using the New-RDSDBSnapshot command. This command simply takes the name of the instance you want to back up and a name to identify the snapshot.

```
New-RDSDBSnapshot -DBSnapshotIdentifier 'MySnapshot' -DBInstanceIdentifier
'SQLServer01'
```

It will take a few minutes to create the snapshot. You can check on the status of the snapshot using the Get-RDSDBSnapshot command. For example, to check on the snapshot we just created, use the following command:

```
Get-RDSDBSnapshot -DBSnapshotIdentifier 'MySnapshot'
```

The Get-RDSDBSnapshot command can also be used to list all the snapshots taken for a given database instance. The following command will list all snapshots taken of the SQLServer01 instance:

```
Get-RDSDBSnapshot -DBInstanceIdentifier 'SQLServer01'
```

You can restore a snapshot using the Restore-RDSDBInstanceFromDBSnapshot command. Remember that restoring a snapshot always creates a new instance. Therefore, we need to include a new identifier. In addition, we can change many of the parameters we specified when we created the database instance.

The following command will restore a RDS snapshot creating a new RDS instance called `SQLServer03`. The new instance will have a new DNS name, and you must update your application to use the new name.

```
Restore-RDSDBInstanceFromDBSnapshot -DBSnapshotIdentifier 'MySnapshot'
-DBInstanceIdentifier 'SQLServer01a' -DBSubnetGroupName 'MySubnetGroup'
```

Note that I had to specify the subnet group in the preceding command. In addition, I could have changed any of the following options. If you leave these options blank, RDS will use the settings that were present on the original instance rather than the defaults defined for `New-RDSDBInstance`:

- `DBInstanceClass`
- `Port`
- `AvailabilityZone`
- `MultiAZ`
- `PubliclyAccessible`
- `AutoMinorVersionUpgrade`
- `LicenseModel`
- `Engine` – Note that the engine must be compatible. You cannot restore an SQL Server snapshot to an Oracle database, but you can move from Standard Edition to Enterprise Edition.
- `IOPS`

Just like EC2, RDS snapshots can be copied to another region for an additional level of redundancy. You can copy a snapshot using `Copy-RDSDBSnapshot`. The copy is always initiated from the target region. Rather than specifying the source region as we did with EC2 snapshots, you must use the fully qualified Amazon Resource Name (ARN) for the source snapshot. The ARN uses the format

```
arn:aws:rds:<region>:<account number>:<type>:<identifier>
```

For example, the following command will copy our snapshot from the Northern Virginia region to the Northern California region:

```
Copy-RDSDBSnapshot -SourceDBSnapshotIdentifier 'arn:aws:rds:us-
east-1:123456789012:snapshot:MySnapshot' -TargetDBSnapshotIdentifier
'MySnapshot' -Region us-west-1
```

Obviously you are charged for the storage required to keep the snapshot. When you no longer need a snapshot, you can delete it using the `Remove-RDSDBSnapshot` command.

```
Remove-RDSDBSnapshot -DBSnapshotIdentifier 'MySnapshot' -Force
```

Snapshots are a great way to back up a database when you can plan for a specific risk. For example, you might take a snapshot before upgrading the application code. But, snapshots are not well suited for unexpected issues. For example, if a disk failed, you might not have taken a snapshot recently. For unexpected issues, we need to take regularly scheduled database backups. In the next section, we will examine how to do this.

Using Point-in-Time Restores

In addition to snapshots, RDS also supports database and transaction log backups. Using these backups, we can restore a database within a second of any point in time within the retention period. The best part is that AWS takes care of all the work required to create and maintain the backups.

When we launched the RDS instance at the beginning of this chapter, we accepted the default backup windows and retention period. Remember that the default retention period is 1 day. As long as the retention period is greater than zero, database backups are enabled. If backups are enabled, RDS will take a full backup of the database once a day during the backup window. In addition, it will back up the transaction log every 5 minutes.

These backups can be used to create a point-in-time restore. Point-in-time restores allow you to specify a specific time you want to restore, and since transaction log backups are taken every 5 minutes, you will never lose more than 5 minutes.

Now, I want to mention a few details specific to SQL Server. First, if your SQL Server has multiple databases, the individual databases will be restored to within 1 second of one another. Second, RDS does not support multi-AZ SQL Server instances. As a result, you should expect a momentary outage when the full backup is taken. This does not occur with multi-AZ databases because the backup is taken on the secondary instance.

Similar to snapshots, RDS point-in-time restores always create a new RDS instance. You cannot overwrite an existing instance. Before restoring an instance, you should check when the last transaction log backup was taken and how many days the backups are retained. You can restore to any point within this period. For example, to check the time of the last transaction log backup and retention period of our SQL database, use the following code:

```
$DBInstance = Get-RDSDBInstance -DBInstanceIdentifier 'SQLServer01'
$DBInstance.LatestRestorableTime
$DBInstance.BackupRetentionPeriod
```

The output of this command, shown as follows, indicates that you can restore to any point within a 1-day window between November 4 at 5:22 p.m. and November 5 at 5:22 p.m.

```
Tuesday, November 5, 2013 5:22:42 PM
1
```

We can use the `Restore-RDSDBInstanceToPointInTime` command to create a new RDS instance restored to any point within this range. For example, to restore to November 5, 2013, at 11:15 a.m., use the following command. This is almost identical to the `Restore-RDSDBInstanceFromDBSnapshot` command except that I am specifying a time and day to restore to. Note that RDS expects the time in UTC.

```
Restore-RDSDBInstanceToPointInTime -SourceDBInstanceIdentifier 'SQLServer01'
    -TargetDBInstanceIdentifier 'SQLServer03' -DBSubnetGroupName 'MySubnetGroup'
    -RestoreTime (Get-date('2013-11-05T11:15:00')).ToUniversalTime()
```

If you omit the `RestoreTime` parameter, RDS will restore to the latest time possible. For example:

```
Restore-RDSDBInstanceToPointInTime -SourceDBInstanceIdentifier 'SQLServer01'
    -TargetDBInstanceIdentifier 'SQLServer04'
    -DBSubnetGroupName 'MySubnetGroup' -UseLatestRestorableTime $true
```

Just like when restoring a snapshot , you are creating a new instance, and you can specify many of the options that were available when we created the original instance, including

- `DBInstanceClass`
- `Port`
- `DBSubnetGroupName`
- `AvailabilityZone`
- `MultiAZ`
- `PubliclyAccessible`
- `AutoMinorVersionUpgrade`
- `LicenseModel`
- `Engine`
- `IOPS`

Unlike snapshots, there is no need to delete database backup files. They are automatically deleted after the retention period. This is the benefit of the RDS platform. AWS takes care of the maintenance for you. In addition, you cannot copy backups to another region.

In the next section, we discuss how to keep track of our RDS instances using tags and how to monitor our instances using events and logs.

Working with Tags, Events, and Logs

As your inventory of servers grows, it will become more and more difficult to keep track of everything. It is really important that you have a strategy for organizing and monitoring your resources. RDS offers tags to help categorize everything and events and logs for monitoring. Let's look at each.

Tags

We saw the power of tags with EC2. The same holds true for RDS. You can use tags to include metadata describing your RDS resources. For example, you might want to tag an instance with the department that owns it so you can create a chargeback report and know whom to contact if something goes wrong.

Creating a tag is similar to EC2. You begin by creating a .Net object used to describe the tag. Then you add a key and value. For example, the following code will create a tag specifying the department=marketing.

```
$Tag = New-Object('Amazon.RDS.Model.Tag')
$Tag.Key = 'Department'
$Tag.Value = 'Marketing'
```

To add the tag to a RDS resource, you use the Add-RDSTagsToResource command. Remember that RDS uses names rather than ids to identify resources. Different resource types can have the same name. For example, I can name both an instance and snapshot "database1." As a result, we have to use the fully qualified Amazon Resource Name (ARN) to uniquely identify a resource. Remember that ARNs follow the format

```
arn:aws:rds:<region>:<account number>:<type>:<identifier>
```

Therefore, to add the department=marketing tag to our instance, use

```
Add-RDSTagsToResource -ResourceName 'arn:aws:rds:us-east-
1:123456789012:db:SQLServer01' -Tags $Tag
```

And, to add the department=marketing tag to our snapshot, use

```
Add-RDSTagsToResource -ResourceName 'arn:aws:rds:us-east-1:123456789012:
snapshot:MySnapshot'-Tags $Tag
```

You can retrieve the tags using the Get-RDSTagForResoure command. For example:

```
Get-RDSTagForResource -ResourceName 'arn:aws:rds:us-east-
1:123456789012:db:SQLServer01'
```

You can also remove a tag using the `Remove-RDSTagsFromResource` command. For example:

```
Remove-RDSTagFromResource -ResourceName 'arn:aws:rds:us-east-
1:123456789012:db:SQLServer01'
    -TagKeys 'Name' -Force
```

Tags are a great way to organize RDS resources. In the next section, we will look at using RDS events to monitor our instances.

Events

It is important that you always know what is going on in the cloud. Events allow us to monitor our RDS instances and receive notifications from SNS when specific events occur. For example, you might want to be notified when the disk is filling up.

To get a list of all events, we use the `Get-RDSEvent` command. For example:

```
Get-RDSEvent
```

You can control how many events are returned using the `Duration` and `MaxRecords` parameters. For example, the following command will return the first 25 events that occurred in the last 15 minutes:

```
Get-RDSEvent -Duration 15 -MaxRecords 25
```

You can also specify a specific range using `StartTime` and `EndTime`, but events are only stored for 15 days. For example:

```
Get-RDSEvent -StartTime '2013-11-01' -EndTime '2013-11-15'
```

RDS captures many event types. Events are organized into source types that correspond to the RDS resource types and include `db-instance`, `db-security-group`, `db-parameter-group`, and `db-snapshot`. Events are further organized into categories. To get a list of categories, use the `Get-RDSEventCategories` command. For example, to get the categories available for an RDS instance

```
(Get-RDSEventCategories -SourceType 'db-instance').EventCategories
```

You can use the parameters of the `Get-RDSEvent` command to limit the events returned. For example, to only retrieve events for the SQL instances we created earlier, use the following command:

```
Get-RDSEvent -SourceType 'db-instance' -SourceIdentifier 'SQLServer01'
```

Similarly you can filter for specific event categories. For example, the following command will return all information about the backup of any RDS instance:

```
Get-RDSEvent -SourceType 'db-instance' -EventCategories 'backup'
```

Of course, you can combine these in various combinations to return the events you want. The following command will return all of the backup events for a specific instance:

```
Get-RDSEvent -SourceType 'db-instance' -SourceIdentifier 'SQLServer01'
-EventCategories 'backup'
```

Being able to query events is great, but we cannot expect someone to sit in front of PowerShell all day looking for issues. We really want a more proactive solution. Luckily RDS allows us to subscribe to events using Simple Notification Service (SNS) with the `New-RDSEventSubscription` command.

For example, let's assume we want to know whenever a failure occurs or the disk space is getting low. More specifically, we want to receive a notification via e-mail so we can respond quickly. First we need to create an SNS topic and e-mail notification. This is exactly what we did in Chapter 8, for example:

```
$Topic = New-SNSTopic -Name 'RDSTopic'
Connect-SNSNotification -TopicArn $Topic -Protocol 'email' -Endpoint
'alerts@brianbeach.com'
```

Now we can create a RDS subscription. The RDS subscription will publish a notification to the SNS topic we just created whenever a new RDS event occurs that matches the criteria we specify. To create the subscription, we use the New-RDSEventSubscription command. For example, the following command will subscribe to all failure and low-storage events and send a notification to our SNS topic:

```
New-RDSEventSubscription -SubscriptionName 'MyRDSSubscription'
    -SnsTopicArn 'arn:aws:sns:us-east-1:123456789012:RDSTopic'
    -SourceType 'db-instance' -EventCategories 'failure', 'low storage'
```

We can also subscribe to events from specific sources. For example, you might have both development and production RDS instances in the same account. You don't want to get a notification in the middle of the night if a development instance fails, so you only set up notifications for the production instances. The following example creates a subscription for a specific instance, SQLServer01:

```
New-RDSEventSubscription -SubscriptionName 'MyRDSSubscription2'
    -SnsTopicArn 'arn:aws:sns:us-east-1:123456789012:RDSTopic'
    -SourceType 'db-instance' -SourceIds 'sqlserver01'
```

Caution   The source ID in the previous example is all lowercase. Your source ID must be lowercase or you will get an error.

As our application changes over time, you may want to add or remove instances from the subscription. You can do this using the Add-RDSSourceIdentifierToSubscripti on and Remove-RDSSourceIdentifierFromSubscription commands. The following two examples add and then remove an instance from the subscription:

```
Add-RDSSourceIdentifierToSubscription -SubscriptionName 'MyRDSSubscription2'
    -SourceIdentifier 'SQLServer03'
Remove-RDSSourceIdentifierFromSubscription -SubscriptionName
'MyRDSSubscription2'
    -SourceIdentifier 'SQLServer03' –Force
```

Finally, you may want to delete a subscription altogether and stop receiving notifications. You can do so using the Remove-RDSEventSubscription command. For example:

```
Remove-RDSEventSubscription  -SubscriptionName 'MyRDSSubscription' –Force
```

Events are a great way to monitor your RDS instances, but you will likely need more detail to debug a failure when it occurs. In the next section, we discuss how to retrieve logs from the database engine.

Logs

With RDS you do not have access to the operating system and therefore cannot access the file system. This means that you cannot see the detailed logs produced by the database engine. In order to access the logs, you need to use an API call.

To list the log files available on the instance, you use the `Get-RDSDBLogFiles` command. This command will list the log files available on the server. For example:

```
Get-RDSDBLogFiles -DBInstanceIdentifier 'SQLServer01'
```

You can also use the `FilenameContains` parameter to find specific files. For example, to find the error log on an SQL Server, use the following command. Note that the file name is case sensitive.

```
Get-RDSDBLogFiles -DBInstanceIdentifier 'SQLServer01' -FilenameContains
'ERROR'
```

Once you know which file you are looking for, you can download the contents using the `Get-RDSDBLogFilePortion` command. For example, to read the error log on our SQL instance, use the following command:

```
$Log = Get-RDSDBLogFilePortion -DBInstanceIdentifier 'SQLServer01'
-LogFileName 'log/ERROR'
$Log.LogFileData
```

As you can see, RDS gives us all the tools we need to manage and monitor our database instance. In the next section, we will briefly discuss Amazon Aurora.

Amazon Aurora

Amazon Aurora is a cloud native database engine that supports both MySQL and PostgreSQL. According to Amazon, Aurora is up to five times faster than MySQL and three times faster than PostgreSQL. To achieve this, Aurora using a different from the RDS databases we have been discussing so far (Figure 10-5).

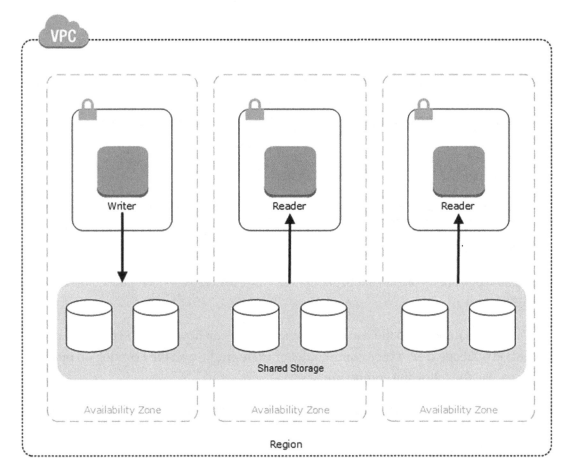

Figure 10-5. *Amazon Aurora Architecture*

Aurora is built on a cloud native shared storage solution that is replicated across three availability zones. This storage solution can scale up to 64TB per database. That's four times the size of traditional RDS databases. In addition, you only pay for storage you are using rather than the storage you provision.

Rather than replicate data between a primary and secondary instance like other RDS databases, Aurora allows you to add up to 15 read replicas to a cluster that share the same storage. If the writer node fails, any of the read replicas can be promoted.

Let's start by creating a new cluster. This is very similar to launching a new RDS database. However, you may notice that I am not specifying an instance size. That is because the cluster only creates the underlying storage, and you add database instances separately.

```
New-RDSDBCluster -DBClusterIdentifier aurora01 -Engine aurora-mysql
-MasterUsername 'sa' -MasterUserPassword 'password' -DBSubnetGroupName
mysubnetgroup -VpcSecurityGroupIds $GroupId
```

Now let's add a database to the cluster. This first instance will become the writer node. This is the node that handles all CRUD operations.

```
New-RDSDBInstance -DBClusterIdentifier aurora01 -DBInstanceIdentifier
aurora01a -Engine aurora-mysql -DBInstanceClass 'db.r4.large'
```

Next, we can add read replicas to the cluster. You can spread read operations over many read replicas. In addition, this instance will be promoted if the writer fails.

```
New-RDSDBInstance -DBClusterIdentifier aurora01 -DBInstanceIdentifier
aurora01b -Engine aurora-mysql -DBInstanceClass 'db.r4.large'
```

If you want to control which instance is promoted on failure of the writer, you can specify a PromotionTier. By default, instances are added as tier 1.

```
New-RDSDBInstance -DBClusterIdentifier aurora01 -DBInstanceIdentifier
aurora01c -Engine aurora-mysql -DBInstanceClass 'db.r4.large'
-PromotionTier 2
```

If we describe the cluster, you will notice that we have three instances. aurora01a is the writer instance. In addition, aurora01b has a higher tier and will be promoted before aurora01c if the writer fails.

```
(Get-RDSDBCluster -DBClusterIdentifier aurora01).DBClusterMembers

DBClusterParameterGroupStatus DBInstanceIdentifier IsClusterWriter
PromotionTier
----------------------------- -------------------- ---------------  --------
in-sync                       aurora01a            True             1
in-sync                       aurora01b            False            1
in-sync                       aurora01c            False            2
```

The `Endpoint` attribute will always return the IP address for the writer instance. This is always the same IP, assuming the writer has not failed. If you run the following command a few times, you will keep getting the same IP address which is the IP address of the `aurora01a` instance:

```
Resolve-DnsName (Get-RDSDBCluster -DBClusterIdentifier aurora01).Endpoint
```

`ReaderEnpoint`, on the other hand, will load balance across the two reader nodes. If you run this command a few times, you notice that you randomly get one of the two reader IP addresses. Of course you can still send read requests to the writer node; however, it's better to distribute your load across all the nodes in the cluster.

```
Resolve-DnsName (Get-RDSDBCluster -DBClusterIdentifier aurora01).
ReaderEndpoint
```

As you can see, RDS and Aurora offer everything you need to build a robust database platform without having to worry about the day-to-day details of system administration and backup. Let's wrap up this chapter with two exercises focused on securing SQL Server. The first will enable SSL to protect your connection and the second will enable Transparent Data Encryption.

EXERCISE 10.1: SQL SERVER AND SSL ENCRYPTION

It is always a good practice to encrypt the connection between your client and server. It is common to do so between the user and a web server, but less common between the web server and database. SQL Server supports encrypting the connection using SSL.

You can enable SSL when using an SQL Server RDS instance. All RDS instances include a self-signed certificate. Of course, your client machine will not trust the self-signed certificate until we import the public key into the trusted store. Let's build a script to do so.

You can download the public key from `https://rds.amazonaws.com/doc/rds-ssl-ca-cert.pem`. Let's use PowerShell to save a copy of the key on our client machine. This command must be run on the client machine.

```
Invoke-WebRequest 'https://rds.amazonaws.com/doc/rds-ssl-ca-cert.pem'
    -OutFile "$env:TEMP\rds-ssl-ca-cert.pem"
```

Next, we can use PowerShell to import the certificate into our trusted store. Note that you must run PowerShell as an administrator on our client machine to complete this step.

```
Import-Certificate -FilePath "$env:TEMP\rds-ssl-ca-cert.pem"
    -CertStoreLocation 'Cert:\LocalMachine\authRoot' -Confirm:$false
```

Finally, we should clean up the temporary copy of the certificate.

```
Remove-Item "$env:TEMP\rds-ssl-ca-cert.pem"
```

That's all there is to it. All you have to do to enable encryption is add two parameters to the connection string: encrypt=true and TrustServerCertificate=true. For example:

```
Server=sqlserver01.cz8cihropmwk.us-east-1.rds.amazonaws.
com;Database=myDataBase;
    User Id=sa;Password=password;encrypt=true;TrustServerCertificate=true"
```

Encrypting your database connection is a simple way to add an extra layer of security. In the next example, I will show you how to encrypt the data that is stored on disk using TDE.

EXERCISE 10.2: SQL SERVER TOTAL DATABASE ENCRYPTION

Earlier in this chapter, we talked about option groups, and I showed you how to create an option group that enables SQL Server Transparent Data Encryption (TDE). In this exercise, we build on that example to fully configure SQL TDE in a new instance. We will create an option group that enables TDE, launch a RDS instance that uses the new option group, create a new database on the RDS instance, and encrypt the new database.

First, we need to accept a few parameters as input to our script. These should all look familiar; they are all the parameters that will be passed to New-RDSDBInstance. Notice that the default engine is SQL Server Enterprise Edition. Remember that TDE is only supported on the Enterprise Edition of SQL Server. In addition, notice that the default instance class is small and I have allocated 200GB of disk. These are the minimum values for SQL Server Enterprise Edition.

```
param(
    [parameter(mandatory=$true)][string]$DBInstanceIdentifier,
    [parameter(mandatory=$false)][string]$DBInstanceClass = 'db.m1.small',
    [parameter(mandatory=$false)][string]$Engine = 'sqlserver-ee',
    [parameter(mandatory=$false)][string]$AllocatedStorage = 200,
```

```
    [parameter(mandatory=$true)][string]$MasterUsername,
    [parameter(mandatory=$true)][string]$MasterUserPassword,
    [parameter(mandatory=$true)][string]$DBSubnetGroupName,
    [parameter(mandatory=$true)][string]$VpcSecurityGroupIds
)
```

Next, we create the new option group just like I did earlier in this chapter. In the following
example, I first check if the option group already exists and, if not, create a new group.

```
Try {
    $OptionGroup = Get-RDSOptionGroup -OptionGroupName 'SQL2012TDE'
}
Catch [Amazon.RDS.Model.OptionGroupNotFoundException]{
    $OptionGroup = New-RDSOptionGroup -OptionGroupName 'SQL2012TDE'
    -OptionGroupDescription "SQL2012 with TDE"
        -EngineName sqlserver-ee -MajorEngineVersion '11.00'
    $Option = New-Object Amazon.RDS.Model.OptionConfiguration
    $Option.OptionName = 'TDE'
    Edit-RDSOptionGroup -OptionGroupName 'SQL2012TDE' -OptionsToInclude $Option
    -ApplyImmediately $true
}
```

Now that the option group has been created, we can launch a new instance using the
parameters passed into the script.

```
New-RDSDBInstance -DBInstanceIdentifier $DBInstanceIdentifier -Engine $Engine
    -AllocatedStorage $AllocatedStorage
    -DBInstanceClass $DBInstanceClass -MasterUsername $MasterUsername
    -MasterUserPassword $MasterUserPassword
    -DBSubnetGroupName $DBSubnetGroupName -VpcSecurityGroupIds
     $VpcSecurityGroupIds
    -OptionGroupName 'SQL2012TDE'
```

It will take a while for the instance to start. Let's add a while loop that will wait for it.

```
While ($Instance.DBInstanceStatus -ne 'available') {$Instance = Get-
RDSDBInstance $DBInstanceIdentifier; Write-Host "Waiting for RDS
instance to launch.";

    Start-Sleep -s 60}
```

Once it's done, we can get the address and report it back to the user so he or she can log into SQL Server and finish the configuration.

```
$Instance = (Get-RDSDBInstance -DBInstanceIdentifier 'SQLServer01').Endpoint.
Address
Write-Host "The RDS instance $DBInstanceIdentifier is ready. The address is
$Address."
```

At this point TDE is enabled on the instance, but the individual databases are not encrypted. TDE allows you to selectively encrypt individual databases on an instance. Each database has its own encryption keys, and the individual encryption keys are protected by the server's certificate, which was created by Amazon when we enabled TDE.

We can use SQL scripts to create and encrypt a database. The remaining scripts in this exercise are SQL scripts that should be run in SQL Management Studio against the RDS instance.

Let's begin getting the name of the server certificate. Make reference of the name that is returned; you will need it later.

```
USE [master]
SELECT TOP 1 Name FROM sys.certificates WHERE name LIKE 'RDSTDECertificate%'
```

Next, we create a new database that we will encrypt. If you already have a database on the instance, you can just skip this step.

```
USE [master]
CREATE DATABASE MyDatabase
```

Then, we create a new encryption key for our database. Replace <<PUT_NAME_HERE>> with the name of the certificate you found earlier.

```
Use [MyDatabase]
CREATE DATABASE ENCRYPTION KEY WITH ALGORITHM = AES_128 ENCRYPTION BY SERVER
CERTIFICATE
    <<PUT_NAME_HERE>>
```

Finally, you can alter the database to enable encryption.

```
ALTER DATABASE MyDatabase SET ENCRYPTION ON
```

That's all there is to it. With TDE enabled, everything SQL writes to disk is encrypted including data files and backups.

Summary

RDS provides a developer everything that he or she needs to launch a database server without the burden of managing it. AWS will take care of the maintenance, backups, replication, and monitoring, so you can concentrate on your application.

We have seen how to launch and configure SQL Server instances. We learned how to restore instances from snapshots and perform point-in-time recovery from database backups. We also learned to create scalable, highly available architectures using multi-AZ instances and read replicas. Finally, we learned how to secure SQL Server using SSL to encrypt the connection and TDE to encrypt files on disk.

In the next chapter, we will focus on Simple Storage Service (S3). S3 is a highly resilient data solution for storing files. This is the data store AWS uses to keep snapshots and RDS backups, but you can use it to store anything you want.

## CHAPTER 11

Simple Storage Service

Simple Storage Service (S3) is used to store in the cloud. S3 can scale to enormous size. You can store an unlimited number of objects and access them from anywhere. You access S3 over HTTP or HTTPS using a REST API.

S3 provides 99.999999999% (that's 11 nines) durability by storing data multiple times across multiple availability zones within a region. A single object can be anywhere from 1 byte to 5 terabytes and you can store an unlimited number of objects.

Unlike Elastic Block Storage, you cannot attach S3 storage to an instance. All access is through the REST API. In this chapter, I will show you how to create and manage buckets, which are used to store data. I will also show you how to upload and download objects and manage storage options.

Next, we will discuss versioning and object life cycle. I will go on to show you how to save money by using Glacier cold storage. Finally, we will talk about security, including encryption at rest and enabling public access to objects in your bucket.

This chapter has two exercises. The first will show you how to host a static web site in S3. We will deploy and configure a web site using PowerShell. The second will discuss how to create pre-signed URLs that allow a user to access data for a specific period of time. At the end of that period, the URL expires, and the user can no longer access the content. Let's get started.

Managing Buckets

S3 stores objects in buckets. It may help to think of a bucket as a drive in a file system. Like a drive, a bucket contains files and the files can be organized into a hierarchy of folders. But that is where the analogy ends. Unlike a drive, a bucket is infinitely large and can store an unlimited number of objects. Buckets are also accessible anywhere in the world using HTTP or HTTPS.

© Brian Beach, Steven Armentrout, Rodney Bozo, Emmanuel Tsouris 2019
B. Beach et al., *Pro PowerShell for Amazon Web Services*, https://doi.org/10.1007/978-1-4842-4850-8_11

Each account can have up to 100 buckets, and each bucket must have a name that is unique across all accounts and regions. To create a bucket, use the New-S3Bucket command. For example, to create a bucket named **pwsh-book-exercises**, I call New-S3Bucket and supply the name.

```
New-S3Bucket -BucketName pwsh-book-exercises
```

Note   Your bucket name must be unique and comply with DNS naming conventions. The name can include 3–63 characters. It must start with a number or letter and cannot include uppercase characters or underscore.

Each bucket is created in a region and data is replicated across multiple availability zones in that region. If you want to specify a region, other than the default region you specified in Chapter 2, you can add a region attribute.

```
New-S3Bucket -BucketName pwsh-book-exercises-02 -Region us-west-2
```

As you might expect, there is a Get-S3Bucket command that can be used to list the buckets in your account. When called without any parameters, it lists all the buckets in your account.

```
Get-S3Bucket
```

If you want to get information about a specific bucket, you can call Get-S3Bucket with the BucketName parameter.

```
Get-S3Bucket -BucketName pwsh-book-exercises
```

If you just want to verify that a bucket exists, there is a separate command, Test-S3Bucket, that will return true if the bucket exists and false if it does not. Of course, you can always use Get-S3Bucket and compare the result to null, but Test-S3Bucket is more convenient.

```
Test-S3Bucket -BucketName pwsh-book-exercises
```

The Get-S3Bucket command returns very little information. It only includes the name and creation date of the bucket. If you want to know where the bucket is located, use the Get-S3BucketLocation command.

```
Get-S3BucketLocation -BucketName pwsh-book-exercises
```

Note   Buckets in the Northern Virginia region will return NULL. This is expected behavior. The Northern Virginia region was the first, and since then AWS has standardized the design. Buckets in all other regions will return the region name (e.g., us-west-1).

Finally, if you want to delete a bucket, you can use the `Remove-S3Bucket` command. The bucket must be empty before you can delete it or you can add the `-DeleteObjects` parameter to delete the contents of a bucket. Of course, you also need to include the `Force` option to avoid being prompted for confirmation.

```
Remove-S3Bucket -BucketName pwsh-book-exercises -Force
```

Enough about buckets. Let's put some data in there already. In the next section, we learn how to read and write objects.

Managing Objects

Now that we have a bucket created, we can start to upload files using the `Write-S3Object` command. For example, the following command uploads the local file HelloWorld.txt to the pwsh-book-exercises bucket and saves it as HelloWorld.txt.

```
Write-S3Object -BucketName pwsh-book-exercises -Key 'HelloWorld.txt' -File 'HelloWorld.txt'
```

You can also use the `Content` parameter to upload data without storing it on the local file system first. For example:

```
Write-S3Object -BucketName pwsh-book-exercises -Key 'HelloWorld.txt' -Content "Hello World!!!"
```

If you want to list the objects in a bucket, you use the `Get-S3Object` command. `Get-S3Object` does not return the objects, but rather lists the objects and a few attributes. This is equivalent of a `dir` in Windows or a `ls` on Linux.

```
Get-S3Object -BucketName pwsh-book-exercises
```

You can also use Get-S3Object to discover information about a specific object. For example, the following command will list information about the HelloWorld.txt file we uploaded earlier.

```
Get-S3Object -BucketName pwsh-book-exercises -Key 'HelloWorld.txt'
```

When you are ready to download a file, you use the Read-S3Object command. Unlike Write-S3Object, Read-S3Object does not support the content parameter and must be used to write to a file on the local file system. For example, the following command will download the HelloWorld.txt file and overwrite the original copy.

```
Read-S3Object -BucketName pwsh-book-exercises -Key 'HelloWorld.txt' -File
'HelloWorld.txt'
```

Obviously we can create a copy of an object by downloading and uploading it with a different name. But, remember that we pay for the bandwidth used. Therefore, it is more efficient to use the Copy-S3Object to create a copy on the server without transferring the data. For example:

```
Copy-S3Object -BucketName pwsh-book-exercises -Key 'HelloWorld.txt'
-DestinationKey 'HelloWorldCopy.txt'
```

We can also use Copy-S3Object to copy an object from one bucket to another. These buckets can even be in different regions allowing you to move data directly from one region to another without making a local copy.

```
Copy-S3Object -BucketName pwsh-book-exercises -Key 'HelloWorld.txt'
-DestinationBucket pwsh-book-exercises-02' -DestinationKey
'HelloWorldCopy.txt'
```

When you no longer need an object, you can delete it using the Remove-S3Object command. Remember to use the Force option to avoid the confirmation prompt.

```
Remove-S3Object -BucketName pwsh-book-exercises -Key 'HelloWorldCopy.txt'
-Force
```

Now that we know how to create and use objects, let's look at how we can use folders to organize them.

Managing Folders

In the previous examples, we copied objects into the root of the bucket. As you add more objects, you will end up with a confusing mess. However, we can use folders to organize objects. For example, we could have uploaded the HelloWorld.txt file into a folder called MyFolder by modifying the Key.

```
Write-S3Object -BucketName pwsh-book-exercises -Key 'MyFolder/HelloWorld.
txt' -File 'HelloWorld.txt'
```

If you want to list the files in a folder, use the KeyPrefix parameter with Get-S3Object.

```
Get-S3Object -BucketName pwsh-book-exercises -KeyPrefix 'MyFolder'
```

Note   Before we go any further, I want to mention that folders don't really exist in S3. At least they do not exist like they do in a traditional file system. There is no folder object. The previous example is simply listing all files that begin with 'MyFolder.' I could just have easily uploaded a file called 'MyFolder_HelloWorld. txt.' AWS would not have cared, and Get-S3Object would still have listed the file because it begins with 'MyFolder.' Folders are just a conversion used by the AWS Management Console. When the console sees a forward slash, it creates a folder icon and groups the files under it. With that said, you will likely find the folders in the console very convenient.

You may find that on occasion you want to make an empty folder appear in the AWS Management Console. To create an empty folder, just create a dummy object that has a key that ends with a slash.

```
Write-S3Object -BucketName pwsh-book-exercises -Key 'EmptyFolder/' -Content
"Dummy Content"
```

The KeyPrefix (or folder) can be really useful. One great feature is the ability to upload an entire directory of files with a single command. For example, the following command will upload all the files in the C:\aws folder and prefix all the files with "utils/."

```
Write-S3Object -BucketName pwsh-book-exercises -KeyPrefix 'utils' -Folder
'c:\aws'
```

The previous command will ignore subfolders, but there is also an option to recursively upload all files in all of the subfolders.

```
Write-S3Object -BucketName pwsh-book-exercises -KeyPrefix 'utils' -Folder
'c:\aws' -Recurse
```

When you read files, you can use the KeyPrefix parameter to download all files that begin with a certain string. Rather than using the File parameter as we did in a previous command, you use the Folder parameter. The Folder parameter specifies where to put the files on the local file system. Note that Read-S3Object is always recursive.

```
Read-S3Object -BucketName pwsh-book-exercises -KeyPrefix 'utils' -Folder
'c:\aws'
```

On occasion you may find that you want to upload files that match a certain pattern. For example, you can upload all executables in the c:\aws folder by using the SearchPattern parameter.

```
Write-S3Object -BucketName pwsh-book-exercises -KeyPrefix 'utils' -Folder
'c:\aws' -SearchPattern '*.exe'
```

Unfortunately, there is no SearchPattern attribute on Read-S3Object. We can use a combination of Get-S3Object and Read-S3Object to produce a little PowerShell magic. For example:

```
Get-S3Object -BucketName pwsh-book-exercises -KeyPrefix 'utils' |
    Where-Object {$_.Key -like '*.exe'} | % {
        Read-S3Object -BucketName $_.BucketName -Key $_.Key -File
        ('C:\' + $_.Key.Replace('/','\'))
    }
```

Note   Obviously these commands that specify C:\ are not going to run on a Linux machine running PowerShell Core. In addition, on a Linux machine there is no need to replace the backslash with forward slash as I did in the last example.

As you can see, folders are a really powerful way to act on multiple objects at once. Next, we will look at how to deal with large numbers of files.

Managing Public Access

Many buckets require public or anonymous access. For example, we might be using S3 to store images for a web site or the installer for our latest application. In both cases we want the objects to be available to the general public. To make an object public, you can add the `PublicReadOnly` attribute to `Write-S3Object` cmdlet. For example:

```
Write-S3Object -BucketName pwsh-book-exercises -Key 'HelloWorld.txt'
-Content "Hello World!!!" -PublicReadOnly
```

In addition, you can make the bucket public read only. That does not make every object in the bucket public; it means anyone can list the contents of the bucket. You still have to mark the individual objects as public when you upload them.

```
New-S3Bucket -BucketName pwsh-book-exercises –PublicReadOnly
```

You can also configure a bucket to allow anonymous users to write to a bucket. For example, you might allow customers to upload log files to your server so you can help debug an issue they are having. In general it is dangerous to allow unauthenticated user to upload files. Not only could the individual files be dangerous, but you are also charged for files they upload. If you allow anonymous uploads, there is nothing stopping a nefarious user from uploading large amounts of data, costing you thousands of dollars. If you still want to create a bucket with anonymous read/write access, you can use the `PublicReadWrite` attribute with `New-S3Bucket`. For example:

```
New-S3Bucket -BucketName pwsh-book-exercises -PublicReadWrite
```

We will discuss Identity and Access Management in detail in the next chapter.

Managing Versions

Often you want to store multiple versions of a document as you make changes. You may have regulatory requirements that demand it, or you may just want the option to roll back. S3 supports this through bucket versioning.

When you enable versioning, S3 stores every version of every document in the bucket. If you overwrite an object, AWS keeps the original. If you delete a document, AWS simply marks the document as deleted, but keeps all the prior versions. When you read a document, AWS returns the latest version, but you can always request a specific version.

Before we enable versioning, let's overwrite the HelloWorld document we created earlier so we have a clean starting point. When you do, the old copy is replaced by this new copy.

```
Write-S3Object -BucketName pwsh-book-exercises -Key 'HelloWorld.txt'
-Content "Hello World Version 1!!!"
```

Now, let's enable versioning. Versioning is always enabled at the bucket. You cannot enable versioning within a specific folder. To enable versioning, use the Write-S3BucketVersioning command.

```
Write-S3BucketVersioning -BucketName pwsh-book-exercises -VersioningConfig_
Status 'Enabled'
```

Now that versioning is enabled, let's overwrite the HelloWorld document. You do not have to do anything special to create a version. Just write the new object and S3 will create a new version and retain the original.

```
Write-S3Object -BucketName pwsh-book-exercises -Key 'HelloWorld.txt'
-Content "Hello Version 2!!!"
```

If you were to call Get-S3Object, you would not see any difference. In fact, all of the commands we have used so far are unaffected by versioning. The following command will return the latest version, which you can verify by checking the date:

```
Get-S3Object -BucketName pwsh-book-exercises -Key 'HelloWorld.txt'
```

To list the versions of all the objects in a bucket, use the Get-S3Version command. Note that Get-S3Version returns a complicated structure. You can ignore most of it and use the Versions property to list the versions. For example:

```
(Get-S3Version -BucketName pwsh-book-exercises).Versions
```

Unfortunately, there is no way to specify a specific object, only a prefix. Often this is enough. For example, you could get the versions of our HelloWorld.txt document like this:

```
(Get-S3Version -BucketName pwsh-book-exercises -Prefix 'HelloWorld.txt').
Versions
```

But, there are times when the prefix is not unique. For example, if we had both HelloWorld.doc and HelloWorld.docx in a folder, it is impossible to list the versions of HelloWorld.doc without getting HelloWorld.docx. Therefore, it is best to check the versions you get back by piping it to Where-Object.

```
(Get-S3Version -BucketName pwsh-book-exercises -Prefix 'HelloWorld.doc').
Versions | Where-Object {$_.Key -eq 'HelloWorld.doc'}
```

If you want to download a specific version of a document, the Read-S3Object accepts a version parameter. First, you have to get the version using Get-S3Version. Note that Get-S3Version returns an array and the array is sorted in reverse order so that the latest version is position 0. Once you find the version you want, you can pass the ID to Read-S3Object. For example:

```
$Versions = (Get-S3Version -BucketName pwsh-book-exercises -Prefix
'HelloWorld.txt').Versions
Read-S3Object -BucketName pwsh-book-exercises -Key 'HelloWorld.txt'
-Version $Versions[1].VersionId -File 'versiontest.txt'
```

If you check the versiontest.txt file, you can verify that it contains the content from version 1, "Hello World version 1!!!" You can delete a version the same way:

```
Remove-S3Object -BucketName pwsh-book-exercises -Key 'HelloWorld.txt'
-VersionId $Versions[1].VersionId
```

When you delete a version, it is physically removed from the bucket. But, when you call Remove-S3Object without specifying a VersionId, S3 simply marks the object as deleted. If you delete an object and then call Get-S3Object, it appears that the object is gone.

```
Remove-S3Object -BucketName pwsh-book-exercises -Key 'HelloWorld.txt' -Force
Get-S3Object -BucketName pwsh-book-exercises
```

However, if you list the versions, you will see that there is a new version called a delete marker.

```
(Get-S3Version -BucketName pwsh-book-exercises -Prefix 'HelloWorld.txt').
Versions
```

Note that the delete marker has the attribute `IsDeleteMaker=True` and a size of 0. You can still access the old versions by specifying a version ID. For example:

```
$Versions = (Get-S3Version -BucketName pwsh-book-exercises -Prefix
'HelloWorld.txt').Versions
Read-S3Object -BucketName pwsh-book-exercises -Key 'HelloWorld.txt'
-Version $Versions[1].VersionId -File 'deletetest.txt'
```

You can also undelete an object by removing the delete marker. Just find the version with `IsDeleteMaker=True` and use `Remove-S3Object` to remove it.

```
$Marker = (Get-S3Version -BucketName pwsh-book-exercises -Prefix
'HelloWorld.txt').Versions | Where-Object {$_.IsDeleteMaker -eq $true}
Remove-S3Object -BucketName pwsh-book-exercises -Key 'HelloWorld.txt'
-VersionId $Marker.VersionId -Force
```

Once you have versioning enabled, you cannot disable it, but you can choose to suspend versioning. When versioning is suspended, the existing versions are maintained but new versions are not created. To suspend versioning, call `Write-S3BucketVersioning` and set the status to `Enabled`.

```
Write-S3BucketVersioning -BucketName pwsh-book-exercises -VersioningConfig_
Status 'Suspended'
```

As you can imagine, versioning, combined with 99.99999999% durability, will ensure that you almost never lose an object again. Of course, storing objects forever can get expensive. In the next section, we will explore life-cycle policies to manage aging objects.

Using Life-Cycle Management and Glacier

Over time you will accumulate a vast collection of objects. Sometimes you want to save these forever, but usually you do not. You may need to keep to certain documents for a specified period of time. For example, the Sarbanes-Oxley Act, enacted after the Enron collapse, recommends that you keep ledgers for 7 years and invoices for 3.

Obviously you have the tools to create a PowerShell script to delete objects older than a certain date. But, S3 also has a built-in life-cycle policy that can manage retention for you. In addition, life-cycle management can be used to copy objects to a cold storage solution called Glacier.

Glacier provides the same high durability as S3 for about 25% the price. The trade-off is that objects stored in Glacier are not immediately available. You have to request that objects be restored, which takes up to 12 hours.

We describe the policy using a series of .Net objects. Let's assume our bucket holds log files from a web server running on EC2. The development team often refers to the logs to diagnose errors, but this almost always happens within a few hours of the error occurring. In addition, the security team requires that we maintain logs for 1 year. Therefore, we decide to keep the logs online, in S3, for 1 week. After 1 week, the logs are moved to cold storage, in Glacier, for 1 year. After 1 year the logs can be deleted.

First, we define a life-cycle transition. The transition defines how long the logs are maintained in S3 and where to move them after. The policy is always defined in days. The transition also defines the storage class to move the document to. In the following example, I am moving the object to Glacier. You can also move an object to Infrequent Access (S3-IA) storage, but I am not going to cover that here.

```
$Transition = New-Object Amazon.S3.Model.LifecycleTransition
$Transition.Days = 7
$Transition.StorageClass = "Glacier"
```

Next, we define the expiration policy. The expiration policy defines how long to keep the object before it is deleted. In this case, I am keeping the object for 365 days. Note that the expiration is defined from the day the object was first uploaded to S3, not the day it was transitioned to Glacier.

```
$Expiration = New-Object Amazon.S3.Model.LifecycleRuleExpiration
$Expiration.Days = 365
```

Now that we have both the transition and expiration defined, we can combine them into a single rule and apply it to the bucket. Note that you do not need to define both the transition and expiration. Some rules only define a transition, and the object is maintained in Glacier until you manually delete it. Other rules only define an expiration and the document is deleted from S3 without being transitioned.

```
$Rule = New-Object Amazon.S3.Model.LifecycleRule
$Rule.Transition = $Transition
$Rule.Expiration = $Expiration
$Rule.Prefix = "
```

```
$Rule.Status = 'Enabled'
Write-S3LifecycleConfiguration -BucketName pwsh-book-exercises
-Configuration_Rules $Rule
```

Sometimes you want to have different rules applied to each folder in a bucket. You can define a folder-level rule by adding a prefix. For example:

```
$Rule = New-Object Amazon.S3.Model.LifecycleRule
$Rule.Transition = $Transition
$Rule.Expiration = $Expiration
$Rule.Prefix = "logs/"
$Rule.Status = 'Enabled'
Write-S3LifecycleConfiguration -BucketName pwsh-book-exercises
-Configuration_Rules $Rule
```

Now, let's assume a user of our web site claims his data was deleted a few months ago and we need to understand why. We need to pull the log files from July 22 to diagnose the cause. First we check if the object exists and where it is by using Get-S3Object. For example:

```
Get-S3Object -BucketName pwsh-book-exercises -Key 'logs/2013-07-22.log'
```

This command returns the following output. Note that the log files have been moved to Glacier, but have not yet been deleted.

```
Key          : logs/2013-07-22.log
BucketName   : pwsh-book-exercises
LastModified : Mon, 22 July 2013 23:59:39 GMT
ETag         : "793466320ce145cb672e69265409ffeb"
Size         : 1147
Owner        : Amazon.S3.Model.Owner
StorageClass : GLACIER
```

To restore the object, we use the Restore-S3Object command. Restore-S3Object requires the bucket and key. In addition, the Days parameter defines how long to keep the object in S3. In the following example, I request that the object be restored for 7 days. This should be plenty of time to figure out what happened to our user's data. After 7 days, the object is automatically deleted from S3, but is still stored in Glacier until the expiration date.

```
Restore-S3Object -BucketName pwsh-book-exercises -Key '/logs/2013-07-22.
log' -Days 7
```

If you want to remove the life-cycle policy from a bucket, you can use the Remove-S3LifecycleConfiguration command. For example:

```
Remove-S3LifecycleConfiguration -BucketName pwsh-book-exercises
```

Life-cycle policies provide an easy solution to managing storage classes and minimizing your S3 spend. Next we look at replicating data from one bucket to another.

Cross-Region Replication

As I already mentioned, S3 provides 99.999999999% durability and 99.99% availability. This is enough for most any use case; however, there may be times that you want even greater durability or availability. S3 replication allows you to replicate objects in one bucket to second bucket. If S3 were to fail in one region, you could still access your objects in another region. Let's set up replication from Northern Virginia to Ohio.

I'll start by creating a new bucket in Northern Virginia (us-east-1) and enabling version. Note that versioning must be enabled on the source bucket.

```
New-S3Bucket -BucketName pwsh-book-exercises-source -Region us-east-1
Write-S3BucketVersioning -BucketName pwsh-book-exercises-source
-VersioningConfig_Status 'Enabled'
```

Next, I will create a second bucket in Ohio (us-east-2). We need to enable replication again.

```
New-S3Bucket -BucketName pwsh-book-exercises-destination -Region us-east-2
Write-S3BucketVersioning -BucketName pwsh-book-exercises-destination
-VersioningConfig_Status 'Enabled'
```

Now that the buckets are created, we need to create an IAM role that grants S3 permission to access our data. The following policy allows S3 read from the source bucket and write to the destination bucket. If you need to review IAM roles and policies, go back to Chapter 9.

```
$AssumeRolePolicy = @"
{
  "Version":"2008-10-17",
  "Statement":[
    {
      "Sid":"",
      "Effect":"Allow",
      "Principal":{"Service":"s3.amazonaws.com"},
      "Action":"sts:AssumeRole"
    }
  ]
}
"@

$AccessPolicy = @"
{
    "Version":"2012-10-17",
    "Statement":[
      {
        "Effect":"Allow",
        "Action":[
          "s3:GetReplicationConfiguration",
          "s3:ListBucket"
        ],
        "Resource":[
          "arn:aws:s3:::pwsh-book-exercises-source"
        ]
      },
      {
        "Effect":"Allow",
        "Action":[

          "s3:GetObjectVersion",
          "s3:GetObjectVersionAcl",
          "s3:GetObjectVersionTagging"
        ],
```

```
      "Resource":[
         "arn:aws:s3:::pwsh-book-exercises-source/*"
      ]
   },
   {
      "Effect":"Allow",
      "Action":[
         "s3:ReplicateObject",
         "s3:ReplicateDelete",
         "s3:ReplicateTags"
      ],
      "Resource":"arn:aws:s3:::pwsh-book-exercises-destination/*"
   }
   ]
}
"@
$Role = New-IAMRole -RoleName 'CrossRegionReplication'
-AssumeRolePolicyDocument $AssumeRolePolicy
Write-IAMRolePolicy -RoleName $Role.RoleName -PolicyName
'ReplicateSourceToDestination' -PolicyDocument $AccessPolicy
```

Now we can configure replication. Similar to life-cycle rules we just covered, we are going to use a .Net object to describe the replication rule. Each rule has an ID to help you keep track of what is being replicated. The destination is a second .Net object and identifies the destination bucket by Arn.

```
$Rule = New-Object  Amazon.S3.Model.ReplicationRule
$Rule.Id = 'MyFirstRule'
$Rule.Status = 'Enabled'
$Rule.Destination = New-Object Amazon.S3.Model.ReplicationDestination
$Rule.Destination.BucketArn = 'arn:aws:s3:::pwsh-book-exercises-destination'
```

Finally, we call Write-S3BucketReplication to configure the rule and specify the source bucket to apply the rule to.

```
Write-S3BucketReplication -BucketName pwsh-book-exercises-source
-Configuration_Rule $Rule -Configuration_Role $Role.Arn
```

289

At this point S3 will begin to replicate changes from the source bucket to the destination bucket. In the preceding rule, I am replicating everything in the bucket. If you want to replicate specific folders, you can modify the prefix. Note that you must delete MyFirstRule before adding this one.

```
$Rule = New-Object  Amazon.S3.Model.ReplicationRule
$Rule.Id = 'MySecondRule'
$Rule.Prefix = 'MyFolder/'
$Rule.Status = 'Enabled'
$Rule.Destination = New-Object Amazon.S3.Model.ReplicationDestination
$Rule.Destination.BucketArn = 'arn:aws:s3:::pwsh-book-exercises-destination'
```

In the following examples, the destination copy is using the same storage class as the source copy. You might want to replicate to a different storage class. For example, you might want to save money on the second copy by using infrequent access. Infrequent access stores data for about half the cost of standard, but you are charged to read the data. This makes sense if the second copy will only be read in the rare case that the primary copy fails.

You can cover destination storage class by specifying it in the destination object. For example:

```
$Rule = New-Object  Amazon.S3.Model.ReplicationRule
$Rule.Id = 'MyThirdRule'
$Rule.Status = 'Enabled'
$Rule.Destination = New-Object Amazon.S3.Model.ReplicationDestination
$Rule.Destination.BucketArn = 'arn:aws:s3:::pwsh-book-exercises-
destination'
$Rule.Destination.StorageClass = 'STANDARD_IA'
```

We are getting close to the end. Before we move on, let's cover tagging.

Tagging

We have seen the power of tagging in EC2. S3 also supports tagging at the bucket and object level. To tag a bucket, create a tag using the Write-S3BucketTagging command and a few .Net classes. For example:

```
$Tag = New-Object Amazon.S3.Model.Tag
$Tag.Key = 'Owner'
```

```
$Tag.Value = 'Brian Beach'
Write-S3BucketTagging -BucketName pwsh-book-exercises -TagSets $Tag
```

You can also get the tags using the Get-S3BucketTagging command

```
Get-S3BucketTagging -BucketName pwsh-book-exercises
```

And, you can remove all tags using the Remove-S3BucketTagging command

```
Remove-S3BucketTagging -BucketName pwsh-book-exercises -Force
```

Tagging individual objects is similar. We can use the Write-S3ObjectTagSet command to add tags to an object. For example:

```
$Tags = New-Object Amazon.S3.Model.Tag
$Tags.Key = "Owner"
$Tags.Value = "Brian Beach"
Write-S3ObjectTagSet -BucketName pwsh-book-exercises -Key 'HelloWorld.txt'
-Tagging_TagSet $Tags
```

Just like buckets, you can query the tags for object using the Get-S3ObjectTagSet command.

```
Get-S3ObjectTagSet -BucketName pwsh-book-exercises -Key 'HelloWorld.txt'
```

And, of course you can delete them as well. Don't forget to add the force attribute to suppress the confirmation dialog.

```
Remove-S3ObjectTagSet -BucketName pwsh-book-exercises -Key 'HelloWorld.txt'
-Force
```

In the next section, we will look at a few miscellaneous commands and then move on to the exercises.

Miscellaneous S3 Options

In this section we will look at a few miscellaneous options, none of which are big enough to warrant their own section.

Pagination

As you add more and more objects to S3, it can become very difficult to sort through them all. AWS gives you the ability to list files in batches. This is really convenient if you are trying to display the objects on a web page or other user interface.

Imagine you have hundreds of files in a bucket and you need to browse through them all. The following example will return the first ten objects in the bucket:

```
$Objects = Get-S3Object -BucketName pwsh-book-exercises  -MaxKeys 10
```

After you browse through these first ten, you want to get ten more. You can use the MaxKeys parameter to tell the S3 to return the next ten objects. For example:

```
$Objects = Get-S3Object -BucketName pwsh-book-exercises -MaxKeys 10 -Marker
$Objects[9].Key
```

Encryption

When you upload an object to S3, you can have S3 encrypt the file before saving it. To enable encryption, use the ServerSideEncryption parameter.

```
Write-S3Object -BucketName pwsh-book-exercises -Key 'HelloWorld.txt'
-Content "Hello World!!!" -ServerSideEncryption AES256
```

Encryption is a critical part of your security strategy, but maintaining an audit log is equally important. Let's look at how to enable logging.

Logging

S3 supports access logs to audit access to the objects in your bucket. When you enable logging, S3 writes log files to the bucket you specify. In this example I am going to create a new bucket to hold all my log files. I am adding the log-delivery-write ACL to grant the logging service the ability to write log files.

```
New-S3Bucket -BucketName pwsh-book-exercises-logging -CannedACLName log-
delivery-write
```

Now I am going to enable logging on pwsh-book-exercises that writes log files to MyLoggingBucket I just created. You should specify a prefix so you can keep track of which logs came from which sources.

292

```
Write-S3BucketLogging -BucketName pwsh-book-exercises -LoggingConfig_
TargetBucketName pwsh-book-exercises-logging -LoggingConfig_TargetPrefix
'Logs/pwsh-book-exercises/'
```

If you do enable logging, you should consider enabling a life-cycle policy to clean up the log files over time. Let's wrap up with a quick look at the ability to manage content types.

Content Type

When you upload an object, the content type is set to "application/octet-stream." You can optionally include the content type to tell the client what type of file it is. For example, your browser will always download files of type "application/octet-stream". If you want the browser to display the file, change the type to "text/plain."

```
Write-S3Object -BucketName pwsh-book-exercises -Key 'HelloWorld.txt'
-Content "Hello World!!!" -ContentType 'text/plain'
```

We will see an example of content type used in Exercise 11.1 where we create a static web site.

EXERCISE 11.1: STATIC HOSTING ON S3

You may have noticed that S3 feels a lot like a web server. We use HTTP or HTTPS to get objects using a URL. In fact, you can use S3 to host a static web site with a few minor alterations. First, we are going to want a vanity URL that does not reference S3. Second, we are going to want to support a default and custom error page. S3 supports all of this and more.

Let's create a simple web site with only two pages. I am going to use the domain name www.pwsh-book-exercises.com, but you can use anything you want. The first thing we need to do is create a bucket. The bucket must be named with the domain name of our web site. For example:

```
New-S3Bucket -BucketName 'www.pwsh-book-exercises.com'
```

Next we need to create a page. A page is just an S3 object with the content type set to "text/html." Remember that if you do not set the content type, it will be set to "application/octet-stream" and your browser will download the file rather than displaying it. You can upload

---

images and other resources, but you have to set the content type correctly for each. We also need to enable the public read-only access to each file. The following example creates a new page called index.htm:

```
$Content = @"
<HTML>
  <HEAD>
    <TITLE>Hello World</TITLE>
  </HEAD>
  <BODY>
    <H1>Hello World</H1>
    <P>Hello from my Amazon Web Services site.</P>
  </BODY>
</HTML>
"@

Write-S3Object -BucketName 'www.pwsh-book-exercises.com' -Key 'index.htm'
-Content $Content -ContentType 'text/html' -PublicReadOnly
```

Next, we need to create an error page. This page will be displayed whenever an error occurs. Once again, remember the content type and public read-only flag.

```
$Content = @"
<HTML>
  <HEAD>
    <TITLE>Oops</TITLE>
  </HEAD>
  <BODY>
    <H1>Oops</H1>
    <P>Something seems to have gone wrong.</P>
  </BODY>
</HTML>
"@

Write-S3Object -BucketName 'www.pwsh-book-exercises.com' -Key 'error.htm'
-Content $Content -ContentType 'text/html' -PublicReadOnly
```

Now that our bucket is all set up, we can enable the Website feature. Write-S3BucketWebsite allows us to identify the default and error documents in the site. The default document will be shown if the user requests http://aws.brainbeach.com without including the path to a document. The error page will be displayed whenever something goes wrong.

```
Write-S3BucketWebsite -BucketName 'www.pwsh-book-exercises.com'
-WebsiteConfiguration_IndexDocumentSuffix 'index.htm' -WebsiteConfiguration_
ErrorDocument 'error.htm'
```

You're almost there. At this point the site is up and running on the URL `http://BUCKET.s3-website-REGION.amazonaws.com`. For example, my site is running on `www.pwsh-book-exercises.com.s3-website-us-east-1.amazonaws.com`. You can create a DNS CNAME from `pwsh-book-exercises.com` to `www.pwsh-book-exercises.com.s3-website-us-east-1.amazonaws.com`, and S3 will begin to respond to the vanity URL. The process will depend on your provider.

Once the CNAME is done, we can test:

- If you navigate to `www.pwsh-book-exercises.com/index.htm`, you should see the welcome page we uploaded.

- If you navigate to `www.pwsh-book-exercises.com`, you should again see the welcome page.

- If you navigate to `www.pwsh-book-exercises.com/DoesNotExist`, you should see our custom error page.

As you can see, S3 is a reliable and inexpensive way to host a static web site. In the next exercise, we will use pre-signed URLs to grant temporary access to a customer without requiring them to log in.

EXERCISE 11.2: USING PRE-SIGNED URLS

At the beginning of this chapter, we discussed enabling anonymous access to a bucket, and I mentioned there is a better way: pre-signed URLs. This is a really simple command to use and does not warrant an exercise of its own, but it is a great opportunity to describe how AWS authentication works using access keys.

Imagine that you run a help desk and you often need to make tools and patches available to customers. You want these tools available only to customers who call the help desk. Furthermore, customers should not be able to download the tools later or share the link with friends. You could create a username and password for the user, but then you have to manage another user. This is a great use case for a pre-signed URL.

A pre-signed URL has been signed with a secret key. In addition, the URL includes an expiration date, after which it can no longer be used. Note that the URL has been signed with the secret key, but does not include the secret key. This allows AWS to prove the authenticity of the URL without exposing the secret key to the customer.

In fact, this is how all AWS web service calls work. Your secret key is never sent to AWS. Whenever we use a PowerShell method, PowerShell creates the request and includes a digital signature to prove that the user knows the secret.

Let's get back to the help desk. You want to create a pre-signed URL. PowerShell has a command for this called Get-S3PresignedURL. You need to pass in your access key and secret key as well as the HTTP verb, bucket, key, and expiration date.

Note   You should use StoredCredentials rather than passing the access keys explicitly. (See Chapter 2 for details.) I am including them here only to help explain how the encryption works.

```
#Authentication Keys
$AccessKey = 'AKIAJ5N3RMX5LGUMP6FQ'
$SecretKey = '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'

#Web Query
$Verb = "GET"
$ExpirationDate = [DateTime]::Parse('2019-01-01')
$Bucket = 'pwsh-book-exercises'
$Key = 'HelloWorld.txt'

Get-S3PreSignedURL -Verb $Verb -Expires $ExpirationDate -Bucket $Bucket -Key
$Key -AccessKey $AccessKey -SecretKey $SecretKey
```

The preceding code will return the following URL, which you can share with your customer. Notice that the URL includes the access key and expiration date we supplied. The expiration date has been converted to seconds from January 1, 1970. In addition, the URL incudes a signature created by the PowerShell command. Also notice that your secret key is not included in the URL.

```
https://s3.amazonaws.com/MyBucket/MyPath/MyFile.txt?AWSAccessKeyId=
AKIAIQPQNCQG3EYO6LIA&Expires=1388552400&Signature=wBUgYztEdlE%2Btw9argXicUKv
ftw%3D
```

You can share this URL with your customer and they can download a single file. They do not have the secret key and therefore cannot use it for anything else. In addition, AWS will refuse it after the expiration date. If the customer changes anything in the URL, he or she will invalidate the signature and AWS will refuse it. What a simple solution to a difficult problem.

While the Get-PreSignedURL method is really simple to use, this is a great opportunity to see how AWS signatures work. Let's write our own code to create a signature so we better understand how it works. If you're not interested, feel free to skip the rest of this example, but remember the Get-S3PreSignedURL method.

First, we will accept the same parameters as the Get-PreSignedURL command. My method only works for GET requests, but you could easily add support for other HTTP verbs.

```
Param
(
    [string][parameter(mandatory=$true)]$AccessKey,
    [string][parameter(mandatory=$true)]$SecretKey,
    [string][parameter(mandatory=$false)]$Verb = 'GET',
    [DateTime][parameter(mandatory=$true)]$Expires,
    [string][parameter(mandatory=$true)]$Bucket,
    [string][parameter(mandatory=$true)]$Key
)
```

Next, we must calculate the expiration. Remember that the expiration is expressed in seconds since January 1, 1970. Also note that I am converting the time to UTC because the AWS servers may be in a different time zone than our client.

```
$EpochTime = [DateTime]::Parse('1970-01-01')
$ExpiresSeconds = ($Expires.ToUniversalTime() - $EpochTime).TotalSeconds
```

Then, we need to canonicalize the input parameters to be signed. Before we can sign the data, we must agree on how the data will be formatted. If both sides don't agree on a common format, the signatures will not match. This process is called canonicalization.

For AWS, we include the following data separated by a newline character:

- HTTP verb

- MD5 hash of the content

- Content type

- Expiration date

- Optional HTTP headers

- URL-encoded path

In our case, we are only supporting GET; therefore, the content and content type will always be blank. In addition, I am not supporting any HTTP headers.

```
$Path = [Amazon.S3.Util.AmazonS3Util]::UrlEncode("/$Bucket/$Key", $true)
$Data = "$Verb`n`n`n$ExpiresSeconds`n$Path"
```

Now that we have the canonicalized data, we can use the .Net crypto libraries to sign it with our secret key. Here I am using the SHA1 algorithm to generate the signature. Note that you must be very careful with how data is encoded. The secret key must be UTF8 encoded, and the resulting signature must be URL encoded.

```
$HMAC = New-Object System.Security.Cryptography.HMACSHA1
$HMAC.key = [System.Text.Encoding]::UTF8.GetBytes($SecretKey);
$signature = $HMAC.ComputeHash(
    [System.Text.Encoding]::UTF8.GetBytes($Data.ToCharArray()))
$signature_encoded = [Amazon.S3.Util.AmazonS3Util]::UrlEncode(
    [System.Convert]::ToBase64String($signature), $true)
```

Finally, we can build the URL. The result should be identical to what Get-PreSignedURL returned earlier.

```
"https://s3.amazonaws.com/$Bucket/$Key" + "?AWSAccessKeyId=$AccessKey&Expires=
$ExpiresSeconds&Signature=$signature_encoded"
```

That may have been a bit more than you wanted to know, but now that you know how to sign a request, you can call the S3 web service methods directly in any language.

Summary

In this chapter, we reviewed Simple Storage Service (S3). S3 allows you to store a seemingly limitless number of objects in the cloud. We learned to create and manage buckets and folders, and we learned to upload and download objects.

We learned how versioning can be used to store multiple versions of a document as it changes over time. We also learned to use life-cycle policies to create retention rules and how to use Glacier cold storage to reduce costs for long-term storage.

In the exercises, we created a static web site hosted entirely in S3 and then learned to create a pre-signed URL that can be shared without needing AWS credentials. We also learned how AWS uses digital signatures in authentication. In the next chapter, we will learn how to use PowerShell to automate Identity and Access Management.

CHAPTER 12

AWS Directory Service

In this chapter, we will cover the AWS Directory Service, which is a highly scalable and managed multi-directory store; it can be used for authentication and Single Sign-On services. As mentioned, there are multiple directories supported by AWS Directory Service, each one helping solve a unique business problem, including authentication services for traditional applications, support for SaaS application developers, and cloud applications with complex authentication relationships. The directories available include Amazon Cloud Directory, AD Connector, Amazon Cognito, Simple AD, and Microsoft AD. As one can imagine, each of these directories has enough depth, nuance, and complexity to warrant a dedicated chapter in this book. However, in this section we will focus on the services that are most frequently used with Microsoft Workloads and managed with PowerShell; these are Microsoft AD, AD Connector, and Simple AD.

In this section we will guide you choose the right directory for your use case, as well as provide you with step-by-step instructions on how to get started with authentication and federation using these directories. The exercises at the end of the chapter will spend time deploying, configuring, and securing Microsoft AD, AD Connector, and Simple AD.

Selecting the Right Directory

As previously mentioned, AWS Directory Service has different options and selecting the right directory for your specific use case and business need is very important, as the wrong choice can result in compatibility problems or expensive rework. To help you make the right choice for your project or workload, we will review specifics of each directory.

301

B. Beach et al., *Pro PowerShell for Amazon Web Services*, https://doi.org/10.1007/978-1-4842-4850-8_12

AWS Directory Service for Microsoft Active Directory

AWS Directory Service for Microsoft Active Directory is a managed service that leverages an actual Microsoft Windows Server Active Directory (AD) infrastructure (Windows Server 2012 R2). As it does on premises, Managed Microsoft AD plays a critical role for Active Directory-aware applications in the AWS Cloud. Some of these applications include Microsoft SQL Server, Microsoft SharePoint, as well as a myriad of .NET applications. AWS Directory Service for Microsoft Active Directory, also known as Managed Microsoft AD, provides directory services for other AWS applications including Amazon WorkSpaces, Amazon QuickSight, and services such as RDS for SQL Server, Amazon Connect, and Amazon Chime.

If there is a requirement to have Active Directory- or LDAP-based directory services for a workload, AWS Managed Microsoft AD tends to be the right choice. There are additional benefits to using this directory option, including US Health Insurance Portability and Accountability Act (HIPAA) and Payment Card Industry Data Security Standard (PCI DSS) compliance eligibility, ability to extend the Active Directory schema, support for Secure LDAP access to the directory, AWS Single Sign-On, and Multi-Factor (MFA) authentication.

AD Connector

The AD Connector is a proxy service that provides on-premises based Active Directory users, access to AWS Enterprise applications, including QuickSight, WorkSpaces, WorkDocs, WorkMail, and Chime. Additionally, the service can also be used to provide seamless domain join to EC2 instances located in your VPC, with requirements being appropriate network connections and a service account to connect to the on-premises domain.

There are additional benefits the AD Connector can provide customers, including the ability to provide Multi-Factor Authentication (MFA) using an existing RADIUS implementation, provide AWS Console access using on-premises credentials, and also continue to leverage your existing domain's security policies, such as password policies.

Simple AD

Simple AD is a fully Managed Microsoft Active Directory compatible directory, which is powered by Samba 4 and provides the ability to use Active Directory features such as users and groups, machine domain join for both Windows and Linux, group policies, LDAP access, and Kerberos-based authentication.

If your use case is to provide your users authentication service to access AWS applications, including Amazon WorkSpaces, Amazon WorkDocs, Amazon QuickSight, and Amazon WorkMail, and perhaps Simple Active Directory functionality, then Simple AD may be the right choice, especially if you're price conscious. Currently, the cost for running a Small deployment of Simple AD is about half of what it costs to run a Standard Edition deployment of Managed Microsoft AD.

Managed Microsoft AD Architecture

Managed Microsoft AD is designed for high availability and is deployed in at least two subnets, in two different availability zones (AZs). At deployment time, the subnets can be explicitly selected or the service can randomly select two subnets. These subnets will be used to host two domain controllers (DCs), each of which will receive an IP address from the subnets specified. Once the directory is created, for greater resiliency, additional DCs can be added to either new or existing availability zones.

The aforementioned subnets can either be part of an existing VPC or a new VPC; VPC must use default hardware tenancy. In addition to a VPC, there is also a requirement to create a security group, which will allow the DCs to communicate with each other. The security group will be automatically created and attached to Managed Microsoft AD during directory creation. Let's begin by configuring the VPC.

Prerequisites

To create a Managed Microsoft AD directory, there are some prerequisites that must be considered:

- AWS created security group.

- Default tenancy is required for the VPC hosting Managed Microsoft AD.

- Directory cannot be created in a VPC using network address range 198.19.0.0/16.

- Network Address Translation with Active Directory is not supported.

Creating a VPC

To create a Managed Microsoft AD directory, we must first configure a VPC to host the domain controllers in separate subnets. Alternatively, these subnets can be placed in existing VPCs (e.g., the VPC created in Chapter 5). For demonstration purposes, we will create a new VPC in the 192.168.0.0 private IP range.

The following line will create a new VPC and store the details in a variable:

```
$VPC = New-EC2Vpc -CidrBlock '192.168.0.0/16'
```

We will continue by creating two subnets in the newly created VPC. For resiliency, these subnets will be in two separate AZs, which is a requirement for the service. (If necessary, review Chapter 5, as we have done this before.)

Creating Private Subnets

The first two variables, delimited with a $, will store the details of the newly created availability zones and will be used when creating the new subnets.

```
$AvailabilityZone1 = 'us-east-1a'
$AvailabilityZone2 = 'us-east-1b'
$FirstSubnet = New-EC2Subnet -VpcId $VPC.VpcId -CidrBlock '192.168.5.0/24'
-AvailabilityZone $AvailabilityZone1
$SecondSubnet = New-EC2Subnet -VpcId $VPC.VpcId -CidrBlock '192.168.6.0/24'
-AvailabilityZone $AvailabilityZone2
```

Creating a Managed Microsoft AD Directory

Once the VPC and the subnets are created, we can move onto setting up the Managed Microsoft AD directory to the subnets.

The following line will create a new domain, with the fully qualified domain name (FQDN) of corp.example.com, a NetBIOS name of CORP, a short description, with the networking settings to use the subnets previously created.

```
New-DSMicrosoftAD -Name corp.example.com -ShortName corp -Password
'password' -Edition Standard -Description "Managed Microsoft AD"
-VpcSettings_VpcId $VPC.VpcID VpcSettings_SubnetId $FirstSubnet.SubnetId,
$SecondSubnet.SubnetId
```

Note   Never use "password" as a password. Please choose something complex and difficult to guess.

The previous command includes the minimum set of the parameters required to set up a Managed Microsoft AD directory into a VPC. These commands are

- **New-DSMicrosoftAD** creates the directory.

- **Name** is the fully qualified domain name used for the directory created, which can be accessed within the VPC.

- **ShortName** is the NetBIOS name and will also be the name of the delegated OU created for your directory.

- **Description** is the freeform text used to identify the directory.

- **Password** is the password used for the Admin account, which is the delegated administrator account used to manage the directory.

- **Edition** is used to set the edition for the directory, either Standard or Enterprise. The Standard Edition is recommended for small and medium size organizations with an estimated 5000 users or 30,000 directory objects. The Enterprise Edition is targeted for large enterprises and can support up to 100,000 users or 500,000 objects.

- **VpcSettings_VpcId** is used to identify the VPC where the directory will be set up.

- **VpcSettings_SubnetId** is used to specify the two subnets where the domain controllers will be deployed. The subnets must be in two separate availability zones, which are used to provide high availability for the service. Once the directory is set up, additional domain controllers can be provisioned for greater resiliency.

Creating Public Subnet

To manage the new Managed Microsoft AD directory, we will need to set up a public subnet and a Remote Desktop Gateway (RDGW), the latter will serve as an administration workstation.

The first step will be to create a new subnet, which will be public.

```
$AvailabilityZone3 = 'us-east-1c'
$PublicSubnet = New-EC2Subnet -VpcId $VPC.VpcId -CidrBlock
'192.168.100.0/24'-AvailabilityZone $AvailabilityZone3
```

Creating Internet Gateway

Once the subnet has been created, the next step is to create an Internet gateway and associating it with the previously created VPC.

The following script will create an Internet gateway and attaching it with the VPC previously created.

```
$InternetGateway = New-EC2InternetGateway
Add-EC2InternetGateway -InternetGatewayId $InternetGateway.
InternetGatewayId -VpcId $VPC.VpcID
```

After the Internet gateway is attached to the VPC, we must make sure the local traffic stays local and traffic intended for the Internet is routed to the Internet gateway as a default route.

Configuring VPC Routing

The next script will create a new routing table, associate it with the VPC we have been working with, and set the default route to use the Internet gateway.

```
$Route = New-EC2RouteTable -VpcId $VPC.VpcID
Register-EC2RouteTable -RouteTableId $Route.RouteTableId -SubnetId
$PublicSubnet.SubnetId
New-EC2Route -RouteTableId $Route.RouteTableId -DestinationCidrBlock
'0.0.0.0/0' -GatewayId $InternetGateway.InternetGatewayId
```

Configuring DNS Hostname Name Resolution

Next, to have DNS name resolution, we will enable DNS Hostnames for the VPC.

```
Edit-EC2VpcAttribute -VpcId $VPC.VpcId -EnableDnsHostnames $true
```

Creating Management Workstation

In order for administrators to connect to the administration workstation (i.e., RDGW), we must make sure there is a security group in place before the management instance is deployed. To create the security group with the appropriate inbound rules, we will run the following commands.

Note   It is recommended the inbound IP ranges are more restrictive than in the example provided.

The script that follows will create a security group to allow inbound Remote Desktop connections via port TCP 3389 to the management workstation.

```
$SecurityGroup = New-EC2SecurityGroup -GroupName RDGW -Description "Remote
Desktop access from Internet" -VpcId $VPC.VpcID

$RDPRule = New-Object Amazon.EC2.Model.IpPermission
$RDPRule.IpProtocol='tcp'
$RDPRule.FromPort = 3389
$RDPRule.ToPort = 3389
$RDPRule.IpRanges = '0.0.0.0/0'

Grant-EC2SecurityGroupIngress -GroupId $SecurityGroup -IpPermissions $RDPRule
```

Once the security group rules are set up, the remote desktop instance can be deployed; we will use the latest version of the Windows Server 2016 Base image (ami-2d360152).

With the following line, we will deploy an EC2 Instance, granting it a public IP address and associating the security group we just created to it.

```
$RDPInstance = New-EC2Instance -ImageId ami-2d360152 -MinCount 1 -MaxCount
1 -KeyName 'key' -AssociatePublicIp $true -SecurityGroupId $SecurityGroup
-InstanceType t2.medium -SubnetId $PublicSubnet.SubnetId
```

Configuring Management Workstation

Once the management instance is deployed, in order to connect to it, we will get the IP address and password of the instance from the AWS Console. See Figures 12-1 and 12-2.

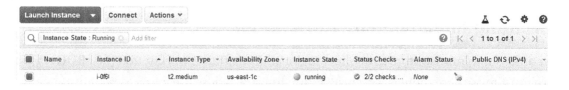

Figure 12-1. *Running EC2 Instance from within the EC2 Console*

Figure 12-2. *Connection information for accessing the EC2 Instance*

Once we get the Public DNS name of the administration instance, as shown in Figure 12-1, we will right-click the instance and use the Connection information to connect to it using the Remote Desktop client. See Figure 12-3.

Figure 12-3. *Example of the Remote Desktop connection client*

Joining EC2 Instance to the Domain

Once connected, we will change the DNS settings of the administration instance to point to the Managed Microsoft AD's domain controller's IP addresses. In order to do this, we can either go to the AWS Console (Figure 12-4) to get the information or run the command shown in the next section (i.e. `Add-Computer -Credential CORP\admin -DomainName corp.example.com -Restart`):

Directory Service > Directories						
Directories					Actions ▼	Set up directory
Q d-90671				×	‹ 1 ›	⚙
Directory ID ▼	Directory name ▼	Type ▼	Size ▼	Status ▼	Launch date ▲	
○ d-906711f2bb	corp.example.com	Microsoft AD	Standard	⊘ Active	Aug 21, 2018	

Figure 12-4. *Managed Microsoft AD details from the Directory Service Console*

The line that follows will provide details of the Active Directory domain we will use in the chapter. We will first get the details of our domain and input them into the $Directory variable (Figure 12-5). Then, we will output the details of the variable.

```
$Directory = Get-DSDirectory -DirectoryID d-906711f2bb
```

The IP addresses of the domain controllers will be listed in the **DNsIPAddrs** section of the output.

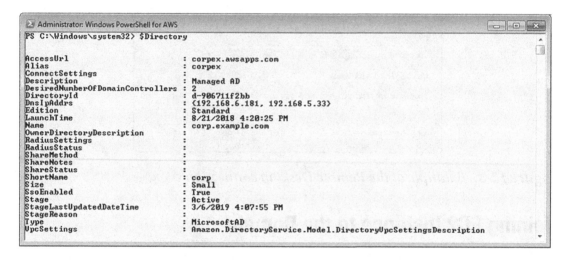

Figure 12-5. *Active Directory domain details*

Once connected to the management workstation/administration instance, we will need to ensure we configure the machine to use the right network interface card to join the domain. To set the IP address on the administration instance, we will need to identify the network interface that will get the DNS servers setting.

The next command will locate the active Ethernet network interface on the server.

```
Get-NetIPAddress | Where-Object {$_.InterfaceIndex -eq 3}
```

If the command does not yield any results, run the command without the filter (e.g., {$_.InterfaceIndex -eq 3}) and locate the active network interface on the public subnet. See Figure 12-6.

```
Get-NetIPAddress
```

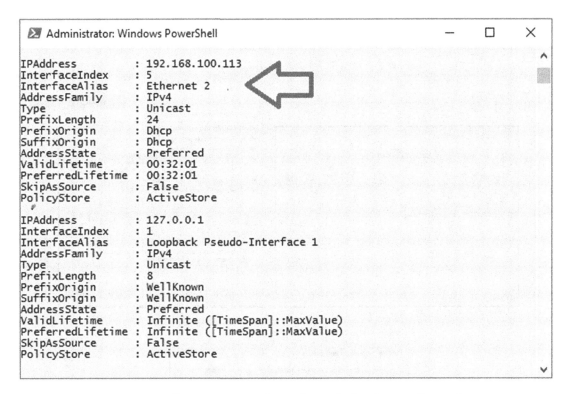

Figure 12-6. *Depicts Ethernet network card needed to be configured*

Once the network interface has been located, run the following command:

```
Set-DnsClientServerAddress -InterfaceAlias "Ethernet 2" -ServerAddresses
192.168.5.33, 192.168.6.181
```

Alternatively, the changes can be made by right-clicking Start and selecting Network Connections and setting the DNS server settings manually. Additional information can be found in the "Manually Join a Windows Instance" documentation page https:// docs.aws.amazon.com/directoryservice/latest/admin-guide/join_windows_ instance.html. See Figure 12-7.

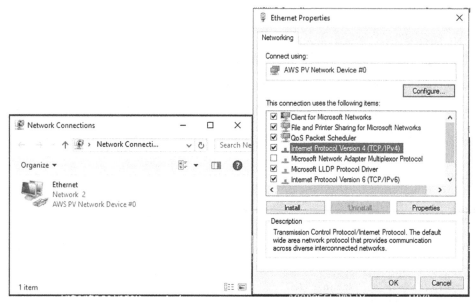

Figure 12-7. *Example of how to configure DNS manually*

Once the DNS settings have been updated, we will use the following command to join the administration instance to the CORP domain.

```
Add-Computer -Credential CORP\admin -DomainName corp.example.com -Restart
```

When prompted, type the appropriate password and click the OK button (Figure 12-8). At this point, the instance will reboot as part of the domain join process.

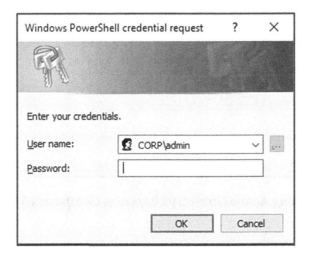

Figure 12-8. *Authentication prompt required to join Corp domain*

Install AD Tools

Once restarted, reconnect using the Remote Desktop client with the CORP\admin account. At this point, we will install the required AD administration tools to manage the directory. To do this, run the following command.

The command installs the Active Directory Windows Server Administration Tools.

```
Add-WindowsFeature RSAT-AD-Tools
```

Once the AD Tools are fully installed, go to Start/Run and type DSA.MSC. See Figure 12-9. This will open the Active Directory Users and Computes Snap-In, which can be used to manage the resources in the domain, including user and computer objects and so on. See Figure 12-10.

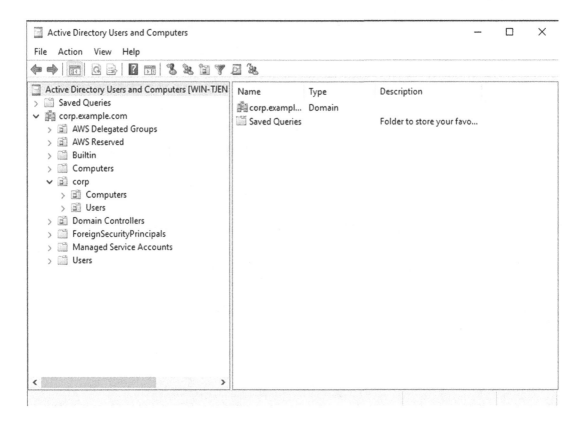

Figure 12-9. *Launching Active Directory Users and Computers Management Console*

Figure 12-10. *Corp domain depicted via Active Directory Users and Computers Management Console*

Additional information can be found in the "Installing the Active Directory Administration Tools" documentation page https://docs.aws.amazon.com/ directoryservice/latest/admin-guide/ms_ad_install_ad_tools.html.

Delegation Model

Because Managed Microsoft AD is a managed service, with a similar delegation model to RDS, customers don't get Domain or Enterprise Administrator access to the directory; therefore, we need to acknowledge some key details about the directory configuration.

Creating a Managed Microsoft AD Domain will result in the creation of a delegated Organizational Unit (OU), with the NetBios name that was specified during domain creation. For example, in our case the NetBios name was CORP. Under the delegated OU, there are a couple of other OUs, which are intended for computers and users. See Figure 12-11.

Along with the deleted OU, there are a set of security groups created to delegate privileges for the routine operational tasks and activities, required to manage domain resources for an organization. Some of these operational tasks include resetting password and unlocking accounts, joining machines to a domain, managing and configuring domain services such as DNS and DHCP, and deploying and administering licensing and certificate services. For a complete list of delegation security groups and their description, visit the "What Gets Created" documentation page `https://docs.aws.amazon.com/directoryservice/latest/admin-guide/ms_ad_getting_started_what_gets_created.html`.

Figure 12-11. *Delegation security groups for the domain we created*

315

As part of providing support services, AWS retains ownership of an OU called AWS Reserved. In this OU resides the administrator account, as well as security groups designated for support purposes; these include the AWSAdministrators and AWS Application and Service Delegated Group security groups. See Figure 12-12.

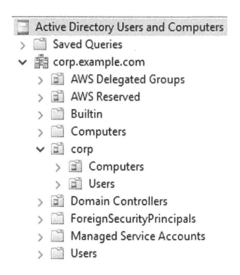

Figure 12-12. *View of Active Directory domain created*

Add Additional Domain Controller

One of the common tasks for Managed Microsoft AD administrators is to add additional domain controllers to the domain for additional resiliency and performance. In this section, we will increase the number of domain controllers in the domain.

The following script will add an additional domain controller to the previously deployed directory.

```
Set-DSDomainControllerCount -DesiredNumber 3 -DirectoryID $Directory.
DirectoryId
```

The list as follows explains in detail the command shown earlier:

- **Set-DSDomainControllerCount** specifies the action that the command will execute, in this case is either add or remove domain controllers to the directory.

- **DesiredNumber** specified the number of desired domain controllers in the directory.

- **DirectoryId** identifies the directory that will get the additional domain controllers, or removal of DCs if appropriate.

Once the command is run, we can verify the number of domain controllers via the AWS Directory Service Console. See Figure 12-13. The "How to Increase the Redundancy and Performance of Your AWS Directory Service for Microsoft AD Directory by Adding Domain Controllers" blog is highly recommended for additional information (https://aws.amazon.com/blogs/security/how-to-increase-the-redundancy-and-performance-of-your-aws-directory-service-for-microsoft-ad-directory-by-adding-domain-controllers/).

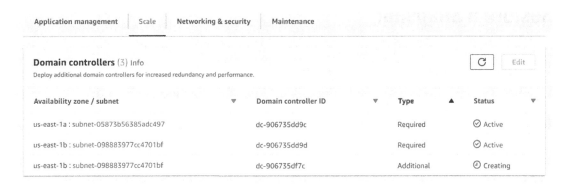

Figure 12-13. *List of additional domain controller being created*

Create a Snapshot

Once the directory is operational, it is critical to make sure that backups are regularly taken. The following command will create a manual snapshot of the directory. There is a limit of five manual snapshots for the directory; once the limit is reached, one of the snapshots must be deleted in order to create any others. There are also daily automatic snapshots that are taken; these are in addition to the manual snapshot limit. Once a directory is deleted, all snapshots associated with that directory will be deleted and cannot be recovered.

The following line creates a manual snapshot of the directory, naming the snapshot "1stManualSnapshot". See also Figure 12-14.

```
New-DSSnapshot -DirectoryId $Directory.DirectoryId -Name 1stManualSnapshot
```

Snapshots (2) Info

Performs a point-in-time backup of your directory that can later be restored.

ID	Name	Created date	Type	Status
s-906560c8e8	1stManualSnapshot	August 22, 2018	Manual	Creating
s-906560de21	-	August 21, 2018	Auto	Completed

Figure 12-14. *Image of manual snapshot being created*

> **Note**   Manual snapshots are highly recommended to be taken prior to any major directory change, such as extending the schema.

Restore a Snapshot

If you have an issue with the data integrity of your directory, a snapshot can be restored from either a manual or automatic snapshot.

The line that follows will restore the manual snapshot previously created:

```
Restore-DSFromSnapshot -SnapshotId s-906560c8e8
```

> **Note**   A snapshot restore does a point-in-time restore of the entire directory, which means there is risk of data loss. Therefore, it is highly recommended that before a snapshot is restored, a support case is created from the AWS Support Center to request assistance with restoring the individual object(s) that may be in question.

Enable Single Sign-On

As previously mentioned in the beginning of the chapter, Managed Microsoft AD can also be leveraged to provide access to the AWS Enterprise applications. In this section, we will discuss the way to grant directory users access to WorkDocs using Single Sign-On; however, one of the requirements is the Creation of an Access URL. Currently, the process of creating an Access URL can only be via the AWS Console. Once the Access URL is created, the Single Sign-On can be configured using the commands in the following sections:

Creating an Access URL

An Access URL can be created by following the next steps. See also Figure 12-15.

1. Go to the AWS Directory Service Console and select the appropriate directory.

2. Go to the Directory details and select the Application Management tab.

3. In the directory alias field, enter the alias appropriate for your organization. In our case, the one selected is corpex.awsapps.com.

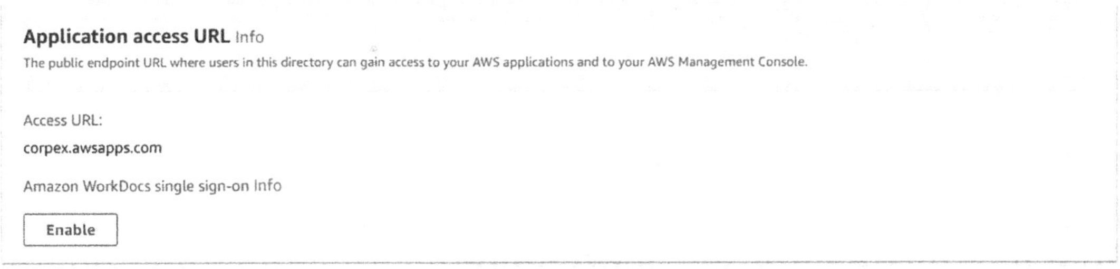

Application access URL Info
The public endpoint URL where users in this directory can gain access to your AWS applications and to your AWS Management Console.

Access URL:
corpex.awsapps.com

Amazon WorkDocs single sign-on Info

Enable

Figure 12-15. *Enabling Application access URL*

Enabling Single Sign-On

The following command provides any machine joined to the domain, access to Amazon WorkDocs, without having to enter credentials separately:

```
Enable-DSSso -DirectoryId $Directory.DirectoryId -Username admin -Password
'password'
```

Disabling Single Sign-On

If required, Single Sign-On can be disabled by running the following command:

```
Disable-DSSso -DirectoryId $Directory.DirectoryId -Username admin -Password
'password'
```

Enabling AWS Apps and Services

Once the Access URL has been created, other AWS Apps and Services can be enabled to integrate with Managed Microsoft AD. Currently, enabling these services can only be performed via the AWS Console. Detailed documentation for enabling these services can be found in the Enable Access to AWS Application and Services documentation page: https://docs.aws.amazon.com/directoryservice/latest/admin-guide/ms_ad_manage_apps_services.html.

- Amazon WorkSpaces

- Amazon WorkSpaces Application Manager

- Amazon WorkDocs

- Amazon WorkMail

- Amazon QuickSight

- Amazon Connect

- RDS SQL Server

- AWS Management Console

Enable Multi-Factor Authentication

Multi-Factor Authentication (MFA) is a mechanism that can be used to increase the security posture of your Microsoft Managed AD workloads, including Amazon Enterprise applications, such as WorkDocs, WorkSpaces, QuickSight, and Single Sign-On to the AWS Console. One of the requirements for enabling MFA is either having an MFA plugin or a Remote Authentication Dial-In User Service (RADIUS), which can be located either in your VPC or on-premises. In this scenario, the RADIUS server would authenticate users via username and one-time passcode. Step-by-step instructions and additional information can be found in the "How to Enable Multi-Factor Authentication for AWS Services by Using AWS Microsoft AD and On-Premises Credentials" blog (https://aws.amazon.com/blogs/security/how-to-enable-multi-factor-authentication-for-amazon-workspaces-and-amazon-quicksight-by-using-microsoft-ad-and-on-premises-credentials/).

The following script will enable RADIUS for your Active Directory domain previously created:

```
Enable-DSRadius -DirectoryId $Directory.DirectoryId -RadiusSettings_
AuthenticationProtocol <RadiusAuthenticationProtocol> -RadiusSettings_
DisplayLabel <String> -RadiusSettings_RadiusPort <Int32> -RadiusSettings_
RadiusRetry <Int32> -RadiusSettings_RadiusServer <String[]>
-RadiusSettings_RadiusTimeout <Int32> -RadiusSettings_SharedSecret <String>
-RadiusSettings_UseSameUsername <Boolean> -PassThru <SwitchParameter>
-Force <SwitchParameter>
```

Disable Multi-Factor Authentication

The Multi-Factor Authentication server can be removed by running a command to disable RADIUS from the directory.

```
Disable-DSRadius -DirectoryId Directory.DirectoryId
```

Reset Admin Password

In some cases, there may be a need to change a user's password, and more importantly there may be a need to change the Admin password. If necessary, the following command will reset the password for the Admin password in the working directory:

```
Reset-DSUserPassword -Username Admin -DirectoryID $Directory.DirectoryId
-NewPassword 'password'
```

The following list of parameters decomposes the command:

- **Reset-DSUserPassword** is the action to change the password for any user in the directory.

- **Username** specifies the username that will get a new password.

- **DirectoryID** identifies the directory where the user is located.

- **NewPassword** sets new password for the user.

Create a Trust Relationship

If there is a need for customers to access resources that belonged to the Managed Microsoft AD using their on-premises credentials, there may be a need to create a forest trust between Managed Microsoft AD or on-premises directories. The forest trust grants access of AWS-based resources to users in a remote forest. To create the trust, the following command can be run to configure the forest trust. The command creates the forest trust between your Managed Microsoft AD and your on-premises domain.

```
New-DSTrust -DirectoryId $Directory.DirectoryId -ConditionalForwarderIpAddr
172.16.1.153 -RemoteDomainName onprem.corporate.local -TrustDirection
OneWayOutgoing -TrustPassword 'password' -TrustType Forest
```

There is an extensive list of prerequisites for creating the trust; these include network connectivity for specific network ports, a user account for creating a trust, and conditional forwarders to route the authentication requests properly. To get a complete list of prerequisites, review the "Create a Trust Relationship Between Your AWS Managed Microsoft AD and Your On-Premises Domain" (`https://docs.aws.amazon.com/directoryservice/latest/admin-guide/ms_ad_tutorial_setup_trust.html`) documentation.

Approve Trust Relationship

Once the forest trust actions have been put in motion, these must be manually approved to running using the commands in the following section:

The command that follows approves the trust previously created:

```
Approve-DSTrust -TrustId <String>
```

Remove a Trust Relationship

An existing forest trust can be deleted by running the following command:

```
Remove-DSTrust -TrustId <String> -DeleteAssociatedConditionalForwarder $true
```

Deleting the Managed Microsoft AD Directory

Once a Managed Microsoft AD directory is no longer needed, the following command can be used to delete the directory. This command will eliminate all components of the directory, including domain objects and domain controllers:

```
Remove-DSDirectory -DirectoryId $Directory.DirectoryId
```

AWS Created Security Group

When a directory is set up, a security group is created to provide communication between the domain controllers and the client machines in EC2 and RDS. The description of the security group should read like the following "AWS created security group for d-xxxxxx directory controllers". This security group is also associated with the network interfaces the domain controllers are using to connect to the assigned subnets. The default ports configured in the security group are the following (subject to change):

- **TCP/UDP 53** – DNS

- **TCP/UDP 88** – Kerberos authentication

- **UDP 123** – NTP

- **TCP 135** – RPC

- **UDP 137–138** – Netlogon

- **TCP 139** – Netlogon

- **TCP/UDP 389** – LDAP

- **TCP/UDP 445** – SMB

- **TCP 636** – LDAPS (LDAP over TLS/SSL)

- **TCP 873** – Rsync

- **TCP 3268** – Global catalog

- **TCP/UDP 1024–65535** – Ephemeral ports for RPC

It is recommended that the default ports of this security group are reviewed and if necessary adjusted to meet your organization's security policy.

AD Connector

Another component part of the AWS Directory Service is the AD Connector, which is a proxy service that can be used to redirect authentication requests to your on-premises Microsoft Active Directory, eliminating the need to have to extend your directory or move data to the cloud. The connector is intended to be used with AWS applications such as Amazon WorkSpaces, Amazon WorkDocs, or Amazon WorkMail. It can also be used to provide your on-premises users access to the AWS Console, leveraging existing credentials and user account and password policies. The AD Connector can also integrate with RADIUS-based Multi-Factor Authentication services to increase the security posture of your AWS applications. The AD Connector also provides the ability to perform EC2 Instance seamless domain join, which can programmatically join instances to the domain during deployment.

Note   If you need authentication services for Windows-based applications, Managed Microsoft Active Directory is recommended.

AD Connector Prerequisites

To deploy the AD Connector, the following prerequisites must be met:

- VPC with at least two subnets, each in a separate availability zone.

- The VPC must be configured in default hardware tenancy.

- Network connectivity between the on-premises site, where Active Directory is hosted, and the VPC.

- On-premises Active Directory domain must be in Windows Server 2003 functional level or higher.

- Service account on the on-premises domain, with the following permissions:

  - Read users and computers

  - Create computer objects

  - Join computers to the domain

- Firewall policies allowing inbound communication to the on-premises network, from the VPC, over the following network ports:

  - **TCP/UDP 53** – DNS

  - **TCP/UDP 88** – Kerberos authentication

  - **TCP/UDP 389** – LDAP

- Kerberos pre-authentication must be enabled.

Creating AD Connector

To create an AD Connector, we will use the VPC and subnets we used in the "Managed Microsoft AD" section of this chapter. See Figure 12-16. We will also mimic the on-premises setup by connecting to the Managed Microsoft AD directory instead of a domain located in your corporate network.

The command that follows will connect AD Connector to Managed Microsoft AD.

```
Connect-DSDirectory -Name corp.example.com -Password 'password'
-ConnectSettings_CustomerDnsIp 192.168.5.33,192.168.6.181 -ConnectSettings_
CustomerUserName admin -Description "AD Connector" -ShortName CORP
-Size Small -ConnectSettings_SubnetId subnet-05873b56385adc497, subnet-
098883977cc4701bf -ConnectSettings_VpcId vpc-0e7632d32bdd1ced6
```

The following are the parameters used in the command just completed:

- **Connect-DSDirectory** is the action to create a new AD Connector.

- **Name** corp.example.com is the fully qualified name of the directory that will be connected to AD Connector.

- **Password** is the password for the service account used for the AD Connector.

- **ConnectSettings_CustomerDnsIp** is for the IP address or addresses of the domain controllers of the on-premises directory.

- **ConnectSettings_CustomerUserName** is the name service account for the AD Connector; it must have the right level of privileges to access the on-premises domain.

- **Description** is the freeform text description of the AD Connector.

- **ShortName** is the NetBIOS name of the on-premises directory.

- **Size** specifies the size of the AD Connector; values can be either Small or Large.

- **ConnectSettings_SubnetId** are the subnet IDs to be used with the AD Connector. Two subnets in separate availability zones must be specified.

- **ConnectSettings_VpcId** is the name of the VPC that is hosting the preceding two subnets listed.

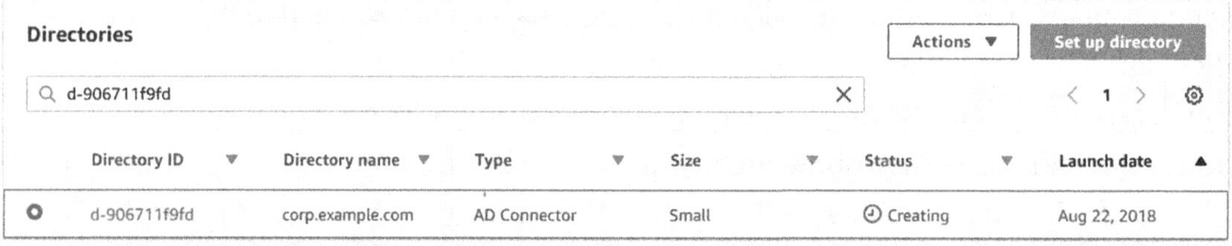

Directories							Actions ▼	Set up directory
Q d-906711f9fd						×	‹ 1 ›	⚙

Directory ID ▼	Directory name ▼	Type ▼	Size ▼	Status ▼	Launch date ▲
◎ d-906711f9fd	corp.example.com	AD Connector	Small	◷ Creating	Aug 22, 2018

Figure 12-16. *AD Connector being created*

Deleting AD Connector

If you no longer need the AD Connector or if you are moving to using Managed Microsoft AD, then the directory can be removed. In order to do this, we will run the commands in the next section:

Because we didn't store the newly created AD Connector into a variable, what we will do is add the directory object into a variable. To do this, we will run the following command:

```
$ADConnector = Get-DSDirectory | where-object {($_.Type -like '*Connector
*')}
```

Once we have the $ADConnector variable storing the right object, then we well run the following command to permanently remove the AD Connector from your AWS account:

```
Remove-DSDirectory -DirectoryId $ADConnector.DirectoryId
```

Simple AD

Simple AD is a managed directory, which is an Active Directory (AD)-compatible service, and allows for many applications and workloads that require AD to use Simple AD in place of full-blown Active Directory. Examples of these applications include AWS applications, such as Amazon WorkSpaces, Amazon WorkDocs, and Amazon WorkMail.

As part of the managed offering, Simple AD provides backup and recovery services, with daily automated snapshots, with point-in-time recovery. High availability, monitoring, and maintenance are also included as part of the managed service.

Creating Simple AD

To launch and manage a new Simple AD directory, we will follow the networking requirements outlined in the "Microsoft AD" section. This includes creating the VPC, subnets, routing configuration, and the management workstation.

Prerequisites

As with the two other directory offerings, Simple AD requires that you have a VPC with multiple subnets, each associated with a separate availability zone for resiliency. Hardware tenancy for the VPC must also be set to default or shared.

Creating a VPC

One of the requirements for hosting Simple AD, the same as Microsoft AD and the AD Connector, is networking. To move forward, what we must do is first create and configure a VPC with separate subnets and place directory controllers in each one of these subnets, which should be in different availability zones for high availability. These subnets can also reside in an existing VPC, such as the VPC created in Chapter 5 or the one created earlier in this chapter. For completeness, we will create a new VPC in the 10.0.0.0 private IP range.

```
$SimpleADVpc = New-EC2Vpc -CidrBlock '10.0.0.0/16'
```

We will continue by creating two subnets in the newly created VPC. As it is always best practice, these subnets should be in separate AZs for resiliency and is a service requirement.

Creating Private Subnets

These sets of commands will create two availability zones with two separate subnets. We will also save the newly created objects into variables we will use in the rest of the chapter.

```
$AvailabilityZone1 = 'us-east-1a'
$AvailabilityZone2 = 'us-east-1b'
$FirstSubnet = New-EC2Subnet -VpcId $SimpleADVpc.VpcId -CidrBlock
'10.0.1.0/24' -AvailabilityZone $AvailabilityZone1
$SecondSubnet = New-EC2Subnet -VpcId $SimpleADVpc.VpcId -CidrBlock
'10.0.2.0/24' -AvailabilityZone $AvailabilityZone2
```

Creating Public Subnet

To manage the new Managed Microsoft AD directory, we will need to set up a public subnet and a Remote Desktop Gateway (RDGW), the latter will serve as an administration workstation.

The first step will be to create a new subnet, which will be public.

```
$AvailabilityZone3 = 'us-east-1c'
$PublicSubnet = New-EC2Subnet -VpcId $SimpleADVpc.VpcId -CidrBlock
'10.0.0.0/24'-AvailabilityZone $AvailabilityZone3
```

Creating Internet Gateway

Once the subnet has been created, the next step is to create an Internet gateway and associating it with the previously created VPC.

```
$InternetGateway = New-EC2InternetGateway
Add-EC2InternetGateway -InternetGatewayId $InternetGateway.
InternetGatewayId -VpcId $SimpleADVpc.VpcID
```

Configuring VPC Routing

After the Internet gateway is attached to the VPC, we must make sure the local traffic stays local and traffic intended for the Internet is routed to the Internet gateway as a default route.

The script that follows will create a new route table and add a default route:

```
$Route = New-EC2RouteTable -VpcId $SimpleADVpc.VpcID
Register-EC2RouteTable -RouteTableId $Route.RouteTableId -SubnetId
$PublicSubnet.SubnetId
New-EC2Route -RouteTableId $Route.RouteTableId -DestinationCidrBlock
'0.0.0.0/0' -GatewayId $InternetGateway.InternetGatewayId
```

Configuring DNS Hostname Name Resolution

Next, to have DNS name resolution, we will enable DNS Hostnames for the VPC:

```
Edit-EC2VpcAttribute -VpcId $SimpleADVpc.VpcId -EnableDnsHostnames $true
```

Creating a Simple AD

To create a Simple AD directory, we need to take the various prerequisite components previously created and use them when running during the directory creation. To do this, we will execute the following PowerShell command:

```
$SimpleAD = New-DSDirectory -Name corp.example.com -Password 'password'
-Description "Simple AD" -ShortName CORP -Size Small -VpcSettings_
SubnetId $FirstSubnet.SubnetId,$SecondSubnet.SubnetId -VpcSettings_VpcId
$SimpleADVpc.VpcId
```

Note   Never use "password" as a password. Please choose a more complex password.

The previous command includes the minimum set of the parameters required to set up a Simple AD directory into a VPC. These commands are

- **New-DSDirectory** creates the directory.

- **Name** is the fully qualified domain name used for the directory created, which can be accessed within the VPC.

- **ShortName** is the NetBIOS name for your directory.

- **Description** is the freeform text used to identify the directory.

- **Password** is the password used for the administrator account used to manage the directory. It is important not to lose this password, as it cannot be retrieved or reset. If this occurs, you will not be able to add objects to the directory.

- **Size** is used to set the edition for the directory, either Small or Large. The Small is recommended organizations that will have a maximum of 500 users and 2000 directory objects, including users, groups, and computers. Large supports up to 5000 users and approximately 20,000 objects.

- **VpcSettings_VpcId** is used to identify the VPC where the directory will be set up.

- **VpcSettings_SubnetId** is used to specify the two subnets where the domain controllers will be deployed. The subnets must be in two separate availability zones, which are used to provide high availability for the service. Once the directory is set up, additional domain controllers can be provisioned for greater resiliency.

Creating Management Workstation

To administer Simple AD, we need a management workstation (i.e., RDGW), where we will have the tools to manage the directory. We will first create the security group to associate with management workstation. Note: It is recommended the inbound IP ranges are more restrictive than in the example provided.

The script that follows will create security group configure a policy to allow port 3389 (the Remote Desktop Protocol (RDP)) from the Internet to the management workstation:

```
$SecurityGroup = New-EC2SecurityGroup -GroupName RDGW -Description "Remote
Desktop access from Internet" -VpcId $SimpleADVpc.VpcID

$RDPRule = New-Object Amazon.EC2.Model.IpPermission
$RDPRule.IpProtocol='tcp'
$RDPRule.FromPort = 3389
$RDPRule.ToPort = 3389
$RDPRule.IpRanges = '0.0.0.0/0'
```

The next command, will allow outbound access from the management workstation to the world.

```
Grant-EC2SecurityGroupIngress -GroupId $SecurityGroup -IpPermissions $RDPRule
```

Once the security group rules are set up, the remote desktop instance can be deployed; we will use the latest version of the Windows Server 2016 Base image (ami-2d360152).

The command that follows will deploy a new instance using a T2.Medium instance type and associate the security group we just created it:

```
$RDPInstance = New-EC2Instance -ImageId ami-2d360152 -MinCount 1 -MaxCount
1 -KeyName 'key' -AssociatePublicIp $true -SecurityGroupId $SecurityGroup
-InstanceType t2.medium -SubnetId $PublicSubnet.SubnetId
```

Configuring Management Workstation

Once the management instance is deployed, in order to connect to it, we will get the IP address and password of the instance from the EC2 Console, where we will right-click the instance we just created and select Get Windows Password. See Figure 12-17.

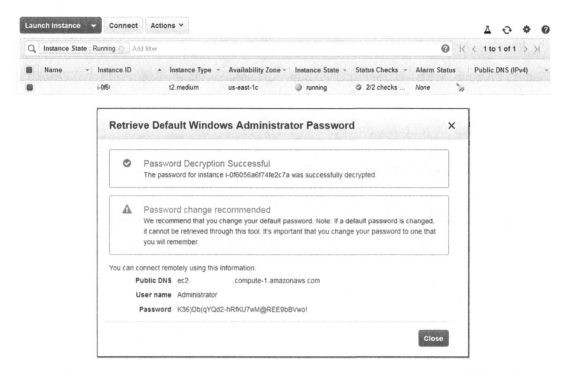

Figure 12-17. *Management workstation connectivity information*

Once we get the Public DNS name of the administration instance, we will use the Remote Desktop client to connect to it. See Figure 12-18.

Figure 12-18. *Remote Desktop client view*

Joining EC2 Instance to the Domain

Once connected, we will change the DNS settings of the administration instance to point to the Simple AD's domain controller's IP addresses. See Figure 12-19. To get the DNS IP addresses, we can either go to the AWS Console or run output the contents of variable $SimpleAD.

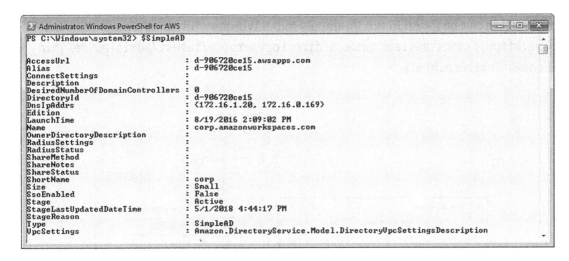

Figure 12-19. *DNS IP address details*

If the variable is empty, you can repopulate it by running the following command:

```
$SimpleAD = Get-DSDirectory -DirectoryId d-906710bc74
```

The IP addresses of the domain controllers will be listed in the **DnsIPAddrs** section of the output, as shown in Figure 12-19.

To change the DNS settings on the management workstation, we will need to identify the network interface that will get DNS servers setting. To get the specific network address, we will run the following set of commands:

The next command will locate the active Ethernet network interface on the server:

```
Get-NetIPAddress | Where-Object {$_.InterfaceIndex -eq 3}
```

If the command does not yield any results, run the command without the filter and locate the active network interface on the public subnet.

```
Get-NetIPAddress
```

Once the network interface has been located, run the following command to set the DNS servers to the Simple AD authentication servers:

```
Set-DnsClientServerAddress -InterfaceAlias "Ethernet" -ServerAddresses
10.0.1.44, 10.0.2.248
```

Alternatively, the changes can be made by right-clicking Start and selecting Network Connections and setting the DNS server settings manually. See Figure 12-20. Additional information can be found in the "Manually Join a Windows Instance" documentation page (https://docs.aws.amazon.com/directoryservice/latest/admin-guide/join_windows_instance.html).

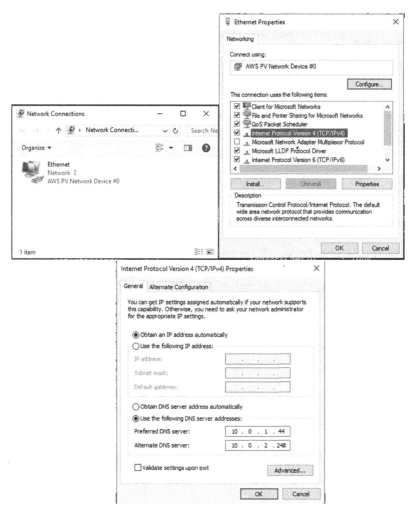

Figure 12-20. *DNS server configuration*

Once the DNS settings have been updated, we will use the following command to join the management workstation/administration instance to the CORP domain:

```
Add-Computer -Credential CORP\administrator -DomainName corp.example.com
-Restart
```

When prompted, type the appropriate password and click the OK button. See Figure 12-21. At this point, the instance will reboot as part of the domain join process. You can use this same process to join additional machines to the domain.

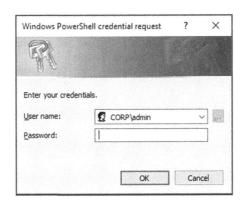

Figure 12-21. *Authentication prompt*

Install AD Tools

Once restarted, reconnect using the Remote Desktop client with the CORP\ administrator account. We will then need to install the required AD administration tools to manage the directory. To do this, run the following command. The command will install the Active Directory Users and Computers Management Console.

```
Add-WindowsFeature RSAT-AD-Tools
```

Once the AD Tools are fully installed, go to Start/Run and DSA.MSC. This will open the Active Directory Users and Computes Snap-In, which can be used to manage the resources in the domain, including user and computer objects and so on. See Figure 12-22.

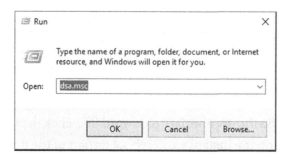

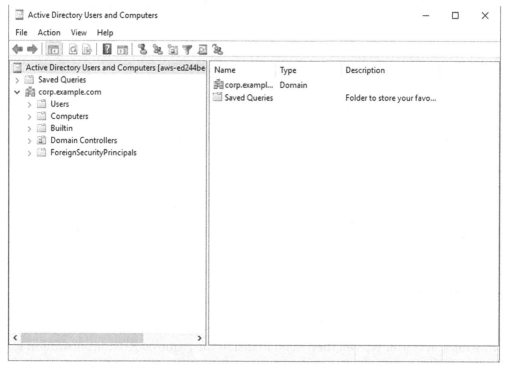

Figure 12-22. *Active Directory Users and Computers Snap-In*

Additional information can be found in the "Installing the Active Directory Administration Tools" documentation page (https://docs.aws.amazon.com/directoryservice/latest/admin-guide/ms_ad_install_ad_tools.html).

AWSAdminD-xxxxxxx

When the Simple AD directory is created, there will be an administrator account created, used by the service to perform various automated maintenance operations. This account should not be disturbed, as it may impact service availability. See Figure 12-23.

Figure 12-23. *AWSAdminD-XXXXX account*

Create a Snapshot

As with Managed Microsoft AD, backups are critical to ensure there is an ability to recover from human error or any other unexpected event. The following command will create a manual snapshot of the directory. There is a limit of five manual snapshots for the directory; once the limit is reached, one of the snapshots must be deleted in order to create any others. There are also daily automatic snapshots that are taken, which are in addition to the manual snapshot limit. Once a directory is deleted, all snapshots associated with that directory will be deleted and cannot be recovered.

The command that follows will create a manual snapshot of the recently created Simple AD directory. Also see Figure 12-24.

```
New-DSSnapshot -DirectoryId $SimpleAD.DirectoryId -Name 1stManualSnapshot
```

Snapshots (1) Info
Performs a point-in-time backup of your directory that can later be restored.

	ID		Name		Created date		Type		Status	
○	s-90655b5c66		1stManualSnapshot		September 30, 2018		Manual		⏲ Creating	

Figure 12-24. *View of snapshot being taken*

Note   Manual snapshots are highly recommended to be taken prior to any major directory change.

Restore a Snapshot

If you have an issue with the data integrity of your directory, a snapshot can be restored from either a manual or automatic snapshot.

The command that follows will restore the directory from a snapshot:

```
Restore-DSFromSnapshot -SnapshotId s-90655b5c66
```

Note   A snapshot restore does a point-in-time restore of the entire directory, which means there is risk of data loss.

Enable Single Sign-On

As with Managed Microsoft AD, Simple AD can be used to grant users in your organizations access to AWS Enterprise applications. In this section, we will configure your directory's users access to WorkDocs using Single Sign-On; however, one of the requirements is the Creation of an Access URL. Currently, the process of creating an Access URL can only be via the AWS Console. Once the Access URL is created, the Single Sign-On can be configured using the commands in the following section.

Creating an Access URL

An Access URL can be created by following these steps:

1. Go to the AWS Directory Service Console and select the appropriate directory.

2. Go to the Directory details and select the Application Management tab.

3. In the Application access URL, click the Create button (Figure 12-25).

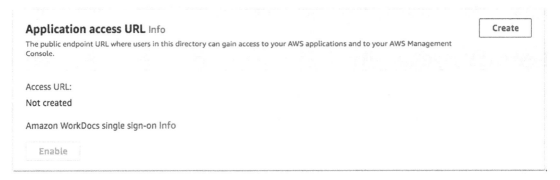

Figure 12-25. *Enable Application access URL*

4. When we get the popup, we will enter excorpo.awsapps.com (Figure 12-26).

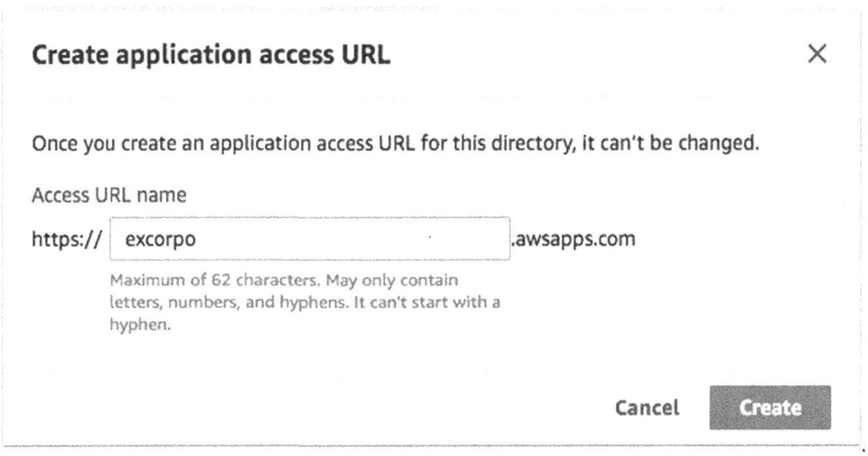

Create application access URL   ✕

Once you create an application access URL for this directory, it can't be changed.

Access URL name

https:// | excorpo | .awsapps.com

Maximum of 62 characters. May only contain letters, numbers, and hyphens. It can't start with a hyphen.

Cancel   **Create**

Figure 12-26. *Configuring custom Application access URL*

5. Once the URL has been created, we will be able to enable Single
    Sign-On to AWS applications for the directory (Figure 12-27).

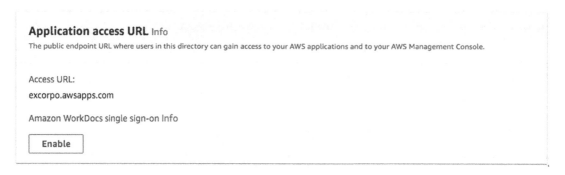

Figure 12-27. *Enabled Application access URL*

Enabling Single Sign-On

The following command provides any machine joined to the domain, access to Amazon
WorkDocs, without having to enter credentials separately:

```
Enable-DSSso -DirectoryId $SimpleAD.DirectoryId -Username administrator
-Password 'passwor'
```

Disabling Single Sign-On

If required, Single Sign-On can be disabled by running the following command:

```
Disable-DSSso -DirectoryId $SimpleAD.DirectoryId -Username administrator
-Password 'password'
```

Enabling AWS Apps and Services

Once the Access URL has been created, the following AWS Apps and Services can be
enabled to integrate with Simple AD. Currently, enabling these services can only be
performed via the AWS Console. Detailed documentation for enabling these services
can be found in the Enable Access to AWS Application and Services documentation page
(https://docs.aws.amazon.com/directoryservice/latest/admin-guide/ms_ad_
manage_apps_services.html).

- Amazon WorkSpaces

- Amazon WorkSpaces Application Manager

- Amazon WorkDocs

- Amazon WorkMail

- Amazon QuickSight

- Amazon Connect

- RDS SQL Server

- AWS Management Console

Enable Multi-Factor Authentication

Simple AD can also be configured to use Multi-Factor Authentication (MFA). One of the requirements for enabling MFA is either having an MFA plugin or a Remote Authentication Dial-In User Service (RADIUS), which can be located either in your VPC or on-premises. In this scenario, the RADIUS server would authenticate users via username and one-time passcode. Step-by-step instructions and additional information can be found in the "How to Enable Multi-Factor Authentication for AWS Services by Using AWS Microsoft AD and On-Premises Credentials" blog (`https://aws.amazon.com/blogs/security/how-to-enable-multi-factor-authentication-for-amazon-workspaces-and-amazon-quicksight-by-using-microsoft-ad-and-on-premises-credentials/`).

The command that follows will enable RADIUS for Simple AD; parameters for the settings used will be specific to the RADIUS solution being used.

```
Enable-DSRadius -DirectoryId $SimpleAD.DirectoryId -RadiusSettings_
AuthenticationProtocol <RadiusAuthenticationProtocol> -RadiusSettings_
DisplayLabel <String> -RadiusSettings_RadiusPort <Int32> -RadiusSettings_
RadiusRetry <Int32> -RadiusSettings_RadiusServer <String[]> -RadiusSettings_
RadiusTimeout <Int32> -RadiusSettings_SharedSecret <String> -RadiusSettings_
UseSameUsername <Boolean> -PassThru <SwitchParameter> -Force <SwitchParameter>
```

Disable Multi-Factor Authentication

The Multi-Factor Authentication server can be removed by running a command to disable RADIUS from the directory.

```
Disable-DSRadius -DirectoryId $SimpleAD.DirectoryId
```

Deleting Simple AD Directory

If the directory is no longer needed, it can be removed from your AWS account using the following PowerShell command. This will permanently delete the entire directory.

```
Remove-DSDirectory -DirectoryId $Simple.DirectoryId
```

AWS Created Security Group

When a directory is set up, a security group is created to provide communication between the domain controllers and EC2 instances. The description of the security group should read like the following "AWS created security group for d-xxxxxx directory controllers". This security group is also associated with the network interfaces the domain controllers are using to connect to the assigned subnets. The default ports configured in the security group are the following (subject to change):

- **TCP/UDP 53** – DNS
- **TCP/UDP 88** – Kerberos authentication
- **UDP 123** – NTP
- **TCP 135** – RPC
- **UDP 137–138** – Netlogon
- **TCP 139** – Netlogon
- **TCP/UDP 389** – LDAP
- **TCP/UDP 445** – SMB
- **TCP 636** – LDAPS (LDAP over TLS/SSL)
- **TCP 873** – Rsync

- **TCP 3268** – Global catalog

- **TCP/UDP 1024–65535** – Ephemeral ports for RPC

It is recommended that the default ports of this security group are reviewed and, if necessary, adjusted to meet your organization's security policy.

Application Compatibility

Because Simple AD is running Samba under the covers, it provides the basic features of Active Directory. If you have a third-party application, which requires advanced Active Directory features, Simple AD may not be a good fit. It is recommended that thorough testing is performed to ensure your third-party application will have no issues. Microsoft services and server applications compatible with Simple AD include IIS, SharePoint, and SQL Server.

EXERCISE 12.1: CREATE DOMAIN USER IN MICROSOFT AD

In this section, we will install and use the Active Directory PowerShell module.

To begin, we will go to the management workstation used for managing the Microsoft AD directory. We will then import the Active Directory module, so we can begin our exercise.

Open PowerShell and run the following command:

```
Import-Module ActiveDirectory
```

Once successfully imported, we use PowerShell to create new domain user and set the title and e-mail address.

```
New-ADUser -Name "Bob Smith" -OtherAttributes
@{'title'="CEO";'mail'="bsmith@corp.example.com"}
```

Once the user is created, we will need to enable the user. However, we won't be able to do that because the account does not have a password set. We will first set a password for the AD account.

```
$NewPassword = (Read-Host -Prompt "Provide New Password" -AsSecureString)

Set-ADAccountPassword -Identity 'Bob Smith' -NewPassword $NewPassword -Reset
```

Once the password is set, we can then enable the user in the directory.

```
Enable-ADAccount -Identity "Bob Smith"
```

Once the user is enabled, it can be used to authenticate to directory resources, assuming the user has been granted privileges to access those resources.

To get a full understanding of the user attributes that can be set when creating an account and also the commands used in this exercise, review the following articles on the Microsoft documentation sites: New-ADUser (`https://docs.microsoft.com/en-us/ powershell/module/addsadministration/new-aduser?view=win10-ps`), Set-ADAccountPassword (`https://docs.microsoft.com/en-us/powershell/ module/addsadministration/set-adaccountpassword?view=win10-ps`), and Enable-ADAccount (`https://docs.microsoft.com/en-us/powershell/module/ addsadministration/enable-adaccount?view=win10-ps`).

Summary

In this chapter, we saw how AWS Directory Service can be used to centralize access and resource management using Managed Microsoft AD, AD Connector, and Simple AD. We also saw how existing on-premises credential can be used to access resources hosted on the AWS Cloud.

Throughout the chapter, we created directories, configured multi-factor authentication, created forest trust between on-premises directories and Managed Microsoft AD, and finally used the AD Connector and Simple AD to grant on-premises users access to AWS applications, such as WorkDocs. As we saw, there are multiple options for access and resource management. It is important to understand how each one option works and what it was designed to do, so you can select the one that fits your use case. Of course, you can always mix and match if your use case justifies the need.

## CHAPTER 13

Amazon WorkSpaces and Amazon AppStream 2.0

An important area in which cloud can add value to your organization is in End-User Computing; this is because you are able to quickly and easily provision virtual desktops, streaming applications, without the need of purchasing expensive hardware and making a long-term financial commitment. There are two specific End-User Computing AWS services which we will focus on, Amazon WorkSpaces and Amazon AppStream 2.0. These services provide users access to their documents, applications, and other resources, from anywhere and anytime, as long as they, users, are on a supported device. These services both provide a pay-as-you-go model and also give you the flexibility to always have the resources running or run them when you need them.

Amazon WorkSpaces is a cloud-based virtual desktop service, which offers both Windows and Linux desktop environments. These virtual desktops can be accessed from any supported client, downloadable from AWS or your favorite mobile app store. Benefits of the service include centralized management, repeatability, and flexibility, as well as the ability to publish or install application packages, with various licensing options.

Amazon AppStream 2.0 is also an End-User Computing service, but unlike Amazon WorkSpaces, there is no need to deploy a desktop environment to grant your users access to your applications. The applications can be imported to AWS and published, made accessible via your favorite HTML5-compatible browser. There are also security benefits for using AppStream 2.0, because data is not stored on the end-user devices.

Amazon WorkSpaces Architecture

We will begin with Amazon WorkSpaces by provisioning virtual desktops via PowerShell. In order to move forward, there are certain things that we need to determine, such as the region and the operating system to use, Windows or Amazon Linux desktops are

© Brian Beach, Steven Armentrout, Rodney Bozo, Emmanuel Tsouris 2019
B. Beach et al., *Pro PowerShell for Amazon Web Services*, https://doi.org/10.1007/978-1-4842-4850-8_13

available. Once we have selected the right region and operating system, we will need to determine the right hardware resource configuration, as this will directly impact the performance of the desktop's user experience.

Once the user experience configuration options have been identified, the next thing to determine is whether Simple AD, AD Connector, or AWS Managed Microsoft AD will be used for authentication and resource management services. Depending on the directory being used, the configuration and management options may vary.

Figure 13-1 depicts the Amazon WorkSpaces architecture, which outlines the WorkSpaces architecture and network requirements which use AWS Directory Service for authentication. If selecting the Quick Setup, which is one of the deployment options, Simple AD will be deployed. If customization for Managed AD or AD Connector is needed, then an Advanced Setup configuration is required.

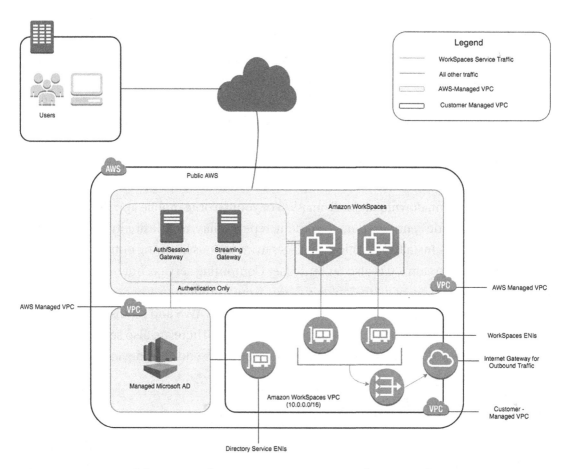

Figure 13-1. *WorkSpaces architecture using Managed Microsoft AD*

Client Requirements

The Amazon WorkSpaces virtual desktop service is accessible via client application that is available for various supported devices.

Client applications are available for the following devices:

- Windows computers
- Mac computers
- Chromebooks
- iPads
- Android tables
- Fire tables
- Zero client devices

Browser-based access is also available for Windows WorkSpaces, for the following supported browsers:

- Chrome 53 and later
- Firefox 49 and later

Managing Amazon WorkSpaces

In order to get started with launching Amazon WorkSpaces, we have to go to the WorkSpaces console to complete this task. Once the WorkSpaces service has been deployed, the management of the resources can be performed via PowerShell.

Basic Setup

The following steps show you how to perform the basic setup:

1. From the Amazon WorkSpaces Console, click the Get Started Now link.

2. Once on the Get Started with Amazon WorkSpaces page, there will be an option for selecting either a Quick Setup or an Advanced Setup. See Figure 13-2.

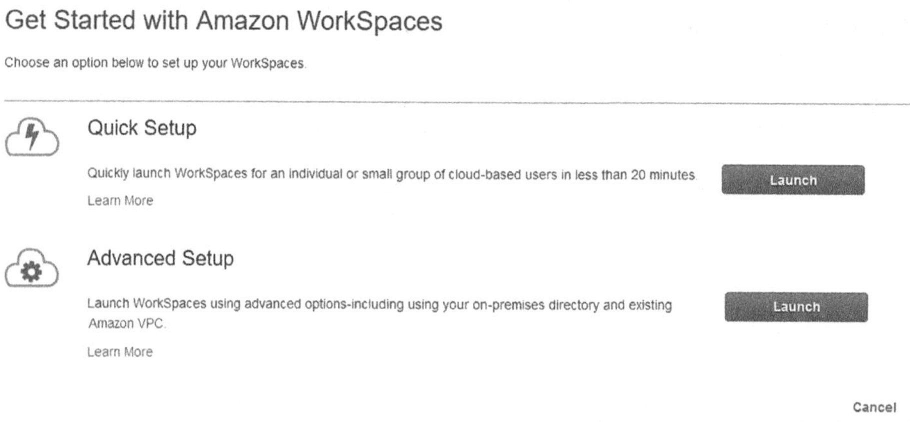

Get Started with Amazon WorkSpaces

Choose an option below to set up your WorkSpaces

Quick Setup

Quickly launch WorkSpaces for an individual or small group of cloud-based users in less than 20 minutes.

Learn More

[Launch]

Advanced Setup

Launch WorkSpaces using advanced options-including using your on-premises directory and existing Amazon VPC.

Learn More

[Launch]

Cancel

Figure 13-2. *Basic or Advanced Setup selection window*

If the Quick Setup is selected, the following tasks will be completed:

a. IAM role, workspaces_DefaultRole, with permissions to create Elastic Network Interfaces and also list WorkSpaces directories.

b. Creates a VPC.

c. Sets up and configures Simple AD, which will be used to store user and WorkSpaces resources objects.

d. A service account will be created to add WorkSpaces to the directory.

e. Creates WorkSpace desktop environments with a public IP address.

f. Sends e-mail communications to the designated WorkSpaces users.

On the other hand, if the Advanced Setup is selected, you will have the flexibility to configure the setup that meets your business needs, including having the ability to determine whether to use an AD Connector, a Simple AD, or a Managed Microsoft AD domain, with or without the use of a Trusted Domain. If the latter option is selected, then you will need to make sure the VPC, subnets, and availability zones, as well as the directory components, are properly configured.

3. The next thing in the Quick Setup option is to select a Bundle, as shown in Figure 13-3, which is a package that is optimized for a particular use case, and comes with a set of predetermined resources (e.g., CPU and Memory) and applications (e.g., Microsoft Office).

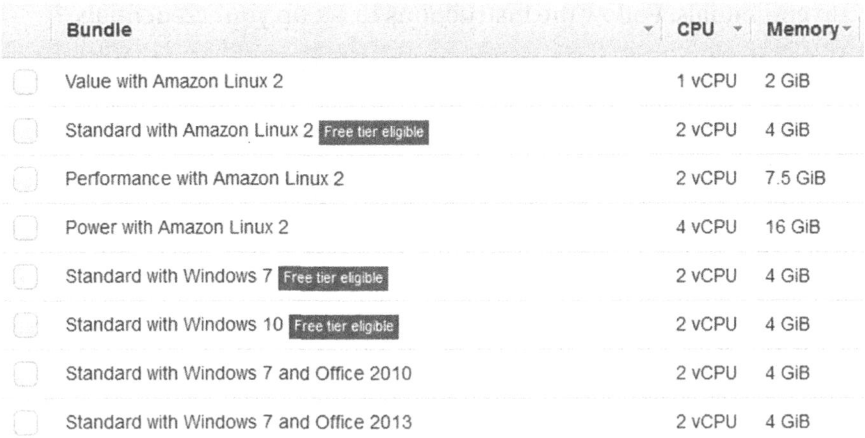

Bundle	CPU	Memory
Value with Amazon Linux 2	1 vCPU	2 GiB
Standard with Amazon Linux 2 Free tier eligible	2 vCPU	4 GiB
Performance with Amazon Linux 2	2 vCPU	7.5 GiB
Power with Amazon Linux 2	4 vCPU	16 GiB
Standard with Windows 7 Free tier eligible	2 vCPU	4 GiB
Standard with Windows 10 Free tier eligible	2 vCPU	4 GiB
Standard with Windows 7 and Office 2010	2 vCPU	4 GiB
Standard with Windows 7 and Office 2013	2 vCPU	4 GiB

Figure 13-3. *Bundle selection window*

4. Once a bundle is selected, the next step will allow you to create an Amazon WorkSpaces user in the Simple AD directory previously created, as well as notify the user about the availability of their WorkSpaces instance. See Figure 13-4.

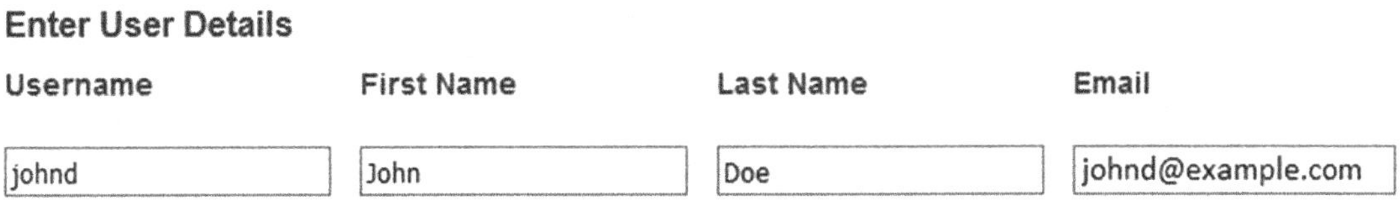

Enter User Details

Username	First Name	Last Name	Email
johnd	John	Doe	johnd@example.com

Figure 13-4. *WorkSpaces user assignment form*

5. The last step is to select the Launch WorkSpaces button to launch the instance.

Connecting to Your WorkSpaces

Once an e-mail invitation is sent, the user who received the invitation can connect to their WorkSpace by downloading their preferred client from the link included in the invitation:

1.   In the invitation e-mail, there will be instructions included to set up credentials. Follow the instructions to set up your credentials.

2.   Once the credentials have been set up, you will be prompted to download the client.

3.   After downloading and installing the WorkSpaces client, start it. At the prompt, enter the registration code included in the e-mail and select Register.

4.   In the sign-in prompt, enter your username and password, and click Sign In.

Advanced Setup

As previously mentioned, the Advanced Setup option offers the flexibility to be explicit on the networking and directory configurations.

Creating WorkSpaces with Microsoft AD

As you may have guessed, the instructions provided in Chapter 12, AWS Directory Service, can be used to create a Microsoft AD directory and leveraged with Amazon WorkSpaces:

1.   To create a Microsoft AD, follow the instructions provided in Chapter 12.

2.   Go to the WorkSpaces Console, and click the Directories link (Figure 13-5).

Directories

Figure 13-5. *Directory selection option*

3. The Directories list should include the list of available directories, including any directory using Microsoft AD, AD Connector, or Simple AD. Select the Microsoft AD directory to be used with WorkSpaces, then click the Actions link, and finally select the Register.

4. When prompted, confirm directory registration by selecting Register (Figure 13-6).

Register directory   ✕

Register your directory for use with WorkSpaces.

                                                    Cancel   **Register**

Figure 13-6. *Directory registration option*

5. The registration will take a few minutes, wait until the registration is complete, as shown in Figure 13-7.

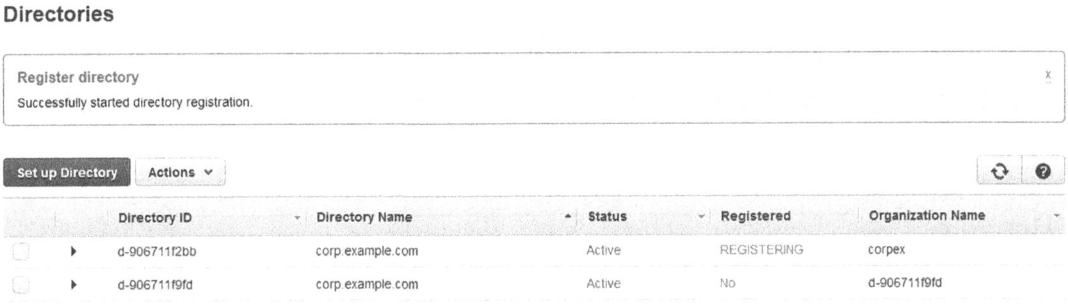

Directories

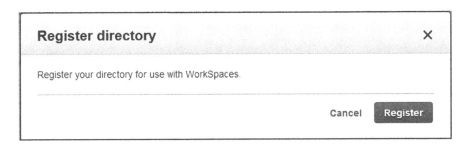

Figure 13-7. *Directory registration confirmation page*

6. Once the registration is complete, we will be able to launch WorkSpaces via PowerShell. See the next section for detailed instructions.

Creating WorkSpaces with AD Connector

The instructions for connecting WorkSpaces to AD Connector were also included in Chapter 12. However, for completeness, we will also provide the instructions in this section:

1. Follow the instructions provided in Chapter 12 to create an AD Connector.

2. Go to the WorkSpaces Console, and click the Directories link (Figure 13-8).

Directories

		Directory ID	▾	Directory Name	▴	Status	▾	Registered	Organization Name	▾
☐	▶	d-906711f2bb		corp.example.com		Active		No	corpex	
☐	▶	d-906711f9fd		corp.example.com		Active		No	d-906711f9fd	

Figure 13-8. *List of directories available to select*

3. The Directories list should include the list of available directories, including any directory using Microsoft AD, AD Connector, or Simple AD. Select the AD Connector to be used with WorkSpaces, then click the Actions link, and finally select the Register.

4. When prompted, confirm directory registration by selecting Register (Figure 13-9).

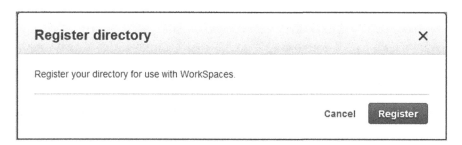

Figure 13-9. *Register directory page*

5. The registration will take a few minutes, wait until the registration is complete. See Figure 13-10.

Directories

Figure 13-10. *Directory registration confirmation page*

6. Once the registration is complete, we will be able to launch WorkSpaces via PowerShell. See the next section for detailed instructions.

Launching New WorkSpace

In order to launch a new WorkSpace, we will store required parameters for deploying a virtual desktop into variables.

The first variable we will store is for the directory object for the active Microsoft AD directory associated with WorkSpaces.

```
$WKSManagedAD = Get-WKSWorkspaceDirectory | where-object {($_.DirectoryType
-like 'MicrosoftAD')}
```

Note   If there are multiple Microsoft AD directories, it would be recommended to filter for a directory ID, instead of filtering by a directory type. See the following example.

```
$WKSManagedAD_Id = Get-WKSWorkspaceDirectory | where-object
{($_.DirectoryId -eq 'd-XXXXXXX')}
```

The next parameter we will need to store as a variable, in order to deploy WorkSpaces, is of the WorkSpaces Bundle. As previously mentioned, a Bundle is a predetermined set of packages that include software and virtual hardware resources (e.g., Windows 7 and 8GB of Memory).

```
$WKSBundle = Get-WKSWorkspaceBundle -Owner Amazon | where-object {($_.Name
-eq 'Value with Windows 7')}
```

Once we have those objects stored in variables, we will use the following command to create a WorkSpace assigned for the CORP\Bob user, which is a domain user in the Microsoft AD directory we previously created.

```
$WorkSpace = New-WKSWorkspace -Workspace @{"BundleID" = $WKSBundle.
BundleId; "DirectoryId" = $WKSManagedAD.DirectoryId; "UserName" = "admin"}
```

Note   Since multiple components need to be created and configured to launch a WorkSpace (e.g., ENI, security groups, etc.), the creation process may take some time.

If deploying the WorkSpace against AD Connector, the directory information can be stored with the following command:

```
$WKSADConnector = Get-WKSWorkspaceDirectory | where-object {($_.
DirectoryType -like 'AD_Connector')}
```

Managing WorkSpace

Once the WorkSpace is fully launched, we can begin managing it.

As an administrator, there are often times when you need uninterrupted access to a system, making sure that other users don't make reboot, start, stop, or rebuild the system. In these cases, the WorkSpace can be put into an ADMIN_MAINTENANCE mode, which prevents the execution of API calls that will run the operations listed previously. See Figure 13-11.

```
Edit-WKSWorkspaceState -WorkspaceId $Workspace.WorkspaceId -WorkspaceState
ADMIN_MAINTENANCE
```

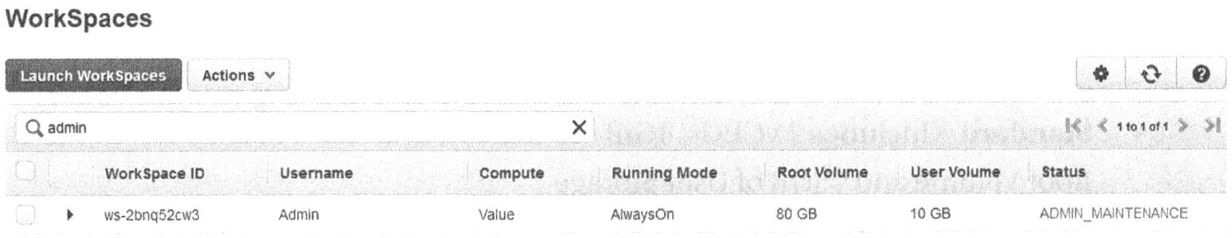

WorkSpaces

	WorkSpace ID	Username	Compute	Running Mode	Root Volume	User Volume	Status
▶	ws-2bnq52cw3	Admin	Value	AlwaysOn	80 GB	10 GB	ADMIN_MAINTENANCE

Launch WorkSpaces   Actions ∨

Q admin

Figure 13-11. *Viewing the Status change triggered by the previous command*

Once the dedicated access to the virtual desktop is no longer required, then with a simple command, as shown as follows, this can be changed.

```
Edit-WKSWorkspaceState -WorkspaceId $Workspace.WorkspaceId -WorkspaceState
AVAILABLE
```

Another example of modifying a workstation is changing the resources associated with the bundle that was selected during deployment. In this example, the command provided as follows can be used to change the compute type from its current value to something that better meets a customer's business needs.

Note   WorkSpace's properties can't be changed within 6 hours of creation (i.e., 21,600 seconds).

Modify Compute Type

The bundle associated with a WorkSpace can be edited by changing the property associated with that setting. The following example will change the compute type from Value, which was specified when created, to Standard:

```
Edit-WKSWorkspaceProperty -WorkspaceId $Workspace.WorkspaceId
-WorkspaceProperties_ComputeTypeName STANDARD
```

Additional values for the compute type property are the following (Figure 13-12):

- **Graphics** – Includes 8 vCPUs, 15GiB of Memory, 1 vGPU, 4GiB of Video Memory, and 100GB of SSD Root Volume and also User Storage

- **Performance** – Includes 2 vCPUs, 7.5GiB of Memory, and 175GB of SSD Root Volume and 100GB of User Storage

355

- **Power** – Includes 4 vCPUs, 16GiB of Memory, and 80GB of SSD Root Volume and 100GB of User Storage

- **Standard** – Includes 2 vCPUs, 4GiB of Memory, and 80GB of SSD Root Volume and 75GB of User Storage

- **Value** – Includes 1 vCPU, 2GiB of Memory, and 80GB of SSD Root Volume and 10GB of User Storage

Amazon WorkSpaces Bundles

	Value	Standard	Performance	Power	Graphics
vCPUs	1	2	2	4	8
Memory GiB	2	4	7.5	16	15
vGPUs					1
Video Memory GiB					4
SSD Root Volume GB*	80	80	80	175	100
SSD User Storage GB*	10	50	100	100	100
Software	Utilities software bundle	Utilities software bundle	Utilities software bundle	Utilities software bundle	Utilities software bundle

* You can change the storage allocation for root and user volumes at launch, or increase any time after that, up to 1,000 GB per volume.

Figure 13-12. *Amazon WorkSpaces Bundles options*

In addition to being able to edit the compute type attribute, the following attributes can also be modified:

- **WorkspaceProperties_RootVolumeSizeGib** – Specifies the size of the root volume, in Gib

- **WorkspaceProperties_RunningMode** – Sets the attribute between ALWAYS_ON and AUTO_STOP

- **WorkspaceProperties_RunningModeAutoStopTimeoutInMinute** – Provides the ability to set the auto stop time, in 60 minutes increments

- **WorkspaceProperties_UserVolumeSizeGib** – Sets the attribute for the user volume, in GiB

As an additional example, we will change the default running mode of the virtual desktop we created and change the WorkSpace to auto stop.

```
Edit-WKSWorkspaceProperty -WorkspaceId $Workspace.WorkspaceId
-WorkspaceProperties_RunningMode AUTO_STOP
```

To view the current properties of the existing WorkSpaces, the following command can be fun:

```
get-wksworkspace | format-list
```

In most cases, organizations will have more than one WorkSpace; therefore, it is important to only focus on getting details of the WorkSpaces we care about. In this case, we will filter on the username property, but we can use any WorkSpace property as a filter.

```
Get-WKSWorkspace | where-object {($_.UserName -eq 'Bob')} | format-list
```

Tagging a WorkSpace

Tagging a WorkSpace is something useful and in some cases required for managing resources effectively. To tag WorkSpaces, we can run the following command to both create the object with the tag and set the properties to the correct values. Once the object has the right data, we can run the New-WKSTag cmdlet to set tag(s) for a WorkSpace.

```
$WKSTag = New-Object Amazon.WorkSpaces.Model.Tag
$WKSTag.Key = "Name"
$WKSTag.Value = "Development"

New-WKSTag -WorkspaceId $Workspace.WorkspaceId -Tag $WKSTag
```

Typical administrator and end-user tasks are starting, stopping, or restarting a WorkSpace.

Starting a WorkSpace

To start a WorkSpace, use the following command:

```
Start-WKSWorkspace -WorkspaceId $Workspace.WorkspaceId
```

Stopping a WorkSpace

On the other hand, if a WorkSpace needs to get stopped, the following command can be used:

```
Stop-WKSWorkspace -WorkspaceId $Workspace.WorkspaceId
```

Restarting a WorkSpace

A WorkSpace virtual desktop can also be restarted in a similar fashion. Of course, if an instance is stopped, it can't be restarted, so it must be in an available status to be restarted. When a rebuild is executed, the latest available image of the original bundle will be used. The user data drive will be restored from a snapshot, which could be as old as 12 hours. This is because currently the automatic snapshot process takes place every 12 hours.

```
Restart-WKSWorkspace -WorkspaceId $Workspace.WorkspaceId
```

Rebuilding a WorkSpace

Another important administration task, especially addressing issues with software or operating system, is of rebuilding a WorkSpace. This can be accomplished by running the following command:

```
Reset-WKSWorkspace -WorkspaceId $Workspace.WorkspaceId
```

Deleting a WorkSpace

When a WorkSpace is no longer needed, the following command can be run to completely eliminate the virtual desktop and the associated user's data:

```
Remove-WKSWorkspace -WorkspaceId $Workspace.WorkspaceId
```

Note   When a WorkSpace is deleted, all of the user data is destroyed. If data persistence is required, a backup of the user data must be performed to an external destination, such as S3.

Amazon AppStream 2.0

Imagine having the ability to run your enterprise applications, without needing to download or install any application files to your workstation. With Amazon AppStream 2.0, you have the ability to do just that. The service is a HTML5 compatible and can stream applications from AWS to any client globally, in a pay-as-you-go model. As typical with AWS managed services, it can easily scale to offer expected performance while at the same time eliminating the need to store any user or application files locally, thus increasing the security posture of your application.

Amazon AppStream 2.0 Architecture

We must understand the following concepts in order to design, deploy, and manage AppStream 2.0 for your organization. The options that affect the settings of the components discussed in this section will determine the behavior of AppStream for users, so it is important to ensure you have a good handle of these concepts.

- **Image** – In a similar vein to the way Amazon Machine Images (AMIs) work, AppStream images contain applications that users can stream. Customers can choose to use custom images or base images provided by AWS. Images are region specific, but can be copied across regions. Also, images can't be changed once they are created. If changes are required, a new image needs to be created. To familiarize yourself with the images available, it is recommended you review the AppStream 2.0 Base Image Version History documentation page (`https://docs.aws.amazon.com/appstream2/latest/developerguide/base-image-version-history.html`).

- **Image Builder** – The images described earlier can be created with an Image Builder, which is a virtual machine used to install and test your applications.

- **Fleet** – The instances streaming your application make up a Fleet, which can either be static or elastic in nature. There is a requirement to have one user per instance.

- **Stack –** The streaming application makes up the stack, which is comprised of a fleet, access policies, and storage configurations.

- **User Pool** – A User Pool is used to manage users and associates Stacks (i.e., streaming applications) to users.

Requirements

Amazon AppStream 2.0 has requirements for publishing applications and for accessing applications that have been published. In this section, we will discuss both sets of requirements.

Publishing Requirements

The first set of requirements for publishing applications are networking requirements, as the streaming instances and Image Builders need to be accessible, and should also be able to access network resources (e.g., databases, network shares, etc.) and the Internet. When deploying fleet instances in a VPC, it is recommended that these instances are deployed in multiple availability zones for high availability and redundancy reasons. One thing to keep in mind is that every instance in your fleet will require an Elastic Network Interface (ENI), so it is important that service limits are reviewed prior to making your application available to your users.

If the streaming application requires domain authentication or resources in a domain, the standard domain port connectivity access is required. The streaming instances must also be able to communicate with the EC2 metadata service, via http://169.254.169.254.

Note   The AppStream service uses two network interfaces, one for local VPC resource access and the Internet and the second one for management (port 8443) and streaming to client devices (port 8300). The management interface uses the IP range of 192.19.0.0/16, so it is critical to prevent conflicts with this network range.

Client Requirements

In order for client devices to connect to the AppStream 2.0 service, port 443 and port 53 are required from the client connectivity. Additionally, in order for both Session Gateway and CloudFront can be accessed correctly, domains *.amazonappstream.com and *.cloudfront.net must be whitelisted, respectively.

Getting Started with AppStream 2.0

In order to get started, we will first go to the AppStream 2.0 Console; once in the console, we will explore the two options for publishing applications. If you're a new customer and need to get familiar with the service, a user-friendly way of starting is by using the Quick Links screen and deploying a stack with sample applications. The second deployment option and the one recommended for production environments is a deployment of a custom stack.

Deploying a Sample Applications Stack

As mentioned before, an easy way to get familiar with AppStream 2.0 is by deploying a stack with sample applications. To do this we will go to the Amazon AppStream 2.0 Console:

1.   Go to the AppStream 2.0 Console.

2.   Click the Get started button (Figure 13-13).

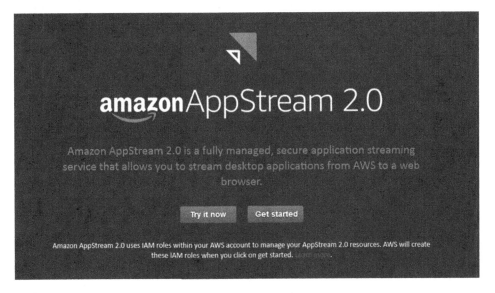

Figure 13-13. *Amazon AppStream 2.0 Get Started page*

3. Click the Agree and Continue button.

4. At this point, you should be on the Quick Links screen (Figure 13-14).

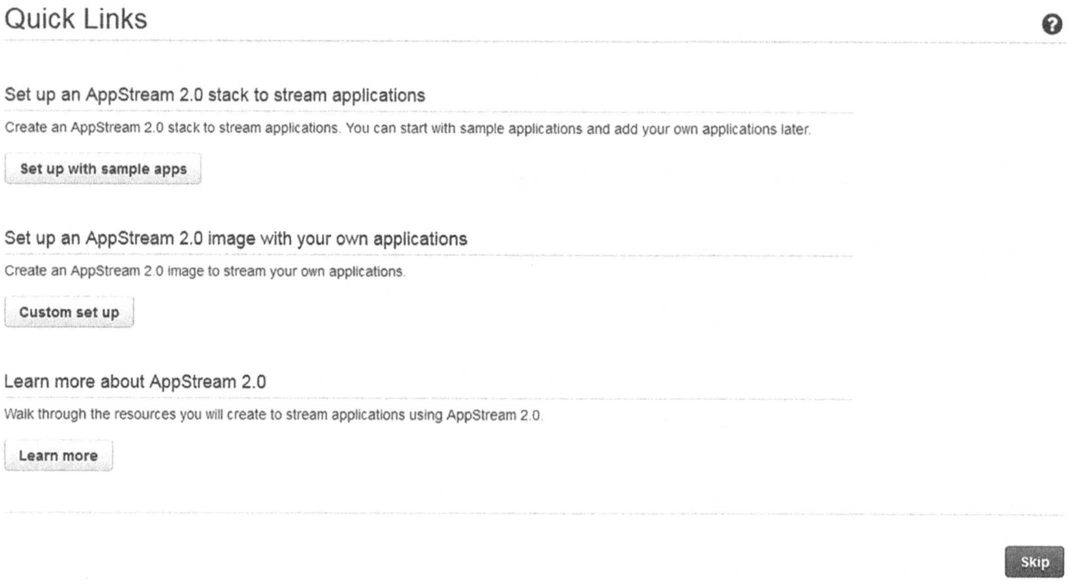

Quick Links   ❓

Set up an AppStream 2.0 stack to stream applications

Create an AppStream 2.0 stack to stream applications. You can start with sample applications and add your own applications later.

Set up with sample apps

Set up an AppStream 2.0 image with your own applications

Create an AppStream 2.0 image to stream your own applications.

Custom set up

Learn more about AppStream 2.0

Walk through the resources you will create to stream applications using AppStream 2.0.

Learn more

Skip

Figure 13-14. *Quick Links page*

Launching Sample Applications

In order to get familiar with the architecture and the service, we will deploy a sample application. To do this, we will use one of the Quick Links options from the previous section:

1. To get started with sample apps, we will click the Setup with sample apps button.

2. Enter Name, Display Name, Description, and optional Redirect and Feedback URLs. Click Next once all the fields have been populated. See Figure 13-15.

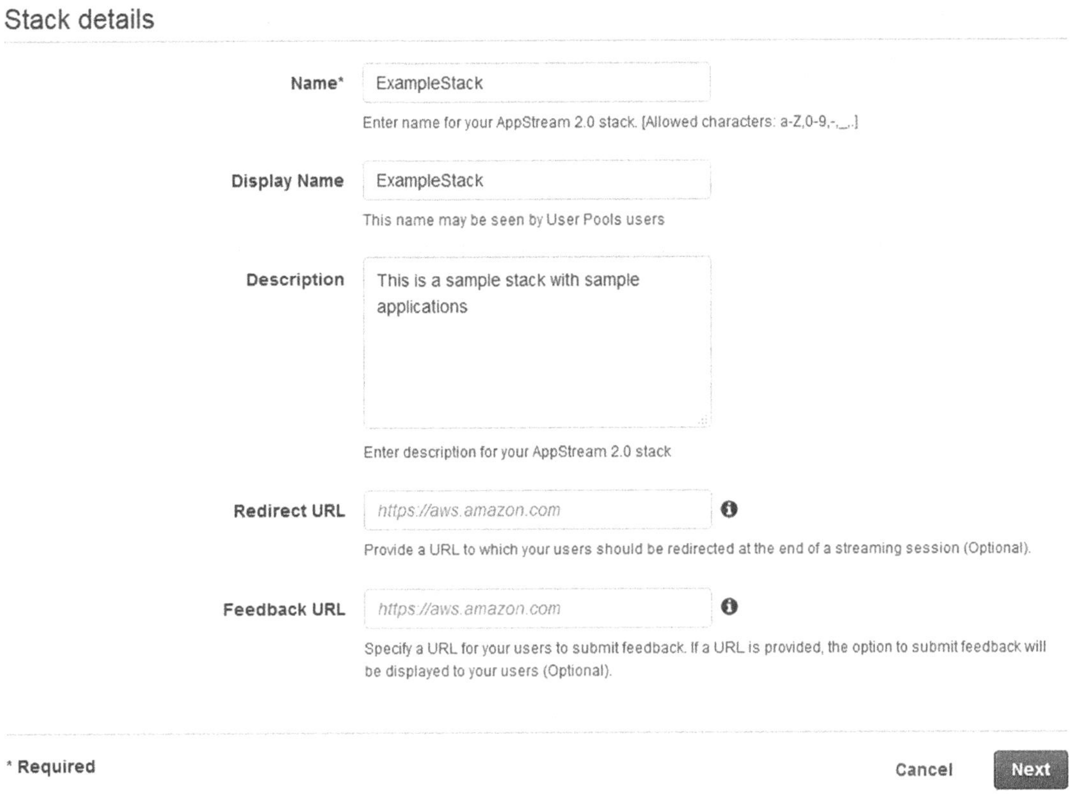

Stack details

Name*	ExampleStack
	Enter name for your AppStream 2.0 stack. [Allowed characters: a-Z,0-9,-,_,.]
Display Name	ExampleStack
	This name may be seen by User Pools users
Description	This is a sample stack with sample applications
	Enter description for your AppStream 2.0 stack
Redirect URL	https://aws.amazon.com ❶
	Provide a URL to which your users should be redirected at the end of a streaming session (Optional).
Feedback URL	https://aws.amazon.com ❶
	Specify a URL for your users to submit feedback. If a URL is provided, the option to submit feedback will be displayed to your users (Optional).

* Required   Cancel   **Next**

Figure 13-15.   *Stack details form*

3. On the next screen, scroll down and select the Amazon-AppStream2-Sample-Image-06-20-2017 image. Click Next.

4. From the Configure fleet page, select the following settings:

   - Instance type: General purpose – stream.standard.medium, 2 vCPUs, 4 Memory (GiB)

   - Fleet type: On-Demand

   - User session details:

     - Maximum session duration: 15 minutes

     - Disconnect timeout: 15 minutes

- Fleet capacity:

  - Minimum capacity: 1

  - Maximum capacity: 2

- Scaling details: Leave default

5. On the Configure network page, select the default settings and click Next.

6. From the Enable Storage page, leave the default settings and click Next.

7. Click Review, to leave the defaults, on the User Settings page.

8. On the Review page, click Create.

9. When prompted, click the check box to acknowledge the charges, and click Create. See Figure 13-16.

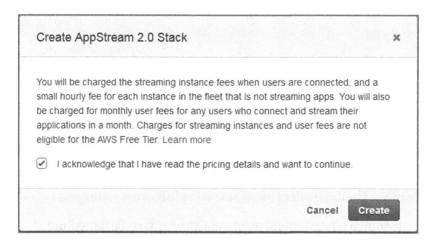

Figure 13-16. *AppStream 2.0 Stack pricing user acknowledgment form*

10. From the Stacks page, select the ExampleStack stack and click Actions, then click Create streaming URL.

11. For the User ID, enter a user ID, and then select an expiration to set the duration of the generated URL.

12. When prompted, click the Copy Link button. See Figure 13-17.

Create streaming URL - ExampleStack   ✕

Link was copied successfully to your clipboard

User ID ▲	URL	▲	
admin	https://appstream2.us-east-1.aws.amazon.com		Copy Link

Figure 13-17. *Unique streaming URL*

13. Go to your favorite HTML5-compatible browser and paste and
     go to the URL. The URL should render a page with the sample
     applications published with the package. See Figure 13-18.

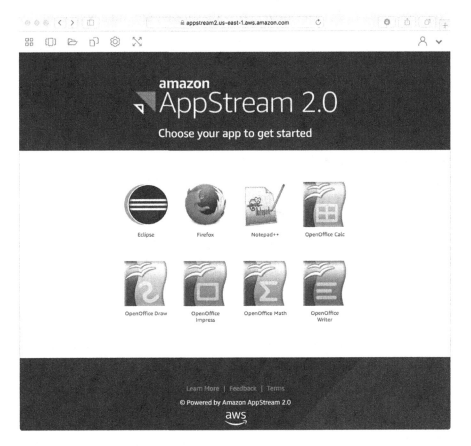

Figure 13-18. *Sample Stack application selection page*

Deploying Custom Applications Stack

When deploying a custom application stack, the first thing to identify is whether the applications being streamed will reside in a new or existing VPC. If the applications will interact with some existing network resources, then it will likely reside in an existing VPC.

If a new VPC is required, one can be created with the instructions provided in the VPC chapter of this book. In order to have high availability and redundancy, it is recommended that streaming instances are placed in at least two availability zones, which means that these will also need to be created in the newly created VPC. The subnets associated with the availability zones must be public, as AppStream 2.0 requires Internet access via an Internet gateway.

If you want to leverage advanced networking configuration, you can also configure the AppStream 2.0 resources to reside in a private subnet, behind a NAT gateway.

The AppStream 2.0 and Active Directory authenticated and SAML 2.0 Single Sign-On Federated implementations have so many layers, that each would require a separate chapter on their own, if covered in depth. For brevity, we will cover a some of the Active Directory integration options, mainly because Active Directory should be used for production implementations of the AppStream 2.0 service.

Creating Directory Configuration

When domain resources are required for the AppStream 2.0 applications, one of the required settings is to create a directory configuration, which will associate a service account with the service. The following commands will create an AppStream directory configuration. If you don't have an Active Directory domain available, one can be created following the instructions provided in Chapter 12.

Once an Active Directory domain is available, the following command can be used to set up an AppStream 2.0 Directory Configuration:

```
$DirectoryConfiguration = New-APSDirectoryConfig -DirectoryName
corp.example.com -ServiceAccountCredentials_AccountName corp\
admin -ServiceAccountCredentials_AccountPassword 'password'
-OrganizationalUnitDistinguishedName OU=Computers,OU=corp,DC=corp,
DC=example,DC=com
```

To verify if the Directory Configuration was created as expected, you can log in to the AWS Console and look at the settings. An example is depicted in Figure 13-19.

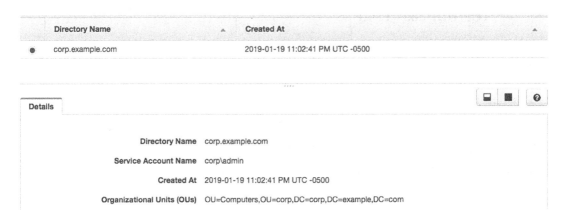

Figure 13-19. *Directory Configuration verification page*

If the streaming applications will leverage Active Directory domain-based resources, it is important to ensure the connectivity between steaming instances and image builders is available and open to the directory services. This means that networking between the subnets that have both AppStream 2.0 resources and Active Directory is configured and security groups are configured to allow port connectivity.

The following port connectivity is required between the AppStream 2.0 VPC and your domain controllers:

- **TCP/UDP 53** – DNS
- **TCP/UDP 88** – Kerberos authentication
- **UDP 123** – NTP
- **TCP 135** – RPC
- **UDP 137–138** – Netlogon
- **TCP 139** – Netlogon
- **TCP/UDP 389** – LDAP
- **TCP/UDP 445** – SMB
- **TCP 1024–65535** – Dynamic ports for RPC

Note   The service account used in the Directory Configuration must have the following minimum permissions to the Organizational Unit (OU) within Active Directory: Create Computer Object, Change Password, Reset Password, and Write Description.

Getting Directory Config List

If you are unsure about the Directory Configurations that have been made, you can run the Get-APSDirectoryConfigList cmdlet to get the list of available configurations.

To get a complete list of configuration, as shown in the code that follows and in Figure 13-20

```
Get-APSDirectoryConfigList
```

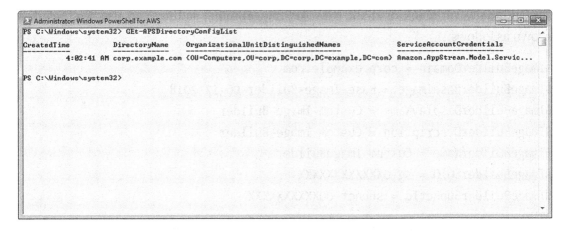

Figure 13-20. *Directory Configuration list*

Launching an Image Builder

The first step to publishing and AppStream 2.0 application is to create an application builder, which will be used to customize an image for the custom application.

In order to avoid issues with running the New-APSImageBuilder command, we will create a variable for the Organizational Unit which will store the computer objects for the AppStream instances.

```
$ImageBuilderOU = OU=Computers,OU=corp,DC=corp,DC=example,DC=com
$ImageBuilder = New-APSImageBuilder -ImageName Base-Image-
Builder-06-12-2018 -AppstreamAgentVersion LATEST -Description
custom-image-builder -DomainJoinInfo_DirectoryName corp.example.com
-DisplayName Custom-Image-Builder -EnableDefaultInternetAccess $true
-InstanceType stream.standard.medium -Name Example -DomainJoinInfo_
OrganizationalUnitDistinguishedName $ImageBuilderOU -VpcConfig_
SecurityGroupId sg-00XXXXXXXXX -VpcConfig_SubnetId subnet-00XXXXXXXXX
```

While the image builder is being created, the Status will be set to pending until the image builder is ready.

Optionally, variables for all the New-APSImageBuilder settings can also be created as shown as follows:

```
$ImageBuilderDomain = corp.example.com
$ImageBuilderBaseImage = Base-Image-Builder-06-12-2018
$ImageBuilderDisplayName = Custom-Image-Builder
$ImageBuilderDescription = Custom-Image-Builder
$ImageBuilderName = Custom-ImageBuilder
$ImageBuilderSGiD = sg-0XXXXXXXXXXXX
$ImageBuilderSubnetId = subnet-00XXXXXXXXXX
```

If you don't need domain resources, the Image Builder can be deployed with as simply as running an appropriate non-domain-based Image Builder launch. See example as follows:

```
$NonDomainImageBuilder = New-APSImageBuilder -ImageName Base-Image-
Builder-06-12-2018 -AppstreamAgentVersion LATEST -Description NonDomain-
image-builder -DisplayName NonDomain-image-builder -InstanceType stream.
standard.medium -Name NonDomain-Image-Builder -EnableDefaultInternetAccess
$true -VpcConfig_SecurityGroupId sg-0XXXXXXXXXXXX -VpcConfig_SubnetId
subnet-00XXXXXXXXXX
```

Once the $NonDomainImageBuilder is deployed, it should come online with a status set to running. Other status states include pending, snapshotting, stopping, starting, and deleting.

Starting Image Builder

Once the image builder is ready, it can be started with the following command:

```
Start-APSImageBuilder -Name $NonDomainImageBuilder.Name
```

- **Start-APSImageBuilder** is for starting the image builder.

- **Name** specifies the name of the image builder to start.

- **AppstreamAgentVersion** is for specifying the AppStream agent version; using LATEST is recommended (optional).

- **Force** overrides confirmation prompts to continue operation (optional).

Stopping Image Builder

To avoid unintended usage charges, an Image Builder can be stopped at any time by running the following command:

```
Stop-APSImageBuilder -Name $NonDomainImageBuilder.Name -Force
```

- **Stop-APSImageBuilder** is for stopping the image builder.

- **Name** specifies the name of the image builder to stop.

- **Force** overrides confirmation prompts to continue operation (optional).

The following sets of parameters can also be used across all the operations (e.g., New-APSImageBuilder, Start-APSImageBuilder, and Stop-APSImageBuilder) to specify region or common credentials:

- **AccessKey** is for the AWS access key for the user account.

- **Credential** AWSCredentials object instance containing access and secret key details.

- **ProfileLocation** specifies the name and location of the ini-format credential file.

- **ProfileName** is the user-defined name (optional).

- **NetworkCredential** is the profile name of the SAML role profile.

- **SecretKey** AWS secret key for the user account.

- **SessionToken** is for the session token if the access and secret keys are used for temporary session-based credentials.

- **Region** is for the AWS region.

- **EndpointURL** specifies the endpoint.

Connecting to the Image Builder

Once an Image Builder is deployed, we will go to the AppStream 2.0 Console and make sure it is in a running state. The next step is to connect to the Image Builder to continue the configuration. To do so, we will go to the App Stream Console, click the Images on the left navigation pane, select the Image Builder, then select the radial button for the Image Builder to connect. Once selected, click the Connect button, as shown in Figure 13-21.

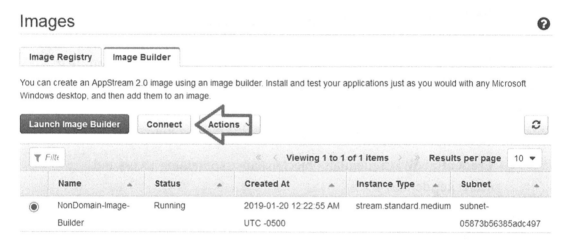

Figure 13-21. *List of Images*

Once connected to the Image Builder, we will select Administrator to install applications using Image Assistant. See Figure 13-22. All applications can be downloaded and installed at this point. The AWS Schema Conversion Tool will be used for demonstration purposes. Once the AWS Schema Conversion Tool is installed, we will use the Image Assistant to AppStream 2.0 Application Catalog.

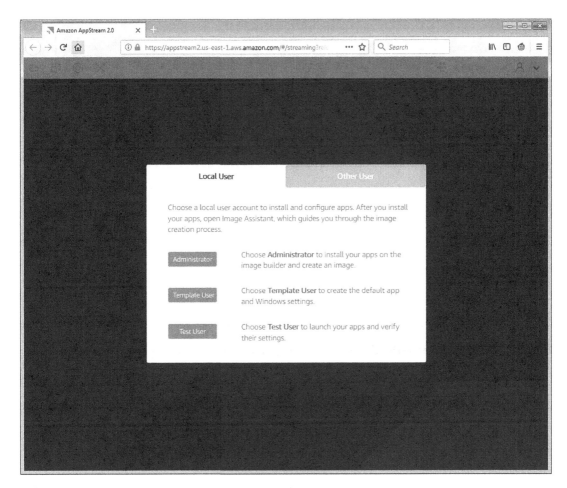

Figure 13-22. *AppStream 2.0 user selection page*

Creating an AppStream 2.0 Application Catalog

To begin, click the Image Assistant icon on the desktop.

Then, we will click Add App and locate and map the executable, as well as the rest of the App Launch Settings (Figure 13-23). Once the settings are selected, we will click the Save button (Figure 13-24).

Figure 13-23. *AppStream 2.0 image installation page*

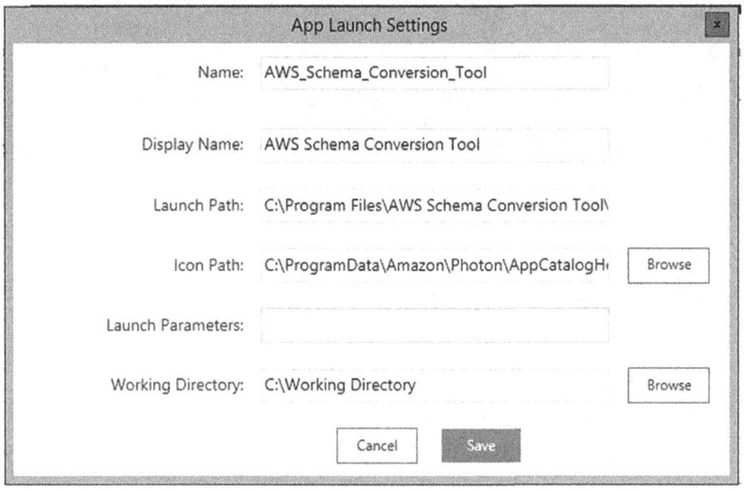

Figure 13-24. *App Launch Settings page*

The next step is to click the Next button (Figure 13-25).

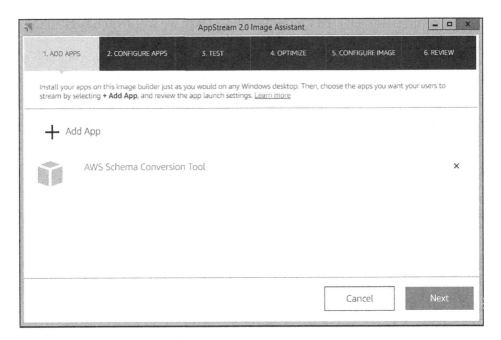

Figure 13-25. *Application installation confirmation*

In the next step, we will follow the instructions to create the default app and Windows settings for your users (Figure 13-26).

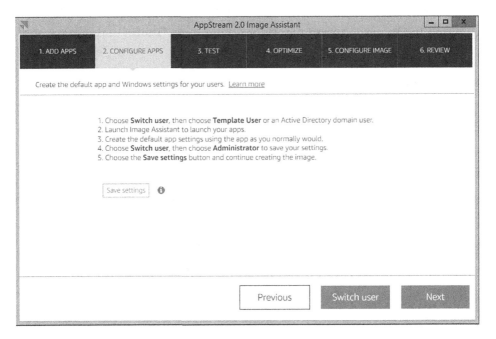

Figure 13-26. *Application Configuration tab*

Once the settings are selected for the Template User, we will switch back to the Administrator user, and click Save settings (Figure 13-27).

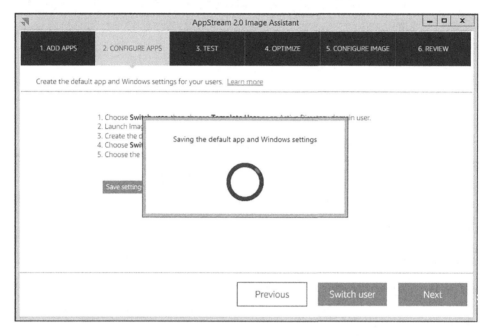

Figure 13-27. *Application Configuration being saved*

Then, click the Next button (Figure 13-28).

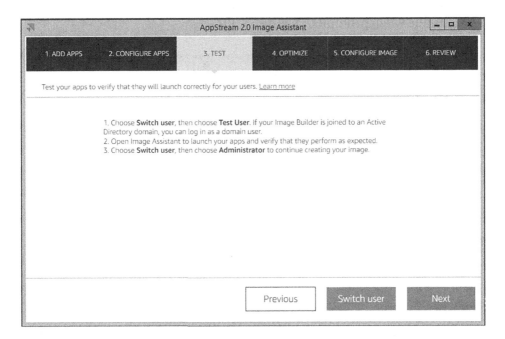

Figure 13-28. *Application image creation*

In the next window, we will be able to optimize the application by clicking the Launch button (Figure 13-29).

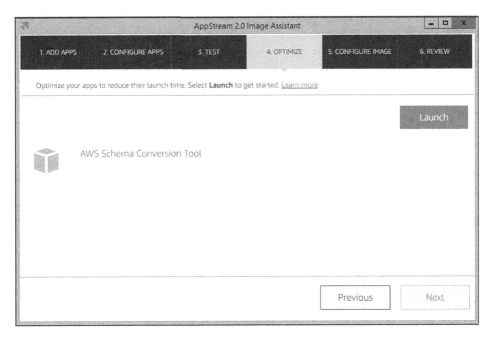

Figure 13-29. *Optional image optimization*

Click Continue when prompted (Figure 13-30).

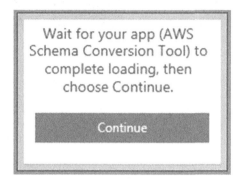

Figure 13-30. Image optimization

In the CONFIGURE IMAGE tab, label the Name, Display name, and Description. Click Next when prompted, as shown in Figure 13-31.

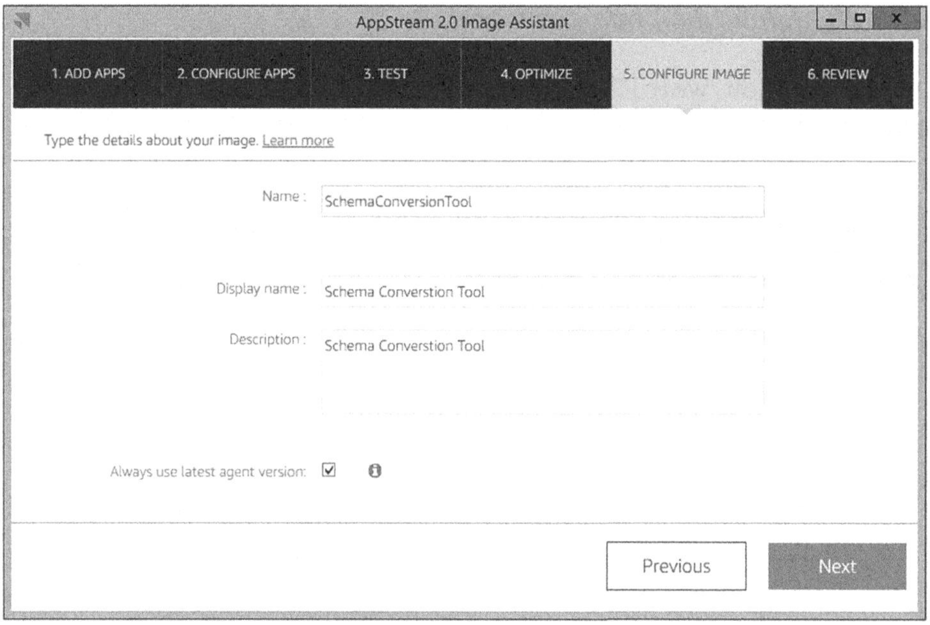

Figure 13-31. Image publishing details

Image Builder must be used to recreate a new Image .

Note   Launch performance can be optimized by specifying the files that need to be included Pre-warm configuration file. To do this, run the following command: `dir -path "C:\Path\Folder\FileToOptimize" -Recurse -ErrorAction SilentlyContinue | %{$_.FullName} | Out-File "C:\ProgramData\Amazon\Photon\Prewarm\PrewarmManifest.txt" -encoding UTF8 -append`

On the REVIEW tab, click the Disconnect and Create Image button (Figure 13-32).

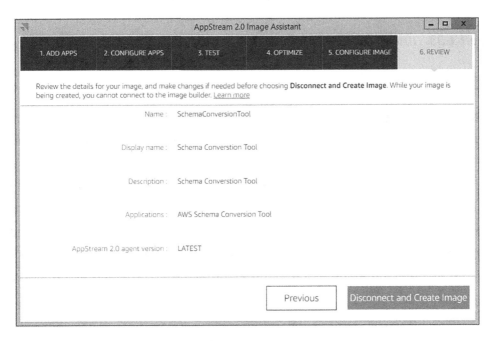

Figure 13-32. *Image Creation finalization*

Once disconnected, the state of the Image Builder will change to Snapshotting (Figure 13-33).

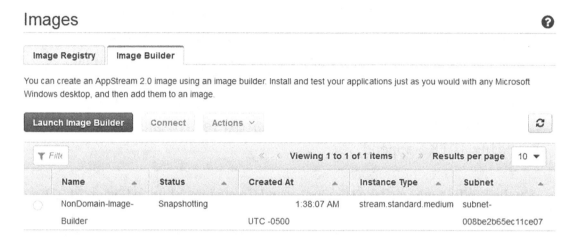

Figure 13-33. *Image Builder confirmation*

Creating Images

Once the previous process is completed, the Images created using the preceding process will be listed in the Image Registry as shown in Figure 13-34. Once an image is created, the settings and configuration are permanent. If a change needs to be made, the Image Builder must be used to recreate a new Image.

Note   If an Image Builder has been deleted, a new Image Builder can be deployed using the Image that was created using the deleted Image Builder.

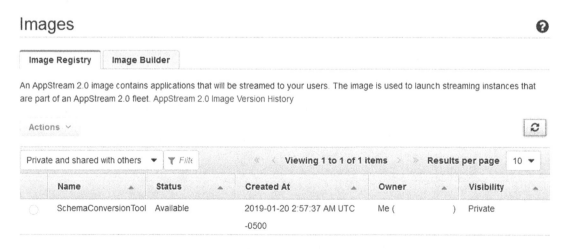

Figure 13-34. *Image Registry page*

Images in the Image Registry can be categorized as either Private, as when once is built and published using the Image Builder; other categories include Public or Shared, with the later shared from another AWS account.

AppStream 2.0 Agent is the software running on the stream instances and is used to stream published applications. There are various versions of this software that can be installed. Ideally, the latest version should be installed; however, you can also customize the version that will be used by redeploying the Image Builder with the appropriate agent version.

Getting Image Builder List

The following command can be used to get the details of an Image Builder; it can also be used to get the complete list by running the command without any options (Figure 13-35):

- **Get-APSImageBuilderList** specifies the list of a single or more Image Builders.

- **Name** is the string name of the Image Builders to describe.

- **MaxResult** is the max integer size of each page results.

- **NextToken** provides string pagination options.

```
Get-APSImageBuilderList -Name $ImageBuilder.Name
```

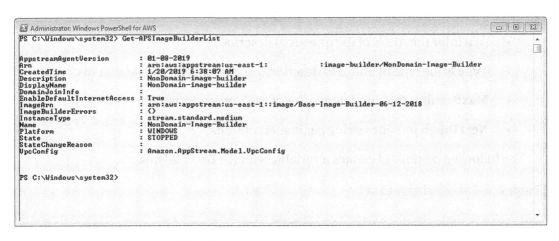

Figure 13-35. *Image Builder list*

Tagging Image Builder List

An Image Builder can be tagged by using the following command:

- **Add-APSResourceTag** is used to add or replace one or many tags.

- **Tag** is the hashable key pair combination for a tag.

- **ResourceArn** is to specify the Image Builder ARN.

- **PassThru** returns passed value (optional).

- **Force** overrides confirmation prompts to continue operation.

The following command creates the key value pair for the tag:

```
$ImageBuilderTag = @{}
$ImageBuilderTag.Add('Name', 'Schema Conversion Tool')
```

The following command adds a tag to a resource:

```
Add-APSResourceTag -Tag $ImageBuilderTag -ResourceArn
```

Getting Images List

The following command can be used to list one or more Images in the Images catalog:

- **Get-APSImageList** specifies the list of a single or more Images.

- **Name** is the string name of the Image Builders to describe.

- **Arn** is for the ARNs of the images to describe.

- **Type** is the type of image to describe (e.g., private, public, or shared).

- **MaxResult** is the max integer size of each page results.

- **NextToken** provides string pagination options.

The following command creates a variable with the list of all images.

```
$Images = Get-APSImageList
```

The following command creates a variable for the working Image we have been working with in this chapter:

```
$SCTImage = Get-APSImageList | Where-Object {$_.Name -eq
'SchemaConversionTool'}
Filters an Image to display the image that was created in this chapter.
Get-APSImageList | Where-Object {$_.Name -eq SchemaConversionTool}
```

Copying Images

Images can be copied within region or across regions within the same AWS account using the following command:

- **Copy-APSImage** is for copying an image.
- **DestinationImageDescription** is for specifying a description of the new image.
- **DestinationImageName** is for specifying the name of the new image.
- **DestinationRegion** specifies a region for the new image.
- **SourceImageName** is for specifying the source image.
- **Force** overrides confirmation prompts to continue operation.

```
$SCTImageCopy = Copy-APSImage -DestinationImageDescription
SchemaConversionToolCopy -DestinationImageName SchemaConversionToolCopy
-DestinationRegion us-east-1 -SourceImageName S
chemaConversionTool
```

Note   An Image can be shared with other AWS accounts by using the AppStream 2.0 Console, selecting the image to share, and going to the Permissions tab.

Removing Images

In order to remove existing Images created in the previous steps, the following command can be run:

- **Remove-APSImage** deletes a specified image.

- **Name** is for the image name.

- **Force** overrides confirmation prompts to continue operation.

```
$SCTImageCopy = Get-APSImageList | Where-Object {$_.Name -eq
'SchemaConversionTool'}
Remove-APSImage -Name $SCTImageCopy -Force
```

Creating Fleets

When creating Fleets, which are comprised of streaming instances, we first have to determine the type of Fleet to have. There are two options that determine how you pay for the instances and when these instances run:

- **Always On** – Instances run all the time and allow users to access their applications immediately.

- **On-Demand** – Instances run when applications are being streamed, when idle they go to a stopped state. If stopped, there is an estimated 1–2-minute hydration time for the instances to become available.

When selecting a Fleet, it is also important to understand the Instance Families available, because the selection made will directly impact the performance of your application; the same is true for the image selected at launch. The following list summarizes the Instance Families available for selection; the selection should match the use case of your application, as well as an appropriate application image.

Instance Family and Use Case

- **General Purpose** – Basic use cases for common business applications

- **Memory Optimized** – Suitable for memory intensive applications

- **Compute Optimized** – Intended for use with compute intensive applications

- **Graphics Design** – AMD FirePro S7150x2 GPU-optimized instances for use with DirectX, OpenGL, or OpenCL

- **Graphics Desktop** – NVIDIA GRID K520 GPU-optimized instances for use with DirectX, OpenGL, or OpenCL

- **Graphics Pro** – NVIDIA Tesla M60 GPU optimized for graphic applications that use DirectX, OpenGL, or OpenCL

Once you have identified fleet type to use and instance family, we will then use the following commands to create the fleet:

- **New-APSFleet** creates a fleet of streaming instances that run on a specific image.

- **Name** sets the fleet name.

- **Description** sets a description for the fleet.

- **ComputeCapacity_DesiredInstance** sets the number of instances for the fleet.

- **DomainJoinInfo_DirectoryName** is for the fully qualified domain name of the directory (e.g., example.com)(optional).

- **DisconnectTimeoutInSecond** sets the amount of time for a session to be considered to have ended. If a user reconnects within the timeout period, then they will reconnect to the previous session. Value can be between 60 to 57,600 seconds.

- **DisplayName** is for the display name for a fleet.

- **EnableDefaultInternetAccess** enables or disables Internet access for a fleet.

- **FleetType** sets the fleet as either ALWAYS_ON or ON_DEMAND.

- **ImageArn** is for the ARN for the image to use.

- **ImageName** is for the name of the image used to create the fleet.

- **InstanceType** sets the instance to one of the available instance types (e.g., stream.standard.medium).

- **MaxUserDurationInSecond** sets the max time a session can last.

- **DomainJoinInfo_OrganizationalUnitDistinguishedName** sets the distinguished name of the Organizational Unit for the computer objects (optional).

- **VpcConfig_SecurityGroupId** is for setting security group for a fleet.

- **VpcConfig_SubnetId** is for the subnet where the network interfaces will be placed.

- **Force** overrides confirmation prompts to continue operation.

```
$Fleet = New-APSFleet -Name NonDomain-Fleet -Description NonDomain-
Fleet -ComputeCapacity_DesiredInstance 2 -DisconnectTimeoutInSecond 60
-DisplayName NonDomain-Fleet -EnableDefaultInternetAccess $true -FleetType
ON_DEMAND -ImageName SchemaConversionTool -InstanceType stream.standard.
medium -MaxUserDurationInSecond 1800 -VpcConfig_SecurityGroupId sg-
00XXXXXXXXXX -VpcConfig_SubnetId subnet-00XXXXXXXXXX
```

Getting Fleet List

There are cases in which you will need to get a list of one or many Fleets. In order to get the list, you can run the **Get-APSFleetList** cmdlet or apply a filter to only get the details for one Fleet.

To get details of the NonDomain-Fleet, apply the following filter and feed the results to the $Fleet variable:

```
$Fleet = Get-APSFleetList | Where-Object {$_.Name -eq 'NonDomain-Fleet'}
```

Starting a Fleet

Once Fleet has been created, it can be started using the following commands:

- **Start-APSFleet** starts a Fleet.

- **Name** specifies the name of the Fleet to start.

- **PassThru** returns the value passed to the Name parameter.

- **Force** overrides confirmation prompts to continue operation.

To start a Fleet that is stopped, run the following command, referencing the $Fleet variable previously created:

```
Start-APSFleet -Name $Fleet.Name
```

Stopping a Fleet

If a Fleet is running, then it can be stopped using the following commands:

- **Stop-APSFleet** starts a Fleet.

- **Name** specifies the name of the Fleet to start.

- **PassThru** returns the value passed to the Name parameter.

- **Force** overrides confirmation prompts to continue operation.

To stop a running Fleet, you can run the following command using the $Fleet variable:

```
Stop-APSFleet -Name $Fleet.Name
```

Creating Stacks

Once a Fleet has been created, the next step is to create a stack to control access to your fleet:

- **New-APSStack** creates a stack to associate fleet, user access policies, and storage configurations.

- **Name** sets the name of the stack.

- **Description** sets the description of the stack.

- **DisplayName** sets the display name for the stack.

- **ApplicationSettings_Enabled** sets the path prefix for the S3 bucket to use for persistency of application settings.

- **FeedbackURL** is for providing a URL where feedback can be provided (optional).

- **RedirectURL** is for the redirect to send a user after a session ends (optional).

- **ApplicationSettings_SettingsGroup** is for enabling or disabling persistent application settings.

- **StorageConnector** identifies the storage connectors to enable. Connectors include Home Folders which stores persistent user data in S3, Google Drive for G suite that stores data in Google Drive, and OneDrive for Business which saves all users data in OneDrive.

- **UserSetting** sets the actions that are enabled or disabled during streaming sessions, enabled by default. These settings include enabling a clipboard, ability to perform file transfers, and printing to a local device.

- **Force** overrides confirmation prompts to continue operation.

The following command creates an object to specify the storage connector setting. The setting can be enabled and disabled from the console.

```
$StackConnectorType = New-Object Amazon.AppStream.Model.StorageConnector
```

The following command will create a stack associated with the non-domain Fleet:

```
$NonDomainStack = New-APSStack -Name NonDomain-Stack -Description
NonDomain-Stack -DisplayName NonDomain-Stack -StorageConnector
$StorageConnectorType
```

Getting Stack List

If you need to get a list of Stacks configured in your account, the **Get-APSStackList** cmdlet can be used to get a list of all Stacks or a filter can be used to only retrieve a single Stack.

To get details of the NonDomain-Stack, apply the following filter and feed the results to the $Stack variable:

```
$Stack = Get-APSStackList | Where-Object {$_.Name -eq 'NonDomain-Stack'}
```

Configuring Persistent Storage

One important setting to identify, which will significantly impact user experience, is whether to have persistent storage (e.g., Home Folders) for your users. There are three options for this setting, which include Google Drive for G Suite, OneDrive for Business, and Home Folders, which is an AWS native solution.

If the latter option is selected, the data stored in the fleet's Home Folders (i.e., C:\Users\PhotonUser\My Files\Home Folder for non-domain instances or C:\Users\%username%\My Files\Home Folder for domain joined instances), then all files stored in this location will be automatically backed up to an S3 bucket that gets created the first time a Stack is created; bucket is in the same region as the stack. The data in transit and at rest will be encrypted, using Amazon S3-managed keys.

By detail the AppStream service creates and attaches a secure S3 bucket policy to the bucket on which persistent files will be saved. For support or security hardening purposes, bucket polices can be further customized to ensure users other than the primary user and the admins can access the files in the S3 bucket. Useful details on how to perform these actions can be found in the "Controlling Access to AppStream 2.0 with IAM Policies and Service Roles" documentation page (https://docs.aws.amazon.com/appstream2/latest/developerguide/controlling-access.html#s3-iam-policy).

If S3 access is required, the following policy can be attached to the VPC endpoint to grant access to the service. Going with this approach, as opposed to accessing S3 via the Internet, may result in unexpected network usage charges.

```
{
  "Version": "2012-10-17",
  "Statement": [
    {
      "Sid": "Allow-AppStream-to-access-home-folder-and-application-
      settings",
      "Effect": "Allow",
      "Principal": {
        "AWS": "arn:aws:sts::account-id-without-hyphens:assumed-role/
        AmazonAppStreamServiceAccess/AppStream2.0"
      },
      "Action": [
        "s3:ListBucket",
        "s3:GetObject",
```

```
        "s3:PutObject",
        "s3:DeleteObject",
        "s3:GetObjectVersion",
        "s3:DeleteObjectVersion"
      ],
      "Resource": [
        "arn:aws:s3:::appstream2-36fb080bb8-*",
        "arn:aws:s3:::appstream-app-settings-*"
      ]
    }
  ]
}
```

Registering Fleet with Stack

Once we have a Stack and a Fleet created, the next step is to associate the Fleet with a Stack. To do this, we will use the Register-APSFleet command:

- **Register-APSFleet** associates a fleet with a specified stack.

- **StackName** is to set the Stack name.

- **FleetName** is to set the Fleet name.

- **PassThru** returns the value passed to the StackName parameter.

- **Force** overrides confirmation prompts to continue operation.

To associate a Stack with a Fleet, we will run the following command and using the $Stack and $Fleet variables we created in previous sections:

```
Register-APSFleet -StackName $Stack.Name -FleetName $Fleet.Name
```

Granting Users Access

Once all the previous steps have been completed, including creating a Stack, users can be granted to the AppStream 2.0 service. Ways in which users can access the service include using a User Pool, Single Sign-On via SAML 2.0 federation, and the AppStream 2.0 API.

Note   AppStream 2.0 User Pool users can't be assigned to Stacks with Fleets that are joined to Active Directory.

Adding AppStream 2.0 User Pool Users

In this section, we will create AppStream 2.0 User Pool users, which can be assigned to the previously created stacks. In order to do this, we will get familiar with the following command:

- **New-APSUser** creates a new user in the user pool.

- **AuthenticationType** is to set the authentication type, which can be API, SAML, or USERPOOL.

- **FirstName** is for the user's first name.

- **LastName** is for the user's last name.

- **MessageAction** specifies whether the welcome e-mail will be sent, resent, or suppressed. If sent, welcome e-mail has a temporary password valid for 7 days.

- **UserName** sets the username.

- **Force** overrides confirmation prompts to continue operation.

In this example, we will create a user for Bob in the AppStream 2.0 User Pool.

The first step to do this is to create an authentication type object and specify the user pool.

```
$AppStreamUserPool =  New-Object Amazon.AppStream.
AuthenticationType('USERPOOL')
```

The next step is to create the actual user for Bob. To do this, we will execute the following command:

```
$Bob = New-APSUser -AuthenticationType $AppStreamUserPool -FirstName Bob
-LastName Smith -UserName Bob@example.com
```

Once the user is created, the AppStream 2.0 Console can be used to verify if the user was created as expected (Figure 13-36).

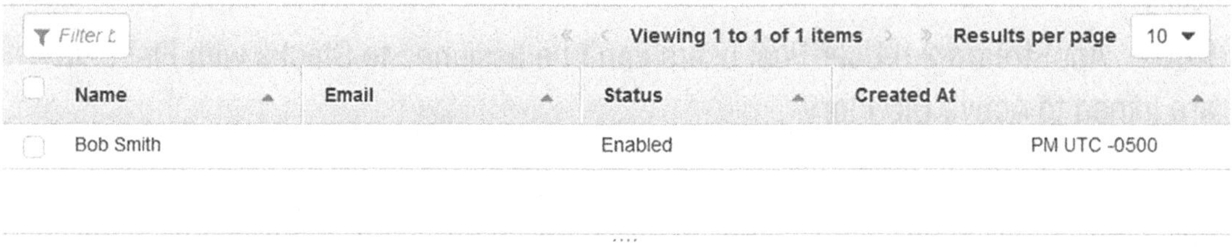

Filter ℓ			Viewing 1 to 1 of 1 items	Results per page	10 ▼
☐ **Name** ▲	**Email** ▲	**Status** ▲	**Created At**		▲
☐ Bob Smith		Enabled		PM UTC -0500	

Figure 13-36. AppStream User Pool account created

The person with the newly created user will receive an e-mail with details on how to access the AppStream 2.0 service (Figure 13-37).

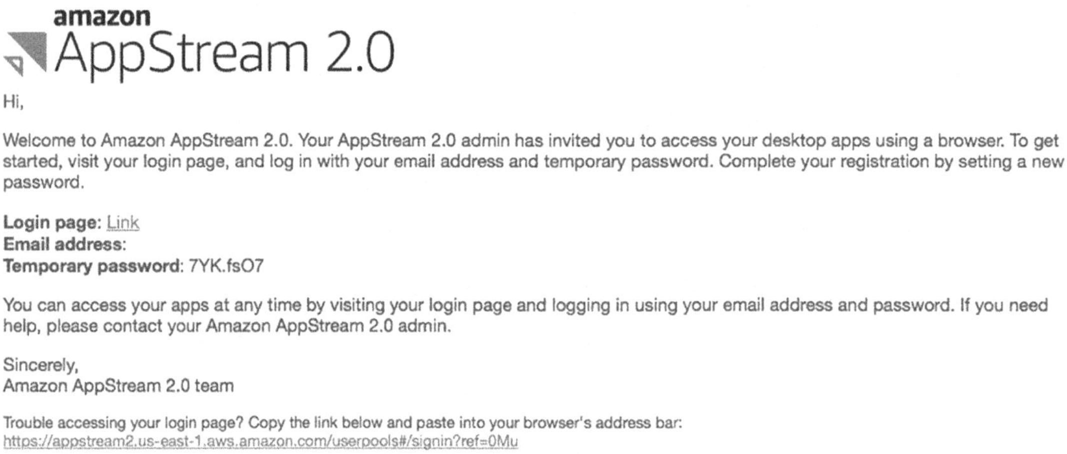

Hi,

Welcome to Amazon AppStream 2.0. Your AppStream 2.0 admin has invited you to access your desktop apps using a browser. To get started, visit your login page, and log in with your email address and temporary password. Complete your registration by setting a new password.

Login page: Link
Email address:
Temporary password: 7YK.fsO7

You can access your apps at any time by visiting your login page and logging in using your email address and password. If you need help, please contact your Amazon AppStream 2.0 admin.

Sincerely,
Amazon AppStream 2.0 team

Trouble accessing your login page? Copy the link below and paste into your browser's address bar:
https://appstream2.us-east-1.aws.amazon.com/userpools#/signin?ref=0Mu

Figure 13-37. AppStream 2.0 automated e-mail

When the user clicks the login page link, they will be prompted to log in with their e-mail address and the temporary password that is provided (Figure 13-38). The temporary password is valid for 7 days from the time issued.

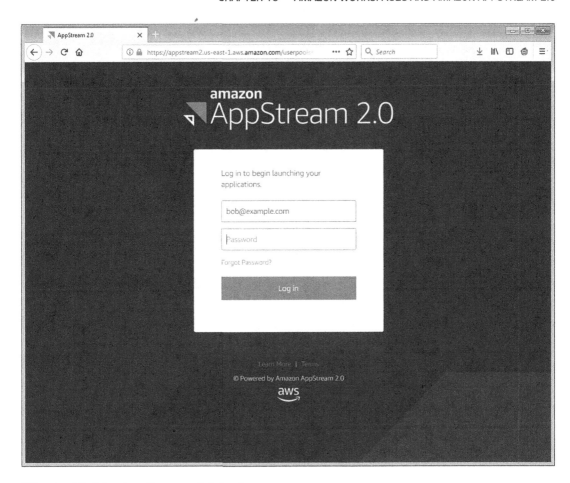

Figure 13-38. *AppStream 2.0 login page*

The user must change their password after successfully authenticating to the service (Figure 13-39).

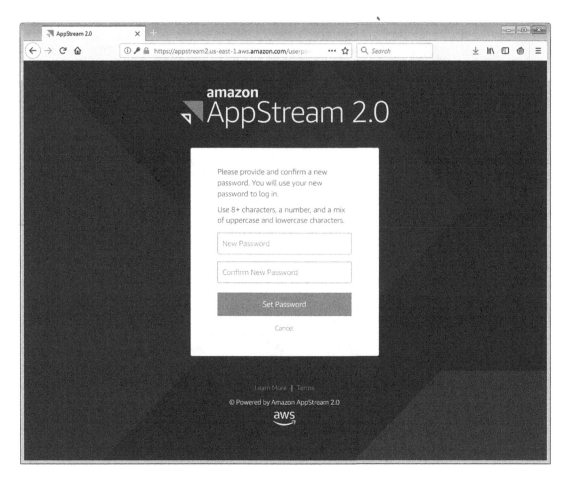

Figure 13-39. Password change page

Disabling AppStream 2.0 User Pool Users

In order to disable AppStream 2.0 User Pool users, we will need to make sure we have an object that specifies the authentication type pointing to the user pool as the location of the user:

- **Disable-APSUser** disables a user.

- **AuthenticationType** is to set the authentication type, which can be API, SAML, or USERPOOL.

- **UserName** specifies the user to disable.

- **Force** overrides confirmation prompts to continue operation.

As a refresher, to create an authentication type object, we will run the following command:

```
$AppStreamUserPool =  New-Object Amazon.AppStream.
AuthenticationType('USERPOOL')
```

The following command will disable the user for username Bob@example.com:

```
Disable-APSUser -AuthenticationType $AppStreamUserPool -UserName Bob@
example.com
```

Enabling AppStream 2.0 User Pool Users

Enabling AppStream 2.0 User Pool users is very similar to disabling the users, except that we perform an action in reverse. We will still need to make sure we have an object that specifies the authentication type pointing to the user pool as the location of the user:

- **Enable-APSUser** disables a user.

- **AuthenticationType** is to set the authentication type, which can be API, SAML, or USERPOOL.

- **UserName** specifies the user to disable.

- **Force** overrides confirmation prompts to continue operation.

The following command will enable the user for username Bob@example.com:

```
Enable-APSUser -AuthenticationType $AppStreamUserPool -UserName Bob@
example.com
```

Assigning AppStream 2.0 User Pool Users to Stacks

One of the ways in which users are granted access to Stacks is by assigning users to specific Stacks. As you can imagine, these assignments can be done either by API, CLI, AWS Console, or PowerShell. To perform the actions in PowerShell, we will leverage the following cmdlet to make this association:

- **Register-APSUserStackBatch** associates a user to a specified Stack.

- **UserStackAssociation** lists the user stack association.

- **Force** overrides confirmation prompts to continue operation.

In order to assign User Pool Users to a Stack, we first have to create a UserStackAssociation object and specify all the parameters required for the association. For example, we will associate user Bob@example.com with the NonDomain-Stack.

```
$APSUserStack = New-Object Amazon.AppStream.Model.UserStackAssociation
$APSUserStack.AuthenticationType = $AppStreamUserPool
$APSUserStack.SendEmailNotification = $true
$APSUserStack.UserName = 'Bob@example.com'
$APSUserStack.StackName = 'NonDomain-Stack'
```

Once we have all the parameters configured as expected, we will run the Register-APSUserStackBatch command.

```
$NonDomainUserStack = Register-APSUserStackBatch -UserStackAssociation
$APSUserStack
```

Once the association is completed, the user associated with a Stack will receive an e-mail to access the login page, as shown in Figure 13-40.

Hi,

Your Amazon AppStream 2.0 admin has assigned new apps to you! To get started visit your login page, and log in with your email address and password.

Sincerely,
Amazon AppStream 2.0 team

Trouble accessing your login page? Copy the link below and paste into your browser's address bar:
https://appstream2.us-east-1.aws.amazon.com/userpools#/signin?ref=0

Figure 13-40. *AppStream 2.0 assignment notification*

Once you log in to the AppStream 2.0 service using the login page in the e-mail, you will be able to access the Schema Conversion Tool published in earlier parts of this section (Figure 13-41).

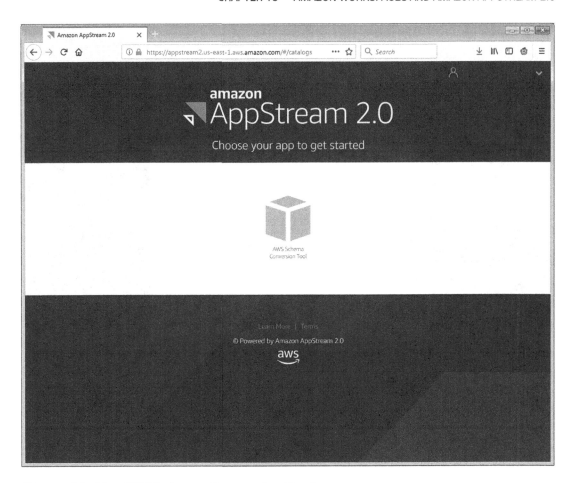

Figure 13-41. *AWS Schema Conversion Tool page*

If we click the application link, we will be able to launch the application which may take several minutes. See Figure 13-42. The application streaming experience can be heavily optimized, but it is outside of the scope of this chapter. If you need additional guidance on optimizing your application, review the Customize an AppStream 2.0 Fleet to Optimize Your Users' Application Streaming Experience documentation page (`https://docs.aws.amazon.com/appstream2/latest/developerguide/customize-fleets.html`).

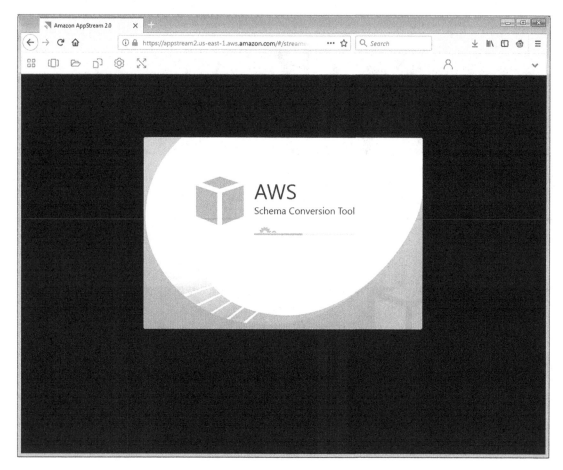

Figure 13-42. *Launching AppStream 2.0 image*

EXERCISE 13.1: LAUNCH CUSTOM STACK, FLEET, AND IMAGE

In this exercise, we will create an Image, launch a Fleet, create a Stack, and associate a non-domain user with an application.

Open the AWS Tools for PowerShell and run the following command:

```
$NonDomainImageBuilder = New-APSImageBuilder -ImageName Base-Image-
Builder-06-12-2018 -AppstreamAgentVersion LATEST -Description 'Description'
-DisplayName 'DisplayName' -InstanceType stream.standard.medium -Name
'Name' -EnableDefaultInternetAccess $true -VpcConfig_SecurityGroupId sg-
0XXXXXXXXXXXX -VpcConfig_SubnetId subnet-00XXXXXXXXXX
```

Once completed, we will start the Image Builder.

Start-APSImageBuilder -Name $NonDomainImageBuilder.Name

Go to the AppStream 2.0 Console connect to the Image Builder and follow the instructions provided in this section to publish a streaming application and Image.

Once an Image has been created and is available in the Image Registry, create a Fleet using the commands as follows:

```
$Fleet = New-APSFleet -Name NonDomain-Fleet -Description 'Description'
-ComputeCapacity_DesiredInstance X -DisconnectTimeoutInSecond 60
-DisplayName 'DisplayName' -EnableDefaultInternetAccess $true -FleetType
ON_DEMAND -ImageName 'ImageName' -InstanceType stream.standard.medium
-MaxUserDurationInSecond 1800 -VpcConfig_SecurityGroupId sg-00XXXXXXXXXX
-VpcConfig_SubnetId subnet-00XXXXXXXXXX
```

Once a Fleet is created, use the following commands to create a Stack:

```
$StackConnectorType = New-Object Amazon.AppStream.Model.StorageConnector
```

```
$Stack = New-APSStack -Name 'Name' -Description 'Description' -DisplayName
'DisplayName' -StorageConnector $StorageConnectorType
```

Once the Stack has been created, associate a Stack with a Fleet.

```
Register-APSFleet -StackName $Stack.Name -FleetName $Fleet.Name
```

Then, we will create a user in the AppStream 2.0 User Pool.

```
$AppStreamUserPool =  New-Object Amazon.AppStream.
AuthenticationType('USERPOOL')
```

```
$User = New-APSUser -AuthenticationType $AppStreamUserPool -FirstName
'FirstName' -LastName 'LastName' -UserName 'user@domain.com'
```

Once a user has been created, we will assign a Stack to a User by running the following commands:

```
$APSUserStack = New-Object Amazon.AppStream.Model.UserStackAssociation
$APSUserStack.AuthenticationType = $AppStreamUserPool
$APSUserStack.SendEmailNotification = $true
$APSUserStack.UserName = user@domain.com'
$APSUserStack.StackName = 'StackName'
```

Once the parameters are configured, the following cmdlet can be run:

```
$UserStack = Register-APSUserStackBatch -UserStackAssociation $APSUserStack
```

Summary

In this chapter, we saw the Amazon Desktop and Application Streaming services, which provide organizations the ability to deliver their workforce secure, centrally managed desktops and applications, at a global scale. Although we spent a lot of time learning about the AppStream Service 2.0 functionality without domain authentication, we also learned how to leverage AWS Directory Services to provide access control to these services, which can help you increase the security posture of your portfolio, by leveraging existing user credentials.

Each section also included a step-by-step walkthrough to help you get started with setting up both Amazon WorkSpaces and Amazon AppStream 2.0. The goal of the step through is to give you a jump start to begin delivering these services to customers within your organization.

CHAPTER 14

Amazon WorkDocs

In the last couple of decades, collaboration platforms have become a necessity to organizations that want to increase productivity with their workforce, by using services that foster collaboration. Amazon WorkDocs is a managed, enterprise storage and sharing service that allows organizations to collaborate on content in a secure and safe fashion, both internally and outside of the organization.

As a managed service, the WorkDocs service is able to scale users and storage easily, from any supported device, and with a pay-as-you-go model and no long-term commitment, organizations can take advantage of full-featured collaboration platform without much risk. In this chapter, we will focus on getting the Amazon WorkDocs provisioned and made available users in your organization. Although some content management can also be performed via PowerShell, we will focus mainly on getting the service up and running with the objective of being to start collaboration.

Client Requirements

Amazon WorkDocs content can be accessed from a supported browser, from any operating system, running a supported version of a browser. Alternatively, content can also be accessed using one of the Amazon WorkDocs apps from either an Android or an iOS device.

The following are the currently supported web browsers for accessing Amazon WorkDocs:

- Google Chrome version 30 or later

- Mozilla Firefox ESR version 24.6 or later

- Mozilla Firefox version 30 or later

- Apple Safari version 7 or later

- Microsoft Internet Explorer 10 or later

© Brian Beach, Steven Armentrout, Rodney Bozo, Emmanuel Tsouris 2019
B. Beach et al., *Pro PowerShell for Amazon Web Services*, https://doi.org/10.1007/978-1-4842-4850-8_14

The Amazon WorkDocs Android and iOS mobile apps can be installed on one of the supported devices.

Mobile phones:

- An Android phone with Android 4.0.3 or later

- An iPhone with iOS 7.0 or later

Tablets:

- An Android tablet with Android 2.3.3 or later

- Kindle Fire HD 7 (2nd Gen) and Kindle Fire HD 8.9 (2nd Gen)

- Kindle Fire HD 7 (3rd Gen)

- Kindle Fire HDX 7 (3rd Gen) and Kindle Fire HDX 8.9 (3rd Gen)

- iPad or iPad 2 with iOS 6.1.2 or later

In addition to the Amazon WorkDocs client and a sync application can be downloaded and installed on a supported Microsoft Windows and macOS devices. The Amazon WorkDocs Sync Client synchronizes files and folders from the WorkDocs service to your desktop, laptop, or tablet.

System requirements for the Sync Client are

- Microsoft Windows 7, Windows 8, or Windows 10

- Microsoft Windows Server 2008

- Microsoft Windows Server 2012 R2 (with Microsoft AD, not Simple AD)

- macOS 10.10 or later

Setting Up WorkDocs

One of the requirements for setting up WorkDocs is to have a directory, to provide access management and authentication to the service. The Directory Service components supported by WorkDocs is Microsoft AD, AD Connector, and Simple AD.

In order to create and deactivate WorkDocs sites, we will need to go to the Amazon WorkDocs Console. From there, users, storage, and security can be managed. In Chapter 12, we set up a Managed Microsoft AD directory. In this section, we will leverage that directory and associate it with WorkDocs, although any other supported directory would work the same way.

Once in the console, we will click the "Get Started Now" link (Figure 14-1).

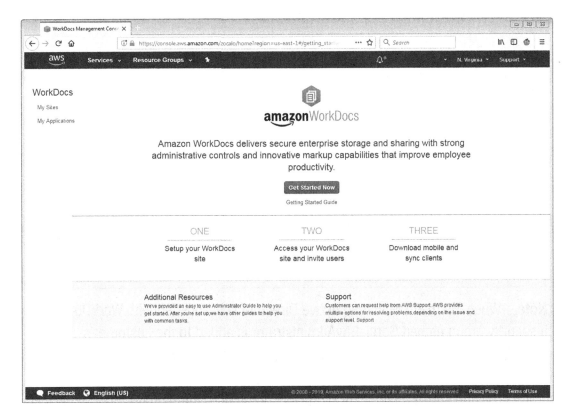

Figure 14-1. *Amazon WorkDocs Get Started page*

On the Select a Directory page, we will select the corp.example.com directory, as this is the Managed Microsoft Active Directory. Once selected, we will click the "Enable Directory" link (Figure 14-2). The corpex.awsapps.com URL was created in Chapter 12.

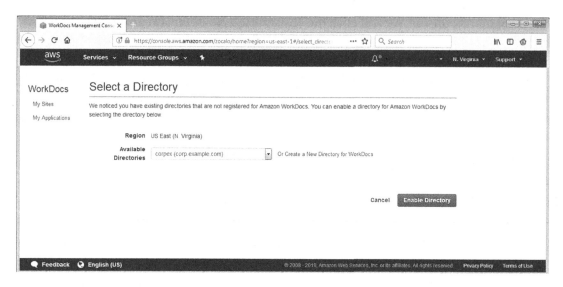

Figure 14-2. *Enable Directory page*

Note   When Microsoft Managed Active Directory is associated with WorkDocs, a security group named GorillaBoyAdministrator is added to the customer's Organizational Unit (OU). The group is a member of the delegated Admins group.

After the directory is enabled for WorkDocs, we assign a domain user as a WorkDocs Administrator. We will type "admin" in the Username field. See Figure 14-3.

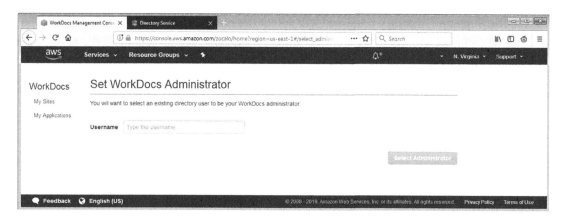

Figure 14-3. *Setting WorkDocs Administrator page*

Once the WorkDocs administrator is set, the WorkDocs administrator will receive an e-mail with details on how to access the WorkDocs site. If the WorkDocs Administrator account selected does not have an e-mail address populated in the active directory's user object, an e-mail will not be sent or received. See Figure 14-4.

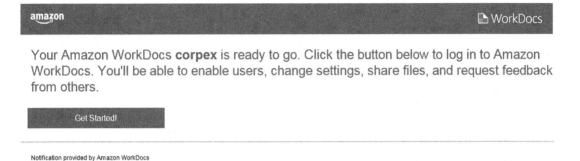

Figure 14-4. *Amazon WorkDocs Administrator notification message*

Once the "Get Started!" link is clicked from inside the WorkDocs e-mail, the administrator will be taken to the WorkDocs site.

When prompted, enter the WorkDocs Administrator's e-mail address and click the "Log in" link. See Figure 14-5.

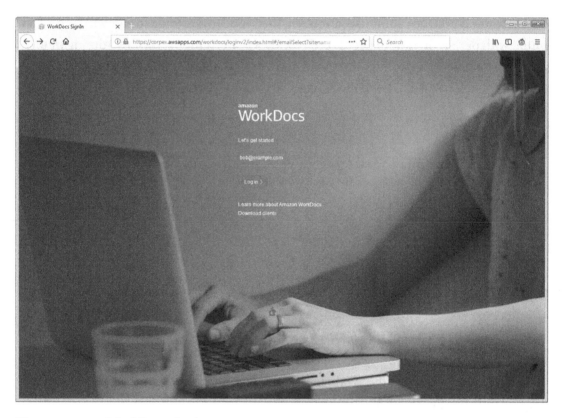

Figure 14-5. *WorkDocs login page*

Then, enter the WorkDocs Administrator's username and password. Click "Sign In".
See Figure 14-6.

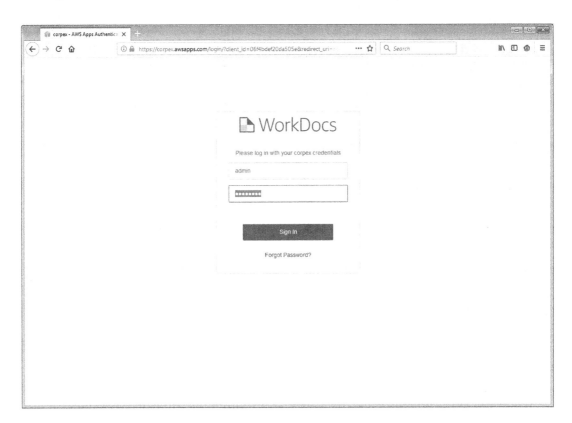

Figure 14-6. *Administrator login page*

Once logged in, the WorkDocs Administrator will be able to access the service, create
and upload content, and begin collaborating. See Figure 14-7.

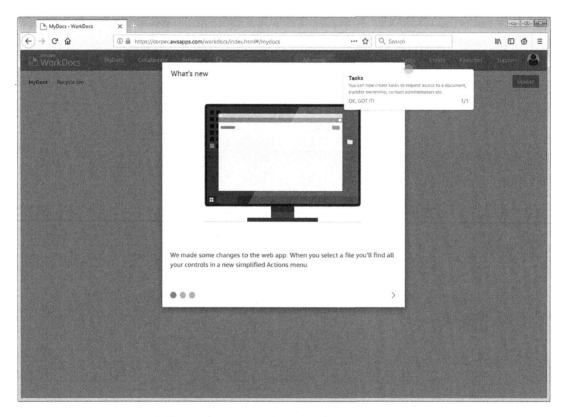

Figure 14-7. *Successfully authenticated to WorkDocs*

WorkDocs sites configured can be viewed from within the Amazon WorkDocs Console. See Figure 14-8.

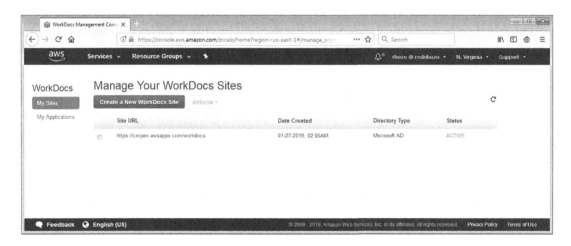

Figure 14-8. *WorkDocs Sites Management page*

Once the WorkDocs service (i.e., site) has been configured, we can begin using PowerShell cmdlets to interact with the service.

Managing WorkDocs Users

In this section, we will view how to list users available in the domain, enable and disable users, and also grant access to the Amazon WorkDocs service.

Getting List of WorkDocs Users

The first PowerShell cmdlet we will use is Get-WDUserList. This command will allow you to get a list of all users in the directory connected to WorkDocs:

- **Get-WDUserList** describes users.

- **OrganizationId** specifies the directory ID, which can be pulled from the Directory Service (e.g., either Managed Active Directory or AD Connector).

- **AuthenticationToken** specifies the WorkDocs authentication token.

- **Field** sets a comma-separated list of values.

- **Include** specifies the state of the users, including specifying "ALL" when querying for inactive users.

- **Order** sets the ordering of the results.

- **Query** can set a query to filter users by user name.

- **Sort** sets the sorting order.

- **UserId** sets the user ID.

- **Limit** sets the maximum number of items to return.

- **Marker** allows to set a market for the next set of results.

To get a list of WorkDocs users, we will run the Get-WDUserList command feeding the results to a variable.

```
$WDUserList = Get-WDUserList -OrganizationID d-XXXXXXX
```

The following command will filter the results to get details of just one user, User1:

```
$User1 = $WDUserList | Where-Object {$_.Username -eq 'user1'}
```

Note   The Get-WDUserList will not show the WorkDocs Administrator user, only standard WorkDocs users.

Adding WorkDocs Users

To create users with access to WorkDocs, we will use the following cmdlet:

- **New-WDUser** creates a user in Simple AD or Managed Active Directory.

- **OrganizationId** sets the ID of the organization.

- **AuthenticationToken** is for the WorkDocs authentication token.

- **EmailAddress** is for the user's e-mail address.

- **GivenName** sets the given name for a user.

- **Password** sets the password for a user.

- **StorageRule_StorageAllocatedInByte** sets the storage allocated by bytes.

- **StorageRule_StorageType** sets the type of storage; the options are UNLIMITED or using a QUOTA.

- **Surname** sets the surname for the user.

- **TimeZoneId** sets the time zone ID of the user.

- **Username** sets the login name for the user.

- **Force** overrides confirmation prompts to continue operation.

To create a user for James, we will execute the following command:

```
$James = New-WDUser -OrganizationId d-906711f2bb -EmailAddress james@
example.com -GivenName James -Password 'password' -StorageRule_
StorageAllocatedInByte 500 -StorageRule_StorageType UNLIMITED -Surname
Smith -Username James
```

Note   Adding WorkDocs accounts using the New-WDUser cmdlet will create a user in the directory associated with WorkDocs. It is only applicable with Microsoft Managed Active Directory and Simple AD. Example is depicted in Figure 14-9.

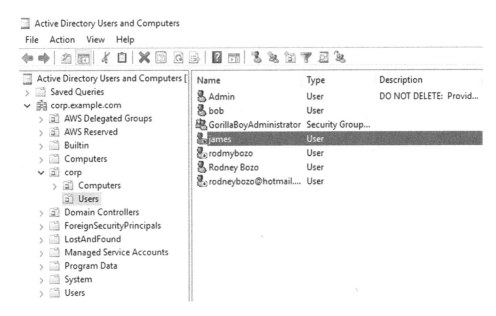

Figure 14-9.   *Domain user created via New-WDUser cmdlet*

Enabling WorkDocs Users

Once a user is created using the cmdlet in the previous example, we will see that the newly created account is disabled. The new WorkDocs user can be enabled by running the Enable-WDUser cmdlet:

- **Enable-WDUser** enables a WorkDocs user.

- **UserId** specifies a user.

- **AuthenticationToken** is for setting the authentication token.

- **Force** overrides confirmation prompts to continue operation.

We will enable the previously created account by running the following command:

```
Enable-WDUser -UserId $James.Id
```

Disabling WorkDocs Users

If necessary, we can also disable a WorkDocs user. To perform this action, we will use the Disable-WDUser cmdlet:

- **Disable-WDUser** enables a WorkDocs user.

- **UserId** specifies a user.

- **AuthenticationToken** is for setting the authentication token.

- **Force** overrides confirmation prompts to continue operation.

The following command will disable James' account:

```
Disable-WDUser -UserId $James.Id
```

Setting Role for WorkDocs Users

After a user has been added to the directory and enabled, the next step will be to assign a role for a user from the User's profile:

- **Guest User** is a user who can only view files.

- **User** is a user who can save files and collaborate.

- **Power User** is a user with special permissions delegated by the administrator.

- **Admin** is the user with administrative permissions for the entire site, which includes user management and site settings.

In order to do this, we will log in to the WorkDocs site using the admin account. Once authenticated, click the My Account icon on the top right hand side of the screen (Figure 14-10).

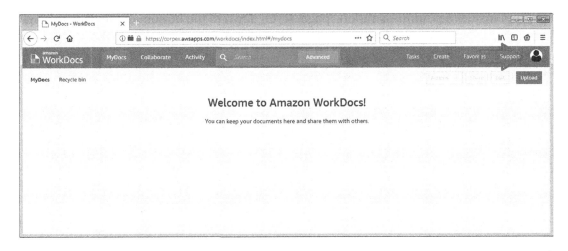

Figure 14-10. *Successfully authenticated user*

After the "My Account" panel comes up, click the "Open admin control panel" link (Figure 14-11).

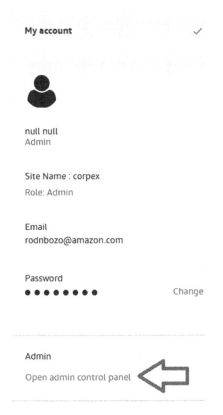

Figure 14-11. *Accessing admin control panel*

From inside the "Administration" page, scroll down to the bottom of the page to view all WorkDocs users. Then, locate the user with Username James, and click the edit profile link (Figure 14-12).

NAME ∧	USERNAME	STATUS	ROLE	STORAGE USED	
AWS_swb_prod_iad	AWS_swb_prod_iad	Inactive	Guest user	0 B of 0 B	
Bob Smith	bob	Active	Guest user	0 B of 0 B	
James Smith	james	Active	Guest user	0 B of 0 B	
Randy Smith	randy	Active	Guest user	0 B of 0 B	
Rodmy Bozo	rodmybozo	Inactive	Guest user	0 B of 0 B	
Rodney Bozo	rbozo	Inactive	Guest user	0 B of 0 B	
rodneybozo@hotmail.com	rodneybozo@hotmail.com	Active	User	0 B of 1 TB	

Figure 14-12. *Edit James Smith's profile*

Once the "Edit user" form comes up, change James' user from "Guest User" to a "User" role. After the role is changed, then James will be able to use WorkDocs and begin collaborating (Figure 14-13).

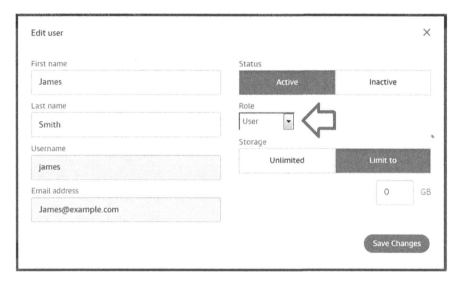

Figure 14-13. *WorkDocs role assignment*

Creating Collaboration Folder

Once James' account is able to create folders within WorkDocs, we will create a parent Folder and will use PowerShell to manage the content within that folder.

In order to do this, click the "Create" folder link and select "Folder" (Figure 14-14).

Figure 14-14. *Creating a Collaboration Folder*

When the "Create Folder" form comes up, type James' name as the name of the folder. Then, click the "Create" link (Figure 14-15).

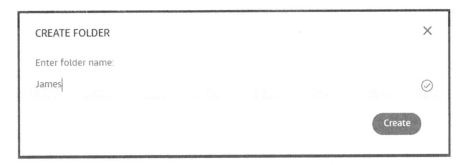

Figure 14-15. *Naming Collaboration Folder*

After the folder has been created, we will click the link to the "James" folder to go inside the folder. Once inside the folder, we will take long alphanumeric folder ID and use PowerShell cmdlets to further manage the content in James' folder. Folder ID is shown as follows in bold:

https://corpex.awsapps.com/workdocs/index.html#/folder/**9674f6123d9faa3a0 bff6d61fa99894258710552167813f0d8a2621127f1d8c7**

Creating New WorkDocs Folder

New WorkDocs folders can be created inside the previously created folder using the **New-WDFolder** cmdlet:

- **New-WDFolder** creates a new WorkDocs folder.

- **ParentFolderId** specifies the unique identifier of the parent folder.

- **AuthenticationToken** is for the WorkDocs authentication token.

- **Name** is the unique name of the folder being created.

- **Force** overrides confirmation prompts to continue operation.

To create a new folder, we will run the following command:

```
$PersonalFolder = New-WDFolder -ParentFolderId
9674f6123d9faa3a0bff6d61fa99894258710552167813f0d8a2621127f1d8c7 -Name
Personal
```

We can verify if the folder has been created by going to the WorkDocs site
(Figure 14-16).

Figure 14-16. *Verifying Folder creation*

Deleting WorkDocs Folder

In order to delete a WorkDocs folder, the Remove-WDFolder cmdlet can be used:

- **Remove-WDFolder** permanently deletes a WorkDocs folder.

- **FolderId** specifies the unique identifier of folder.

- **AuthenticationToken** is for the WorkDocs authentication token.

- **PassThru** returns passed value (optional).

- **Force** overrides confirmation prompts to continue operation.

To delete a folder, we will run the following command:

```
Remove-WDFolder -FolderId
9674f6123d9faa3a0bff6d61fa99894258710552167813f0d8a2621127f1d8c7
```

Listing WorkDocs Folders Metadata

If you need to get the metadata for a folder, you can use the Get-WDFolder cmdlet and store the results in a variable:

- **Get-WDFolder** retrieves metadata for a specific folder.

- **FolderId** sets the unique folder ID.

- **AuthenticationToken** is for the WorkDocs authentication token.

- **IncludeCustomMetadata** specifies whether the command should include custom metadata.

The following command will store the results of the Get-WedFolder in a variable:

```
$JamesFolder = Get-WDFolder -FolderId
9674f6123d9faa3a0bff6d61fa99894258710552167813f0d8a2621127f1d8c7
-IncludeCustomMetadata $true
```

We can then view the contents of the metadata by viewing the contents of the $JamesFolder variable. See Figure 14-17.

```
$JamesFolder.Metadata
```

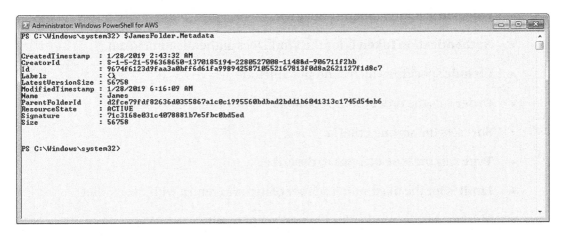

Figure 14-17. *Collaboration Folder details*

417

Custom metadata can also be viewed, if it has been added for the folder. See Figure 14-18.

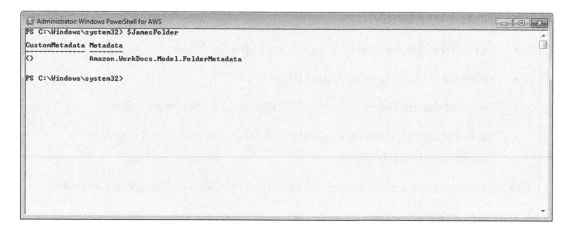

Figure 14-18. *Custom metadata details*

Describing WorkDocs Folders Contents

If you need to get a list of the contents of a folder, the Get-WDFolderContent can be used:

- **Get-WDFolderContent** describes the contents of a folder.

- **FolderId** is for the unique folder ID.

- **AuthenticationToken** is for the WorkDocs authentication token.

- **Include** specifies which content to include.

- **Order** sets the order for the contents.

- **Sort** sets the sorting criteria.

- **Type** sets the type of items to describe.

- **Limit** is for the maximum number of items to return with the cmdlet.

- **Marker** sets the marker for the next set of results.

In order to view the contents of the James folder, we will store the results of the Get-WDFolderContent into a variable.

```
$JamesFolderContents = Get-WDFolderContent -FolderId
9674f6123d9faa3a0bff6d61fa99894258710552167813f0d8a2621127f1d8c7 -Type ALL
```

We can then view the contents by seeing what's stored in the $JamesFolderContents variable. As we can see in Figure 14-19, there are two folders in the James folder, Shared and Personal.

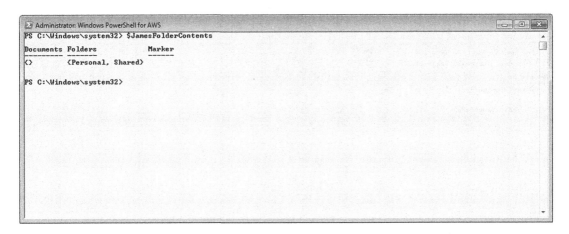

Figure 14-19. Describing Folder contents

Getting WorkDocs Folder Path

There are cases in which you will need to get a list of all the WorkDocs folder IDs for the folders that make up the hierarchy of a specific folder. For example, getting the folder hierarchy may help to identify a path for getting additional lists of content and narrow down on a particular structure for creating other folders, as well as other administrative functions, to name a few. In order to get a folder path, we will use the Get-WDFolderPath cmdlet:

- **Get-WDFolderPath** gets the folder path information.

- **FolderId** is for the unique folder ID.

- **AuthenticationToken** is for the WorkDocs authentication token.

- **Field** can be used as a comma-separated list of values; name can be used to include folder names in the output.

- **Limit** is for the maximum number of items to return with the cmdlet.

- **Marker** sets the marker for the next set of results.

We will run the following command and store the results in the $FolderPath variable. See Figure 14-20.

```
$FolderPath = Get-WDFolderPath -FolderId
94655552f6d553500f619fa0718e9d2b993d6d656d6c96b1b25bd4b7f82aa5b9 -Field NAME
```

Figure 14-20. *Folder content path*

We can then view the content of the $FolderPath.Components, as shown in Figure 14-21.

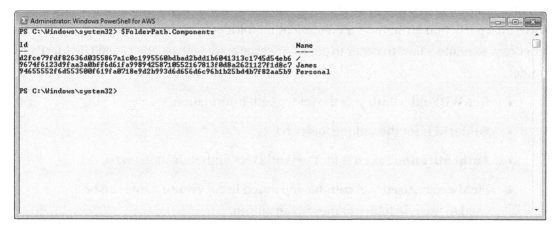

Figure 14-21. *Viewing Folder components*

Removing WorkDocs Folder Contents

If there is ever a need to remove all the content from a specified folder, the Remove-WDFolderContent cmdlet can be used to do so:

- **Remove-WDFolderContent** removes content from a specified folder.

- **FolderId** sets the unique folder ID.

- **AuthenticationToken** is for the WorkDocs authentication token.

- **PassThru** returns passed value (optional).

- **Force** overrides confirmation prompts to continue operation.

We will run the following command to delete all contents from the personal folder:

```
Remove-WDFolderContent -FolderId
94655552f6d553500f619fa0718e9d2b993d6d656d6c96b1b25bd4b7f82aa5b9
```

Managing WorkDocs Content

This chapter provides enough context and insight to get started with the Amazon WorkDocs service. Currently, there are some content management API operations exposed to PowerShell, but those are outside of the scope of this chapter. If you need to manage content via available cmdlets, further reading of the PowerShell Reference documentation for Amazon WorkDocs page is recommended (`https://docs.aws.amazon.com/powershell/latest/reference/items/Amazon_WorkDocs_cmdlets.html`).

EXERCISE 14.1: LAUNCHING AMAZON WORKDOCS

In this exercise, we will associate an Amazon WorkDocs to an existing Microsoft Managed Active Directory forest.

For provisioning a Managed Microsoft Active Directory forest, follow the steps provided in Chapter 12.

Once completed, follow the following steps to associate WorkDocs with the managed Directory Service.

From the WorkDocs Console, we will click the "Get Started Now" link.

On the Select a Directory page, we will select the directory you created in Chapter 12. Once selected, we will click the "Enable Directory" link.

After the directory is enabled for WorkDocs, assign a domain user as a WorkDocs Administrator. Type a user of your choice.

Once the WorkDocs Administrator is set, follow the steps in the welcome e-mail received.

Once logged in to the WorkDocs service, create some folders and upload content.

Summary

In this chapter, we saw how Amazon WorkDocs can be deployed quickly and easily to provide collaboration services to the enterprise in a secure and globally scale fashion. We configured WorkDocs to authenticate against Managed Microsoft AD because it most likely will be the choice for a production deployment. There are also other Directory Service components supported, including AD Connector and Simple AD and the setup process is the same as the process used with Managed Microsoft AD. For example, the PowerShell commands used to manage users stored in AD can also be used with Simple AD. As the AD Connector does not perform any write operations, some of the commands, such as creating new WorkDocs users, are not applicable with the AD Connector.

CHAPTER 15

Systems Manager Basics

Now that you've been creating resources in the cloud with PowerShell, you'll need a simple and secure way to manage all those resources. AWS Systems Manager is a convenient set of management tools that lets you configure and manage your AWS resources at scale.

In this chapter, I'll explain some basics to get you started with Systems Manager. We'll begin by going over some important prerequisites, and then I'll show you how to get organized by grouping your resources using AWS Resource Groups. We'll walk through Session Manager which allows you to connect and run PowerShell on your Amazon EC2 instances. Finally, I'll show you a few ways to use Parameter Store with your PowerShell scripts.

There are two exercises in this chapter. In the first, I'll show you how to use Parameter Store to find the latest Windows AMI and use it to launch an EC2 instance. In the second exercise, you'll create a resource group to list resources that match a certain resource query.

To explore and learn more about the many features we'll be talking about, open your browser and head over to the AWS Systems Manager Console at `https://console.aws.amazon.com/systems-manager`.

Note If you've been using AWS for a while, you'll remember AWS Systems Manager under its former name: Amazon EC2 Systems Manager.

Systems Manager Prerequisites

Remember when we covered IAM in detail back in Chapter 11? Well before you begin using Systems Manager, there are a few IAM permissions you'll need to set up.

© Brian Beach, Steven Armentrout, Rodney Bozo, Emmanuel Tsouris 2019
B. Beach et al., *Pro PowerShell for Amazon Web Services*, https://doi.org/10.1007/978-1-4842-4850-8_15

IAM Access to Systems Manager

If your IAM user or role has full administrative access to your AWS account, you won't need to add any additional permissions. For those of you who need to configure your IAM user with the least amount of privileges, there are a few permissions you'll need to add depending on the specific features you'll be using. You can find the details at https://docs.aws.amazon.com/systems-manager/latest/userguide/sysman-access-user.html.

Creating an IAM Instance Profile for Systems Manager

Systems Manager won't be able to do anything with your Amazon EC2 instances by default. The way you allow Systems Manager to take action, connect, or manage your instances is with an IAM instance profile. You can create one or many roles with the specific permissions you need. We talked about IAM and instance profiles back in Chapters 2 and 3. We'll cover it again in the next few steps, focusing on the permissions needed for Systems Manager.

We'll first define a policy that will allow the Systems Manager service to assume a role. Once we have that policy in JSON format, we'll create the new role and attach the policy. Then we must create a new instance profile and add the IAM role to that instance profile.

```
$assumeRolePolicy = @{}
$assumeRolePolicy['Version'] = "2012-10-17"
$assumeRolePolicy['Statement'] = @{}
$assumeRolePolicy['Statement']['Effect'] = "Allow"
$assumeRolePolicy['Statement']['Principal'] = @{}
$assumeRolePolicy['Statement']['Principal']['Service'] = "ssm.amazonaws.com"
$assumeRolePolicy['Statement']['Action'] = "sts:AssumeRole"
```

Next, we create the new IAM role with the assume role policy JSON. The assume role policy allows the Systems Manager service (ssm.amazonaws.com) to assume the new role we are creating.

```
$role = New-IAMRole -RoleName "MySystemsManagerRole"
-AssumeRolePolicyDocument ($assumeRolePolicy | ConvertTo-Json) -Region us-
east-1
```

Now, attach the AmazonEC2RoleforSSM managed policy to the role using Register-IAMRolePolicy, and pass in the ARN for the managed policy. This managed policy permits communication to the Systems Manager API.

```
Register-IAMRolePolicy -RoleName $role.RoleName -PolicyArn
'arn:aws:iam::aws:policy/service-role/AmazonEC2RoleforSSM' -Region us-east-1
```

Then we create a new instance profile with New-IAMInstanceProfile. This is what we'll be attaching to our EC2 instance to enable Systems Manager.

```
$instanceProfile = New-IAMInstanceProfile -InstanceProfileName
"MyNewInstanceProfile" -Region us-east-1
```

Finally, we use Add-IAMRoleToInstanceProfile to add the IAM role to the instance profile, which finishes up our new instance profile.

```
Add-IAMRoleToInstanceProfile -InstanceProfileName $instanceProfile.
InstanceProfileName -RoleName $role.RoleName -Region us-east-1
```

Note   The Systems Manager profile in this example doesn't allow access to other services such as Amazon S3. Be sure to create instance profiles that have access to only the services needed in each specific use case.

To use this profile with Systems Manager, you'll need to either launch a new instance with the profile attached as discussed in Chapter 3, or attach it to an existing EC2 instance.

AWS Resource Groups

Now that you've been creating resources, you need a way to group them and keep things organized. With AWS Systems Manager Resource Groups, you're able to group your many AWS resources by tags. You can use Resource Groups in many different ways that will help you manage your cloud resources at scale. Some examples for grouping your resources are to group them by application, by environment (development, test, production), or for billing (by customer, department, or cost center).

> **Note**   Systems Manager Resource Groups are regional, so you'll only see AWS resources in the same region. To view resources in other regions, you'll need to create a resource group in those regions as well.

Creating New Resource Groups

In order to create a new resource group, we'll need a JSON query which represents the tags by which we'll group resources. I've built the JSON using PowerShell hashtables, but you can just as easily pass the JSON from a file or string.

First, let's begin by defining a hashtable for the tag we'll be filtering on.

```
$tagFilter = @{}
$tagFilter["Key"] = "Application"
$tagFilter["Values"] = @("MyApplication")
```

Next, we'll define another hashtable that represents the query and we'll reference our tag filter hashtable. In this query we're limiting the resources to EC2 instances and S3 buckets. These resource filters follow the standard naming scheme found in AWS ARNs. You can find a complete list of supported resources at `https://docs.aws.amazon.com/ARG/latest/userguide/supported-resources.html`.

```
$query = @{}
$query["ResourceTypeFilters"]=@("AWS::EC2::Instance", "AWS::S3::Bucket")
$query["TagFilters"]=@($tagFilter)
```

Now that we have our query constructed, we can convert it to JSON. We need to make sure we have the depth set with ConvertTo-Json, and we'll also use the compress switch to remove whitespace.

```
$queryJSON = $query | ConvertTo-Json -Depth 4 -Compress
```

If we look at the contents of the $queryJSON variable, we can see the resource types specified in the hashtable, along with the tag values.

```
PS C:\> $queryJSON
```

```
{"ResourceTypeFilters":["AWS::EC2::Instance","AWS::S3::Bucket"],"TagFilters":
[{"Key":"Application","Values":["MyApplication"]}]}
```

Next, we'll define our query type.

```
$queryType = [Amazon.ResourceGroups.QueryType]::TAG_FILTERS_1_0
```

Tip   If you receive an invalid operation exception in PowerShell telling you that it is unable to find [Amazon.ResourceGroups.QueryType], then you are most likely using an older version of the AWS PowerShell module which is missing the object we are trying to create. The way to fix this error is to update your AWS PowerShell module.

Now it's time to put it all together into a resource query object. We'll do that by using New-Object and assigning $queryType and $queryJSON to the type and query properties, respectively.

```
$resourceQuery = New-Object Amazon.ResourceGroups.Model.ResourceQuery
$resourceQuery.Type = $queryType
$resourceQuery.Query = $queryJSON
```

Finally, we can create our resource group using New-RGGroup and passing our resource query object.

```
New-RGGroup -DescNew-RGription "My Resource Group Description" -Name
"MyFirstResourceGroup" -ResourceQuery $resourceQuery -Region us-east-1
```

Updating Resource Groups

Let's take a look at how to update a resource groups. In the previous section, we constructed a query with hashtables and converted the hashtables to JSON. An alternative method is to pass the query as a string already formatted as JSON.

We'll begin by defining our query type.

```
$queryType = [Amazon.ResourceGroups.QueryType]::TAG_FILTERS_1_0
```

Then we'll create a resource query object, and pass $queryType, which is the query type we just defined.

```
$resourceQuery = New-Object Amazon.ResourceGroups.Model.ResourceQuery
$resourceQuery.Type = $queryType
```

We're going to pass the query as a JSON-formatted string. In the previous example, we passed EC2 instances and S3 buckets as the resource type filters; this time let's limit to just EC2 instances.

```
$resourceQuery.Query = '{"ResourceTypeFilters":["AWS::EC2::Instance"],
"TagFilters":[{"Key":"Department"}]}'
```

Once we have our new resource query object, we can update the resource group query by passing the resource query and resource group name to Update-RGGroupQuery.

```
Update-RGGroupQuery -ResourceQuery $resourceQuery -GroupName
"MyFirstResourceGroup" -Region us-east-1
```

Finding Resources with a Resource Query

There may be times when you want to test a resource query or quickly search for resources without first creating a resource group. Using Find-RGResource, you can do just that. Just as we did before, we'll define a query type for tag filters.

```
$queryType = [Amazon.ResourceGroups.QueryType]::TAG_FILTERS_1_0
```

Then we'll create a new resource query object using New-Object and set its type property to $queryType and also pass the query JSON.

```
$resourceQuery = New-Object Amazon.ResourceGroups.Model.ResourceQuery
$resourceQuery.Type = $queryType
$resourceQuery.Query = '{"ResourceTypeFilters":["AWS::EC2::Instance"],
"TagFilters":[{"Key":"Department"}]}'
```

Finally, we'll pass the resource query object to Find-RGResource.

```
Find-RGResource -ResourceQuery $resourceQuery
 -Region us-east-1
```

Listing Resource Groups

To list resource groups in your account, use `Get-RGGroupList` which returns the name, description, and ARN of the groups.

```
Get-RGGroupList -Region us-east-1
```

Deleting Resource Groups

Use `Remove-RGGroup` to delete groups. PowerShell will ask you to confirm the action to be sure you really want to delete the group. You can use the `-Force` switch to override the confirmation.

```
Remove-RGGroup -GroupName "MyFirstResourceGroup" -Region us-east-1

Confirm
Are you sure you want to perform this action?
Performing the operation "Remove-RGGroup (DeleteGroup)" on target
"MyFirstResourceGroup".
[Y] Yes [A] Yes to All [N] No [L] No to All [S] Suspend [?] Help (default
is "Yes"): Y

Description      GroupArn         Name
-----------      --------         ----
Test Description arn:aws:reso...  MyFirstResourceGroup
```

Listing Resources in a Resource Group

There are a few ways to view resources in resource groups. With the Systems Manager Console, you get a rich visual view of your resources. For scripting and automation, you'll want to use `Get-RGGroupResourceList` and pass the group name.

```
Get-RGGroupResourceList -GroupName "MyFirstResourceGroup" -Region us-east-1
| Format-List

ResourceArn  : arn:aws:ec2:us-east-1:12...:instance/i-11...
ResourceType : AWS::EC2::Instance
```

Built-In Insights

Within the Systems Manager Console, under the "Resource Groups" section, you'll find Insights. We'll go into detail on some of these in the next chapter, but there's one feature here that directly ties into the Resource Groups we just learned about. That's the Built-In Insights as shown in Figure 15-1. From the Built-In Insights, you first choose a resource group and can then view AWS Config rule compliance, Resource compliance, and Config history. This is a powerful feature to keep track of your resources and the changes made to them.

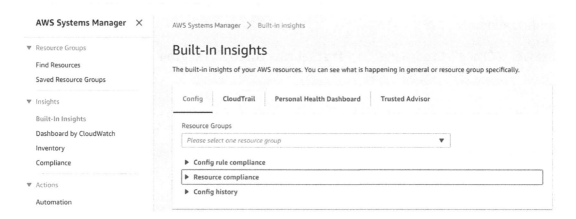

Figure 15-1. *The Built-In Insights within AWS Systems Manager Console*

Session Manager

Using Session Manager, you're able to connect to your Windows and Linux EC2 instances with a powerful web-based interactive shell. We'll take a look at Session Manager with a Windows instance, which gives us a PowerShell command-line interface in a web browser!

Tip   Session Manager gives you command-line access to your instances. If you typically use RDP or SSH to run command and scripts, you may be able to keep those inbound ports closed and just use Session Manager instead!

Connecting with Session Manager

Head over to the Systems Manager Console and, as shown in Figure 15-2, you'll find Session Manager under the Actions. You can also go directly via the URL `https://console.aws.amazon.com/systems-manager/session-manager`.

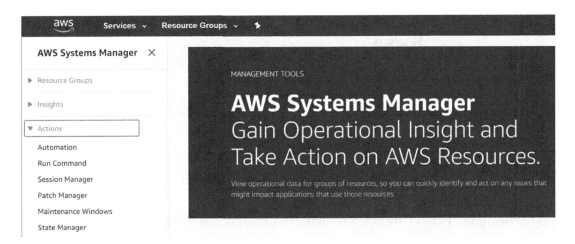

Figure 15-2. *The AWS Systems Manager Console, where Session Manager can be found*

Figure 15-3 shows you the Preferences tab. You have the option to set an S3 bucket for storing output, configure encryption, and enable CloudWatch logging.

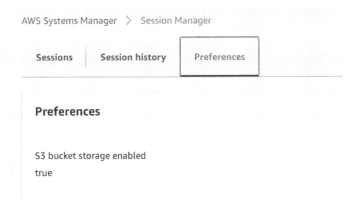

Figure 15-3. *The Session Manager Preferences tab allows you to configure a location for storing output and enabling CloudWatch Logs*

Back on the Sessions tab in Figure 15-4, you'll see a list of sessions and their status.

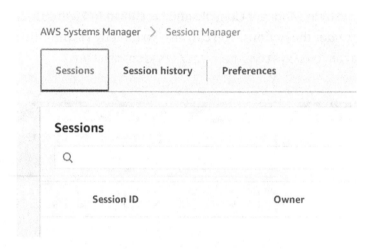

Figure 15-4. *The Sessions tab shows you a list of current sessions*

On the upper right of the Session Manager Console, you'll see the Start session button as shown in Figure 15-5. Click the button and select an instance to connect to.

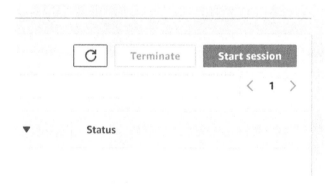

Figure 15-5. *The Start session button allows you to begin a new session*

Once connected, as in Figure 15-6, you'll have a regular PowerShell session in your web browser. From here, you can run any of the usual commands you would run on an instance. Two great aspects of this feature are that you don't need remote desktop and you don't need to open port 3389 on your security group.

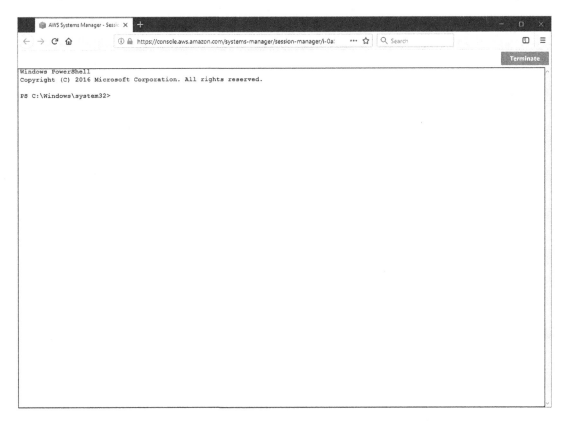

Figure 15-6. *A PowerShell session from your instance in a web browser*

Note   Connecting to an instance with Session Manager requires that you have the Systems Manager agent installed and running on your instance. The agent is preinstalled on Amazon-provided AMIs by default. You'll also need to launch your instance with an instance profile that has Systems Manager permissions associated with it. See the previous section in this chapter on "Creating a Systems Manager IAM instance profile."

Parameter Store

Parameter Store is a powerful shared feature within AWS Systems Manager and is designed to store configuration parameters for anything you build in the cloud. People often use it for application settings, database connection strings, passwords, license keys, and other runtime parameters. Parameter Store also features public parameters that can help you find the latest Windows or Linux AMI. You'll find Parameter Store at the bottom of the AWS Systems Manager Console, under Shared Resources as shown in Figure 15-7.

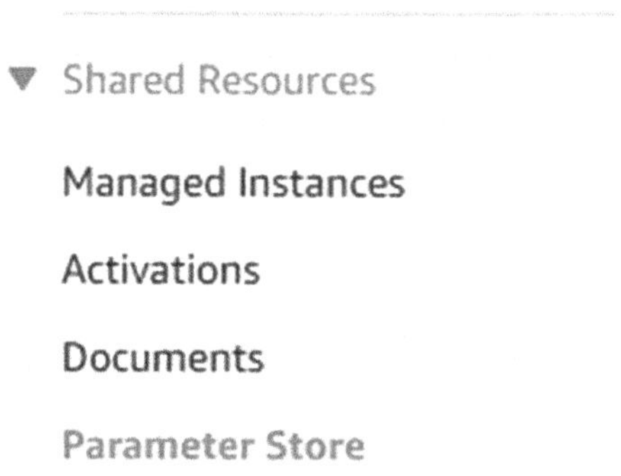

▼ Shared Resources

    Managed Instances

    Activations

    Documents

    Parameter Store

Figure 15-7. *Parameter Store can be found under the Shared Resources menu*

Using Parameter Store

A parameter's name follows a hierarchical format. This allows you to get all parameters matching the hierarchical path. You create entries in Parameter Store with `Write-SSMParameter`, though keep in mind as with most AWS resources, your parameters are stored in the region you create them.

```
Write-SSMParameter -Name "/Test/ParameterName" -Description
"MyParameterDescription" -Value "ParameterValue" -Type String -Region us-east-1
```

Now, let's look at using that hierarchical path to get any parameters that begin with /Test. This returns a parameter object where the value we set is stored in the value property.

```
Get-SSMParametersByPath -Path "/Test" -Region us-east-1
```

If you want to get the specific parameter, then `Get-SSMParameter` is the right cmdlet here, and we just need to pass the parameter name.

```
Get-SSMParameter -Name "/Test/ParameterName" -Region us-east-1
```

Finally, to remove a parameter, you call `Remove-SSMParameter`. PowerShell will prompt you to confirm. If you would like to suppress the confirmation prompt, remember to use the `-Force` switch.

```
Remove-SSMParameter -Name "/Test/ParameterName" -Region us-east-1
```

Finding the Latest Windows AMI

One of the Parameter Store features I use the most is finding the latest Windows AMI published by Amazon using a public parameter. Let's take a look at how this works using `Get-SSMParametersByPath`, which will return all the entries with the path `/aws/service/ami-windows-latest`, and the respective AMI Ids.

```
Get-SSMParametersByPath -Path "/aws/service/ami-windows-latest" -region us-east-1
```

From the list returned by `Get-SSMParametersByPath`, we can pick a specific parameter and use `Get-SSMParameter` to return the AMI ID for that specific entry.

```
Get-SSMParameter -Name /aws/service/ami-windows-latest/Windows_Server-2016-English-Full-Base -region us-east-1
```

Finding the Latest Linux AMI

We saw how we were able to retrieve the latest Windows AMI using `Get-SSMParametersByPath`, we can do the same for Amazon Linux AMIs which are under the path `/aws/service/ami-amazon-linux-latest`:

```
Get-SSMParametersByPath -Path "/aws/service/ami-amazon-linux-latest" -region us-east-1
```

Referencing Values with Systems Manager

Systems Manager has quite a few capabilities such as Run Command, Automation, and State Manager where you can reference Parameter Store values by using a specific syntax of `{{ssm:ParameterName}}`.

For a parameter with the name of /Test/ParameterName, you would use the following syntax:

```
{{ssm:/Test/ParameterName }}
```

We'll dive deeper into Run Command, Automation, and State Manager in the next couple of chapters, so remember that syntax for Parameter Store.

EXERCISE 15.1: LAUNCH AN EC2 INSTANCE WITH THE LATEST AMI

When running Windows, it's important to use the latest AMI which contains the latest Microsoft Updates along with the latest drivers for Amazon EC2. If you've ever run Get-EC2Image without specifying a filter or specific image ID for an AMI, you'll know that there are quite a few AMIs available! If you're new to AWS, it can indeed be difficult to determine which AMI to use when launching a new Amazon EC2 Instance.

In this exercise, we'll be using Parameter Store to quickly and easily find the latest Windows AMI and launch a new instance using it. In order to keep track of this new instance, we'll also use what we learned about tagging an EC2 instance in earlier chapters to apply a couple of tags.

Write Some Reusable Values to Parameter Store

First, let's create a variable to use for our region. Then we'll store a few values in Parameter Store to reuse in our script.

```
$region = "us-east-1"
```

The first value will be the name of our application.

```
Write-SSMParameter -Name "/Test/Application/Name" -Description "The
application name." -Value "MyTestApplication" -Type String -Region $region
```

The second value is what we'll use to set the name of our application server instance.

```
Write-SSMParameter -Name "/Test/Application/ServerName" -Description "The
application server name." -Value "MyTestApplicationServer" -Type String
-Region $region
```

Third, we'll need to set the instance type to use when spinning up an EC2 instance for the application server. We'll set this in Parameter Store, so when we need to scale up the instance type in future launches, we can do so without needing to modify the script.

```
Write-SSMParameter -Name "/Test/Application/ServerInstanceType" -Description
"The application server instance type." -Value "t3.large" -Type String
-Region $region
```

Get the Parameter Store Values

Here, we're going to grab the application server name, the application name, and instance type from Parameter Store.

```
$applicationServerName = (Get-SSMParameter -Name "/Test/Application/
ServerName" -Region $region).Value
```

```
$applicationName = (Get-SSMParameter -Name "/Test/Application/Name" -Region
$region).Value
```

```
$instanceType = (Get-SSMParameter -Name "/Test/Application/
ServerInstanceType" -Region $region).Value
```

Create a Tag Specification for Our New Instance

Let's create a name and application tag using a couple of hashtables and use our Parameter Store values to set them.

```
$nameTag = @{Key="Name"; Value=$applicationServerName}
```

```
$applicationTag = @{Key="Application"; Value=$applicationName}
```

In this step, we'll create a tag specification using New-Object and reference the tag specification type. Then we'll set the resource type to instance, since this is being used with an EC2 instance.

```
$tagSpec = New-Object Amazon.EC2.Model.TagSpecification
```

```
$tagSpec.ResourceType = "instance"
```

Now it's time to add the hashtables we created earlier.

```
$tagSpec.Tags.Add($nameTag)
$tagSpec.Tags.Add($applicationTag)
```

Find the Latest AMI Using Parameter Store

To find the latest AMI from Parameter Store, we'll need to reference the parameter path. parameterPath.

```
$parameterPath = "/aws/service/ami-windows-latest/Windows_Server-2016-
English-Full-Base"
```

Next, we'll use the parameter path we just defined with Get-SSMParameter and store the result. The object returned has a few different properties and we only need the image ID for the AMI in the next step, so we'll use the value property.

```
$latestImageId = (Get-SSMParameter -Name $parameterPath -Region $region).Value
```

Launch the EC2 Instance

Using our tag specification and latest Windows AMI, we're now ready to launch an EC2 instance. We'll do that with New-EC2Instance.

```
$newInstance = New-EC2Instance -ImageId $latestImageId -InstanceType
$instanceType -TagSpecification $tagSpec -Region $region
```

Finally, we can assign the RunningInstances property of the newly created instance to a variable.

```
$runningInstance = $newInstance.RunningInstance
```

If we look at this $runningInstance variable, we will see details for the running instance. If we wanted to build more automation around our running instance, we could use this variable to pass the Instance ID to another function. For now, we'll keep it simple and stop here.

Now we have seen how easy it is to create Parameter Store values and use them to launch an EC2 Instance. Our instance has two tags, the first one is a name that shows up in the main EC2 Console view, and the second is an application tag that we'll use in the next exercise.

```
EXERCISE 15.2: CREATING AND USING A RESOURCE GROUP
```

When building in the cloud with all the different AWS services, we need an easy way to group all of our resources together. Luckily, we can use Resource Groups to do just that!

Creating a Resource Group

Begin by creating a region variable and retrieving the application name from Parameter Store. Remember, we wrote to Parameter Store in Exercise 15.1.

```
$region = "us-east-1"

$applicationName = (Get-SSMParameter -Name "/Test/Application/Name" -Region $region).Value
```

Next, we'll create our tag filter and query hashtables.

```
$tagFilter = @{}
$tagFilter["Key"] = "Application"
$tagFilter["Values"] = @($applicationName)

$query = @{}
$query["ResourceTypeFilters"]=@("AWS::EC2::Instance", "AWS::S3::Bucket")
$query["TagFilters"]=@($tagFilter)
```

Since the query accepts a JSON-formatted string, we'll convert our hashtable to JSON, with a depth of 4, and the compress switch to remove whitespace.

```
$queryJSON = $query | ConvertTo-Json -Depth 4 –Compress
```

Now we can create our resource query.

```
$queryType = [Amazon.ResourceGroups.QueryType]::TAG_FILTERS_1_0

$resourceQuery = New-Object Amazon.ResourceGroups.Model.ResourceQuery
$resourceQuery.Type = $queryType
$resourceQuery.Query = $queryJSON
```

Finally, we're going to create the resource group using the same application name to prepend the name of the resource group.

```
New-RGGroup -Name "$applicationName -ResourceGroup" -Description "My Resource Group Description" -ResourceQuery $resourceQuery -Region $region
```

Listing Resources in a Resource Group

In this next activity, we are going to use the resource group we just created to list what resources are picked up by the query. First, we'll create a variable for our region.

```
$region = "us-east-1"
```

Then we'll grab our application name from Parameter Store.

```
$applicationName = (Get-SSMParameter -Name "/Test/Application/Name" -Region $region).Value
```

Finally, we'll get the resources in our resource group.

```
Get-RGGroupResourceList -GroupName "$applicationName -ResourceGroup" -Region $region
```

Remember, you can also view your resources using the "Resource Groups" section of the Systems Manager Console at `https://console.aws.amazon.com/resource-groups/`.

In this exercise you learned how to use Resource Groups to group resources for an application using a common tag. To better explore how resource groups can help you manage your resources, you can try tagging an Amazon S3 bucket with the same tag as the resource group query and see if it shows up in the resource group.

Summary

We saw that Resource Groups are a powerful way to group your AWS resources by using queries based on tags. With Built-In Insights, we saw how we can use our Resource Groups to look at some useful insights that are built right into the Systems Manager Console. Taking a look at Session Manager, we learned how we can run PowerShell from a web-based console without the need for RDP to our Windows instance. We wrapped up the chapter with Parameter Store and learned how to find the latest Windows or Linux AMIs, store custom application settings, and use those settings in our script. These are just a few of Systems Manager's powerful tools to help you manage your fleet of resources.

In the next chapter, we'll continue to dive into Systems Manager, occasionally coming back to both Parameter Store and Resource Groups as we discuss the different features that integrate with them.

CHAPTER 16

Systems Manager: Run Command, Automation, and State Manager

AWS Systems Manager includes several powerful features which can help you manage fleets of Amazon EC2 instances. In this chapter, we'll take a look at AWS Systems Manager Run Command, Automation, and State Manager which are all built upon an common object known as Systems Manager (SSM) documents. Since SSM documents are a common thread between all these features, it makes sense to dive into them first. So we'll look at what documents are and how to work with them, and then we'll see how they are used with Run Command, Automation, and State Manager.

Finally, we'll end the chapter with an exercise that shows you how to start an automation that builds an updated Windows AMI.

Note The previous chapter covered AWS Systems Manager basics which also included an important prerequisite, the IAM instance profile. By default, AWS Systems Manager isn't able to do anything with your EC2 Instances, so to enable connectivity between the AWS Systems Manager and the Amazon SSM Agent on your EC2 instances, you'll need that IAM instance profile discussed in the previous chapter, with the correct IAM role attached.

© Brian Beach, Steven Armentrout, Rodney Bozo, Emmanuel Tsouris 2019
B. Beach et al., *Pro PowerShell for Amazon Web Services*, https://doi.org/10.1007/978-1-4842-4850-8_16

AWS Systems Manager (SSM) Documents

Before we dive into Run Command, Automation, and State Manager, let's go over AWS Systems Manager (SSM) documents. SSM documents are a JSON based object used by the various features within AWS Systems Manager and define how actions are performed by Systems Manager.

There are a good number of predefined documents provided by Amazon which can help you manage your fleet of Amazon EC2 instances and perform all sorts of activities. SSM documents also have the ability to use parameters which allow you to pass configuration settings at runtime. Let's talk about the different document types and then look at how to work with these documents using either the AWS Systems Manager Console or PowerShell.

SSM Document Types

SSM documents come in a few different types which correspond to specific Systems Manager features. Document types can include command documents, policy documents, and automation documents which we'll be learning about later in this chapter.

A printed list of document types might never be up to date since Systems Manager, like many AWS Services, grows and has new feature added. These features might introduce new document types or use existing ones. As new features are added, you can always take a look at the "AWS Systems Manager User Guide" `https://docs.aws.amazon.com/systems-manager/latest/userguide/sysman-ssm-docs.html` which gives you information on the various document types.

Command Documents

Command documents define the commands that the SSM Agent should run on a targeted instance. Both Run Command and State Manager use these types of documents. The command document `AWS-RunPowerShellScript`, for example, allows you to execute PowerShell commands on one or more instances in your fleet.

Policy Documents

Policy documents are used by State Manager to enforce policies on your targeted instances. A policy is basically a configuration that you define, and Systems Manager makes sure that your instances match that configuration. An example use of policy documents would be to configure newly launched instances to match a standard configuration, optimize instances in an Auto Scaling group with a certain configuration, or even join Windows instances to a domain.

Automation Documents

Automation documents are used by Systems Manager Automation, a feature that you can use to automate systems management workflows. One popular use of Systems Manager Automation is to create custom AMIs by defining steps that can launch the latest Windows AMI from Amazon, add your custom software to it, update it, and then create a new AMI from that updated instance.

Working with Documents in the AWS Systems Manager Console

Let's open up the AWS Systems Manager Console using our web browser and going to `https://console.aws.amazon.com/systems-manager`. If we look under Shared Resources, we'll see a link to the Documents page, where we can browse any documents we've created as well as those created by Amazon (Figure 16-1). From here we can also create a new document by clicking the Create document button.

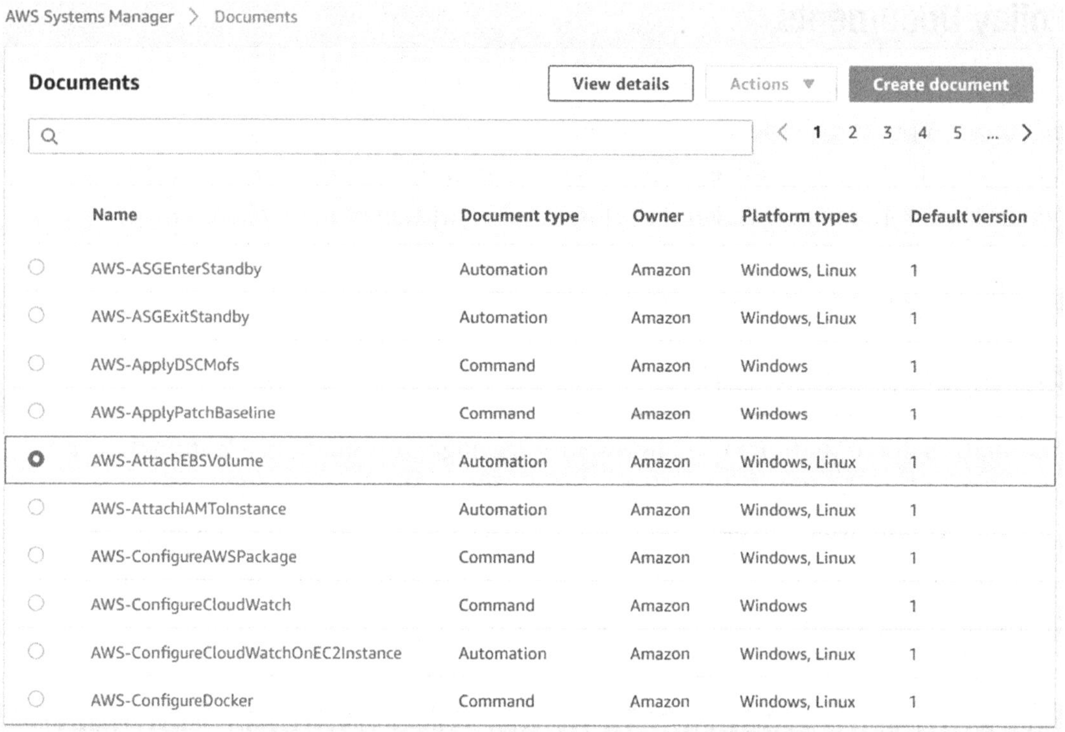

AWS Systems Manager > Documents

Documents

View details   Actions ▼   **Create document**

Q				< **1** 2 3 4 5 … >	

	Name	Document type	Owner	Platform types	Default version
○	AWS-ASGEnterStandby	Automation	Amazon	Windows, Linux	1
○	AWS-ASGExitStandby	Automation	Amazon	Windows, Linux	1
○	AWS-ApplyDSCMofs	Command	Amazon	Windows	1
○	AWS-ApplyPatchBaseline	Command	Amazon	Windows	1
◉	AWS-AttachEBSVolume	Automation	Amazon	Windows, Linux	1
○	AWS-AttachIAMToInstance	Automation	Amazon	Windows, Linux	1
○	AWS-ConfigureAWSPackage	Command	Amazon	Windows, Linux	1
○	AWS-ConfigureCloudWatch	Command	Amazon	Windows	1
○	AWS-ConfigureCloudWatchOnEC2Instance	Automation	Amazon	Windows, Linux	1
○	AWS-ConfigureDocker	Command	Amazon	Windows, Linux	1

Figure 16-1. *Documents in the AWS Systems Manager Console*

When we click the name of a document in the list, such as AWS-AttachEBSVolume, we'll be taken to a details page for that document (Figure 16-2). This details page shows us the Description, Parameters, Permissions, Content, Versions, and Tags for the document.

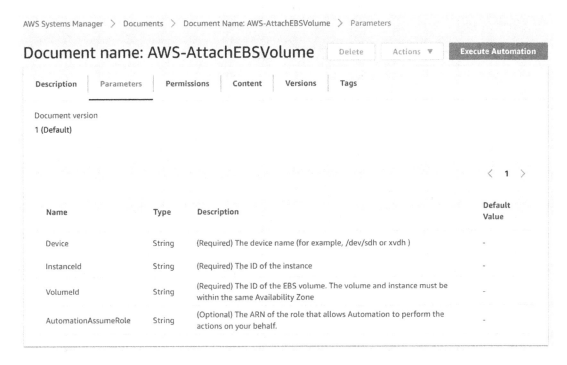

Figure 16-2. *Automation Document Parameters in the AWS Systems Manager Console*

If we click the Parameters tab, we can see the parameters that the document accepts. Some parameters might be required, while others are optional. These are defined by the document author within the document's content. In this case, we're looking at an automation document created by Amazon. Automation documents (to little surprise) are used by Systems Manager Automation. Now let's take a look at the Content tab (Figure 16-3).

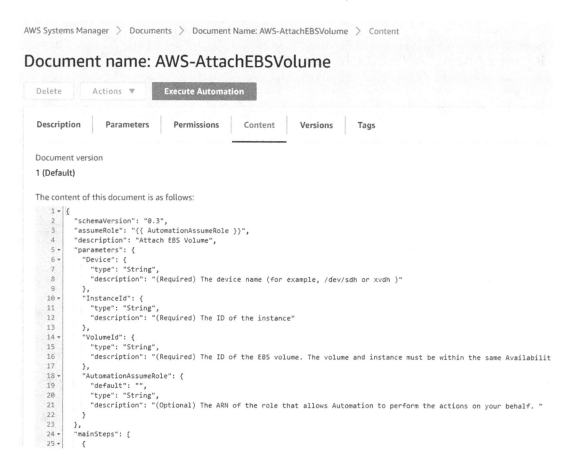

Figure 16-3. *Automation Document Content in the AWS Systems Manager Console*

We can see that the Content tab shows us a document version (not to be confused with the schema version), along with a blob of JSON.

The JSON content defines parameters and actions for the document and include a schema version. This schema version is important since the document schema might change with newer versions of Systems Manager to support new features. So if you're looking at two documents and notice the formats are different, look at the document type and the schema version.

Now, scroll down through the JSON, you'll see a section where the steps of the document are defined (Figure 16-4). For automation documents with a schema version of 0.3, each step is made up of a step name, actions, and inputs. If we go back and look at a command document with a version of 1.2, AWS-ApplyPatchBaseline, for example, we'll see it not only has different schema version, but the JSON structure is also a bit different.

Document name: AWS-ApplyPatchBaseline

| Description | Parameters | Permissions | Content | Versions | Tags |

Document version

1 (Default)

The content of this document is as follows:

```
 1 ▾ {
 2      "schemaVersion": "1.2",
 3      "description": "Scans for or installs patches from a patch baseline.",
 4 ▾    "parameters": {
 5 ▾      "Operation": {
 6          "type": "String",
 7          "description": "(Required) The update or configuration to perform on the instance.
 8 ▾        "allowedValues": [
 9            "Scan",
10            "Install"
11          ]
12        },
```

Figure 16-4. *Command Document Content in the AWS Systems Manager Console*

Documents can have different schema versions, and each version can be used with a specific document type; we can see a mapping of document types and the schemas that they can use in Table 16-1.

Table 16-1. *AWS Systems Manager Document Schema Versions*

Document Type	Uses Schema Versions
Command	1.2, 2.0, 2.2
Automation	0.3
Policy	2.0

Each schema version may have a different structure, support different features, and may use different section names in the content. You can read more about these document schemas and their features on the "AWS Systems Manager User Guide" https://docs.aws.amazon.com/systems-manager/latest/userguide/document-schemas-features.html.

Working with Documents Using PowerShell

While the AWS Systems Manager Console provides a rich GUI interface to browse and work with documents, often we'll want a programmatic way to automate our work with PowerShell scripts.

Listing SSM Documents

We can easily list documents using Get-SSMDocumentList, which returns a list of documents and includes properties such as document name, owner, and the type of document.

```
$documents = Get-SSMDocumentList -Region us-east-1
```

To see only the different types of documents available, we can use Group-Object along with the output of Get-SSMDocumentList.

```
$documents | Group-Object -Property DocumentType | Select-Object Name, Count
```

Listing SSM Documents with Document Filters

If we want to get a list of documents that match certain filter criteria, we can do so with a document filter. For example, to get all the command documents, create an Amazon.SimpleSystemsManagement.Model.DocumentFilter object. Then set the key to DocumentType, and set the value to Command. When we use –DocumentFilterList to pass the document filter to Get-SSMDocumentList, we'll only see command documents.

```
$documentFilter = New-Object Amazon.SimpleSystemsManagement.Model.
DocumentFilter
```

```
$documentFilter.Key = "DocumentType"
$documentFilter.Value = "Command"
```

```
Get-SSMDocumentList -DocumentFilterList $documentFilter -Region us-east-1
```

We can also combine document filters in an array. This allows us to filter on multiple properties. Say, for instance, we want to list all command documents that begin with "AWSSupport".

```
$docTypeFilter = New-Object Amazon.SimpleSystemsManagement.Model.
DocumentFilter
```

448

```
$docTypeFilter.Key = "DocumentType"
$docTypeFilter.Value = "Command"

$docNameFilter = New-Object Amazon.SimpleSystemsManagement.Model.
DocumentFilter

$docNameFilter.Key = "Name"
$docNameFilter.Value = "AWSSupport"

$docFilters = @($docTypeFilter,$docNameFilter)

$documents = Get-SSMDocumentList -DocumentFilterList $docFilters -Region
us-east-1
```

Getting an SSM Document Object

To take a closer look at a document, we can use Get-SSMDocument and pass it the name of a document, in this case we'll look at **AWS-RunPowerShellScript**. One detail we can see is that the content property is the same JSON string containing details that define the document actions similar to what we saw on the Content tab in the console.

```
$ssmDoc = Get-SSMDocument -Name "AWS-RunPowerShellScript" -Region us-east-1

$ssmDoc.Content
```

If you'd prefer to see the content formatted as YAML instead of JSON, you can set the -DocumentType parameter to **YAML**.

```
Get-SSMDocument -Name "AWS-RunPowerShellScript" -DocumentFormat "YAML"
-Region us-east-1
```

Creating a New SSM Document

When we want to create a new SSM Document, we must first create the document JSON content. A command document with a schema version of 2.2 looks something like this:

```
{
    "schemaVersion": "2.2",
    "description": "This is an example Run Command document.",
    "parameters": {
        "MyParameter": {
```

```
            "type": "String",
            "description": "(Optional) An example parameter.",
            "default": "Hello World!",
            "maxChars": 256
        }
    },
    "mainSteps": [
        {
            "name": "MyNewCommandDocument",
            "action": "aws:runPowerShellScript",
            "precondition": {
                "StringEquals": [
                    "platformType",
                    "Windows"
                ]
            },
            "inputs": {
                "timeoutSeconds": 300,
                "runCommand": [
                    "Write-Host '{{MyParameter}}'",
                    "Write-Host 'This is a new Run Command document'"
                ]
            }
        }
    ]
}
```

Then using New-SSMDocument, we would create a new document with our JSON content and set the name of the document and the correct document type (in this case, we are creating a Run command document, so we'll set it to Command).

```
$docJson = Get-Content .\MyNewCommandDocument.json | Out-String

New-SSMDocument -Content $docJson -DocumentType Command -Name
"MyNewCommandDocument"
```

Run Command

Run Command is one of the oldest and original AWS Systems Manager features. It's both powerful and secure, giving you the ability to run commands on your Amazon EC2 Instances and on-premises computers. A Run command document simply includes the details and instructions needed for the Amazon SSM Agent to perform actions on your behalf. As we'll learn later, Automation, State Manager, and other Systems Manager features build upon Run Command as a foundation. You'll find there are many documents predefined and published by Amazon. We also saw how you can create your own documents to meet your specific needs. You might want to use Run Command to enable server roles, install applications, perform routine maintenance, or even troubleshoot issues.

Note   The following sections require your EC2 Windows Instance have an IAM instance profile with the appropriate roles and trust in order for AWS Systems Manager to function. If you skipped the previous chapters on IAM and Systems Manager Basics, it might be a good idea to go back and review those. Without the IAM instance profile, the Amazon SSM Agent on your EC2 instances won't be able to communicate with the backend services.

Run Command Using the AWS Systems Manager Console

If we go back to the AWS Systems Manager Console, under the Actions sub-heading, we'll find Run Command (Figure 16-5).

Figure 16-5. *Run Command in the AWS Systems Manager Console*

On the Run Command page, we can run a new command, view currently running commands, and view command history. To run a new command, we simply click the Run command button and we'll be taken to the next page which shows us a list of command documents that we can select from (Figure 16-6).

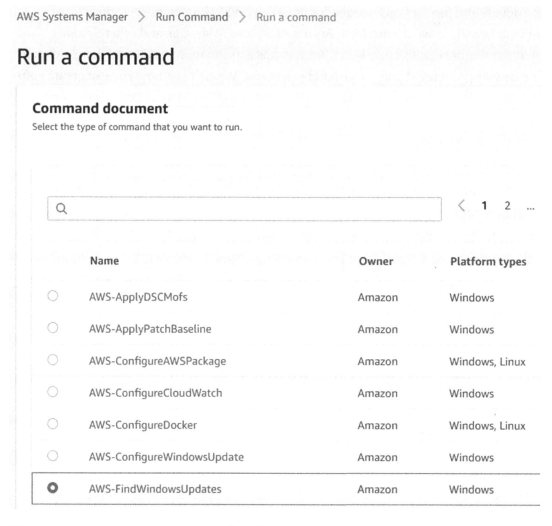

Figure 16-6. Running a command in the AWS Systems Manager Console

As we learned earlier, we can click the Name of a command document, and we will see a details page. Now if we want to run a command document, we must click the radio button to select it. Let us look closer at `AWS-FindWindowsUpdates`, a document which searches for missing Windows Updates on an instance we choose. Once selected, we can scroll down the page and see document details including its Command parameters (Figure 16-7).

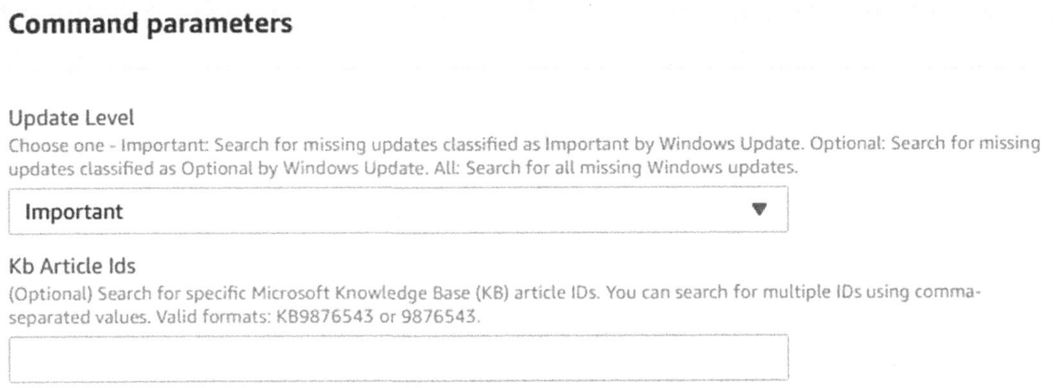

Command parameters

Update Level
Choose one - Important: Search for missing updates classified as Important by Windows Update. Optional: Search for missing updates classified as Optional by Windows Update. All: Search for all missing Windows updates.

Important ▾

Kb Article Ids
(Optional) Search for specific Microsoft Knowledge Base (KB) article IDs. You can search for multiple IDs using comma-separated values. Valid formats: KB9876543 or 9876543.

Figure 16-7. *Command parameters for running a command*

These Command parameters map to the command document's parameters we discussed earlier in the section on SSM Documents. The AWS Systems Manager Console shows parameters as input fields. For this document, we can see that the document author has added two parameters, one sets the Update Level and the other specifies Microsoft Knowledge Base (KB) articles. Continuing to scroll down, we'll see the Targets section (Figure 16-8).

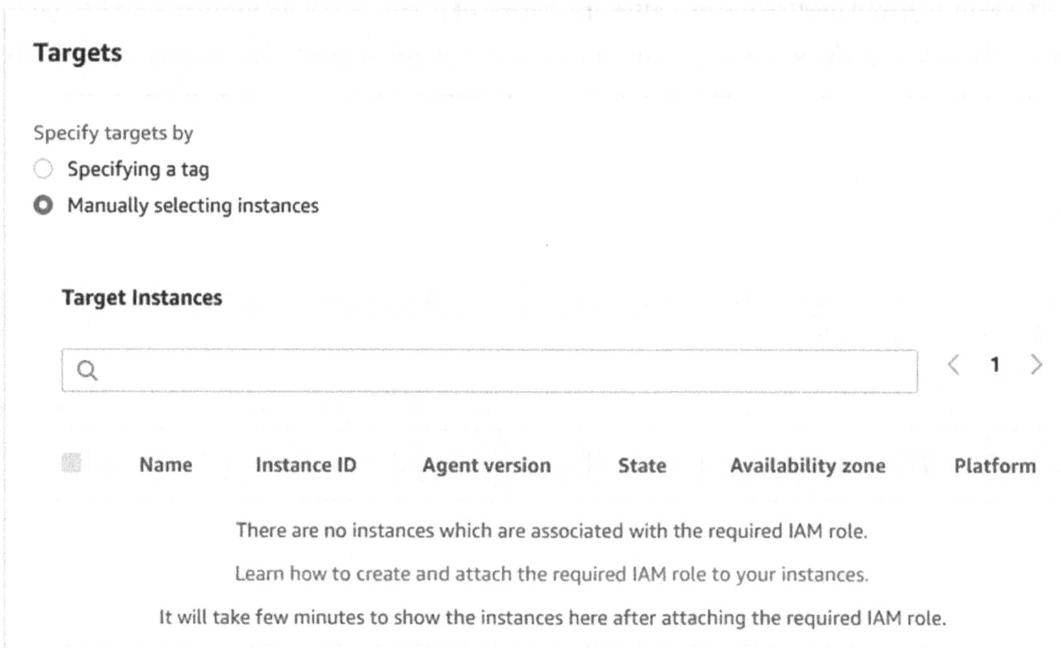

Targets

Specify targets by
○ Specifying a tag
⦿ Manually selecting instances

Target Instances

| 🔍 | | | | | | ‹ 1 › |

	Name	Instance ID	Agent version	State	Availability zone	Platform

There are no instances which are associated with the required IAM role.

Learn how to create and attach the required IAM role to your instances.

It will take few minutes to show the instances here after attaching the required IAM role.

Figure 16-8. *Targets for running a command*

This is where we define which instances (or targets) we want to run the command on. We can use two methods for selecting targets. We can use a tag, and any instances with that tag will be selected, or we can manually choose manually using instance ID, activation ID, Amazon SSM Agent version, IAM role name, platform, or even resource type.

In the other parameters section, we can optionally enter a comment or set the timeout for the command. We'll also find a rate control section, which gives us options to limit the number of concurrent targets (this is useful if we are to throttle our command and have only a few run the command at a time). Error threshold also gives us the ability to stop running the command if we get a set number of errors (or percentage).

From here, we also get output options which can enable writing command output to an S3 bucket, CloudWatch Logs, and even trigger an SNS notification that we can use to kick off other workflows or connect to other AWS services.

Finally, there's a Run button at the bottom of the page that runs the command. Once running, we can view the status of the command from the console, and eventually when it's done running, we can look at the output.

Run Command Using PowerShell

Since this is a PowerShell book, let's take a deeper look at how we can use Run Command from our PowerShell scripts. There's one particular command document that we should look at, and that's `AWS-RunPowerShellScript`. As the name implies, this document lets you run PowerShell scripts on your target instances. If you want to run shell commands on Linux, there's a document for that too!

Now we can run this command document using the console just as we learned a little bit ago, but let's look at how we can run it using PowerShell.

The document has a few parameters which can be seen in the content section of the document properties either by reading the JSON content or by converting it to an object using `ConvertFrom-JSON`.

```
$ssmDoc = Get-SSMDocument -Name "AWS-RunPowerShellScript" -Region us-east-1
```

```
$ssmDoc.Content | ConvertFrom-Json | Select-Object parameters
```

The parameters you'll find in the content property match up with those parameters you'll find in AWS Systems Manager Console (Figure 16-9).

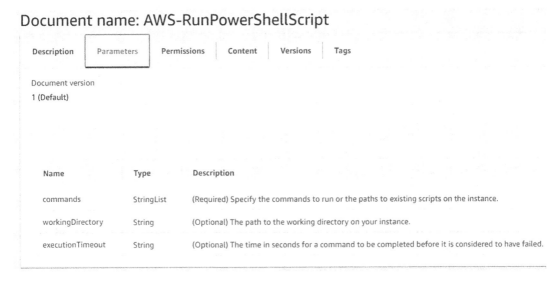

Figure 16-9. *Parameters for AWS-RunPowerShellScript*

We can see that the only required parameter is the one named `commands`. This is a string list (or array) of PowerShell commands. There are also two optional parameters, `workingDirectory` and `executionTimeout`. Working directory is simply the path to a working directory on your instance. So if you want your script to start in a specific directory, you will set that here. Execution timeout has a default value of 1 hour, which means if your script is going to run longer than an hour, you'll need to set this accordingly; otherwise, execution of the command might timeout. The maximum timeout you can set is 48 hours.

Sending an SSM Command

Now, let's send an SSM command that tells the Amazon SSM Agent to run some PowerShell script using, you guessed it, the AWS-RunPowerShellScript document.

For convenience, let's define an instance ID in a PowerShell variable. Remember, you must use an instance ID that's running and has an appropriate IAM instance profile attached. Then we'll define a variable which represents the document parameters. The only required one is `commands`, and we'll use it to pass `Get-Date` and `Get-Service`.

```
$instanceId = "your instance id"
$parameter = @{'commands'=@('Get-Date', 'Get-Service')}
```

Next, let's use `Send-SSMCommand` to run the PowerShell commands on your instance. Pay close attention to the region parameter; it must be the same region as your instance. Also, by returning the result into a variable, you can easily use the `CommandId` later to get status of the command. In addition, if you pass an array of instance ids, you will run the command on all of them.

```
$ssmCommand = Send-SSMCommand -DocumentName AWS-RunPowerShellScript
-Parameter $parameter -Comment 'Testing Run Command' -InstanceId
$instanceId -Region us-east-1
```

Examine the command output by printing the contents of the `$ssmCommand` variable. You'll see the status and status details are both pending. To get the status, we would use `Get-SSMCommand` with the `CommandId` property.

```
Get-SSMCommand -CommandId $ssmCommand.CommandId –Region us-east-1
```

When the Status is no longer pending, you're able to view command invocation details with `Get-SSMCommandInvocation`.

```
$commandInvocation = Get-SSMCommandInvocation -CommandId $ssmCommand.
CommandId -Detail $true -Region us-east-1
```

The command invocation details have a property named `CommandPlugins`; if we expand the property, we can see the output returned by our PowerShell commands.

```
$commandInvocation | Select-Object -ExpandProperty CommandPlugins
```

Handling Run Command Output

If output is longer than 2500 characters, it'll be truncated. You'll know it was truncated because Systems Manager adds `---Output truncated---` as the last entry in the output to let you know. You can get the full output in a couple of ways, either by using an S3 bucket or with CloudWatch Logs. Both of these methods require that your IAM instance profile have the appropriate access roles to allow writing to the S3 bucket or CloudWatch Logs depending on which you choose to use.

Sending Output to an S3 Bucket

To save the output in an S3 bucket, make sure your IAM instance profile has write access to the S3 bucket, and use the `–OutputS3BucketName` property with `Send-SSMCommand`. You'll get the full output of the PowerShell commands stored in your bucket.

```
Send-SSMCommand -DocumentName AWS-RunPowerShellScript -Parameter $parameter
-Comment 'Testing Run Command' -InstanceId $instanceId -OutputS3BucketName
"MyTestBucket12345" -OutputS3KeyPrefix "SomeKeyPrefix" –Region us-east-1
```

Sending Output to CloudWatch Logs

To use CloudWatch Logs, configure the two CloudWatch properties of `Send-SSMCommand` `-CloudWatchOutputConfig_CloudWatchOutputEnabled` and `-CloudWatchOutputConfig_ CloudWatchLogGroupName`. If we don't pass a CloudWatch Log Group Name, Systems Manager uses the default log group name `/aws/ssm/<document name>`. So in this case, it would be `/aws/ssm/AWS-RunPowerShellScript`.

```
Send-SSMCommand -DocumentName AWS-RunPowerShellScript -Parameter
$parameter -Comment 'Testing Run Command' -InstanceId $instanceId
-CloudWatchOutputConfig_CloudWatchOutputEnabled $true -Region us-east-1
```

AWS Systems Manager Automation

AWS Systems Manager Automation executes automation workflows that string together actions to perform a more complex task. Automation uses SSM Documents much like Run Command, and those documents can perform a wide variety of activities such as creating a new instance, stopping that instance, updating it with the latest drivers or patches, and then creating an AMI from that newly updated instance.

User Access to Automation

If you are using an IAM user account, group, or role with administrator permissions, then you should be able to use the Automation service without any access issues; otherwise, you'll need to grant your account, group, or role access to the Automation service. You can grant access using an AWS managed policy named `AmazonSSMFullAccess`.

Automation Roles

Much like Run Command, Automation needs an instance profile for any instances that you are launching or targeting with an Automation. Creating that instance profile is covered in the previous chapter under prerequisites. Remember, if you're using CloudWatch, SNS, or other AWS services with Automation, you'll also need to grant your instance profile access to those services. The "AWS Systems Manager User Guide" also contains information on how to configure those needed roles and even provides a CloudFormation template to get you started. See "Configuring Access for Systems Manager Automation" at `https://docs.aws.amazon.com/systems-manager/latest/userguide/automation-setup-user.html`.

Listing Automation Documents

As we learned in the section on SSM documents, listing automation documents with PowerShell can be done easily using the `Get-SSMDocumentList` command and a document filter.

```
$docFilter = New-Object Amazon.SimpleSystemsManagement.Model.DocumentFilter
$docFilter.Key = "DocumentType"
$docFilter.Value = "Automation"
```

```
$documents = Get-SSMDocumentList -DocumentFilterList $ docFilter -Region
us-east-1
```

```
$documents | Select-Object Name
```

To see the details for each document, look at "Systems Manager Automation Documents Reference" located within the "Systems Manager User Guide" `https://docs.aws.amazon.com/systems-manager/latest/userguide/automation-documents-reference-details.html`.

Starting an Automation Execution

To start an Automation workflow, we can use `Start-SSMAutomationExecution` and pass it a document name and parameters. The specific parameters will vary depending on the document.

```
$params = @{'InstanceId' = "i-12345", 'InstanceType' = "t3.xlarge"}
```

```
$execId = Start-SSMAutomationExecution -DocumentName "AWS-ResizeInstance"
-Parameter $params -Region us-east-1
```

This example uses the SSM automation document `AWS-ResizeInstance` which executes the following steps:

- Creates a CloudFormation Stack

- Changes the Instances State to stopped

- Invokes a Lambda function that changes the Instance Size

- Changes the Instance State to Running

- Deletes the CloudFormation Stack

See the "Systems Manager User Guide" for details on each automation document; for example, the details on `AWS-ResizeInstance` can be found at `https://docs.aws.amazon.com/systems-manager/latest/userguide/automation-aws-resizeinstance.html`.

Getting Automation Execution Status

We can view execution status of our automation using `Get-SSMAutomationExecution` and pass it the automation execution ID we got from `Start-SSMAutomationExecution`.

```
Get-SSMAutomationExecution -AutomationExecutionId $execId
```

AWS Systems Manager State Manager

Managing a fleet of instances, whether they are in the cloud or on-premises can be challenging. State Manager can help you define policies and enforce those policies to ensure your systems remain in the state you desire. Remember those documents we were talking about? Well State Manager allows you to associate those documents with your instances. You can add a schedule to do things like keep software up to date or perform some routine maintenance task.

Creating an Association

Let's look at how we can use New-SSMAssociation to create an association with State Manager. We'll define a tag which will be used for the association (so any instances with that tag will run the document), pass the document name, and create a schedule. This association will run the AWS-UpdateSSMAgent document every 24 hours and target any instances that have a tag named UpdateSSM with a value set to true.

```
$targetTags = @{Key = "tag:UpdateSSM"; Values = @("true")}

New-SSMAssociation -AssociationName TestAssociation1 -Name AWS-
UpdateSSMAgent -Target $targetTags -ScheduleExpression "rate(24 hours)"
```

State Manager supports a number of cron and rate expressions. Table 16-2 outlines the field positions and possible values you can use to construct a cron expression. Cron expressions, as shown in Table 16-3, are composed of six required fields separated by spaces and can also feature a seventh optional field which represents seconds (and comes first before the other six). For a few examples of cron expressions, see Table 16-4. Rate expressions are a little different where you specify the rate and unit; to see some examples of rate expressions, take a look at Table 16-5.

Table 16-2. *Cron Expression Values for Systems Manager*

Field	Wildcards	Possible Values
Minutes	, - * /	0–59
Hours	, - * /	0–23
Day of the Month	, - * ? / L W	1–31
Month	, - * /	1–12 or JAN–DEC
Day of the Week	, - * ? / L	1–7 or SUN–SAT
Year	, - * /	1970–2199

Table 16-3. *Cron Field Positions for Systems Manager*

Minutes	Hours	Day of the Month	Month	Day of the Week	Year
*	*	*	*	*	*

Table 16-4. *Cron Examples for Systems Manager*

Expression	Meaning
cron(0/15 * * * ? *)	Every 15 minutes
cron(0/30 * * * ? *)	Every 30 minutes
cron(0 0/1 * * ? *)	Every hour
cron(30 5 ? * * *)	Every day at 5:30 a.m.

Table 16-5. *Rate Examples for Systems Manager*

Expression	Meaning
rate(30 minutes)	Every 30 minutes
rate(1 hour)	Every hour
rate(14 days)	Every 14 days

To learn more about "Cron and Rate Expressions for Systems Manager," check out the user guide at https://docs.aws.amazon.com/systems-manager/latest/userguide/ reference-cron-and-rate-expressions.html.

EXERCISE 16.1: BUILD A WINDOWS AMI USING AUTOMATION

Amazon provides a great number of Windows AMIs that are maintained monthly and kept up to date. There are cases where you may want to build your own customized AMI and keep it up to date with the latest patches and AWS software. In this exercise, we are going to use AWS Systems Manager Automation to take an AMI as input and build us a new AMI.

Create an IAM Instance Profile

We'll create an IAM instance profile. If you already have one created, feel free to skip this and substitute your instance profile throughout the exercise.

First, we'll begin by defining our assume role policy, which allows the AWS Systems Manager service (ssm.amazonaws.com) to assume the role we're going to create.

```
$assumeRolePolicy = @"
{
    "Version": "2012-10-17",
    "Statement": {
        "Effect": "Allow",
        "Principal": {
            "Service": [
                "ec2.amazonaws.com",
                "ssm.amazonaws.com"
            ]
        },
        "Action": "sts:AssumeRole"
    }
}
"@
```

Next, we'll create a new role and apply the assume role policy document we defined in $assumeRolePolicy.

```
$role = New-IAMRole -RoleName "DemoSSMRole" -AssumeRolePolicyDocument
$assumeRolePolicy
```

Now, let's add the AmazonEC2RoleforSSM managed policy.

```
Register-IAMRolePolicy -RoleName $role.RoleName -PolicyArn
'arn:aws:iam::aws:policy/service-role/AmazonEC2RoleforSSM'
```

To allow our managed instances to write to CloudWatch, we'll also add the CloudWatch Managed Policy.

```
Register-IAMRolePolicy -RoleName $role.RoleName -PolicyArn
'arn:aws:iam::aws:policy/CloudWatchFullAccess'
```

Once we've registered all the needed policies, let's create the instance profile. This profile will be attached to an Amazon EC2 instance and will enable the Amazon SSM Agent.

```
$instanceProfile = New-IAMInstanceProfile -InstanceProfileName
"DemoSSMInstanceProfile"
```

Finally, we'll add the role to the instance profile.

```
Add-IAMRoleToInstanceProfile -InstanceProfileName $instanceProfile.
InstanceProfileName -RoleName $role.RoleName
```

Finding the Latest Windows Server 2019 AMI

While you can use your own custom AMI ID, let's use the latest Windows Server 2019 AMI. Remember Parameter Store? We'll go back to what we learned in the previous chapter to use Parameter Store which is kept up to date with the latest AMI ID in each region.

```
$parameterPath = "/aws/service/ami-windows-latest/Windows_Server-2019-
English-Full-Base"
```

```
$latestImageId = (Get-SSMParameter -Name $parameterPath -Region $region).
Value
```

Configure the Automation Document Parameters

Automation documents feature parameters, which allow you to pass values to the document. We'll be using the automation document AWS-UpdateWindowsAmi which has a number of parameters; there are two in particular that we need to set to ensure the automation doesn't fail. That's the source AMI ID, which will be used to launch an instance, and the IAM instance profile we just created. The other parameters either have default values or are optional, so we'll leave them out to keep things simple.

```
$parameters = @{
    SourceAmiId=$latestImageId;
    IamInstanceProfileName="DemoSSMInstanceProfile";
}
```

Kick Off the Automation Document

Let's kick off the automation and pass the parameters.

```
$execId = Start-SSMAutomationExecution -DocumentName "AWS-UpdateWindowsAmi"
-Parameter $parameters
```

Finally, let's get Automation Execution Status to see progress of our automation workflow.

```
Get-SSMAutomationExecution -AutomationExecutionId $execId
```

When our automation is complete, we'll find a new AMI that has been created which contains the latest AWS Drivers and Software, along with the latest Microsoft Updates.

Summary

In this chapter, we learned about SSM documents and how they are used with AWS Systems Manager Run Command, Automation, and State Manager. We went through the steps of taking an AMI and running it through an automation workflow that updated the operating system and AWS software. In the next chapter, we'll wrap up our look at AWS Systems Managers with some of the remaining features we haven't covered yet including Patch Manager.

CHAPTER 17

Systems Manager: Inventory and Patch Manager

Two AWS Systems Manager features that help manage your fleet at scale are Systems Manager Inventory and Systems Manager Patch Manager. With Systems Manager Inventory, you can specify the type of metadata you want to collect from your instances, which instances to collect it from, and when to collect it. AWS Systems Manager Patch Manager gives you the tools you need to automate the process of scanning or installing patches on your instances.

In this chapter, we'll first look at how we can use AWS Systems Manager Inventory to collect some information from our instances. Secondly, we'll run through the basics of configuring and using AWS Systems Manager Patch Manager to keep our instances up to date on a regular schedule. Finally, we'll end the chapter with two exercises. The first one walks us through configuration of inventory, and the second one focuses on a common patch management scenario.

Note   AWS Systems Manager Inventory and AWS Systems Manager Patch Manager both build on the concepts discussed in earlier chapters, specifically Systems Manager prerequisites and AWS Systems Manager (SSM) documents. These previous chapters covered an important prerequisite, the IAM instance profile. By default, AWS Systems Manager is not able to do anything with your EC2 Instances; so to enable connectivity between the AWS Systems Manager and the Amazon SSM Agent on your EC2 instances, you'll need that IAM instance profile discussed in those chapters, with the correct IAM role attached.

© Brian Beach, Steven Armentrout, Rodney Bozo, Emmanuel Tsouris 2019
B. Beach et al., *Pro PowerShell for Amazon Web Services*, https://doi.org/10.1007/978-1-4842-4850-8_17

AWS Systems Manager Inventory

Systems Manager Inventory gives you the ability to define metadata collection rules. Assuming you've attached correct IAM instance profile needed by the Amazon SSM Agent, inventory collection will occur based on the rules and schedule you specify. In the next section, we'll take a look at how we define those both in the console and using PowerShell.

Systems Manager Inventory in the Console

Open up the "AWS Systems Manager Console" at `https://console.aws.amazon.com/systems-manager`, and you'll find Inventory listed under the Insights sub-heading. See Figure 17-1.

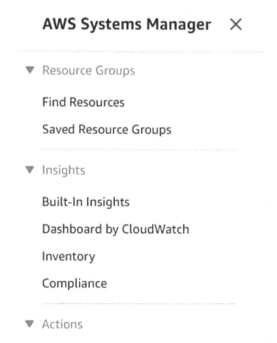

Figure 17-1. *Finding Systems Manager Inventory in the console*

Once you click Inventory, you'll be taken to the AWS Systems Manager Inventory Dashboard, where you can set up inventory or look at data. See Figure 17-2.

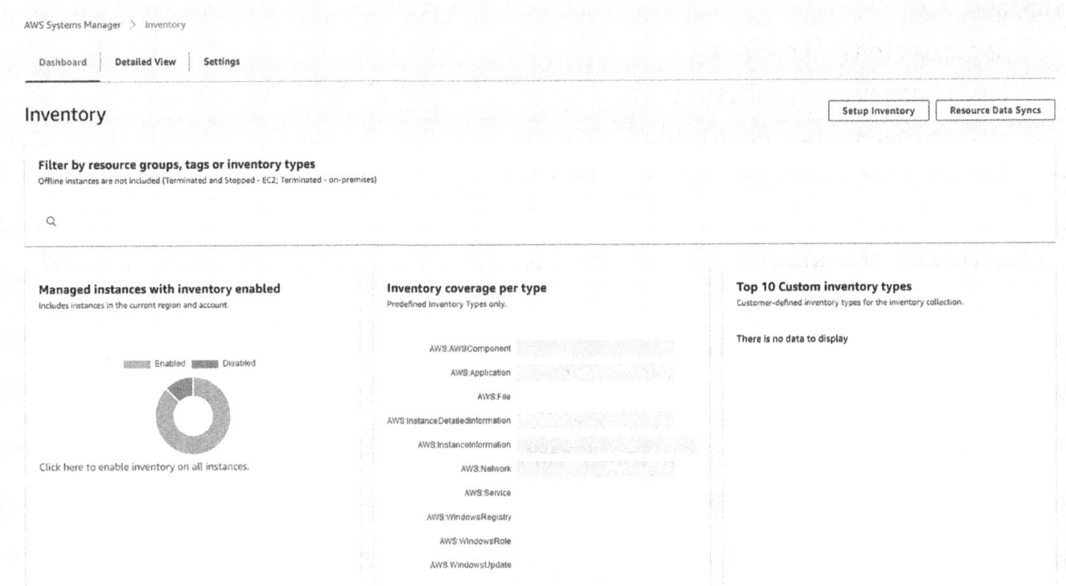

Figure 17-2. *Systems Manager Inventory Dashboard in the console*

Creating an Inventory Association

Assuming you have one or more managed instances already running in a particular region, here's how you can enable Inventory by creating an Inventory Association. We are going to focus on what's referred to as a global inventory association, and that means that all instances in a particular region will begin collecting inventory data. We can also specify a specific instance, and we'll see how to do that in the next few steps.

If you'd like to inventory all of your instances in a particular region, you can create a global inventory association by using `New-SSMAssociation` and specifying a wildcard for the Instance ID.

```
$target = @{Key = "InstanceIds"; Values = "*"}
```

We'll define a schedule using the rate format.

```
$schExp = "rate(30 minutes)"
```

Define parameters that tell SSM what items to inventory (applications, AWS components, etc.).

467

```
$params = @{
    applications='Enabled';
    awsComponents='Enabled';
    customInventory='Enabled';
    instanceDetailedInformation='Enabled';
    networkConfig='Enabled';
    services='Enabled';
    windowsRoles='Enabled';
    windowsUpdates='Enabled'
}
```

Then, we create an association for the AWS-GatherSoftwareInventory document, passing the target, schedule, and parameters.

```
New-SSMAssociation -Name AWS-GatherSoftwareInventory -Target $target
-ScheduleExpression $schExp -Parameter $params -Region us-west-2
```

Inventory Schemas

In order to understand what inventory types are available, we can look at the schemas available to us in a particular region using Get-SSMInventorySchema.

```
Get-SSMInventorySchema -Region us-west-2
```

If we want to look at just the type names available in a nice list, we can simply look at the TypeName property.

```
PS C:\> (Get-SSMInventorySchema -Region us-west-2).TypeName

AWS:AWSComponent
AWS:Application
AWS:ComplianceItem
AWS:File
AWS:InstanceDetailedInformation
AWS:InstanceInformation
AWS:Network
AWS:PatchCompliance
AWS:PatchSummary
AWS:ResourceGroup
```

```
AWS:Service
AWS:Tag
AWS:WindowsRegistry
AWS:WindowsRole
AWS:WindowsUpdate
```

When working with these schemas, we'll need to know the attributes for each schema type. We can do that by looking ata specific schema's attributes.

```
PS C:\>(Get-SSMInventorySchema -TypeName "AWS:AWSComponent" -Region us-
west-2).Attributes
```

```
DataType Name
-------- ----
string   Name
string   ApplicationType
string   Publisher
string   Version
string   InstalledTime
string   Architecture
string   URL
```

To view the inventory schemas that support the use of an aggregator, we just pass $true to the -Aggregator parameter. An aggregator groups and summarizes larger amounts of inventory data.

```
Get-SSMInventorySchema -Aggregator $true -Region us-west-2
```

Viewing Inventory Data

Once inventory has completed, we'll want to look at what's been collected. We can do that using Get-SSMInventory.

```
Get-SSMInventory -Region us-west-2
```

For convenience, let's assign the result to an array of Inventory Result Entity data types, which helps us work with the data structure.

```
[Amazon.SimpleSystemsManagement.Model.InventoryResultEntity[]]$invResults =
Get-SSMInventory -Region us-west-2
```

To keep things simple, let's look at the first object in the array.

```
$inventoryResultEntity = $invResults | Select-Object -First 1
```

Looking at the inventory result entity data structure, we can see two properties. There's an ID which corresponds to the Instance ID, and a data property.

```
PS C:\> $inventoryResultEntity | Format-List

Data : {[AWS:InstanceInformation, Amazon.SimpleSystemsManagement.Model.
       InventoryResultItem]}
Id   : i-1234567890
```

The Data property contains a key value pair. We can look at this property to see the specific inventory schema data type (key) and inventory data (value). You might see different data types and values depending on the specific inventory data that has been collected in your account.

```
PS C:\>$inventoryResultEntity.Data | Format-List

Key   : AWS:InstanceInformation
Value : Amazon.SimpleSystemsManagement.Model.InventoryResultItem
```

Now let's look at the content stored within the value property.

```
$inventoryResultItem = ($inventoryResultEntity.Data).Values
$inventoryContent = $inventoryResultItem.Content
```

When we look at $inventoryContent, we can see various key value pairs which contain our inventory data. For example, the AWS:InstanceInformation data type gives us AgentType, AgentVersion, InstanceStatus, IpAddress, PlatformName, PlatformType, and other relevant properties related to an Amazon EC2 Instance.

To look at a specific data type, for a specific instance, we can use Get-SSMInventoryEntryList.

```
$instInv = Get-SSMInventoryEntryList -TypeName "AWS:InstanceInformation"
-InstanceId i-1234567890 -Region us-west-2
$instInv.Entries
```

You can also use Get-SSMInventoryEntryList with a filter.

```
$invFilter = New-Object -TypeName Amazon.SimpleSystemsManagement.Model.
InventoryFilter
```

To define the filter, simply set its properties which are a key, list of value, and type (which defines how to evaluate the filter).

```
$invFilter.Key = "AWS:WindowsUpdate.HotFixId"
$invFilter.Values = @("KB4091664")
```

To set the type, we'll create a InventoryQueryOperatorType object, which can be set to Equal, NotEqual, BeginWith, LessThan, GreaterThan, or Exists.

```
$invFilter.Type = [Amazon.SimpleSystemsManagement.InventoryQueryOperator
Type]::Equal
```

Then, we just pass the type name, filter, instance ID to Get-SSMInventoryEntryList.

```
$instInv = Get-SSMInventoryEntryList -TypeName "AWS:WindowsUpdate" -Filter
$invFilter -InstanceId i-1234567890 -Region us-west-2
```

We can see the results by looking at the Entries property.

```
PS C:\>$instInv.Entries

Key           Value
---           -----
Description   Update
HotFixId      KB4091664
InstalledBy   NT AUTHORITY\SYSTEM
InstalledTime 2019-01-01T00:00:00Z
```

Aggregating Inventory Data

Oftentimes, you'll have a lot of inventory data and need to look at a summary (or aggregate) of that data. We first need to create an InventoryAggregator object.

```
$inventoryAggregator = New-Object Amazon.SimpleSystemsManagement.Model.
InventoryAggregator
```

Then, we'll need to set the expression property to a schema type along with an attribute in the format "SchemaTypeName.Attribute".

```
$inventoryAggregator.Expression = "AWS:InstanceInformation.PlatformType"
```

Now we can pass the aggregator to Get-SSMInventory.

```
$invAggResults = Get-SSMInventory -Aggregator $inventoryAggregator -Region us-west-2
```

Let's look at the values property of the object we get back.

```
$invAggResultItem = ($invAggResults.Data).Values
```

Now, look at the content property. If you have multiple Windows and Linux instances that have run inventory, you'll see a count of those.

```
PS C:\>$invAggResultItem.Content

Key            Value
---            -----
Count          2
PlatformType   Linux
Count          18
PlatformType   Windows
```

AWS Systems Manager Patch Manager

Keeping your running instances up to date can be a challenge, especially at scale. Having a systems management solution at your fingertips can not only save you time, but keep your infrastructure and applications secure. AWS Systems Manager Patch Manager helps you automate the actions you'd normally have to take on your Windows and Linux systems to keep them up to date.

Before we begin, we'll dive a little deeper into some of the basic concepts of Patch Manager: patch baselines, patch groups, and maintenance windows.

Patch Baselines

There are two sorts of patch baselines with AWS Systems Manager, one is the default baseline, and the other is a custom patch baseline. With the default baseline, you get a set of predefined patch baselines for various operating systems. A custom patch baseline is one that you define, and tell Patch Manager how and what to patch. This can give you the granularity, for example, to make sure a certain operating system patch doesn't take down your application.

Viewing Existing Patch Baselines

To view the patch baselines available to us in a given region, we can use Get-SSMPatchBaseline, and it will return a list of our baselines in addition to the default ones provided by AWS.

```
Get-SSMPatchBaseline -Region $region
```

In the list, we'll see a number of patch baselines, including the default ones for Windows and Amazon Linux.

```
BaselineDescription : Default Patch Baseline Provided by AWS.
BaselineId          : arn:aws:ssm:us-west-2:280605243866:patchbaseline/
                      pb-04fb4ae6142167966
BaselineName        : AWS-DefaultPatchBaseline
DefaultBaseline     : True
OperatingSystem     : WINDOWS

BaselineDescription : Default Patch Baseline for Amazon Linux 2 Provided
                      by AWS.
BaselineId          : arn:aws:ssm:us-west-2:280605243866:patchbaseline/
                      pb-0e930e75b392d70da
BaselineName        : AWS-AmazonLinux2DefaultPatchBaseline
DefaultBaseline     : True
OperatingSystem     : AMAZON_LINUX_2
```

Creating a New Patch Baseline

To create a new custom patch baseline, we'll need to set up a few variable first to make things a little easier. First, we'll set up a name, description, and tags for our new patch baseline.

```
$pbName = "Development-Baseline"
$pbDesc = "My Patch Baseline"

$pbTags = @{Key="Environment";Value="Production"}
```

Now, we'll need a couple of patch filters which consist of key/value pairs. For a list of valid options, take a look at the class reference for Amazon.SimpleSystemsManagement. Model.PatchFilter in the AWS SDK for .Net.

```
$pFilter1 = New-Object Amazon.SimpleSystemsManagement.Model.PatchFilter
$pFilter1.Key = "MSRC_SEVERITY"
$pFilter1.Values = @("Critical","Important")

$pFilter2 = New-Object Amazon.SimpleSystemsManagement.Model.PatchFilter
$pFilter2.Key = "CLASSIFICATION"
$pFilter2.Values = @("SecurityUpdates","Updates","UpdateRollups","Critical
Updates")
```

The patch filters will be grouped together in a patch filter group.

```
$pfGroup = New-Object Amazon.SimpleSystemsManagement.Model.PatchFilterGroup
$pfGroup.PatchFilters = @($pFilter1,$pFilter2)
```

Now we can create a patch rule. The Patch Compliance Level property can be set to Critical, High, Medium, Low, Informational, or Unspecified.

```
$patchRule = New-Object Amazon.SimpleSystemsManagement.Model.PatchRule
$patchRule.ComplianceLevel = [Amazon.SimpleSystemsManagement.
PatchComplianceLevel]::HIGH
$patchRule.PatchFilterGroup = $pfGroup
$patchRule.ApproveAfterDays = 7
```

We'll put the patch rule into an array of rules.

```
$patchRules = @($patchRule)
```

Finally, using the New-SSMPatchBaseline cmdlet, we can create our new patch baseline using the variables we've just set up.

```
$pBaseline = New-SSMPatchBaseline -Name $pbName -Description $pbDesc
-OperatingSystem WINDOWS -Tags $pbTags -ApprovalRules_PatchRules
$patchRules -Region $region
```

Deleting a Patch Baseline

To remove (or delete) a patch baseline, we simply use the Remove-SSMPatchBaseline cmdlet and pass it a valid baseline ID. If you want to remove the patch baseline without PowerShell prompting you to confirm, simply add the -Force switch.

```
Remove-SSMPatchBaseline -BaselineId pb-1234567890 -Region $region
```

Patch Groups

When patching your servers, you may find yourself needing a way to group your instances by some arbitrary grouping strategy.

Some common groupings might include

- Production, Testing, and Development Server Groups

- Frontend and Backend Server Groups

- Web and Database Server Groups

- Windows and Linux Server Groups

Patch groups are simply created with Amazon EC2 tags. If you have spent a lot of time tagging your instances into some logical grouping, this capability gives you the power to use those tags for your patch and update management needs.

Viewing Patch Groups

To see patch groups (or a specific patch group), we use the Get-SSMPatchGroup cmdlet.

```
Get-SSMPatchGroup -Region $region
```

If we are looking for a high-level aggregated patch compliance state for a patch group, then we can use the Get-SSMPatchGroupState cmdlet.

```
Get-SSMPatchGroupState -PatchGroup <patchGroup> -Region $region
```

Registering a Patch Baseline to a Patch Group

For registering (or associating) a patch baseline to a patch group, we can use the Register-SSMPatchBaselineForPatchGroup cmdlet and pass it the baseline ID, along with a patch group name.

```
Register-SSMPatchBaselineForPatchGroup -BaselineId $pBaseline -PatchGroup
"Production" -Region $region
```

Viewing Patch Baselines by Patch Group

When we need to find a patch baseline for a given patch group, we can use the Get-SSMPatchBaselineForPatchGroup cmdlet.

```
Get-SSMPatchBaselineForPatchGroup -PatchGroup "Production" -Region $region
```

Maintenance Windows

AWS Systems Manager Patch Manager uses maintenance windows to define when software updates should be applied to instances. This allows us to pick a reasonable schedule for any activities which might impact users or business processes. Maintenance windows are defined with a schedule, a maximum duration, registered targets (instances), and tasks. There are four distinct tasks we can use with maintenance windows: Run Command, AWS Systems Manager Automation workflows, AWS Lambda functions, and tasks within AWS Step Functions.

Viewing Maintenance Windows

Listing all of the maintenance windows in a given account for a specific region is done using the Get-SSMMaintenanceWindowList cmdlet.

```
Get-SSMMaintenanceWindowList -Region $region
```

Getting information for an existing maintenance window is done using the Get-SSMMaintenanceWindow cmdlet and passing it an existing maintenance window ID.

```
Get-SSMMaintenanceWindow -WindowId <window ID> -Region $region
```

Creating Maintenance Windows

When we want to create a maintenance window, we can do so by using the New-SSMMaintenanceWindow cmdlet and passing a cron or rate expression as the schedule, duration in hours, and cutoff which defines the number of hours before the end of a window when SSM should stop scheduling new tasks.

```
$fridayNights = "cron(0 0 21 ? * FRI *)"
```

```
New-SSMMaintenanceWindow -Name "Production-Fridays" -Schedule $fridayNights
-Duration 1 -Cutoff 0 -Region $region
```

Registering Instances with Maintenance Windows

In order for instances to be associated with a maintenance window, we must register them using the Register-SSMTargetWithMaintenanceWindow cmdlet and pass a maintenance window ID, target, owner information, and resource type.

Here, we'll define a task target using a maintenance window target ID.

```
$taskTarget = @{Key="WindowTargetIds";Values=$mwTargetWed}
```

Then, we'll create a task parameters hashtable that contains instructions for a scan operation.

```
$taskParameters = @{}
```

```
$taskParam = New-Object Amazon.SimpleSystemsManagement.Model.
MaintenanceWindowTaskParameterValueExpression
$taskParam.Values = @("Scan")
```

```
$taskParameters.Add("Operation", $taskParam)
```

Finally, we can register the task with our maintenance window, where $mWinId is our maintenance window ID.

```
Register-SSMTaskWithMaintenanceWindow -WindowId $mWinId -Target $taskTarget
-TaskArn "AWS-ApplyPatchBaseline" -TaskType RUN_COMMAND -MaxConcurrency 2
-MaxError 1 -Priority 1 -TaskParameter $taskParameters -Region $region
```

EXERCISE 17.1: COLLECTING INVENTORY DATA

Oftentimes, you'll have instances running in your AWS account and will need to know what's on those instances. In this exercise, we'll look at enabling inventory for a single Amazon EC2 instance. Once inventory has been collected, we'll look for some applications and settings using the inventory data.

Do We Have Managed Instances Running?

Before we can configure inventory, we'll need at least one (or more) Amazon EC2 instances. The instances must have an instance profile attached with the correct role. This enables AWS Systems Manager (SSM) to communicate with the agent running on the instance. If you'd prefer to use an EC2 instance you already have running, feel free to do so, but just make sure it has the necessary instance profile attached.

Launch a Windows Instance with SSM Enabled

To begin this exercise, we'll first define the region we'll be working in.

```
$region = "us-west-2"
```

Next, let's define the AWS Systems Manager Parameter Store path which will give us the latest Windows Server 2016 AMI.

```
$parameterPath = "/aws/service/ami-windows-latest/Windows_Server-2016-
English-Full-Base"
```

Using that parameter path, we'll get the image ID.

```
$latestImageId = (Get-SSMParameter -Name $parameterPath -Region $region).
Value
```

Now, let's create a hashtable representing the necessary IAM role policy (we'll convert it to JSON later).

```
$assumeRolePolicy = @{}
$assumeRolePolicy['Version'] = "2012-10-17"
$assumeRolePolicy['Statement'] = @{}
$assumeRolePolicy['Statement']['Effect'] = "Allow"
$assumeRolePolicy['Statement']['Principal'] = @{}
$assumeRolePolicy['Statement']['Principal']['Service'] = "ssm.amazonaws.com"
$assumeRolePolicy['Statement']['Action'] = "sts:AssumeRole"
```

Here's where we define our new IAM role and give it the policy which is our hashtable converted to JSON.

```
$role = New-IAMRole -RoleName "MySystemsManagerRole"
-AssumeRolePolicyDocument ($assumeRolePolicy | ConvertTo-Json) -Region
$region
```

We'll need to register the managed SSM policy to our newly created role.

```
Register-IAMRolePolicy -RoleName $role.RoleName -PolicyArn
'arn:aws:iam::aws:policy/service-role/AmazonEC2RoleforSSM' -Region $region
```

With the role created and the AmazonEC2RoleforSSM registered, we can create the instance profile which is what we will attach to our instance.

```
$instanceProfile = New-IAMInstanceProfile -InstanceProfileName
"MyNewInstanceProfile" -Region $region
```

Our instance profile still doesn't have a role, so let's add the role we just created.

```
Add-IAMRoleToInstanceProfile -InstanceProfileName $instanceProfile.
InstanceProfileName -RoleName $role.RoleName -Region $region
```

Remember, if we want to get the password to our instance, we'll need to use a key pair. Let's create one (or you can use an existing one).

```
(New-EC2KeyPair -KeyName "MyNewKeyPair"  -Region $region).KeyMaterial | Out-
File .\MyNewKeyPair.pem
```

Using our latest Windows AMI, we're now ready to launch an EC2 instance and attach the new instance profile. We'll do that with New-EC2Instance.

```
$newInstance = New-EC2Instance -ImageId $latestImageId -InstanceType "t3.
medium" -InstanceProfile_Name "MyNewInstanceProfile" -KeyName "MyNewKeyPair"
-Region $region
```

We can see the instance ID by looking at the RunningInstances property of the newly created instance.

```
$runningInstance = $newInstance.RunningInstance
```

Configure Inventory by Association

To begin our inventory configuration, we'll define our target as the instance we just launched using the $runningInstance variable.

```
$target = @{Key = "InstanceIds"; Values = ($runningInstance.InstanceId)}
```

Now we'll define a cron or rate expression for the inventory collection schedule. We'll use 30 minutes here, but in production work, you'd want to spread the inventory schedule out a little more.
$schExp = "rate(30 minutes)"

Let's enable a few inventory items.

```
$params = @{
    applications='Enabled';
    awsComponents='Enabled';
    customInventory='Enabled';
    instanceDetailedInformation='Enabled';
    networkConfig='Enabled';
    services='Enabled';
    windowsRoles='Enabled';
    windowsUpdates='Enabled'
}
```

Now we'll associate the AWS Systems Manager document, AWS-GatherSoftwareInventory, to our running instance using the parameters we just set.

```
New-SSMAssociation -Name AWS-GatherSoftwareInventory -Target $target
-ScheduleExpression $schExp -Parameter $params -Region $region
```

Since we configured it to run inventory every 30 minutes, we'll need to wait at least that long before we can see any inventory data for this instance.

Checking Inventory Status

We can look at the SSM associations which will include the one we created for inventory collection.

```
Get-SSMAssociationList -Region $region
```

By passing the association ID of our association, we can view the status of it.

```
Get-SSMAssociationExecution -AssociationId <id> -Region $region
```

Look at Inventory Data

Finally, let's see what inventory we have.

```
$instInv = Get-SSMInventoryEntryList -TypeName "AWS:InstanceDetailed
Information" -InstanceId ($runningInstance.InstanceId) -Region $region
```

```
$instInv.Entries
```

You can see now that when inventory is complete, we have some interesting data which can help us manage our instances. Many features within AWS Systems Manager work together to give you a complete systems management solution. Inventory, just like many of the other Systems Manager features, uses documents and associations, one of the foundational concepts of how SSM works.

EXERCISE 17.2: PATCHING DURING A MAINTENANCE WINDOW

Let's take a look at how we would patch servers using a custom patch baseline, some patch groups, and a maintenance window. Since Microsoft releases patches the second Tuesday of the month, we'll create two maintenance windows. One will be a recurring Wednesday night scan task, and the other will be a patching task on every Friday night.

Create a Custom Patch Baseline

First, we'll begin by defining our region.

```
$region = "us-west-2"
```

Next, let's create a name and description for our patch baseline.

```
$pbName = "Production-Patch-Baseline"
$pbDesc = "My Patch Baseline"
```

We'll give our patch baseline a production tag, so we know which environment we've created it for.

```
$pbTags = @{Key="Environment";Value="Production"}
```

Now, we'll need a patch filter to define what patches this will be applicable to. Let's set the first filter to only include Critical and Important patches (as rated by the Microsoft Security Response Center), represented by MSRC_SEVERITY.

```
$pFilter1 = New-Object Amazon.SimpleSystemsManagement.Model.PatchFilter
$pFilter1.Key = "MSRC_SEVERITY"
$pFilter1.Values = @("Critical","Important")
```

The second filter specifies patches that have a classification of Security Updates, Updates, Update Rollups, and Critical Updates.

```
$pFilter2 = New-Object Amazon.SimpleSystemsManagement.Model.PatchFilter
$pFilter2.Key = "CLASSIFICATION"
$pFilter2.Values = @("SecurityUpdates","Updates","UpdateRollups","CriticalUp
dates")
```

482

We'll add both of these new filters to a patch filter group.

```
$pfGroup = New-Object Amazon.SimpleSystemsManagement.Model.PatchFilterGroup
$pfGroup.PatchFilters = @($pFilter1,$pFilter2)
```

Our new patch group then gets added to a patch rule. The rule will specify how many days should pass before approving the patch and also specify the compliance level.

```
$patchRule = New-Object Amazon.SimpleSystemsManagement.Model.PatchRule
$patchRule.ComplianceLevel = [Amazon.SimpleSystemsManagement.
PatchComplianceLevel]::HIGH
$patchRule.PatchFilterGroup = $pfGroup
$patchRule.ApproveAfterDays = 3
```

The rules need to be in an array, so we'll add them to one.

```
$patchRules = @($patchRule)
```

Now, we can create our new patch baseline and pass all of our parameters we've created.

```
$pBaseline = New-SSMPatchBaseline -Name $pbName -Description $pbDesc
-OperatingSystem WINDOWS -Tags $pbTags -ApprovalRules_PatchRules $patchRules
-Region $region
```

Register the Patch Baseline in a Patch Group

We'll create a patch group named Production Group and register our patch baseline with that group.

```
Register-SSMPatchBaselineForPatchGroup -BaselineId $pBaseline -PatchGroup
"Production" -Region $region
```

Creating Two Maintenance Windows

Let's create a tag that will let us know our maintenance windows are for our production environment.

```
$tags = @{Key="Environment";Value="Production"}
```

Now, we can create our Wednesday morning maintenance window by creating a cron expression for 9 p.m. every Wednesday. The duration of the maintenance window will be 2 hours after it begins, and we'll set the cutoff to 0.

```
$wednesdayMornings = "cron(0 0 21 ? * WED *)"
$mWinWed = New-SSMMaintenanceWindow -Name "Production-Wednesdays" -Schedule
$wednesdayMornings -Tags $tags -Duration 3 -Cutoff 1 -AllowUnassociatedTarget
$false -Region $region
```

We'll do it again, but this time we're creating a Friday night maintenance window. Since this will be our patching Window, let's give it 3 hours with a cutoff of 1 hour. The cutoff prevents any new tasks from starting after 11 p.m.

```
$fridayNights = "cron(0 0 21 ? * FRI *)"
$mWinFri = New-SSMMaintenanceWindow -Name "Production-Fridays" -Schedule
$fridayNights -Tags $tags -Duration 3 -Cutoff 1 -AllowUnassociatedTarget
$false -Region $region
```

Registering Servers with Our New Maintenance Windows

Now we can register the production servers with our two maintenance windows, using the patch group as the target.

```
$target = @{Key="tag:Patch Group";Values=@("Production")}
```

Then, we can register our patch group target to our Wednesday maintenance window.

```
$mwTargetWed = Register-SSMTargetWithMaintenanceWindow -WindowId $mWinWed
-Target $target -OwnerInformation "Production Servers" -ResourceType INSTANCE
-Region $region
```

Next, we'll register our patch group target to our Friday maintenance window.

```
$mwTargetFri = Register-SSMTargetWithMaintenanceWindow -WindowId $mWinFri
-Target $target -OwnerInformation "Production Servers" -ResourceType INSTANCE
-Region $region
```

Register the Wednesday Scan Task

For our scan task, we'll run a scan on our production servers every Wednesday night. Let's define a task target by creating a hashtable where WindowTargetIds is the key and our target registered to our Maintenance Window for Wednesday is the value.

```
$ttWed = @{Key="WindowTargetIds";Values=$mwTargetWed}
```

Now, we'll define a scan task operation.

```
$scanTasks = @{}

$scanTask = New-Object Amazon.SimpleSystemsManagement.Model.
MaintenanceWindowTaskParameterValueExpression
$scanTask.Values = @("Scan")

$scanTasks.Add("Operation", $scanTask)
```

Next, we'll register the scan task with our Wednesday maintenance window.

```
Register-SSMTaskWithMaintenanceWindow -WindowId $mWinWed -Target $ttWed
-TaskArn "AWS-ApplyPatchBaseline" -TaskType RUN_COMMAND -TaskParameter
$scanTasks -MaxConcurrency 2 -MaxError 1 -Priority 1 -Region $region
```

Register the Friday Patch Task

The Friday patch task will be very similar to the task we just created, except we are going to specify our Friday maintenance window target.

```
$ttFri = @{Key="WindowTargetIds";Values=$mwTargetFri}
```

Create a patch task operation.

```
$patchTasks = @{}

$patchTask = New-Object Amazon.SimpleSystemsManagement.Model.
MaintenanceWindowTaskParameterValueExpression
$patchTask.Values = @("Patch")

$patchTasks.Add("Operation", $patchTask)
```

Then, register our Friday maintenance window with the patch task we just defined.

```
Register-SSMTaskWithMaintenanceWindow -WindowId $mWinFri -Target $ttFri
-TaskArn "AWS-ApplyPatchBaseline" -TaskType RUN_COMMAND -TaskParameter
$patchTasks -MaxConcurrency 2 -MaxError 1 -Priority 1 -Region $region
Tag an EC2 Instance to be Included in the Group
```

Associate an EC2 Instance with Our Patch Group

Since we specified when we created our maintenance window, we'll need our EC2 instances to have a patch group tag. Let's tag an instance with Patch Group as the key and Production (our patch group name) as the value.

```
$tag = New-Object Amazon.EC2.Model.Tag

$tag.Key = "Patch Group"
$tag.Value = "Production"

New-EC2Tag -Resource "i-1234567890" -Tag $tag -Region $region
```

Get the State of Our Patch Group

We now have scan and patch tasks set up in our maintenance windows. Let's view the state of our production patch group.

```
Get-SSMPatchGroupState -PatchGroup "Production" -Region $region
```

Once our scanning and patch maintenance windows have completed, we'll be able to look at the state of our patch groups and also be able to tie it into inventory data for a more complete picture of our servers.

Summary

In this chapter, we learned about AWS Systems Manager Inventory and Patch Manager, two features you can use to manage your fleet of instances. We went through some steps to configure inventory and query that data. We also took a deep look at patch management and maintenance windows. Using PowerShell, you can automate some of the more complex tasks related to systems management and manage your servers in the cloud. This information coupled with the other chapters on AWS Systems Manager gives you a starting point to building a cloud-based systems management solution for your specific needs.

CHAPTER 18

Lambda with PowerShell

With AWS Lambda you can deploy and execute code that can be triggered from a multitude of event sources without provisioning or the need to maintain any host servers. Lambda functions can run a number of different languages to include PowerShell Core. In this chapter, we'll explain how to set up AWS Lambda using PowerShell and to execute PowerShell code as a Lambda function.

We'll begin by going over prerequisites to set up your development environment and install required packages and modules. Then we'll show you a couple ways to generate and deploy a PowerShell-Based Lambda function. We'll walk through the execution of this Lambda function. We will evaluate the function execution and resultant output logs. Finally, we will set up an execution schedule for our new Lambda function.

There is one exercise at the end of this chapter. We'll show you how to use AWS PowerShell on Lambda function to update an AWS Auto Scaling group ImageId that is triggered by an SNS notification.

To explore and learn more about the many features we'll be talking about, open your browser and head over to the AWS Lambda console at `https://console.aws.amazon.com/lambda`.

PowerShell-Based Lambda Prerequisites

Lambda's support for PowerShell is based on the cross-platform PowerShell Core. Because PowerShell Core is built on top of .NET Core, we will also need .NET Core installed. There are several new PowerShell publishing cmdlets to generate and deploy PowerShell-Based Lambda functions, and these require the .NET Core SDK.

We can download and install the latest .NET Core SDK from `www.microsoft.com/net/download`.

© Brian Beach, Steven Armentrout, Rodney Bozo, Emmanuel Tsouris 2019
B. Beach et al., *Pro PowerShell for Amazon Web Services*, https://doi.org/10.1007/978-1-4842-4850-8_18

Once download and installation is complete, we need to install PowerShell Core. Downloads for various Linux and Windows installers can be found at `https://github.com/PowerShell/PowerShell/releases`.

Instructions for installing PowerShell Core on your specific development environment can be found at `https://docs.microsoft.com/en-us/PowerShell/scripting/setup/installing-PowerShell?view=PowerShell-6`.

Once both the SDK and PowerShell Core are installed, we open a PowerShell Console session and verify the .NET Core SDK version installed meets the minimum requirements by executing the dotnet.exe with version parameter.

```
dotnet.exe --version
```

Note   Lambda support for PowerShell requires version 2.1 or greater of the .NET Core SDK.

We initialize the PowerShell Core executable from the PowerShell Console by executing pwsh.exe.

```
pwsh.exe
```

We can verify the current PowerShell version by reviewing the output of the $PSVersionTable variable.

```
write-output $PSVersionTable
```

Note   Lambda support for PowerShell requires PowerShell Core Edition 6.0 or greater. This version number can be seen as the PSVersion key value of the $PSVersionTable variable.

Next we install the AWS Lambda Core Module and import it into our current session. Confirm the request to install the NuGet package provider and trust the PSGallery repository modules if prompted. We then verify the AWS Lambda PowerShell Core module is found in the available module list using the Get-Module cmdlet.

```
Install-Module AWSLambdaPSCore -Scope CurrentUser -Force
Get-Module -ListAvailable -Name AWSLambdaPSCore
```

Finally, we complete the requirements by installing the AWSPowerShell.NetCore module from the PSGallery and verifying its version.

```
Install-Module AWSPowerShell.NetCore -MinimumVersion 3.3.270.0 -Scope
CurrentUser -Force
Get-Module -ListAvailable -Name AWSPowerShell.NetCore
```

Note   Be sure to use version 3.3.270.0 or greater of AWSPowerShell.NetCore, which optimizes the cmdlet import process. If you use an older version, you will experience longer cold starts. To update your existing install to the latest version, run `Update-Module AWSPowerShell.NetCore -Force`.

The AWSPowerShell.NetCore module provides the SDK PowerShell cmdlets to interact with AWS infrastructure and services.

Authoring PowerShell-Based Lambda Functions

There are four new cmdlets available that we now have access to as a result of installing these prerequisites. Each of these cmdlets provides the tools necessary to quickly build, package, and deploy a PowerShell-Based Lambda function.

Creating a Script Template

First, we are going to list the common templates using the Get-AWSPowerShellLambdaTemplate cmdlet. A number of templates will be listed, and they can be distinguished by the type of trigger we expect to use for our Lambda function.

```
Get-AWSPowerShellLambdaTemplate
```

You should see a number of template listed as seen in Table 18-1.

Table 18-1. *Lambda Templates*

Template	Description
Basic	Bare bones script
CloudFormationCustomResource	PowerShell handler base for use with CloudFormation custom resource events
CodeCommitTrigger	Script to process AWS CodeCommit Triggers
DetectLabels	Use Amazon Rekognition service to tag image files in S3 with detected labels
KinesisStreamProcessor	Script to process a Kinesis Stream
S3Event	Script to process S3 events
S3EventToSNS	Script to process SNS Records triggered by S3 events
S3EventToSNSToSQS	Script to process SQS Messages, subscribed to an SNS Topic that is triggered by S3 events
S3EventToSQS	Script to process SQS Messages triggered by S3 events
SNSSubscription	Script to be subscribed to an SNS Topic
SNSToSQS	Script to be subscribed to an SQS Queue, that is, subscribed to an SNS Topic
SQSQueueProcessor	Script to be subscribed to an SQS Queue

We are now going to create a script named LatestAMIID using the basic template.

```
Set-Location $env:HOMEPATH
New-AWSPowerShellLambda -ScriptName LatestAMIID -Template Basic
```

Using Windows Explorer, when we look at our home directory we should now see a folder named LatestAMIID. The folder contains a corresponding named ps1 starter script and a Readme.txt file containing some additional details on the generated starter script. When we open the LatestAMIID.ps1 script template in the PowerShell ISE editor, we see content similar to Figure 18-1.

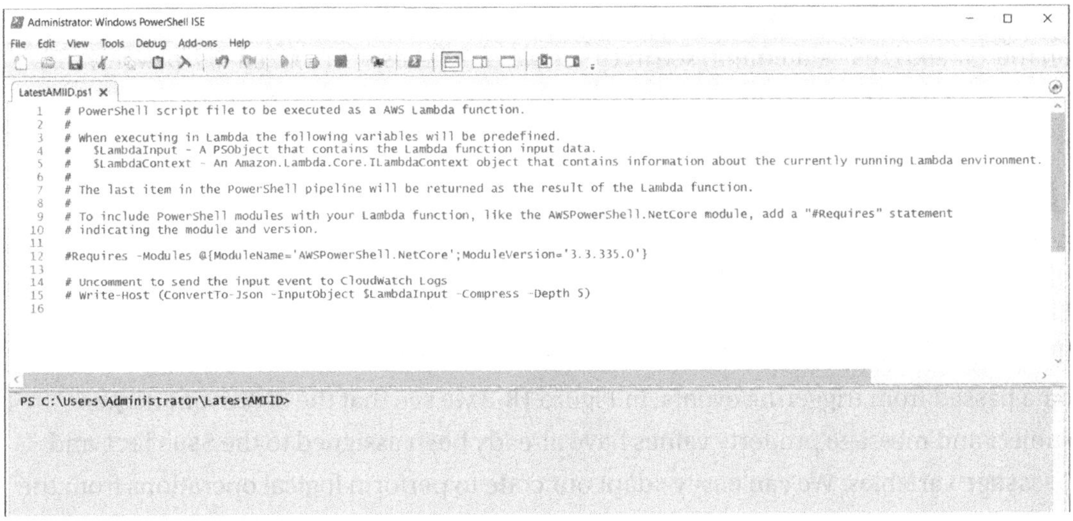

Figure 18-1. *Latest AMI ID template*

Included in the script are a number of comments that will guide us in creating our PowerShell-Based Lambda function. In the next sections, we will investigate and understand the components of this template. We will also be adding some of our own code before saving it.

Understanding Modules

Near the top of the script template is the `"#Requires"` statement. This statement lists the modules that are needed by the PowerShell script and loads them when the Lambda function is executed. There can be many requires statements in a single script, and these modules must be packaged with your Lambda function for it to execute properly. These same statements are read by the AWS commands Publish-AWSPowerShellLambda and New-AWSPowerShellLambdaPackage that we will learn about later in this chapter. In our script templates, we see the following statement:

```
#Requires -Modules @{ModuleName='AWSPowerShell.NetCore';ModuleVersi
on='3.3.335.0'}
```

This statement indicates that the script requires the AWSPowerShell.NetCore module with a version of 3.3.335.0 or greater, we had installed earlier in this chapter. Note that 3.3.335.0 is the minimum version at the time of this books writing and any value greater than this in the script template is acceptable. For more information on the "#Requires" statement, see https://docs.microsoft.com/en-us/powershell/module/microsoft.powershell.core/about/about_requires?view=powershell-6.

Understanding Input

At the top of the script template, we see how input is defined in a PowerShell-Based Lambda function. The $LambdaInput variable is a PSObject that contains all the data that is passed as input to the Lambda function when executed. This includes the data passed from triggering events. In Figure 18-2 we see that the SNS event trigger subject and message property values have already been assigned to the $subject and $message variables. We can easily adapt our code to perform logical operations from the $LambdaInput variable or one of its properties.

We may not know all the input properties and values from a triggering event so we will write them all as a JSON-formatted document upon execution of the Lambda function. To allow all input data to be written to CloudWatch Logs as output, we will uncomment or remove the # mark in front of the following statement in our script:

```
Write-Host (ConvertTo-Json -InputObject $LambdaInput -Compress -Depth 5)
```

Understanding Output and Logging

Lambda functions write their log data to CloudWatch Logs service. The write cmdlets that do not place data in the pipeline are written as logs. Cmdlets such as Write-Host and Write-Information as well as Write-Verbose and Write-Error if enabled are all written to CloudWatch Logs. Each CloudWatch Logs entry will also display its corresponding log level such as Information, Warning, or Verbose. See Figure 18-2 for example of CloudWatch Logs output.

▶	21:02:01	START RequestId: 8b0cb1a2-dee2-11e8-b448-b3cc011ca194 Version: $LATEST
▶	21:02:01	[Information] - {"AliasName":""}
▶	21:02:01	[Warning] - @{AliasName=} AliasName value missing. Using default Alias Name
▶	21:02:01	[Information] - Getting latest regional ImageId for public Amazon Machine Image with alias:Windows_Server-2016-English-Full-Base
▶	21:02:01	[Verbose] - Invoking AWS Systems Manager operation 'GetParameter' in region 'us-east-1'
▶	21:02:01	[Verbose] - Latest ImageId for Alias Windows_Server-2016-English-Full-Base is ami-050202fb72f001b47
▶	21:02:01	END RequestId: 8b0cb1a2-dee2-11e8-b448-b3cc011ca194
▶	21:02:01	REPORT RequestId: 8b0cb1a2-dee2-11e8-b448-b3cc011ca194 Duration: 101.75 ms Billed Duration: 200 ms Memory Size: 512 MB Max Memory Used: 175 MB

Figure 18-2. *Lambda CloudWatch Logs*

Write-Output places data into the pipeline so it does not get written to CloudWatch Logs. It shares a similar characteristic to the return statement in that it can be used in place of a return. Lambda function output will either be the last item added to the pipeline such as the last Write-Output statement or from a return statement if utilized. More details on Lambda function logging using PowerShell can be found at `https://docs.aws.amazon.com/lambda/latest/dg/PowerShell-logging.html`.

Understanding Errors

Lambda function executions end in either a succeeded or failed result. Failure to execute, timeouts, or script-level terminating errors are some of the ways that a Lambda function will result in a failed state. A successful execution of a Lambda function is all that's needed for a passing result.

You can control the result of your Lambda function by using the throw or write-error statement in your script. The throw statement is a terminating error that will exit your script and Lambda function immediately. The write-error statement will continue executing your Lambda function script but will ultimately result in your function ending with a failed result. For more information on Lambda function errors in PowerShell, see `https://docs.aws.amazon.com/lambda/latest/dg/PowerShell-exceptions.html`.

The LambdaContext Variable

We also have the $LambdaContext variable listed at the top of our script templates. This variable provides runtime details about the overall execution of the Lambda function. This includes context object properties such as FunctionName, MemoryLimitInMB, and RemainingTime. Like the $LambdaInput object, the $LambdaContext is also an object that can be converted to a JSON document and written to CloudWatch Logs. For our testing purposes, we want to add the following line of code after the Write-Host for $LambdaInput statement in our script.

```
Write-Host (ConvertTo-Json -InputObject $LambdaContext -Compress -Depth 5)
```

Additional data on the Lambda Context Object for PowerShell can be found at `https://docs.aws.amazon.com/lambda/latest/dg/PowerShell-context-object.html`.

The script should now look similar to Figure 18-3.

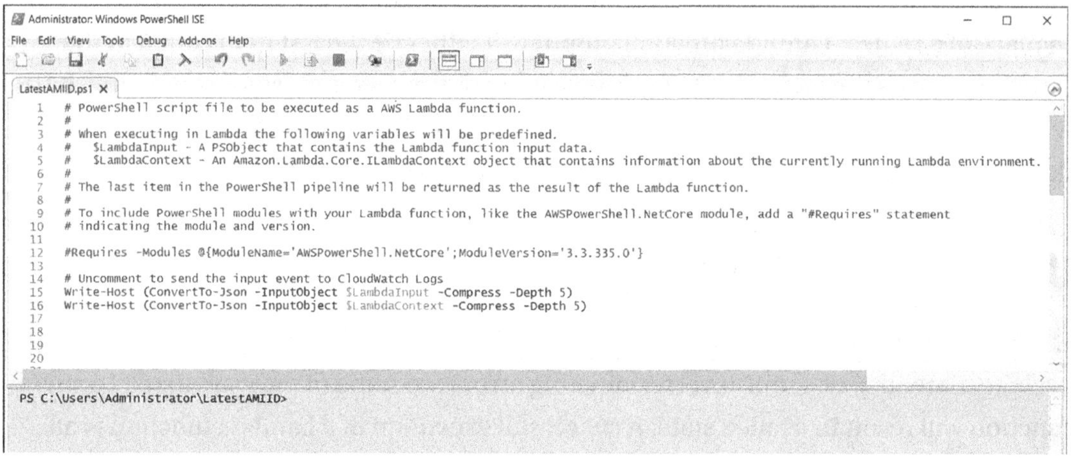

Figure 18-3. *Log Only Template*

Creating a PowerShell Lambda Package

Now we have a basic template script that can be used in a Lambda function, but does not perform any real actions other than importing modules and writing logs. Add the following lines of code to our LatestAMIID.ps1 script:

```
$VerbosePreference = "continue"
If ([string]::IsNullOrEmpty($LambdaInput.AliasName))
{
    [string]$AliasName = "Windows_Server-2016-English-Full-Base"
    Write-Warning "AliasName value missing. Using default Alias Name"
}
Else
{
    [string]$AliasName = $LambdaInput.AliasName
}
Write-information "Getting latest regional ImageId for public Amazon
Machine Image with alias:$($AliasName)"
$ImageId=(Get-SSMParameter -Name /aws/service/ami-windows-
latest/$($AliasName)).Value
Write-Verbose "Latest ImageId for Alias:$($AliasName) is:$($ImageId)"
return $ImageId
```

494

In this example script, we are going to return the latest Public ImagId for a matching alias name. You may recognize this code from Chapter 15 in the section titled "Finding the Latest Windows AMI." Note that we are using a few different logging types for demonstration. Your final script should look similar to the following:

```
# PowerShell script file to be executed as a AWS Lambda function.
#
# When executing in Lambda the following variables will be predefined.
#   $LambdaInput - A PSObject that contains the Lambda function input data.
#   $LambdaContext - An Amazon.Lambda.Core.ILambdaContext object that
     contains information about the currently running Lambda environment.
#
# The last item in the PowerShell pipeline will be returned as the result
  of the Lambda function.
#
# To include PowerShell modules with your Lambda function, like the
  AWSPowerShell.NetCore module, add a "#Requires" statement
# indicating the module and version.

#Requires –Modules @{ModuleName='AWSPowerShell.NetCore';ModuleVersi
  on='3.3.335.0'}

# Uncomment to send the input event to CloudWatch Logs
Write-Host (ConvertTo-Json -InputObject $LambdaInput -Compress -Depth 5)
Write-Host (ConvertTo-Json -InputObject $LambdaContext -Compress -Depth 5)
$VerbosePreference = "continue"
If ([string]::IsNullOrEmpty($LambdaInput.AliasName))
{
    [string]$AliasName = "Windows_Server-2016-English-Full-Base"
    Write-Warning "AliasName value missing. Using default Alias Name"
}
Else
{
    [string]$AliasName = $LambdaInput.AliasName
}
Write-information "Getting latest regional ImageId for public Amazon
Machine Image with alias:$($AliasName)"
```

```
$ImageId=(Get-SSMParameter -Name /aws/service/ami-windows-
latest/$($AliasName)).Value
Write-Verbose "Latest ImageId for Alias:$($AliasName) is:$($ImageId)"
return $ImageId
```

Now that we have a better understanding of PowerShell-Based Lambda functions script components and a completed script, save the changes and close it.

Before we can deploy our function, we first need to create a deployment package. There are a couple cmdlets to create a Lambda package. The first cmdlet Publish-AWSPowerShellLambda will create a temporary package and then publish it to Lambda automatically. The second cmdlet New-AWSPowerShellLambdaPackage will only create a named package we can deploy later. New-AWSPowerShellLambdaPackage is primarily used to generate packages as a part of an automated deployment package such as a CI/CD pipeline or as a part of a CloudFormation template. We are going to start with the New-AWSPowerShellLambdaPackage cmdlet so we can look at the generated package components and demonstrate a couple different deployment options.

To generate a Lambda package using our LatestAMIID.ps1 script, execute the following code in the PowerShell 6 Core Console we opened earlier in this chapter.

```
$LambdaPackage = New-AWSPowerShellLambdaPackage -ScriptPath .\LatestAMIID\
LatestAMIID.ps1 -OutputPackage .\LatestAMIIDPackage.zip
```

Upon completion of the package creation, we see console output detailing the steps to creating the package. Make note of the reference to the handler value in the output. We will be using this value to deploy this package in future steps. We can also see this value by looking at the LambdaHandler property of the $LambdaPackage variable output as seen in Figure 18-4.

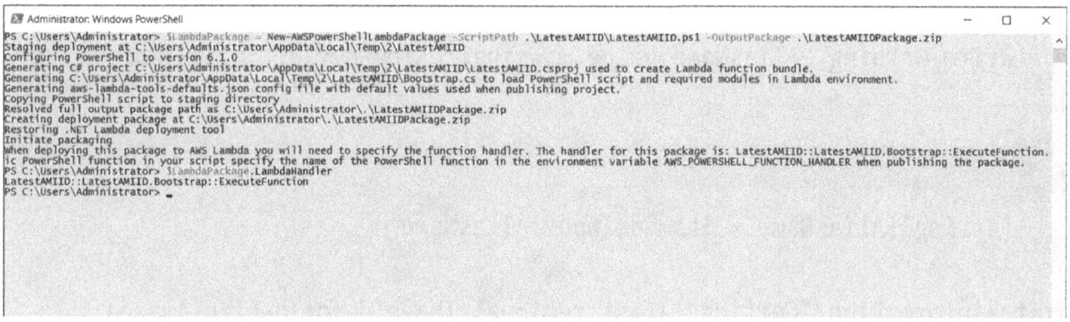

Figure 18-4. *New Lambda Package Output*

Open the output package LatestAMIIDPackage.zip and review its contents. Among the many dll assemblies needed to host PowerShell Core, notice that our LatestAMIID. ps1 file is contained in this package as well as a folder labelled "Modules". The modules folder contains the AWSPowerShell.NetCore module that is listed in our script requires statement. When we use either the New-AWSPowerShellLambdaPackage or Publish-AWSPowerShellLambda cmdlets, the requires statement is read from the script and those modules are placed into the packaged modules directory.

Publishing a PowerShell-Based Lambda Function

We are now ready to publish our new package. We will be working through a couple PowerShell-Based methods to publish a PowerShell Lambda package. The first method will use the package we just created and publish using some of the legacy AWS PowerShell Lambda cmdlets. The second method will use the newer Publish-AWSPowerShellLambda cmdlet.

Note   The remainder of this chapter will require administrative-level privileges to make modification to your AWS account. If you have not done so already, load your credentials in the current PowerShell 6 Core Console and set your default region to us-east-1. Lambda is a regional service, and the following chapter activities will be performed in the us-east-1 region.

Lambda functions require some privileges to access AWS resources. Required permissions will vary greatly depending on the Lambda function activities. For the sake of completion, we included the code to create a least privilege IAM role that will be assigned to our new Lambda function. To better understand the IAM role creation process, refer back to Chapter 2. Create a new IAM role with the name of "Lambda_LatestAMIID_Role" by using the following code:

```
$assumeRolePolicy = @"
{
    "Version": "2012-10-17",
    "Statement": {
        "Effect": "Allow",
        "Principal": {
```

```
            "Service": "lambda.amazonaws.com"
        },
        "Action": "sts:AssumeRole"
    }
}
"@

$rolepolicy = @"
{
    "Version": "2012-10-17",
    "Statement": [{
        "Effect": "Allow",
        "Action": [
            "logs:CreateLogStream",
            "logs:CreateLogGroup",
            "logs:PutLogEvents",
            "ssm:GetParameter"
        ],
        "Resource": "*"
    }]
}
"@

Import-Module AWSPowerShell.NetCore
$role = New-IAMRole -RoleName "Lambda_LatestAMIID_Role"
-AssumeRolePolicyDocument $assumeRolePolicy
$newpolicy = New-IAMPolicy -PolicyName Lambda_LatestAMIID_Policy
-PolicyDocument $rolepolicy
Register-IAMRolePolicy -rolename $role.RoleName -PolicyArn $newpolicy.arn
```

We now have an IAM role that only has write access to CloudWatch Logs and read access to AWS Systems Manager Parameter Store. To deploy the Lambda package we previously generated, we first assign a function name to the LMFunctionName variable that we will reuse.

```
$LMFunctionName = 'LatestAMIID'
```

Note   Due to the large number of parameters, many of the remaining examples in this chapter will pass parameters as a hashtable. This is known as PowerShell Splatting. More information on Splatting can be found at `https://docs.microsoft.com/en-us/powershell/module/microsoft.powershell.core/about/about_splatting`.

We will now use the Publish-LMFunction cmdlet and pass it a few parameters to create our new Lambda function using the following code:

```
$PublishLMParams = @{
"ZipFilename" = ".\LatestAMIIDPackage.zip"
"Handler" = $LambdaPackage.LambdaHandler
"MemorySize" = 256
"Timeout" = 30
"Runtime" = "dotnetcore2.1"
"Role" = $role.arn
}

$PublishLM = Publish-LMFunction -FunctionName $LMFunctionName @PublishLMParams
```

Let's spend a minute talking about some of the Publish-LMFunction parameters before continuing. The ZipFilename parameter identifies the location of our Lambda package zip. Handler defines what script Lambda calls as the entry point in our package to begin execution. If you recall, this value was defined when we created the Lambda package earlier in this chapter. The Role parameter gets assigned the ARN value of the IAM role we just created.

Timeout is the maximum amount of time the Lambda function can execute before force stopping with a failure result. Runtime is the environment our function will execute under. For PowerShell code we use the dotnetcore2.1 value.

MemorySize determines how performant our function will be as this value determines both available memory and the CPU power available but increases the cost of an execution. CPU power will effectively double every 128MB of memory allocated and can have considerable impact on how quickly your function executes. Too little memory can result in unexpected failures or hitting the function timeout, while too much results in costly unutilized capacity.

PowerShell modules and script executions require a bit more resources than the defaults allow. We increase the timeout from the default of 3 seconds to 30 seconds and increased the MemorySize from the default of 128 to 256.

For more details on configuration settings go to `https://docs.aws.amazon.com/lambda/latest/dg/resource-model.html`.

We now have successfully deployed a PowerShell-Based Lambda function. When we open the Lambda service in the AWS Management Console and select the LatestAMIID function, we see configuration data similar to Figure 18-5.

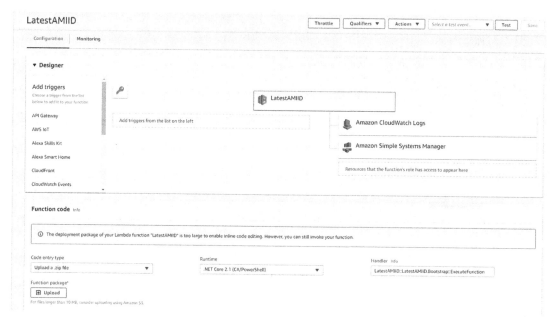

Figure 18-5. *Lambda Function Console View*

While we are reviewing the console, let's run a manual invocation. In the upper right corner of the LatestAMIID Lambda console window, select the Test button. When prompted by the Configure Test Event window, input "test1" into the event name box and click the Create button to close the window. The Lambda test console requires a Test Event configured before we can execute even if our function does not require any input.

In the upper right corner of the LatestAMIID Lambda function console, select the Test button again and the Lambda function will execute automatically. After a short time, you should see a green "Execution result: succeeded" message at the top. Clicking the arrow under this message expands the details similar to Figure 18-6.

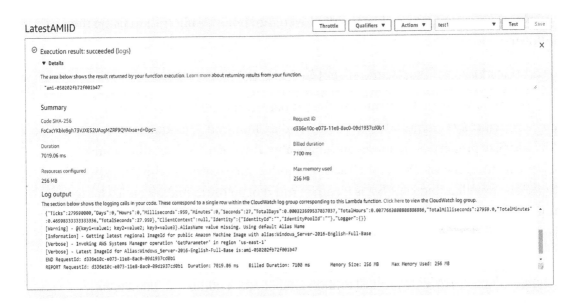

Figure 18-6. *Lambda Execution Console View*

Now that we know the function works, let's run some PowerShell describe cmdlets to review the function configuration from the cmd line. Execute the following cmdlet:

```
Get-LMFunctionConfiguration -FunctionName $LMFunctionName
```

We see that the parameter values we used to publish the function match the console and Get-LMFunctionConfiguration output.

We are now going to remove this Lambda function and demonstrate deployment using the new Publish-AWSPowerShellLambda cmdlet. To remove the LatestAMIID Lambda function, execute:

```
Remove-LMFunction -FunctionName $LMFunctionName -Force
```

We executed with the force switch to automatically accept confirmation prompts. If we check the console or try the Get-LMFunctionConfiguration query again, we find the function no longer exists.

To deploy our script with Publish-AWSPowerShellLambda, we do not need the package we previously generated. This cmdlet automatically generates a package during the publication process for us. To redeploy our Lambda function, we execute the following example:

```
Publish-AWSPowerShellLambda -ScriptPath .\LatestAMIID\LatestAMIID.ps1 -Name
$LMFunctionName -IAMRoleArn $role.arn
```

Now let's once again look at the deployed functions configuration using the following code:

```
Get-LMFunctionConfiguration -FunctionName $LMFunctionName
```

We can now see that a number of the properties we had to define earlier are automatically configured for us. The Handler, Runtime, Timeout, and MemorySize properties are all set automatically with default values that would allow executing a basic PowerShell script. Another nice feature of the Publish-AWSPowerShellLambda cmdlet is it can be run repeatedly to make a code change or update modules. It will automatically update the target Lambda function with whatever components that need changed.

Note   Publish-AWSPowerShellLambda cmdlet has a number of additional parameters to publish and update PowerShell-Based Lambda functions. For a full list, review the cmdlet help by executing *"get-help Publish-AWSPowerShellLambda -full"*.

Before we get into executing our Lambda function using PowerShell cmdlets, we will set the Timeout and MemorySize parameters to the values we originally set using the following command:

```
Update-LMFunctionConfiguration -FunctionName $LMFunctionName -MemorySize
256 -Timeout 30
```

Invoking Lambda Functions

Now that we have seen a couple ways to create and publish a PowerShell-Based Lambda function, let's see how we can manually execute it and review the output.

Normally Lambda functions are invoked as a result of an event trigger such as an SNS notification, CloudWatch event, or write to an S3 bucket, to name a few. We can also invoke a Lambda function manually. This can be useful for debugging, testing or even creating our own code to initiate a Lambda function when appropriate.

The cmdlet we will be using to execute our newly published function is Invoke-LMFunction. First, let's execute without any input payload by executing:

```
$ExecuteLMFunction = Invoke-LMFunction
-FunctionName  $LMFunctionName  -LogType Tail
```

The LogType parameter with "Tail" value tells our script to wait for the Lambda function to complete and retrieves the last 4KB of log data written during the execution. To see these logs, we need to review the LogResult property of our execution. The LogResult data is Base64Encoding so we need to wrap it in a decoder by executing the following:

```
[System.Text.Encoding]::UTF8.GetString([System.Convert]::FromBase64String($
ExecuteLMFunction.LogResult))
```

We then see several lines of text where some are labelled as Information and others as Warning or Verbose. Remember that our code uses several different approaches to write log, and we can see here how Lambda automatically tags the log entry with the log level it was written under. Make note of the log entry labelled with Warning.

Now we are going to run our Lambda function again, but this time we are going to give it an input payload and capture its output data.

The Payload parameter allows us to pass JSON-formatted input to our Lambda function. In our example we will define an AMI AliasName with value as "Windows_ Server-2012-R2_RTM-English-64Bit-Base" by executing the following parameter JSON coded for PowerShell:

```
$LMPayload = @"
{"AliasName": "Windows_Server-2012-R2_RTM-English-64Bit-Base"}
"@
```

We also add the InvocationType parameter. InvocationType can be set to one of three options:

- **RequestResponse** – Executes and collects the output data upon completion

- **Event** – Performs a quick asynchronous execution with no output data

- **DryRun** – Used to test execution without actually executing the function

We will be using RequestResponse value for InvocationType so we can review the return data. Define the parameters and execute the Lambda function with the following code:

```
$ExecuteLMParams = @{
"FunctionName" = $LMFunctionName
```

```
"LogType" = "Tail"
"InvocationType" = "RequestResponse"
"Payload" = $LMPayload}
```

```
$ExecuteLMFunction = Invoke-LMFunction @ExecuteLMParams
```

Once again we decode the logs.

```
[System.Text.Encoding]::UTF8.GetString([System.Convert]::FromBase64String($
ExecuteLMFunction.LogResult))
```

We no longer see the Warning log entry and now see that one of the Information entries that was previously empty now contains data. Remember the "Write-Host (ConvertTo-Json -InputObject $LambdaInput -Compress -Depth 5)" and "Write-Host (ConvertTo-Json -InputObject $LambdaContext -Compress -Depth 5)" that we uncommented and added earlier to our script? These have correlating log entries we now see. LambdaInput object contains the data we passed as input with the Payload parameter. We also have another log entry that contains JSON-formatted data that includes FunctionName, LogGroupName, and MemoryLimitInMB, among many other attributes of the Lambda execution. This correlates to writing the LambdaContext object to logs.

The Lambda execution output data is assigned to the Payload property. If we look at $ExecuteLMFunction.Payload, we see that Payload is defined as a System.IO.MemoryStream. We cannot simply read it as a string value, so to read the output data, we wrap it in a StreamReader. Executing the following code will show a single ImageId value was returned.

```
([System.IO.StreamReader]::new($ExecuteLMFunction.Payload)).ReadToEnd()
```

Lambda CloudWatch Logs

As we know, all log outputs for Lambda functions are recorded in CloudWatch Logs automatically. There will be times when we will need to check the history of a Lambda execution or need more granular data to debug our function. While this is not specific to Lambda, it can be difficult to find relevant examples for searching CloudWatch Logs using PowerShell. We will filter for and return the CloudWatch Logs for our recent Lambda execution as a demonstration.

First we need to identify the RequestID for the last Lambda function execution we invoked. This is actually a property of our last invocation. It can be found under the ResponseMetadata property using the following query:

```
$LMRequestId = $ExecuteLMFunction.ResponseMetadata.RequestId
```

CloudWatch Logs are separated as log groups. All AWS Lambda functions write to the /aws/lambda/{Function Name} log group. Log groups are further broken down as log streams. Log streams in Lambda log groups are a collection of executions and their events that occurred within a time range.

To get our execution event logs, we need to filter through all of CloudWatch Logs and get the CloudWatch Logs log stream name that contains our recent Lambda execution request ID. We can only search through 1MB of logs per query so we use a do while loop to keep searching through the logs. The loop runs until we find a matching log entry or we complete searching through all log streams.

The following code returns the log stream events matched by our request ID string:

```
do {
    $MatchingLogs = (Get-CWLFilteredLogEvent -LogGroupName /aws/
    lambda/$LMFunctionName @args -FilterPattern "'"$($LMRequestId)'"")
    if ($MatchingLogs.Events){
        $LogStreamName = $MatchingLogs.Events[0].LogStreamName
        $LogStream = (Get-CWLLogEvent -LogGroupName /aws/
        lambda/$LMFunctionName -LogStreamName $LogStreamName)
        write-output $LogStream.Events | Format-Table -Wrap

        break
    }
    $args = @{"NextToken"=$([string]$MatchingLogs.Nexttoken)}
} While($MatchingLogs.Nexttoken)
```

Notice how we formatted the request ID as the FilterPattern value. This is because CloudWatch Logs filtering requires string matching searches to be in double quotes. We used escape characters to ensure that the double quotes were retained in the query. When we find matching logs, we identify the log stream name from the first matching log found and write the entire log stream as output. The matching log stream output will be formatted as a table so we can wrap the text to our screen for review.

Using this query, we can see the complete log for our Lambda execution.

Lambda Event Trigger

Up to this point, we have created a Lambda PowerShell script and packaged and published it. We also manually executed our Lambda function and evaluated output and log data. For our function to be useful, we also have to define a trigger. There are many Amazon services and conditions that can be used as triggers for Lambda functions. The configurations of these different triggers could easily span several chapters of their own. In this final topic and the chapter exercise, we will demonstrate two of the possible options.

Lambda service does not support schedules but the CloudWatch service does. In the following steps, we will be creating a CloudWatch Rule that will target our Lambda function every 60 minutes. We will then set a policy on our function allowing the 60 minute CloudWatch rule to invoke it.

Retrieve the ARN of our Lambda function by using the Get-LMFunctionConfiguration we executed earlier and retrieving the FunctionArn property.

```
$LambdaArn = (Get-LMFunctionConfiguration -FunctionName $LMFunctionName
-Region us-east-1).FunctionArn
```

Now we create a CloudWatch Event Rule. We will define the name as "60MinuteTimer". The ScheduleExpression parameter takes a rate or cron expression. In our example, we define a rate expression of 60 minutes. For details on Schedule Expressions, go to https://docs.aws.amazon.com/lambda/latest/dg/tutorial-scheduled-events-schedule-expressions.html.

The State parameter sets the Event Rule to either enabled or disabled. We intend to use this rule so we will set it to enabled with the following code:

```
$CWRuleName = "60MinuteTimer"
$CWRuleParams = @{
 ScheduleExpression = "rate(60 minutes)"
State = "ENABLED"
}
```

Now that we have defined our parameters, run the Write-CWERule cmdlet and evaluate that the $NewCWERule variable contains an ARN value for the new rule.

```
$NewCWERule = Write-CWERule -name $CWRuleName @CWRuleParams
Write-Output $NewCWERule
```

Set our Lambda function ARN as the target for the CloudWatch rule using the following code:

```
$CWEventTarget = New-Object Amazon.CloudWatchEvents.Model.Target
$CWEventTarget.Arn = $LambdaArn
$CWEventTarget.Id = (Get-random)
Write-CWETarget -Rule $CWRuleName -Target $CWEventTarget
```

We can verify the configuration for our CloudWatch event rule using the following two commands:

```
Get-CWERuleDetail -Name 60MinuteTimer
Get-CWETargetsByRule -Rule 60MinuteTimer
```

Finally, we need to set a policy on our Lambda function allowing our new 60MinuteTimer to invoke it. The Action parameter indicates that our function can be invoked. The Principal parameter is the source service being given permissions to invoke it. The SourceArn limits the invoke permissions to the 60MinuteTimer CloudWatch Rule. The FunctionName parameter limits the permissions to invoke our Lambda function ARN. The StatementId is a unique value we provide for this policy. We will fill it with a randomly generated number for this example. We now execute:

```
$LMPermissionParams = @{
Action = 'lambda:InvokeFunction'
Principal = "events.amazonaws.com"
SourceArn = $NewCWERule
FunctionName = $LMFunctionName
StatementId = (Get-Random)
}
Add-LMPermission @LMPermissionParams
```

All done. Our PowerShell-Based Lambda function will execute every 60 minutes. You can easily verify this by reviewing the function CloudWatch Logs for hourly entries.

EXERCISE 18.1: UPDATE AUTO SCALE GROUP WITH LATEST IMAGEID

In Chapter 8 we learned how to create an Auto Scaling group and corresponding Launch Configuration. In Chapter 15 we learned how to get the latest ImageId using SSM Parameter Store. In this exercise we will combine what we learned from those two chapters along with what we learned in this chapter to create a new Lambda function. This new function will automatically update our Auto Scale group with the latest ImageId whenever a new version is announced through a public SNS topic subscription.

Create the Script

First let's identify the new Lambda function name and generate a script using the SNSSubscription template.

```
$FunctionName = "AutoUpdateASG"
New-AWSPowerShellLambda -ScriptName $FunctionName -Template SNSSubscription
```

Open the .\AutoUpdateASG\AutoUpdateASG.ps1 script in an editor and uncomment the following line of code:

```
Write-Host (ConvertTo-Json -InputObject $LambdaInput -Compress -Depth 5)
```

Add the following lines of code and save it:

```
$VerbosePreference = "continue"
[string]$AliasName = "Windows_Server-2012-RTM-English-64Bit-Base"
[string]$ASGroupName = "MyAutoScalingGroup"
Write-information "Getting latest regional ImageId for public Amazon Machine
Image with alias:$($AliasName)"
$ImageId = (Get-SSMParameter -Name /aws/service/ami-windows-
latest/$($AliasName)).Value
Write-Verbose "Latest ImageId for Alias:$($AliasName) is:$($ImageId)"
$MyASGroup = Get-ASAutoScalingGroup -AutoScalingGroupName $ASGroupName
$MyASLaunchConfig = Get-ASLaunchConfiguration -LaunchConfigurationName
$($MyASGroup.LaunchConfigurationName)
$MyASLCImageID = $MyASLaunchConfig.ImageId
Write-Verbose "ImageId for Auto Scaling Group:$($ASGroupName)
is:$($MyASLCImageID)"
If ($MyASLCImageID -ne $ImageId)
```

```
{
    $MyNewASLaunchConfigName = "MyLaunchConfig_$(Get-Date -format yyyy.MM.dd.
    hh.mm.ss)"
    Write-information "New ImageId available. Updating Auto Scaling group
    $($ASGroupName) with new Launch Configuration $($MyNewASLaunchConfigName)"
    $ASLaunchConfigParam = @{
    LaunchConfigurationName = $MyNewASLaunchConfigName
    ImageId = $ImageId
    KeyName = $MyASLaunchConfig.KeyName
    SecurityGroup = $MyASLaunchConfig.SecurityGroups
    Userdata = $MyASLaunchConfig.UserData
    InstanceType = $MyASLaunchConfig.InstanceType
    }
    $NewASLaunchConfig = New-ASLaunchConfiguration @ASLaunchConfigParam
    $UpdateASGroup = Update-ASAutoScalingGroup -AutoScalingGroupName
    $ASGroupName -LaunchConfigurationName $MyNewASLaunchConfigName
}
```

You can see in the script that we find the latest public ImageId from Parameter Store and compare it to the value set in the Auto Scale groups Launch Configuration we created in Chapter 8. The two ImageId values are compared, and if they do not match, a new Launch Configuration is created. The new Launch Configuration is then assigned to the Auto Scale group.

Create the IAM Role

Before we deploy this function, we need to create an IAM role with the required permissions. This new IAM role is an extension of the IAM role we created earlier in Chapter 18. The new role includes full control permissions for the AWS Auto Scaling service. Execute the following code to create our new IAM role:

```
$assumeRolePolicy = @"
{
    "Version": "2012-10-17",
    "Statement": {
        "Effect": "Allow",
        "Principal": {
            "Service": "lambda.amazonaws.com"
        },
```

```
        "Action": "sts:AssumeRole"
    }
}
"@
$labrole = New-IAMRole -RoleName "$($FunctionName)_Role"
-AssumeRolePolicyDocument $assumeRolePolicy
$labrolepolicy = @"
{
    "Version": "2012-10-17",
    "Statement": [{
            "Effect": "Allow",
            "Action": [
                    "logs:CreateLogStream",
                    "logs:CreateLogGroup",
                    "logs:PutLogEvents",
                    "ssm:GetParameter"
"autoscaling:*"
            ],
            "Resource": "*"
    }]
}
"@
$newlabpolicy = New-IAMPolicy -PolicyName "$($FunctionName)_Policy"
-PolicyDocument $labrolepolicy
Register-IAMRolePolicy -rolename $labrole.RoleName -PolicyArn $newlabpolicy.
arn
```

Publish the Lambda Function

We now publish our Lambda function using the Publish-AWSPowerShellLambda cmdlet using the new IAM role we just created. We also set the memory and timeout values to ensure our function has enough time and resources to execute completely.

```
Publish-AWSPowerShellLambda -ScriptPath .\AutoUpdateASG\AutoUpdateASG.ps1
-Name $FunctionName -IAMRoleArn $labrole.Arn -Memory 512 -Timeout 10
```

Subscribe to the SNS Topic

Get the details of our new Lambda function and assign them to the $LMFunctionConfig variable.

```
$LMFunctionConfig = Get-LMFunctionConfiguration -FunctionName $FunctionName
```

Our Lambda function is ready so we subscribe its ARN to the public SNS topic used to announce new Amazon Machine Image Windows versions.

```
$SNSTopicARN = "arn:aws:sns:us-east-1:801119661308:ec2-windows-ami-update"
$Subscription = @{
  Protocol = 'lambda'
  Endpoint = $LMFunctionConfig.FunctionArn
  TopicArn = $SNSTopicARN
}
Connect-SNSNotification @Subscription
```

Note   This is a public SNS topic used by AWS to announce when new versions of public Amazon Machine Images have been released. This occurs at least once a month, and more details can be found at `https://docs.aws.amazon.com/AWSEC2/latest/WindowsGuide/windows-ami-version-history.html`.

Permit SNS Invocation

Finally, we give our Lambda function the permissions to be invoked by an SNS notification.

```
$LMPermission = @{
  FunctionName = $FunctionName
  Action = 'lambda:InvokeFunction'
  Principal = 'sns.amazonaws.com'
  StatementId = 1
}
Add-LMPermission @LMPermission
```

In this exercise we learned how to build and deploy a Lambda function that will update our Auto Scaling group with a new Amazon Machine Image. We also learned how to subscribe to and enable SNS as a trigger for our Lambda function.

Summary

In this chapter, we saw how to install the prerequisites for creating and deploying PowerShell-Based Lambda functions. We saw how to create a script, understand its components, and deploy it as a Lambda function. Using a few cmdlets, we saw how to execute our function and review the output as well as parse resulting CloudWatch Logs. Finally, we demonstrated how to create and assign a schedule trigger for our function. Lambda is a truly powerful tool to execute PowerShell code without owning or managing a single server.

Index

A

AccessKeyId command, 201

Account access, IAM
  AWS management Console, 233
  AWS web site, 233
  support, 234, 235
  viewbilling/viewusage, 234

Active directory (AD), 101, 302

AD connector
  creation, 325, 326
  deletion, 326
  prerequisites, 324
  proxy service, 324

ADMIN_MAINTENANCE mode, 354

Amazon AppStream 2.0, 345
  architecture, 359, 360
  client requirements, 361
  custom application stack (*see* Custom application stack, AppStream 2.0)
  pay-as-you-go model, 359
  publishing requirements, 360

Amazon Aurora
  architecture, 268
  cloud database engine, 267
  cluster, 268, 269
  CRUD operations, 269
  robust database platform, 270
  TDE, 270

Amazon EC2 security groups, 118

Amazon Glacier, 5

Amazon machine images (AMIs), 27, 229, 359
  image dialog box, creation, 166
  New-EC2Instance command, 167
  listing, 158
    Get-EC2ImageByName, 160, 161
    limiting the number of instance, 159
    name filter, 160
    owner-alias filters, 160
  scripted build, 157
    benefits and drawbacks, 158
    DSC, 158
    prepared image, 158
  sharing image, 168, 169
  VMware or Hyper-V, 157

AmazonProvidedDNS, 103

Amazon resource name (ARN), 209, 259

Amazon Web Services (AWS)
  account, creation, 9
  AZs, 3
  creating IAM user account
    add user button, 10, 12
    AdministratorAccess, 22
    create role button, 21
    credentials, 12, 13
    logging in, 13, 14
    selecting EC2 role, 23
    services, 10

© Brian Beach, Steven Armentrout, Rodney Bozo, Emmanuel Tsouris 2019
B. Beach et al., *Pro PowerShell for Amazon Web Services*, https://doi.org/10.1007/978-1-4842-4850-8

S

Printed in the United States
By Bookmasters